Feeling and Thinking

The role of affect in how people think and behave in social
been a source of fascination to laymen and philosophe
immemorial. Surprisingly, most of what is known abou
feelings in social thinking and behavior has been discovere
the past two decades. This book reviews and integrates the
research and theories on this exciting topic and feat
contributions from leading researchers active in the area. The
fundamental issues such as the nature of and relationship be
and cognition, the cognitive antecedents of emotion, and the c
of affect for social cognition and behavior. It offers a highl
and comprehensive coverage of the field and is suitable as a c
in advanced courses dealing with the role of affect in co
behavior.

Joseph P. Forgas is Professor of Psychology at the Univers
South Wales, Sydney, Australia.

STUDIES IN EMOTION AND SOCIAL INTERACTION
Second Series

Series Editors

Keith Oatley
University of Toronto

Antony Manstead
University of Amsterdam

This series is jointly published by the Cambridge University Press and the Editions de la Maison des Sciences de l'Homme, as part of the joint publishing agreement established in 1977 between the Fondation de la Maison des Sciences de l'Homme and the Syndics of the Cambridge University Press.

Cette collection est publiée co-édition par Cambridge University Press et les Editions de la Maison des Sciences de l'Homme. Elle s'intègre dans le programme de co-édition établi en 1977 par la Fondation de la Maison des Sciences de l'Homme et les Syndics de Cambridge University Press.

Titles published in the Second Series:

The Psychology of Facial Expression
Edited by James A. Russell and José Miguel Fernández-Dols

Emotions, the Social Bond, and Human Reality: Part/Whole Analysis
Thomas J. Scheff

Intersubjective Communication and Emotion in Early Ontogeny
Stein Bråten

The Social Context of Nonverbal Behavior
Edited by Pierre Philippot, Robert S. Feldman, and Erik J. Coats

Communicating Emotion: Social, Moral, and Cultural Processes
Sally Planalp

For a list of titles in the First Series of Studies in Emotion and Social Interaction, see the page following the index.

Feeling and Thinking

The Role of Affect in Social Cognition

Edited by

Joseph P. Forgas
University of New South Wales
Sydney, Australia

& Editions de la Maison des Sciences de l'Homme
Paris

PUBLISHED BY THE PRESS SYNDICATE OF THE UNIVERSITY OF CAMBRIDGE
The Pitt Building, Trumpington Street, Cambridge, United Kingdom

CAMBRIDGE UNIVERSITY PRESS
The Edinburgh Building, Cambridge CB2 2RU, UK
40 West 20th Street, New York, NY 10011-4211, USA
10 Stamford Road, Oakleigh, Melbourne 3166, Australia
Ruiz de Alarcón 13, 28014 Madrid, Spain
Dock House, The Waterfront, Cape Town 8001, South Africa

http://www.cambridge.org

First published 2000
First paperback edition 2001
Reprinted 2001

Printed in the United States of America

Typeface Palantino 10/13 pt.   *System* DeskTopPro $/_{UX}$ [BV]

A catalog record for this book is available from the British Library

Library of Congress Cataloging in Publication data is available

ISBN 0 521 64223 X hardback
ISBN 2 7351 0830 9 hardback (France only)
ISBN 0 521 01189 2 paperback

To Teeshie, Paul, and Peter

Contents

Contributors

Mahzarin R. Banaji Department of Psychology, Yale University
Leonard Berkowitz Department of Psychology, University of Wisconsin-Madison
Jim Blascovich Department of Psychology, University of California, Santa Barbara
Herbert Bless Department of Psychology, University of Trier
Eric Eich Department of Psychology, University of British Columbia
Shelly D. Farnham Department of Psychology, University of Washington
Klaus Fiedler Department of Psychology, University of Heidelberg
Joseph P. Forgas School of Psychology, University of New South Wales
Daniel T. Gilbert Department of Psychology, Harvard University
Anthony G. Greenwald Department of Psychology, University of Washington
Jamin H. Halberstadt Department of Psychology, University of Otago, New Zealand
Sara Jaffee Department of Psychology, University of Wisconsin-Madison
Eunkyung Jo Department of Psychology, University of Wisconsin-Madison
Leslie D. Kirby Department of Psychology and Human Development, Vanderbilt University
Mark R. Leary Department of Psychology, Wake Forest University
Dawn Macaulay Department of Psychology, University of British Columbia

Leonard L. Martin   Department of Psychology, University of Georgia

Wendy Berry Mendes   Department of Psychology, University of California, Santa Barbara

Paula M. Niedenthal   Department of Psychology, Indiana University

Brian A. Nosek   Department of Psychology, Yale University

Marshall Rosier   Department of Psychology, Yale University

Laurie A. Rudman   Department of Psychology, Rutgers University

Carolin J. Showers   Department of Psychology, University of Oklahoma

Craig A. Smith   Department of Psychology and Human Development, Vanderbilt University

Bartholomeu T. Troccoli   Department of Psychology, University of Wisconsin-Madison

Timothy D. Wilson   Department of Psychology, University of Virginia

Robert B. Zajonc   Department of Psychology, Stanford University

Preface

Writing a preface is the last task to be done and should be a source of cheerful mood for any editor; I am certainly no exception. Such moods inevitably color how we see, remember, and judge situations and people in our daily lives – and this is just what this book is about. The relationship between mental faculties such as affect and cognition has of course been the source of endless speculation among philosophers, writers, and artists throughout human history. Surprisingly, empirical psychology has largely assumed that fundamental faculties of the human mind, such as feeling and thinking, affect and cognition, can be adequately studied in separation from each other. Neither of the two traditionally dominant paradigms in the discipline – behaviorism and the more recent cognitivist framework – assigned much importance to the study of affect. Affect was kept firmly inside the "black box" by most behaviorists, and cognitive researchers often saw affect as little more than a disruptive influence on normal, that is, affect-less, cognition.

Fortunately, there has been a dramatic increase in interest in affect during the past 20 years or so. Today we know more about the intricate relationship between affect and cognition than at any time in the past, and most of the evidence has been accumulated in the last two decades. Research on affect and cognition is now one of the most rapidly growing endeavors in psychology, providing a unifying focus for researchers working in a variety of disciplines such as social, cognitive, developmental, clinical, and neuropsychology.

However, despite extensive interest in affective phenomena in recent years and the growing popularity of university courses dealing with this issue, the field is still rather fragmented and there have been relatively few attempts at presenting a comprehensive review and integration of what we know about the links between affect and cognition. This book seeks to provide an informative, scholarly, yet readable overview of recent advances in affect-cognition research, based on invited contributions from this eminent group of investigators. This is not simply an edited book in the usual sense, however, so perhaps a few words are in order about the genesis of this volume, the first in a new series entitled the Sydney Symposium of Social Psychology, organized at the University of New South Wales, Australia.

The project has been carefully planned over a 2-year period, and has benefited from substantial financial support from granting agencies, including a Special Investigator award from the Australian Research Council and support from the University of New South Wales, Sydney. This allowed the careful selection and funding of a small group of leading researchers as contributors. Draft papers by all contributors were prepared well in advance of the symposium and were made available to all participants. A critical part of the preparation of this book has been an intensive face-to-face meeting between all invited contributors. The purpose of this, the first Sydney Symposium of Social Psychology, was to allow free-ranging and critical discussion among all participants, with the objective to explore points of integration and contrast among the proposed papers. Revised versions of the chapters, incorporating many of the points that emerged in our discussions, were prepared soon after the symposium. Thanks to these collaborative procedures, the book does not simply consist of a set of chapters prepared in isolation. Rather, the volume presents a collaborative effort by this leading group of international researchers intent on producing a comprehensive and up-to-date review of affect and social cognition research. The same integrative strategy will be followed in other forthcoming titles in the Sydney Symposium of Social Psychology series.

The volume covers most of the key issues in contemporary affect-cognition research and theorizing. The chapters discuss the fundamental nature of the relationship between affect and cognition as well as the role of cognitive appraisal processes in the generation of affective states and physiological responses. The influence of affect and mood on thinking, memory, judgments, and behavior is analyzed in several chapters. The reasons why people often find it difficult to accurately forecast their affective reactions to future events receive special attention. Affect plays not merely an informational role in influencing the *content* of cognition, but it can also have a direct processing role, impacting on *how* people think. Several chapters offer theoretical explanations for the nature and consequences of mood effects on information processing strategies. Affect is also intimately involved in how social information is cognitively represented, and plays a key role in the way attitudes, stereotypes, and self-concept are organized according to theories and evidence outlined by several of this book's contributors.

A better understanding of how affect and cognition interact is also of considerable applied importance, as several chapters emphasize. If affect is indeed *the* primary medium of interpersonal behavior, then the interface between affect and cognition by necessity lies at the heart of many professional applications of psychology. The chapters included here should have direct relevance to key applied domains such as counseling and clinical psychology, organizational research, health psychology, and marketing and advertising research.

Given the coverage of the book, the main target audience groups for this volume are practitioners, professionals, students, and researchers in psychology, sociology, communication studies, and cognitive science. The primary audience is likely to be practitioners and students in social, cognitive, personality, counseling, and clinical psychology, both at the undergraduate and at the graduate level. The book will also have considerable textbook potential for the growing number of undergraduate and graduate courses dealing with affect.

I want to express my gratitude to several people and organizations who have helped to make the Sydney Symposium of Social Psychology, and this inaugural volume in particular, a reality. The idea of organizing such a symposium owes much to discussions with, and encouragement by Kevin McConkey, and subsequent support by Chris Fell, Merilyn Sleigh, and numerous others at the University of New South Wales. My colleagues at the School of Psychology at UNSW, Kip Williams, Ladd Wheeler, Stephanie Moylan, Joseph Ciarrochi, and Natalie Freer, as well as many others, have helped with advice, support, and sheer hard work to share the burden of preparing and organizing the symposium and the ensuing book. Financial support from the Australian Research Council (Special Investigator Award) and the University of New South Wales was of course essential to get this project off the ground, and additional support by the Alexander von Humboldt Foundation (Germany) and by the University of Heidelberg and the University of Mannheim is gratefully acknowledged. I am particularly indebted to Julia Hough at Cambridge University Press for her enthusiastic support for this book and the Sydney Symposium of Social Psychology series, and to Helen Wheeler, Kelly Hamilton, Alan Gold, and others at Cambridge University Press for all their wonderful work on this project. Most of all, I am grateful for the love and support of my wife, Letitia, and my children, Paul and Peter, who have put up with me during the months I worked on this book. I expect I was even more difficult to have around than usual, and frequently my moods must have been less than cheerful. . . . Although this may not be a consolation to them, it is my sincere hope that in some small way this book may help them and others to understand just how and why our moods have such a pervasive effect on our thoughts and behaviors!

Joseph P. Forgas
Heidelberg, Germany
July 1999

1. Introduction

The Role of Affect in Social Cognition

JOSEPH P. FORGAS

Introduction

What is the role of affect in the way we think and act in social situations? Since time immemorial, philosophers, writers, and laymen have been fascinated by the complex interaction between feeling and thinking, affect and cognition, in human affairs. On the one hand, it is frequently assumed that affect has a disruptive, dangerous influence on thinking and behavior, leading some theorists to suggest that whenever emotions are "directly involved in action, they tend to overwhelm or subvert rational mental processes" (Elster, 1985, p. 379). Thus, feelings may have an invasive, "disturbing role," as "noisome, irrational agents in the decision-making process" (Toda, 1980, p. 133). Some even speculated that our inability to fully understand and manage our affective states indicates a fatal flaw in the evolution of our species (Koestler, 1978). A contrary view, however, suggests that openness to feelings is a useful, and even necessary, adjunct to rationality and to effective social thinking (Damasio, 1994; De Sousa, 1987; Oatley & Jenkins, 1992, 1996). These ideas reflect a long-held belief that "the heart has its reasons which reason does not understand" (Pascal, 1643/1966, p. 113). There can be little doubt that the delicate interplay between cognition and affect has also been the moving force

This project was supported by a Special Investigator Award from the Australian Research Council and by the Research Prize from the Alexander von Humboldt Foundation, Germany. The contribution of Stephanie Moylan is gratefully acknowledged.

Further information on this research project can be found at http://www.psy.unsw.edu.au/~joef.jforgas.htm.

Correspondence concerning this article should be addressed to Joseph P. Forgas, School of Psychology, University of New South Wales, Sydney 2052, Australia. Electronic mail may be sent to jp.forgas@unsw.edu.au.

1

behind many of the great artistic achievements throughout the ages. Surprisingly, psychologists were rather late to explore empirically the interface of affect and cognition, despite the abundance of speculative theorizing on this question.

This book is about the role of affect in social thinking. It is organized into four main parts. After this introductory chapter, Part 1 will consider some *basic conceptual issues* about the interplay of affect and cognition. The three chapters here take different, complementary approaches, emphasizing either the primary, preconscious aspects of affect (Zajonc, Chapter 2) analyzing the role of psychophysiological processes in affective experience (Blascovich and Mendes, Chapter 3), or focusing on cognitive appraisal processes in the generation of affect (Smith & Kirby, Chapter 4). Part II looks at the role of *affect as a source of information* in cognitive functioning, with chapters discussing evidence for mood congruency in memory (Eich & Macaulay, Chapter 5), as well as some of the mechanisms capable of producing mood-incongruent outcomes (Berkowitz et al., Chapter 6). A theory outlining the use of affect as a configural input to cognitive processes is discussed (Martin, Chapter 7) and the mechanisms involved in affective forecasting are analysed (Gilbert & Wilson, Chapter 8). Part III considers the links between *affect and information processing strategies,* suggesting that affect also plays a critical role in such fundamental cognitive processing dichotomies as assimilation and accommodation (Fiedler, Chapter 10) and top-down and bottom-up processing (Bless, Chapter 9). Different processing strategies in turn often mediate affective influences on thinking and behavior (Forgas, Chapter 11). The relationship between *affect and social knowledge structures* is explored in Part IV, which first looks at the role of affect in self-organization (Showers, Chapter 12) and in the organization and use of attitudes, stereotypes, and beliefs (Greenwald et al., Chapter 13). The influence of emotions in self-relevant thoughts is explored by Leary (Chapter 14), and evidence for the critical importance of emotional reactions in cognitive categorization is reviewed by Niedenthal and Halberstadt (Chapter 15). A general review and integration of the material is the task of a final, concluding chapter (Forgas, Chapter 16). Each of the chapters will present a comprehensive theoretical overview of the authors' orientation, as well as summarize relevant empirical evidence. Few attempts have been made so far to review, integrate, and link these convergent research domains. This is one of the main objectives of this volume.

The aim of this introductory chapter is to set the scene for much of what follows. The chapter begins with a brief summary of the historical antecedents of theorizing about affect and cognition, and early psychoanalytic and conditioning explanations of these phenomena are considered. We shall then move to a brief overview of contemporary affect-cognition research that provides the background to this volume, with special emphasis on the cognitive, information processing theories that have been proposed to explain both the informational and the processing consequences of affect on cognition. The chapter concludes with a brief summary of the structure of the book, and the main themes covered in each chapter will be outlined.

Historical Background

Affect and Cognition: Distinct Faculties?

Ever since antiquity, many great philosophers have been intrigued by the question of how feeling and thinking, affect and cognition, are related. Fascination with this issue can be traced throughout the Western philosophical tradition, from the work of Aristotle to St. Augustine, Descartes, Pascal, and Kant. A key development in this field has been the idea that human mental life can be separated into three distinct and complementary faculties: feeling, knowing, and willing (affect, cognition, and conation). This notion first emerged in a concrete form in the eighteenth-century philosophy of the Enlightenment. Christian Wolff (1714–1762) was among the first to distinguish between a *facultas cognoscivita* and a *facultas appetiva* – knowing and desire (Hilgard, 1980). A few decades later, Moses Mendelssohn (1729–1789) introduced a three-fold classification of the fundamental faculties of soul, consisting of understanding, feeling, and will. Kant, perhaps the most influential philosopher of his period, explicitly accepted this tripartite division of the human mind. For Kant, "pure reason corresponds to intellect or cognition, practical reason to will, action or conation, and judgment to feeling pleasure or pain, hence affection" (Hilgard, 1980, p. 109). Indeed, Kant's main philosophical works clearly reflect this tripartite categorization of human mental life into cognition, conation, and affect (*Critique of Pure Reason*, 1788; *Critique of Practical Reason*, 1788; *Critique of Judgment*, 1790).

This classification of psychology's subject matter into affect, cognition, and conation has survived in our discipline to this day. One unfortunate consequence has been the tendency for psychologists to treat these three mental faculties as if they were fundamentally separate, distinct entities that can be studied in separation from each other. In contrast, most of the contributions to this volume bear clear testimony to the need to study affect and cognition as inseparable, interwoven dimensions of human social life. Interestingly, in the work of Wundt and Titchener introspective accounts in the cognitive, conative, and affective modalities were still considered as complementary, reflecting on unitary underlying experiences. Subsequent paradigms however increasingly focused on affect, cognition, and conation as isolated faculties, largely ignoring the interdependence between them.

Not surprisingly, then, the twentieth-century history of psychology came to be dominated by two major paradigms: behaviorism, which is explicitly concerned with motivated, goal-oriented action (conation); and cognitivism, which deals predominantly with the study of cold, affect-less ideation. Neither of these two paradigms assigned much importance to the study of affective phenomena. From the perspective of the radical behaviorist, all unobservable mental events – such as feelings and affect – were by definition of little interest. Although early behaviorist research did explore the environmental conditioning of emotional responses, as in Watson's "little Albert" studies, subsequent work merely focused on the behavioral consequences of powerful and easily manipulated drive states such as hunger and thirst. In consequence, behaviorist research and theory contributed little to our understanding of the functions and consequences of affect in everyday social life.

Until recently, the alternative cognitive paradigm was also characterized by a consistent lack of interest in affect. Emotions, if considered at all, were seen as a disruptive influence on "proper," that is, affect-less, thinking. However, the fiction of such "cold" cognition as the ideal could not be maintained forever. Most everyday thinking also involves feelings, desires, and affect, a fact that was to be explicitly recognized in the work of such influential researchers as Bruner (1957) and Neisser (1982). Several chapters in this volume advocate such an integrated theoretical treatment of affective and cognitive phenomena (see chapters by Eich & Macaulay, Fiedler, Forgas, Greenwald, and Niedenthal & Halberstadt in particular). When considered from a proper historical perspective, the recent emergence of research on the interaction of affect and cognition represents a belated recognition that these mental faculties do not operate in isolation (Oatley & Jenkins,

1992, 1996). By exploring the close interdependence of feeling and thinking in human social life, this book tackles one of the age-old puzzles that continue to command our attention.

The Contemporary Status and Definitions of Affect

No doubt it was partly in reaction to the historical neglect of affective phenomena that psychologists have in the past decade made a concentrated attempt to reintegrate affect into the mainstream of psychological inquiry. One highly controversial issue in this field concerns whether affect should be seen as an integral part of the cognitive-representational system (see, e.g., Smith & Kirby, Gilbert, Leary, and Showers, this volume), or should be considered as a separate, and in some ways, primary response system in its own right (see Zajonc, this volume). Some theorists, such as Zajonc (1980, this volume), argue for a "separate-systems" view, proposing that affective reactions often precede, and are psychologically and neuroanatomically distinct from, cognitive processes. Many other theorists however espouse a more interactionist conceptualization (see, e.g., Blascovich & Mendes, Smith & Kirby, Fiedler, Forgas, and Greenwald et al., this volume). Of course, one's position in this debate depends at least in part on how broadly the domain of "cognition" is defined. Affect can be considered a primary and separate response system only if cognition is defined as excluding early attentional and interpretational processes that are inevitably involved in stimulus identification before any response is possible (Lazarus, 1984).

Even if we do accept the more challenging view that affect and cognition are at least partly independent response systems, affect could still fulfill an important informational role in inferential social thinking and judgments. Indeed, there is a long tradition in psychological theorizing that does recognize the close interdependence of feeling, thinking and behavior. These ideas were present in the writings of many philosophers, and were clearly manifest in some of the work of William James (1890). Most contemporary affect-cognition models also define affect as part of a single, integrated cognitive representational system (Bower, 1981; Isen, 1984; Mayer, 1986), at least in the sense that "the experience of an emotion *is* a cognition" (Laird & Bresler, 1991, p. 24).

Another crucial issue affecting research is the lack of broad agreement as to how terms such as *affect, feelings, emotion,* and *mood* may be psychologically defined (Fiedler & Forgas, 1988; Forgas, 1991a; Frijda, 1986). One commonly accepted view is that affect is a broad and inclusive concept referring to both moods and emotions (Forgas, 1995a; Mayer, 1986). Moods in turn can be defined as relatively low-intensity, diffuse, and enduring affective states that have no salient antecedent cause and therefore little cognitive content (such as feeling good or feeling bad, being in a good or a bad mood). In contrast, distinct emotions are more short-lived, intense phenomena and usually have a highly accessible and salient cause, as well as clear, prototypical cognitive content (e.g., disgust, anger, or fear). Both emotions and moods may have an impact on social cognition, but the nature of this influence is quite different.

Interestingly, the conceptual distinction between moods and emotions is to some extent also reflected in contemporary research on affect and cognition. Emotion researchers are typically interested in the cognitive *antecedents* and appraisal strategies that lead to an emotional reaction (see, e.g., Blascovich & Mendes, Smith & Kirby, and Leary, this volume). In contrast, a lot of the existing research and theorizing on the *consequences* of affect for social cognition has focused on low-intensity, general *mood* states, rather than specific emotions. This is most likely because moods seem to be less subject to conscious monitoring and control and therefore have potentially more insidious, enduring, and subtle effects on social thinking, memory, and judgments than do distinct emotions. Many of the contributors to this volume share a concern with how nonspecific moods, rather than distinct emotions, influence social thinking (see especially the chapters by Berkowitz, Bless, Fiedler, Forgas, and Martin). Despite these differences, it is not always easy to draw a sharp distinction between mood states and emotional states. Strong emotions often leave a lingering mood state in their wake, and moods in turn can determine how an individual responds to emotional stimuli.

The available research clearly points to a bidirectional rather than a unidirectional link between affect and cognition. There is much evidence for affect influencing attention, memory, thinking, associations and judgments (see Berkowitz et al., Eich & Macaulay, Fiedler, Forgas, Greenwald et al., Niedenthal & Halberstadt, and Showers, in this volume). Equally, however, cognitive processes are integral to the elicitation of affective states, as people's appraisal and analysis of situational information activate appropriate emotional responses (see, e.g., Zajonc, Blascovich & Mendes, Leary, and Smith & Kirby, this volume). Many of these research approaches seek to discover and systematize the cognitive contents and processes that underlie various affect elicitation rules. Whether one is concerned with the antecedents of emotions or the consequences of moods, both approaches have clear historical antecedents. We shall next turn to a brief review of early psychological theories that inform contemporary research.

Early Psychological Theories Linking Affect and Cognition

Although people always had a common-sense awareness of the infusion of affect in their social lives, psychologists largely studied affect and cognition in isolation from each other. However, there have been several lines of empirical evidence suggesting the possibility of an interaction between affective and cognitive phenomena. Such a relationship was perhaps first demonstrated by Razran (1940) almost 60 years ago. Using a free lunch (!) or aversive smells to induce good or bad moods, Razran found that the positive or negative affect produced had a marked mood-congruent influence on subsequent social judgments. Two major theories were traditionally invoked to explain such affect-cognition interactions in early research. One influential account was couched in terms of psychoanalytic principles. An alternative paradigm suggested that conditioning mechanisms may be the key to understanding how affect and cognition are linked.

Psychodynamic Accounts: The Hydraulic Principle

The interplay between affect and cognition played a central role in Freud's elaborate psychodynamic theories. In a sense, it was psychoanalytic theory that first placed emotions in the spotlight of psychological theorizing. According to this dynamic framework, affective states were primarily located within the id, and were thought of as seeking expression and exerting "pressure" against the countervailing force of rational, controlled ego mechanisms. Psychoanalytic theory suggests that attempts at controlling and channeling affective reactions require psychological resources and may not always be successful. In psychodynamic terms, affect can thus be thought of as having an invasive, dynamic quality that can potentially influence and invade a wide variety of cognitive processes and behaviors unless adequate psychological effort and resources are employed to control it.

Freud's original ideas about affect gave rise to a great deal of speculative psychoanalytic theorizing, and eventually were also incorporated into some mainstream psychological research, for example, in the work of Murray (1933). Psychodynamic theories also stimulated a number of empirical attempts to demonstrate the dynamic character of affect infusion. In an excellent example of this approach, Feshbach and Singer (1957) predicted that powerful emotional states may invade unrelated cognitive judgments, and, paradoxically, that these affect infusion effects should be greater when people make a conscious effort to suppress their feelings. According to the hydraulic principle of psychoanalytic thinking, this should occur because attempts at emotional repression will create increased pressure for the emotional state to find an alternative expression. On the basis of these ideas, Feshbach and Singer (1957) induced the emotional state of fear and anxiety in their subjects by using electric shocks. Subjects were then either instructed to repress their fear or not, before making social judgments about a target person.

Results showed that fearful subjects were more likely to "perceive another person as fearful and anxious" (p. 286), and this effect was particularly marked precisely when they were trying to suppress their fear. Feshbach and Singer (1957) took this finding to be consistent with the psychodynamic process of projection, as "suppression of fear facilitates the tendency to project fear onto another social object" (p. 286). Indeed, in a prescient passage they describe this process as indicating the "infusion of affect into cognition." It is interesting that it took several more decades of research before the precise cognitive mechanisms responsible for such affect infusion or its absence could be systematically explored (see, e.g., Berkowitz et al., Bless, Fiedler, Forgas, and Martin, this volume).

Feshbach and Singer's (1957) psychodynamic study was not the only one to show that affect can infuse unrelated cognitive and judgmental processes. Wehmer and Izard (1962) manipulated the behavior of the experimenter to induce an affective state. This study also showed that subjects induced to feel good subsequently made more positive judgments than did subjects who were in a negative mood. In a similar procedure, Izard (1964) used the behavior of a trained confederate (an actress) to induce affect. He, too, found that judgments and performance were more positive after positive mood induction. Perceptions of the self and judgments about various social activities were also positively related to self-rated mood over time (Wessman & Ricks, 1966). Karl Popper's devastating criticisms of psychoanalytic theory and the lack of convincing empirical support for Freud's theories caused dynamic explanations of affect infusion to decline in popularity. In keeping with the changing zeitgeist in psychology, conditioning theories became the major alternative theoretical explanation of such affectively induced biases in thinking and judgments.

Conditioning Accounts

The idea that powerful associations between preexisting, unconditioned affective reactions and new, previously neutral stimuli could be readily established as a result of temporal and spatial contiguity alone was first demonstrated by Watson in his well-known "little Albert" studies. The same fundamental idea was explored in the judgmental studies of Byrne and Clore (1970) and Clore and Byrne (1974). These authors suggested that conditioning principles may explain how affective states triggered by unrelated events can influence unrelated judgments, such as evaluations of others. Thus, an unconditioned affective reaction elicited by an aversive environment can result in a more negative evaluation of a person encountered in that environment, due to the temporal and spatial contiguity between the two stimuli. Supporting this prediction, Griffitt (1970) found that people in whom unconditioned negative affect was induced by exposure to excessive heat and humidity made more negative judgments of a target person encountered in that environment. This suggests that "evaluative responses are . . . determined by the positive or negative properties of the total stimulus situation" (Griffitt, 1970, p. 240). Similarly, Gouaux (1971) demonstrated mood-congruent effects on social judgments following exposure to happy or depressing films, concluding that "interpersonal attraction is a positive function of the subject's affective state" (p. 40). In other studies, Gouaux and Summers (1973) used manipulated interpersonal feedback to induce mood, with very similar results. Although such "blind" conditioning principles are now rarely emphasized to explain affect infusion in contemporary research, somewhat similar ideas continue to exert considerable influence on recent social cognition theorizing (Berkowitz, 1993; Clore, Schwarz, & Conway, 1994; Wyer & Srull, 1989). In particular, the affect-as-information model proposed by Schwarz and Clore (1983) also implies a direct link between affective states and evaluative judgments that is strongly reminiscent of Clore and Byrne's (1974) earlier associationist approach.

Despite such strong early evidence for mood effects on social judgments, explanations based on conditioning or psychodynamic principles remained inconclusive. For example, most conditioning explanations assume that the simultaneous presence of affect-eliciting stimuli and the judgmental targets (the UCS and the CS) is necessary for affect infusion to occur. Yet it is clear from other studies that affective states can have significantly delayed cognitive and judgmental consequences even in the absence of spatial or temporal contiguity (e.g., Forgas & Bower, 1988; Wessman & Ricks, 1966). The conditioning model was also criticized for its lack of attention to exactly how affective states are integrated with other kinds of information in the construction of judgments (Abele & Petzold, 1994; Kaplan, 1991). Although conditioning may well play a role in mediating some affective reactions (Berkowitz, 1993), it cannot provide a complete theory of mood effects on social judgments because of the absence of a well-articulated cognitive dimension mediating these effects (Forgas, 1992a, 1992c). Surprisingly, it is the psychodynamic theorizing of Feshbach and Singer (1957) that came closest to anticipating contemporary thinking, by suggesting that cognition in a sense becomes "infused" with affect. Contemporary social cognitive theories were developed to deal with this precise problem: the explanation of how, and under what circumstances, such affect infusion into social cognition occurs.

Contemporary Cognitive Approaches

During the past 20 years or so, a number of theories have been proposed to explain how affective states come to influence social cognition. Most of the early work was concerned with the impact of affective states on the *content* of cognition. In particular, the need to theoretically explain affect congruity effects or their absence were the focus of most early affect-cognition theorizing. We may call these theories informational theories, because their aim is to explain how affect may inform the content of people's thinking, judgments, and decisions. Two major kinds of such informational theories have been proposed: memory-based theories (e.g., the affect-priming model; see Eich & Macaulay, Forgas, this volume), and inferential models (e.g., the affect-as-information model; see Martin, this volume).

As affect-cognition research progressed, it soon became clear that in addition to informational effects, affect may also influence the *process* of cognition, that is, *how* people think (see chapters by Fiedler, and by Bless, this volume). Theorizing about the impact of positive and negative affect on information-processing style continues to be an active area, drawing on a number of principles, such as functional, motivational, and cognitive capacity explanations. We shall briefly review the various informational theories of affect and social cognition, before turning to processing effects.

Affect and Memory

Perhaps the most powerful and enduring idea in recent affect-cognition research is that affective states are intimately linked to people's memory representations. The notion that affect and cognition may become linked within an integrated cognitive representational system was first formalized by Bower (1981) and by Isen (1984). However, the roots of cognitive network theories can be found in earlier behavioral research based on associationist paradigms (Berkowitz, 1993). It was Gordon Bower at Stanford University who most clearly specified and elaborated this model, and who derived from it a series of testable hypotheses. The associative network principle suggests that the links between affect and cognition are neither motivationally based, as psychodynamic theories suggest, nor are they the result of merely incidental associations, as conditioning theories imply. Rather, affect and cognition are integrally linked within an associative network of cognitive representations (see also Eich & Macaulay, and Greenwald et al., this volume). Thus, material that is associatively linked to the current mood is more likely to be activated, preferentially recalled, and used in various constructive cognitive tasks, leading to a potential mood congruency in attention, learning, memory, associations, evaluations, and judgments. In other words, affect is not an incidental, but an inseparable, part of how we see and represent the world around us; how we select, store, and retrieve information; and how we use stored knowledge structures in the performance of cognitive tasks.

Network models can also accommodate evidence that some affective reactions may be biologically wired into the brain. These reactions are activated by a range of situational triggers that become greatly elaborated as a result of cultural learning (a view that clearly resonates with Watson's early work on affective conditioning). Affective states can also spread activation to related physiological and automatic reactions, facial and postural expressions, verbal labels, action tendencies, and memories associated with that affect in the past (Berkowitz,

1993; Blascovich & Mendes, this volume). When one is trying to retrieve a memory, affect-related information is more likely to be accessed as it receives more total activation from the retrieval cue, plus the current affective state. As a result of such summation of activation, affect can infuse cognitive processes by facilitating access to related cognitive categories (Bower, 1981; Isen, 1987). As Bower (1981) suggests, affective states have a "specific node or unit in memory that . . . is also linked with propositions describing events from one's life during which that emotion was aroused. . . . Activation of an emotion node also spreads activation throughout the memory structures to which it is connected" (p. 135). Several important consequences follow from this basic principle.

Affect-state dependent retrieval occurs when retrieval mood matches the original encoding mood. Several studies have found that memory is improved when recall mood matches encoding mood. People also seem better at selectively recalling autobiographical memories that match their prevailing mood (Bower, 1981). Although some problems have arisen in replicating mood-state dependent retrieval with simple stimuli such as word lists (Bower & Mayer, 1985), more complex social stimuli and more realistic encoding and recall contexts have produced reliable mood-state dependent effects (Fiedler, 1990, 1991; Forgas, 1991c, 1992d, 1993; Forgas & Bower, 1987). It seems that affective states can most effectively function as a differentiating context in learning and recall when people are dealing with a richer set of encoding and retrieval cues than are available in standard memory experiments, as originally suggested by Bower (1981; see also Eich & Macaulay, this volume).

Affect-congruent retrieval is a related process that occurs when affective state facilitates the recall of affectively congruent material from memory. Thus, depressed subjects are faster to retrieve unpleasant memories, and anxious patients show a similar bias for recalling negative autobiographic memories. Experimental studies have also found that people are more likely to recall negative information when in a bad mood, and positive information when in a good mood (Forgas, Bower, & Krantz, 1984; Forgas & Bower, 1987). Support for this prediction also comes from implicit memory tasks. For example, depressed people are more likely to produce negative rather than positive words when completing word stems (Ruiz-Caballero & Gonzalez, 1994) and also show a similar mood-congruent tendency in lexical decisions (Niedenthal & Setterlund, 1994).

Because social cognition typically involves highly selective information processing, mood effects on *selective attention and learning effects* are also important. Thus, affect-congruent information may receive greater attention and preferential encoding owing to the selective activation of a mood-related associative base (Bower, 1981, 1991; Forgas & Bower, 1987; Forgas, 1992b). These effects occur because "concepts, words, themes, and rules of inference that are associated with that emotion will become primed and highly available for use . . . /in/ . . . top-down or expectation-driven processing. . . . /acting/. . . . as interpretive filters of reality" (Bower, 1983, p. 395). To the extent that social cognitive tasks require people to "go beyond the information given," affect will also have an impact on *associations, inferences, and interpretations*. Studies show an affect-congruent bias in associations to an ambiguous word like "life," as well as associations produced in response to Thematic Apperception Test (TAT) pictures (Bower, 1981). Such associative mood effects can also influence impressions about people (Forgas, et al., 1984; Forgas & Bower, 1987), as well as self-perceptions (Sedikides, 1995). However, this effect is diminished as the targets to be judged become more clear-cut and thus require less constructive processing (Forgas, 1994a, 1994b, 1995b).

A major advantage of associative network theories is that they can provide a relatively simple and parsimonious framework for understanding a wide variety of affective influences on social cognition, both at the encoding and at the retrieval stage. However, network models are notoriously difficult to falsify. Some empirical findings also present difficulties for associative network models. Several experiments show that mood congruence is not always obtained when network principles posit that they should occur (e.g., Parrott & Sabini, 1990). Further, numerous studies suggest that the extent of affect priming can vary, depending on contextual factors such as the nature of the task, the complexity of the information, and the motivation of the subjects (Blaney, 1986; Fiedler, 1991; Forgas, 1998a, 1998b, in press; Forgas et al., 1984).

Although the associative network model provides a robust, parsimonious, and well-supported explanation for a wide variety of affect-congruity effects, it is now also clear that affect priming does not occur in every situation. It is most likely to occur in circumstances that facilitate an open, constructive information processing style that encourages the generative and constructive use of previously stored and affectively primed information (Fiedler, 1991). Recent integrative affect-cognition theories, such as the Affect Infusion Model (AIM; Forgas, 1995a), were specifically designed to explain when and how affect infusion effects occur. The underlying principle seems to be that tasks that require more elaborate, constructive processing also allow more extensive reliance on affectively primed information and tend to produce greater affect infusion effects (Eich & Macaulay, this volume; Forgas, 1994a, 1994b, 1995b). However, affect priming is not the sole mechanism of affect infusion.

Affective Inferences

A competing theoretical explanation of how affective states may come to influence the content of cognition and judgments is based on the "affect-as-information" hypothesis (Clore & Parrott, 1991; Schwarz & Clore, 1983, 1988; Wyer & Srull, 1989). The affect-as-information model assumes that "rather than computing a judgment on the basis of recalled features of a target, individuals may ... ask themselves: 'How do I feel about it?' /and/ in doing so, they may mistake feelings due to a preexisting state as a reaction to the target" (Schwarz, 1990, p. 529). Unlike memory-based explanations, these theories suggested that affective states may be inferentially used as information in some circumstances. Such "direct" affective influences on behavior and judgment were first studied in associationist research in the 1960s and 1970s (see the preceding section; Clore & Byrne, 1974). The model also has some affinity with research on judgmental heuristics and attributions: it assumes that affect may function as a simple, judgment-simplifying heuristic device, as if people used their mood to infer an evaluative judgment (Clore & Parrott, 1991; Schwarz & Clore, 1988). In a further extension of this idea, Clore and Parrott (1991, 1994) suggest that just as "affective feelings concern how much ... something is good or bad, ... cognitive feelings indicate the status of one's knowledge, understanding or expectations" (1994, p. 102).

The affect-as-information account is primarily a theory of mood effects on evaluative judgments. Because the affect-as-information model accounts for mood effects at the retrieval or judgmental stage only, it cannot account for the kind of encoding, learning, and attention effects predicted by affect-priming theories. A key prediction of the model is that only unexplained, unattributed moods that are capable of misattribution should produce judgmental consequences. Some studies supported this prediction (Clore & Parrott, 1991, 1994;

Schwarz & Clore, 1988). However, other experiments report mood effects even after mood manipulations that are likely to be highly salient and thus correctly attributed (such as the Velten technique, behavior of a confederate, or false feedback about performance) (Fiedler, 1990, 1991; Forgas et al., 1984; Forgas & Bower, 1987; Sedikides, 1992, 1994). When correctly attributed affect can still have an impact on judgments, affect-as-information is unlikely to be the mechanism involved.

The affect-as-information account also implies a simple, categorical mood effect, where mood either informs or does not inform judgments. Thus, the model may have difficulty in accounting for the kind of context-sensitive, gradual, and target-specific mood effects most commonly reported in the literature. In response to these criticisms, the affect-as-information model has undergone a number of major revisions in recent years. Martin (this volume) argued that the actual informational value of an affective state depends largely on the configural situation in which it is experienced. Thus, the same affective state can produce mood congruity or incongruity, depending on its configural meaning. In a somewhat related vein, Abele and Petzold (1994) recently suggested that the informational role of affect must be understood in combination with a variety of other informational cues simultaneously considered by people. It is only through such an information integration perspective (Anderson, 1974) that the informational role of affect can be properly analyzed. It seems that the affect-as-information model has a somewhat limited capacity to explain affect infusion beyond simple evaluative judgments. This kind of affect infusion is most likely to occur when the judgment is global and indeterminate, and judges have neither the capacity nor the motivation to engage in more detailed, substantive processing and choose to adopt a simplified affect-as-information heuristic instead.

Affect and Processing Style

Affect not only plays an informational role in social cognition, but it can also influence processing strategies. Until recently, many researchers believed that people in a positive mood tend to think more rapidly and perhaps superficially, reach a decision more quickly, use less information, avoid demanding, systematic processing, and are more confident about their decisions. Negative moods in turn were assumed to generate more systematic, analytic, and vigilant processing strategies (Forgas, 1989, 1991b, 1998c; Isen, 1984, 1987; Schwarz, 1990; Schwarz & Bless, 1991; Sinclair & Mark, 1992). However, the simple juxtaposition of these two processing styles is not without its critics. It has been repeatedly noted that positive mood can also produce distinct processing advantages, as people are more likely to adopt more creative, open, constructive, and inclusive thinking styles when feeling good (Fiedler, in press and this volume; Isen, 1987). Nor are the processing consequences of negative moods unequivocally beneficial. More than 10 years ago, Ellis and Ashbrook (1988) argued that dysphoria is likely to selectively activate negative thoughts and memories and thus take up scarce attentional and processing resources and impair processing capacity.

In recent years, there have been several attempts to rethink the processing consequences of affect. Fiedler (in press; this volume) suggested that positive and negative affect do not simply produce more or less sytematic, analytic processing. Rather, positive moods facilitate assimilative, generative, productive and top-down thinking allowing the creative use of existing information. In contrast, negative affect tends to produce a more inductive and externally focused thinking style, involving greater attention to situational information (Fiedler, 1990, 1991). In a somewhat similar vein, Bless (this volume) proposed that the key processing difference between positive and negative affective states is the extent to which they facilitate the use of stored, schematic information. Whereas positive affect triggers more schematic thinking, negative mood has the opposite effect, producing greater reliance on detailed, piecemeal information in social cognition. These recent formulations provide a more subtle account of the processing consequences of affect than did previous theories that simply emphasized differences in the extent to which processing is analytic, systematic, and vigilant.

But why exactly should positive or negative affect produce any differences in processing strategies at all? One explanation emphasizes the *cognitive load* produced by affective states, which may limit attention, memory, and processing capacity. However, as both positive and negative affective states may take up scarce processing capacity (Ellis & Ashbrook, 1988; Mackie & Worth, 1991), excess cognitive load is not a plausible explanation of the different, asymmetric processing consequences of positive and negative affect often found in the literature. Alternatively, affect may also function as *an evolutionary signal*, providing shorthand information about the kind of response required to deal with more or less challenging situations (Frijda, 1986; Oatley & Jenkins, 1992, 1996; Schwarz, 1990). Thus, positive affect suggests that "all is well with the world," cueing more top-down, schematic, and heuristic information processing, and providing greater scope to engage in unusual, unorthodox, and creative thinking (Fiedler, in press). Negative affect in turn signals problematic, difficult situations, triggering more attentive, piecemeal, externally focused, and "tight" cognitive strategies. To the extent that affective reactions are themselves cognitively mediated (Blascovich & Mendes, Smith & Kirby, and Leary, this volume), the processing consequences of affect may not be as robust or uniform as evolutionary, functionalist accounts suggest. Affect may also influence cognitive processing styles owing to its *motivational* consequences. Positive affect may motivate directed strategies designed to maintain a favorable mood, for example, by avoiding cognitive effort. In a negative mood, controlled processing may involve a more careful, attentive, and motivated search for external information (Clark & Isen, 1982), as found in several of our studies looking at mood effects on social judgments (Forgas, 1989, 1991b, 1998c).

It appears, then, that positive and negative affective states have a variety of informational and processing consequences for social cognition. The reverse link is equally important: Cognitive appraisal processes and "emotion production rules" are also heavily implicated in the way people perceive and construe situations, and in the nature of their resulting affective reactions. A central aim of this book is to bring together some of the most recent research and theorizing about the interaction between affective and cognitive processes in social thinking and behavior, as the next section will suggest.

Outline of the Book

The book is organized into four complementary sections. Part I addresses some fundamental conceptual issues concerning the links between affect and cognition. Subsequent sections explore the informational (Part II), processing (Part III), and representational (Part IV) influence of affect on social thinking.

Fundamental Issues: The Interplay of Affect and Cognition (Part I)

In Chapter 2, Robert Zajonc addresses one of the key issues in affect-cognition research: what is the status of affect in relation to cognition? Zajonc returns to the theme of his highly influential paper in 1980, and further develops his arguments that affective states represent a distinct response system, and can exert an influence on behavior in the absence of cognition and awareness. This chapter critically reviews recent experimental evidence consistent with this view, including psychological, neuroanatomical, and neurophysiological evidence suggesting the independence of affect from cognition.

Jim Blascovich and Wendy Mendes's biopsychosocial model of affect and cognition, discussed in Chapter 3, implies a complementary orientation. In a series of recent psychophysiological experiments, these authors identified distinct physiological markers associated with affective experiences such as challenge and threat. Specifically, they found that during experiences of challenge relatively strong increases in cardiac performance are accompanied by arterial dilation, whereas during threat relatively weak increases in cardiac performance are accompanied by unchanging or increased arterial constriction. Their results also show that cognitive variables can significantly mediate these visceral affective responses to challenge and threat. The idea that even affect-specific physiological reactions are subject to cognitive inferences illustrates the key role that social cognition plays in affective responses.

Chapter 4, by Craig Smith and Leslie Kirby, also emphasizes the role of cognitive appraisals in affective reactions. Smith and his collaborators are among the founders and major contributors to this thriving literature. This chapter presents a new, process model of affect appraisal that goes beyond existing structural, content theories. Specifically, schematic processing is proposed as the key mechanism whereby memory representations associated with affect can be automatically primed and activated, producing emotional reactions without conscious cognitive processing. Smith and Kirby also emphasize the role of emotion-related memory structures in triggering appraisal and emotion elicitation. Their focus on affective memory structures represents a major new integrative link between researchers interested in the cognitive antecedents of affect (appraisal theories) and those investigating the cognitive consequences of affect (e.g., affect-priming theories).

The Informational Role of Affect (Part II)

The role of affect in memory is addressed by Eric Eich and Dawn Macaulay (Chapter 5). Many of the studies demonstrating that events experienced in a specific mood state are more easily retrieved in the same mood came out of Eich's laboratory at the University of British Columbia. Eich and Macaulay review two approaches to studying mood-dependent memory (MDM) here. Laboratory studies using experimentally induced moods focus on the cognitive factors that produce MDM. Complementary research concentrates on clinical studies involving naturally occurring moods. Based on overwhelming empirical evidence, Eich and Macaulay conclude that there are real and robust affective influences on memory processes that are generally consistent with associative network formulations. However, these effects are most likely to be detected in tasks in which affect has a real function and "casual belonging" linking it to the memory structures in question, and in which constructive, generative cognitive processing style allows affect infusion to occur (Fiedler, 1991; Forgas, 1995a).

Despite strong evidence for affect congruence in memory and judgments, as the Eich and Macaulay chapter shows, these effects are certainly not universal. Why do we sometimes get no mood effects, or affect-incongruent effects in memory and social judgments? This is the topic of Chapter 6 by Leonard Berkowitz, Sara Jaffee, Eunkyung Jo, and Bartholomeu Troccoli. Their research suggests that at times an affect-congruent bias is reversed, and in some instances affect actually leads to incongruent cognitive outcomes. Looking at a variety of mood inductions and judgment contexts, Berkowitz and his colleagues show that when people become highly aware of their feelings or are highly motivated to be accurate, they attempt to "correct for" their affect and consequently make affect-incongruent judgments. Simply calling attention to an internal state often seems sufficient to trigger such an overcorrection effect. The authors propose a model of overcorrection that goes some way toward explaining why affect infusion is not always found and helps to reconcile affect-congruent and affect-incongruent findings in the available literature.

The question of why we sometimes get affect-congruent cognitive biases and sometimes the opposite is also discussed by Leonard Martin in Chapter 7. Most existing models of mood and cognition treat one effect as basic (e.g., affect congruence) and treat all other effects as exceptions to the rule. In contrast, Martin's configural affect-as-input model accounts for a variety of affective influences through a single mechanism, a configural role fulfillment model. Martin suggests that the nature of affective influences on cognition depends on how a person interprets the informational value of his or her affective state in the light of other, contextual information available at the time. Thus, the informational value of affect does not simply lie in its positive or negative valence, as Clore et al. (1994) and Schwarz (1990) suggested, but depends on whether affect is or is not congruent with what would be expected in a given context. These ideas go beyond existing formulations that simply emphasize the intrinsic informational value of positively and negatively valenced states and may thus be regarded as a major reformulation of the earlier affect-as-information hypothesis (Clore et al., 1994).

Nowhere is the informational value of affective states more critical than when it comes to forecasting reactions to future events, as Dan Gilbert explains in Chapter 8. He argues that the ability to transform, invent, and ignore emotionally relevant information provides an invisible shield against enduring negative affect, but that the invisibility of that shield also promotes a durability bias in affective forecasting, leading people to overestimate the intensity and duration of their future affective reactions. Gilbert presents evidence suggesting a clear tendency by people to overestimate the duration of their affective reactions to such events as the dissolution of a romantic relationship, the failure to achieve tenure, an electoral defeat, the receipt of negative personality feedback, and rejection by a prospective employer. He also describes studies that suggest these forecasting biases are caused by the participants' failure to correctly recognize that they will be able to ameliorate future negative affect.

Affect and Information Processing (Part III)

The chapters in Part III explore the role of affective states in information-processing strategies. For example, why are happy people more likely than sad people to rely on general knowledge structures such as heuristics and stereotypes when making judgments? Previous researchers have explained this effect by assuming that happy mood reduces processing motivation or capacity. In Chapter 9, Herbert Bless argues against this explanation, proposing instead that individuals are more likely to process new information in a bottom-up fashion when the situation is perceived as problematic, which is partly a function of being in a sad mood. In contrast, individuals are more likely to rely on preexisting general knowledge structures when the situation is perceived as safe, an inference that is partly a function of being in a happy mood. Bless describes a series of recent experiments that support his theoretical position and integrates his model with other recent processing theories.

In Chapter 10, Klaus Fiedler presents his new, dual-force model of how mood states influence cognitive style and memory performance. In Fiedler's view, cognitive processes can be decomposed into two complementary components: conservation and active generation. His model argues that positive affective states support the second component (generative thinking, creativity, top-down inferences), whereas negative affect promotes the first component (conserving stimulus details, vigilance, sticking to the facts). The complementary processes of accommodation and assimilation are modeled within a connectionist framework. Fiedler argues that such a dual-force model can explain numerous empirical findings, including enhanced stereotype and priming effects under positive mood, the greater sensitivity of negative mood subjects to strong and weak arguments in persuasion, constructive memory effects and enhanced generation effects in positive mood, and the accentuation of mood congruence for self-generated information. In addition to providing new, parsimonious interpretations of previous findings, Fiedler's model also makes several novel predictions and highlights underlying communalities between a number of existing affect/cognition theories.

In Chapter 11, Joseph Forgas discusses the bidirectional relationship between affect and processing strategies. He outlines a multiprocess model of affect and social cognition that highlights the role of different processing strategies in determining what kind of influence an affective state may have on cognitive activity. Four distinct processing strategies are identified: (1) direct access to crystallized information, (2) motivated processing in the service of a preexisting goal, (3) heuristic or simplified processing, and (4) substantive or elaborate processing. The theory also specifies how contextual features of the target, the judge, and the situation recruit different processing strategies. Forgas reviews a number of empirical studies stimulated by the AIM, demonstrating how different processing strategies produce different patterns of affect infusion into social cognition, social judgments, and even interpersonal behaviors. The complementary influence of affect on processing strategies is also discussed, and several studies illustrating this effect are reviewed. He argues that differences in processing style are the key to an integrative understanding of the bidirectional relationship between affect and social thinking.

Affect and Social Knowledge Structures (Part IV)

The previous two sections dealt with the informational, and the processing implications of affect, respectively. Part IV turns to a complementary issue: How is affect implicated in the cognitive representation and organization of social information? In Chapter 12, Carolin Showers discusses her intriguing work on the role of affect in the organization of self-knowledge. She differentiates between compartmentalized self-organization, when knowledge in a particular category is uniformly positive or negative, and integrative self-organization, when knowledge in a category is both positive and negative. In a series of experiments, using a variety of methods, Showers shows that compartmentalization may be effective for dealing with negative mood and negative beliefs about the self or others. However, when compartmentalization breaks down (e.g., when negative self-aspects are important and unavoidable), it may become necessary to integrate positive and negative self-beliefs. The chapter highlights the key role that affective valence plays in the way people construct and store self-knowledge.

Chapter 13 – by Tony Greenwald, Mahzarin Banaji, Laurie Rudman, Shelly Farnham, Brian Nosek, and Marshall Rosier – presents an exciting new theory that seeks to account for the role of affective, valenced representations in three of social psychology's central cognitive constructs: attitudes, stereotypes, and self-concept. The authors reach back to classic balance theories to account for the ways in which implicit associations between self-esteem and self-concept may distort the semantic representational space of social objects in at least two ways. First, social objects that are linked to the self are pulled toward the position of self in semantic space. Second, objects that are dissociated from self are repelled from the self's position in this space. Distortions in representations are most likely to occur in the evaluative (affective) dimension. Greenwald and his colleagues review recent findings supporting such a unified associative theory of cognitive representations of social objects. Recently developed empirical techniques, such as the Implicit Associations Test (IAT), offer an interesting method for quantifying the strength of such implicit evaluative links.

Although many emotions may be experienced as a result of either impersonal or interpersonal events, certain affective states (e.g., loneliness, embarrassment, and jealousy) occur only as the result of real, anticipated, or imagined interactions with other people. Much theory and research have examined the cognitive processes that precipitate social emotions, but little attention has been devoted to the reciprocal effects of interpersonal emotions on cognition. In Chapter 14, Mark Leary reviews recent work on the role of social emotions in how people think about themselves and about their relationships with others. He then provides a new theoretical framework for understanding the reciprocal effects of interpersonal emotions, social cognitions, and self-relevant thoughts.

Affect is intimately involved in the way we cognitively represent all social objects, as Paula Niedenthal and Jamin Halberstadt point out in Chapter 15. Traditional theories of categorization based on perceptual similarity ignore an important basis for conceptual structure: the discrete emotion that a stimulus elicits in the perceiver. Niedenthal and Halberstadt argue that emotional responses are salient features of stimuli that can also be used as the basis of categorization. The authors summarize a series of experiments investigating the nature and theoretical characteristics of emotional response categories, and explore the conditions under which they are used. These studies also show that emotional perceivers are more likely to base their categorization on affective characteristics. Multidimensional scaling analyses have shown that emotional categorization is not only tenable, but also is necessary for a complete account of conceptual coherence.

The last chapter (Forgas; Chapter 15) presents an overview and conceptual integration of the preceding discussion. The contributions within each of the four sections of the book will be critically reviewed, and integrative principles capable of linking them will be highlighted. The chapter will also discuss parallel developments in other fields that have implications for an emerging understanding of the affect-cognition interface. Finally, the chapter will also discuss the specific implications of the papers presented here for a number of substantive areas of research in psychology, and future prospects for affect-cognition research will be outlined.

References

Abele, A., & Petzold, P. (1994). How does mood operate in an impression formation task? An information integration approach. *European Journal of Social Psychology, 24*, 173–188.

Anderson, N. H. (1974). Cognitive algebra: Integration theory applied to social attribution. In L. Berkowitz (Ed.), *Advances in experimental social psychology* (Vol. 7, pp. 1–101). New York: Academic Press.

Berkowitz, L. (1993). Towards a general theory of anger and emotional aggression. In T. K. Srull & R. S. Wyer (Eds.), *Advances in social cognition* (Vol. 6, pp. 1–46). Hillsdale, NJ: Erlbaum.

Blaney, P. H. (1986). Affect and memory: A review. *Psychological Bulletin, 99,* 229–246.

Bower, G. H. (1981). Mood and memory. *American Psychologist, 36,* 129–148.

Bower, G. H. (1983). Affect and cognition. *Philosophical Transactions of the Royal Society, 302*(B), 387–403.

Bower, G. H. (1991). Mood congruity of social judgments. In J. P. Forgas (Ed.), *Emotion and social judgments* (pp. 31–53). Oxford: Pergamon Press.

Bower, G. H., & Mayer, J. D. (1985). Failure to replicate mood-dependent retrieval. *Bulletin of the Psychonomic Society, 23,* 39–42.

Bruner, J. S. (1957). On perceptual readiness. *Psychological Review, 64,* 123–152.

Byrne, D., & Clore, G. L. (1970). A reinforcement model of evaluation responses. *Personality: An International Journal, 1,* 103–128.

Clark, M. S., & Isen, A. M. (1982). Towards understanding the relationship between feeling states and social behavior. In A. H. Hastorf & A. M. Isen (Eds.), *Cognitive social psychology* (pp. 73–108). New York: Elsevier-North Holland.

Clore, G. L., & Byrne, D. (1974). The reinforcement affect model of attraction. In T. L. Huston (Ed.), *Foundations of interpersonal attraction* (pp. 143–170). New York: Academic Press.

Clore, G. L., & Parrott, G. (1991). Moods and their vicissitudes: Thoughts and feelings as information. In J. P. Forgas (Ed.), *Emotion and social judgments* (pp. 107–123). Oxford: Pergamon Press.

Clore, G. L., & Parrott, G. (1994). Cognitive feelings and metacognitive judgments. *European Journal of Social Psychology, 24,* 101–116.

Clore, G. L., Schwarz, N., & Conway, M. (1994). Affective causes and consequences of social information processing. In R. S. Wyer & T. K. Srull (Eds.) *Handbook of social cognition* (2nd ed., pp. 323–417). Hillsdale, NJ: Erlbaum.

Damasio, A. R. (1994). *Descartes' error.* New York: Grosset/Putnam.

De Sousa, R. (1987). *The rationality of emotion.* Cambridge, MA: MIT Press.

Ellis, H. C., & Ashbrook, T. W. (1988). Resource allocation model of the effects of depressed mood state on memory. In K. Fiedler & J. P. Forgas (Eds.), *Affect, cognition and social behaviour* (pp. 25–43). Toronto: Hogrefe.

Elster, J. (1985). Sadder but wiser? Rationality and the emotions. *Social Science Information, 24,* 375–406.

Feshbach, S., & Singer, R. D. (1957). The effects of fear arousal and suppression of fear upon social perception. *Journal of Abnormal and Social Psychology, 55,* 283–288.

Fiedler, K. (1990). Mood-dependent selectivity in social cognition. In W. Stroebe & M. Hewstone (Eds.), *European review of social psychology* (Vol. 1, pp. 1–32). Chichester: Wiley.

Fiedler, K. (1991). On the task, the measures and the mood in research on affect and social cognition. In J. P. Forgas (Ed.), *Emotion and social judgments* (pp. 83–104). Oxford: Pergamon Press.

Fiedler, K., & Forgas, J. P. (Eds.). (1988). *Affect, cognition and social behavior.* Toronto: Hogrefe International.

Fiedler, K. (in press). Affect and processing strategies. In L. L. Martin & G. Clore (Eds.), *Affect theories.* Mahwah, NJ: Erlbaum.

Forgas, J. P. (1989). Mood effects on decision-making strategies. *Australian Journal of Psychology, 41,* 197–214.

Forgas, J. P. (Ed.). (1991a). *Emotion and social judgments.* Oxford: Pergamon Press.

Forgas, J. P. (1991b). Mood effects on partner choice: Role of affect in social decisions. *Journal of Personality and Social Psychology, 61,* 708–720.

Forgas, J. P. (1991c). Affect and cognition in close relationships. In G. Fletcher & F. Fincham (Eds.), *Cognition in close relationships* (pp. 151–174). Hillsdale, NJ: Erlbaum.

Forgas, J. P. (1992a). Affect in social judgments and decisions: A multi-process model. In M. Zanna (Ed.), *Advances in experimental social psychology* (Vol. 25, pp. 227–275). New York: Academic Press.

Forgas, J. P. (1992b). On bad mood and peculiar people: Affect and person typicality in impression formation. *Journal of Personality and Social Psychology, 62,* 863–875.

Forgas, J. P. (1992c). Affect and social perceptions: Research evidence and an integrative model. In W. Stroebe & M. Hewstone (Eds.), *European review of social psychology* (Vol. 3, pp. 183–224). Chichester: Wiley.

Forgas, J. P. (1992d). Mood and the perception of unusual people: Affective asymmetry in memory and social judgments. *European Journal of Social Psychology, 22,* 531–547.

Forgas, J. P. (1993). On making sense of odd couples: Mood effects on the perception of mismatched relationships. *Personality and Social Psychology Bulletin, 19,* 59–71.

Forgas, J. P. (1994a). Sad and guilty? Affective influences on the explanation of conflict episodes. *Journal of Personality and Social Psychology, 66,* 56–68.

Forgas, J. P. (1994b). The role of emotion in social judgments: An introductory review and an Affect Infusion Model (AIM). *European Journal of Social Psychology, 24,* 1–24.

Forgas, J. P. (1995a). Mood and judgment: The affect infusion model (AIM). *Psychological Bulletin, 117*(1), 39–66.

Forgas, J. P. (1995b). Strange couples: Mood effects on judgments and memory about prototypical and atypical targets. *Personality and Social Psychology Bulletin, 21,* 747–765.

Forgas, J. P. (1998a). On feeling good and getting your way: Mood effects on negotiation strategies and outcomes. *Journal of Personality and Social Psychology, 74,* 565–577.

Forgas, J. P. (1998b). Asking nicely? The effects of mood on responding to more or less polite requests. *Personality and Social Psychology Bulletin, 24,* 173–185.

Forgas, J. P. (1998c). On being happy and mistaken: Mood effects on the fundamental attribution error. *Journal of Personality and Social Psychology*, 75, 318–331.

Forgas, J. P. (in press). On being sad and polite? Affective influences on language use and requesting strategies. *Personality and Social Psychology Bulletin*.

Forgas, J. P., & Bower, G. H. (1987). Mood effects on person perception judgements. *Journal of Personality and Social Psychology*, 53, 53–60.

Forgas, J. P., & Bower, G. H. (1988). Affect in social judgements. *Australian Journal of Psychology*, 40, 125–145.

Forgas, J. P., Bower, G. H., & Krantz, S. (1984). The influence of mood on perceptions of social interactions. *Journal of Experimental Social Psychology*, 20, 497–513.

Frijda, N. H. (1986). *The emotions*. Cambridge: Cambridge University Press.

Gouaux, C. (1971). Induced affective states and interpersonal attraction. *Journal of Personality and Social Psychology*, 20, 37–43.

Gouaux, C., & Summers, K. (1973). Interpersonal attraction as a function of affective states and affective change. *Journal of Research in Personality*, 7, 254–260.

Griffitt, W. (1970). Environmental effects on interpersonal behavior: Ambient effective temperature and attraction. *Journal of Personality and Social Psychology*, 15, 240–244.

Hilgard, E. R. (1980). The trilogy of mind: Cognition, affection, and conation. *Journal of the History of the Behavioral Sciences*, 16, 107–117.

Isen, A. (1984). Towards understanding the role of affect in cognition. In R. S. Wyer & T. K. Srull (Eds.), *Handbook of social cognition* (Vol. 3, pp. 179–236). Hillsdale, NJ: Erlbaum.

Isen, A. (1987). Positive affect, cognitive processes and social behaviour. In L. Berkowitz (Ed.), *Advances in experimental social psychology* (Vol. 20, pp. 203–253). New York: Academic Press.

Izard, C. E. (1964). The effect of role-played emotion on affective reactions, intellectual functioning and evaluative ratings of the actress. *Journal of Clinical Psychology*, 20, 444–446.

James, W. (1890). *Principles of psychology*. New York: Holt.

Kaplan, M. F. (1991). The joint effects of cognition and affect on social judgment. In J. P. Forgas (Ed.), *Emotion and social judgment* (pp. 73–82). Oxford: Pergamon.

Koestler, A. (1978). *Janus: A summing up*. London: Hutchinson.

Laird, J. D., & Bresler, C. (1991). The process of emotional experience: A self-perception theory. In M. Clark (Ed.), *Review of Personality and Social Psychology* (Vol. 14, pp. 213–234). Beverly Hills, CA: Sage.

Lazarus, R. S. (1984). On the primacy of cognition. *American Psychologist*, 39, 124–129.

Mackie, D., & Worth, L. (1991). Feeling good, but not thinking straight: The impact of positive mood on persuasion. In J. P. Forgas (Ed.), *Emotion and social judgments* (pp. 201–220). Oxford: Pergamon Press.

Mayer, J. D. (1986). How mood influences cognition. In N. E. Sharkey (Ed.),

Advances in cognitive science (Vol. 1, pp. 290–314). Chichester: Ellis Horwood.

Murray, H. A. (1933). The effects of fear upon estimates of the maliciousness of other personalities. *Journal of Social Psychology, 4*, 310–329.

Neisser, U. (1982). Memory: What are the important questions? In U. Neisser (Ed.), *Memory observed*. San Francisco: Freeman.

Niedenthal, P. M., & Setterlund, M. B. (1994). Emotion congruence in perception. *Personality and Social Psychology Bulletin, 20*(4), 401–411.

Oatley, K., & Jenkins, J. M. (1992). Human emotions: Function and dysfunction. *Annual Review of Psychology, 43*, 55–85.

Oatley, K., & Jenkins, J. M. (1996). *Understanding emotions*. Oxford: Blackwell.

Parrott, W. G., & Sabini, J. (1990). Mood and memory under natural conditions: Evidence for mood incongruent recall. *Journal of Personality and Social Psychology, 59*, 321–336.

Pascal, B. (1966/1643). *Pensées*. Baltimore: Penguin Books.

Razran, G. H. S. (1940). Conditioned response changes in rating and appraising sociopolitical slogans. *Psychological Bulletin, 37*, 481.

Ruiz Caballero, J. A., & Gonzalez, P. (1994). Implicit and explicit memory bias in depressed and non-depressed subjects. *Cognition and Emotion, 8*, 555–570.

Schwarz, N. (1990). Feelings as information: Informational and motivational functions of affective states. In E. T. Higgins & R. Sorrentino (Eds.), *Handbook of motivation and cognition: Foundations of social behaviour* (Vol. 2, pp. 527–561). New York: Guilford Press.

Schwarz, N., & Bless, H. (1991). Happy and mindless, but sad and smart? The impact of affective states on analytic reasoning. In J. P. Forgas (Ed.), *Emotion and social judgments* (pp. 55–71). Oxford: Pergamon Press.

Schwarz, N., & Clore, G. L. (1983). Mood, misattribution and judgments of well-being: Informative and directive functions of affective states. *Journal of Personality and Social Psychology, 45*, 513–523.

Schwarz, N., & Clore, G. L. (1988). How do I feel about it? The informative function of affective states. In K. Fiedler & J. P. Forgas (Eds.), *Affect, cognition, and social behavior* (pp. 44–62). Toronto: Hogrefe.

Sedikides, C. (1992). Changes in the valence of self as a function of mood. *Review of Personality and Social Psychology, 14*, 271–311.

Sedikides, C. (1994). Incongruent effects of sad mood on self-conception valence: It's a matter of time. *European Journal of Social Psychology, 24*, 161–172.

Sedikides, C. (1995). Central and peripheral self-conceptions are differentially influenced by mood: Tests of the differential sensitivity hypothesis. *Journal of Personality and Social Psychology, 69*(4), 759–777.

Sinclair, R. C., & Mark, M. M. (1992). The influence of mood state on judgment and action. In L. L. Martin & A. Tesser (Eds.), *The construction of social judgments* (pp. 165–193). Hillsdale, NJ: Erlbaum.

Toda, M. (1980). Emotion in decision-making. *Acta Psychologica, 45*, 133–155.

Wehmer, G., & Izard, C. E. (1962). *The effect of self-esteem and induced affect on interpersonal perception and intellective functioning.* Nashville, TN: Vanderbilt University.

Wessman, A. E., & Ricks, D. F. (1966). Mood and personality. *Experimental Aging Research, 10,* 197–200.

Wyer, R. S., & Srull, T. K. (1989). *Memory and cognition in its social context.* Hillsdale, NJ: Erlbaum.

Zajonc, R. B. (1980). Feeling and thinking: Preferences need no inferences. *American Psychologist, 35,* 151–175.

PART I

Fundamental Issues: The Interplay of Affect and Cognition

2. Feeling and Thinking

Closing the Debate Over the Independence of Affect

ROBERT B. ZAJONC

Historical Antecedents of Affective Primacy

This chapter seeks to close the debate about the independence of affect from cognition. It focuses on the conjecture, proposed almost 20 years ago (Zajonc, 1980), that cognition and affect are distinct, conceptually separable processes. At that time it was argued that affective reactions can take place virtually without the participation of any cognitive input, although no direct neuroanatomical or neurophysiological evidence was available to support these ideas. Since then, much behavioral, neuroanatomical, and neurophysiological evidence has been found – evidence that is clear and robust – and that substantiates many of the suppositions that derive from the original conjecture that "preferences need no inferences."

It is perplexing, in retrospect, that this conjecture invited such agitated opposition (e.g., Lazarus, 1982, 1991). "Passion" and "reason" were acknowledged as separate domains for at least 2,500 years, with "passion" emerging as an independent source of conduct, often unruly and harmful. The independence of these two realms of influence was affirmed by supposing without much contradiction that "reason" could be called upon as an autonomous process capable of modulating and moderating the "passions" (e.g., Aristotle, trans. 1991). And "reason" only came to the rescue after a potentially undesirable course of action was instigated by the "passions." So the "passions" were primary and "reason" followed. Not always, of course, but often.

Gustave Le Bon (1995/1895), to whom social psychology owes a

Communication in connection with this work may be sent to Robert B. Zajonc, Department of Psychology Stanford University, Stanford, California 94305, USA.

great deal, expressed himself quite clearly on the matter more than 100 years ago: "The individual forming part of a crowd descends several rungs in the ladder of civilization. Isolated, he may be a cultivated individual; in a crowd he is a barbarian – that is, a creature acting by instinct" (p. 52). This view of the interplay between "reason" and "passion" persisted over the centuries and appears as an indisputable axiom in a variety of philosophical, economic, psychological, sociological, and anthropological literature. Since the time of the early Greek philosophers, we have taken it for granted that it is the passions that make people similar, whereas reason or intellect is the source of individual differences (Zajonc, 1997).

In seeking to establish the independence of affect and cognition, I relied on the assumption that emotions are often unconscious, that they are often the first reactions of the organism to an instigating stimulus, and that if we can devise an experimental paradigm in which behavioral effects that are brought about by such early and nonconscious affective instigations can be observed, questions about the independence of affect from cognition could be answered at least in part. The conclusions that this chapter draws about the relationship between affect and cognition derive from a series of experimental findings in which specific affective experiences are induced at such low levels of energy that the person is not aware of them. Since there is no recognition or recognition memory of the sources of these experiences, we might say that there is no corresponding cognition to which the person has any access. Yet these experiences, which do not have conscious cognitive representations, generate marked changes in the person's affective dispositions to their sources.

For the present purposes – namely, to establish that there are conditions under which an affective reaction can occur prior to and independently of the participation of cognitive processes – I define affect and cognition by contrasting them in terms of prototypes. Thus, the prototype of affective response is the individual's expressed or inferred *preference* for one stimulus over another or others. "I like A better than B" is an instance of an affective response because it reveals 2that the individual invests greater positive affect for A than for B. In contrast, the prototype of a cognitive response is the evidence of *recognition* of a given stimulus as familiar and thus confirming its retrieval from memory. "I have seen A previously, but I have never seen B" is a prototype of a cognitive reaction.

Is Cognitive Judgment Better Evidence Than Affective Reaction of an Individual's Experience with a Stimulus?

The phenomena defined in this way have profound implications, not only for the question of the independence of affect from cognition, but more generally for what we take to be the evidence of the person's past history of experience. These implications are developed in the following assertions, with which almost all of psychology would readily agree.

Assertion 1. All of us, psychologists, are interested in the effects of past experience. We all want to know what traces experiences leave on people. How do these experiences affect them? What sort of changes in behavior are we to expect as a result of these experiences? This is really the basic focus of all psychology.

Assertion 2. This universal interest is fully reflected in our fundamental experimental paradigm. All of us have committed ourselves to the same basic procedure: We present some stimuli (or take it for granted that the individual had been somehow exposed to some stimuli in the past), and we record responses that we take for granted to be reactions to these stimuli. These stimuli might be words, pictures, objects, smells, tastes, nonsense syllables, figures, stories, life events – all sorts of things. But no matter what they are, they have the conceptual status of stimuli that will have some influence on the individual's reactions and responses.

Assertion 3. Sometimes these stimuli are shown once, sometimes more than once. And the person is required to make particular responses that are constrained in various ways: Sometimes the response is recall, when the subject is asked to reproduce the items previously presented. And usually that is all the subject does. Nothing more. Sometimes the response is a choice among alternatives, sometimes it is a judgment, perhaps, or an eye-blink, or the EEG, or an MRI record. But on all occasions psychologists constrain the subject to come up with one or two responses from a particular class of responses of this type.

Assertion 4. Whereas the key experimental focus of all psychologists is the person's experience with the stimulus, not everyone observes and records the same outcomes. In cognitive psychology, for example, the major outcomes of interest are recall, recognition, lexical decision, and cognitive judgment. Most of these outcomes are measured in some form of accuracy and response time. For the cognitive paradigm, the focus is on understanding how the individual absorbs the world. In the paradigm dedicated to the understanding of the mind as a reasoning machine, psychologists study the ways people *get to know the world around them*. Its model is psychophysics, and its paradigmatic method is signal detection. All other forms of cognitive inquiry are simply special cases of this basic psychophysical paradigm.

Assertion 5. But there is another paradigm, best exemplified by more traditional social psychology. Here, too, psychologists begin by presenting some stimulus, sometimes once, sometimes more often. But our focus is not on recall or recognition. It is most often on people's affective dispositions, or their liking, their preferences, their attitudes. We are interested in seeing how past experience with a given stimulus changes the person's *affective disposition* to that stimulus. In short, the two paradigms of psychology differ in their focal perspectives: The first focuses on how we come to *understand* and represent the world around us. The second focuses on how we *relate* to that world. Hence, because our scientific goals are different, our dependent measures are different as well.

Assertion 6. Now, these distinctions carry certain implications, which are not so obvious. Cognitive psychologists do not care what happens to the participants' affective dispositions to the given word, picture, or story. They could not care less how well the participants like the 10 nonsense syllables or 8 three-dimensional shapes they were asked to memorize. It is simply irrelevant to an experimental psychologist that participants might have particular preferences for some of these stimuli and feel contempt for others. But the participants do! It is no secret that whether we ask the participants about their preferences and dispositions or not – they do exist, and they, too, change as a result of experience. Participants do not restrict their behavior to suit the experimenter's convenience. They do not confine their reactions to the experimental paradigms that we inflict on them. They change their cognitive representations with experience, and they also change their affective dispositions. When bombarded with some experimental manipulation, participants respond with all they have to respond with, whether it is recorded or not. And since those of us of the cognitive persuasion do not ask questions about the participants' affective reactions or dispositions, and since the changes in these dispositions are often not accessible to the participants' awareness, we are simply ignorant of the affective influences that we have inflicted on our subjects.

Now, even if we are only interested in knowing how individuals represent the world around them, can we ignore this affective source of variation? There just might be an interaction here such that the three-dimensional shapes the person happens to like might be remembered better. Also, the affective disposition of a person to a particular stimulus is quite different when that stimulus has been presented for a second time. You cannot step in the same river twice. But this is not because the river is different. You cannot step in it twice because *you* are different. After having encountered a given stimulus, the person is significantly different from a person who has never encountered it. The person is subjectively, behaviorally, and neurophysiologically different. This is demonstrated, for example, by a marked increment in the liking for Chinese ideographs after they had been presented only once before, for only 4 msec and with a red filter – a condition of exposure that did not allow for any recognition memory whatsoever (Murphy, Monahan, & Zajonc, 1995).

In this chapter, I argue that for many important purposes, and under many conditions, the change in preference of an affective disposition is a *more revealing* indicator of the cognitive, memorial, or representational effects of past experience than is a recognition or recall test. This is particularly true when the person is not aware of his or her experience with the stimulus.

The Consequences of Repeated Stimulus Exposure

It is now well established that changes in affective dispositions can be produced by absurdly minimal procedures. Research has consistently shown that when a particular stimulus is shown over and over again, for instance, it gets to be better liked (Zajonc, 1968). This "mere exposure" effect has been demonstrated in a variety of contexts, using a wide assortment of stimuli, populations, and procedures (Harrison, 1977). Exposure effects were found for geometric figures, random polygons, Chinese and Japanese ideographs, numbers, letters of the alphabet, letters of one's own name, random sequences of tones, nonsense syllables, odors, flavors, colors, foods, faces, actual persons, and many others. And, according to cross-cultural psychologists (Smith & Bond, 1993), the mere exposure effect is valid in all cultures thus far examined. American undergraduates, nationals of 12 countries, sons of alcoholics, amnesiacs, dieters, chicks, ducklings, and goslings were all found responsive to exposure effects. Exposure effects were also found with human neonates and were induced prenatally in fetuses (Rajecki, 1972).

The typical experiments are quite simple. Some novel objects that are not familiar to the participants – say, Chinese ideographs – are shown to participants several times, and afterward they are simply asked how much they like these objects. In all these experiments, the objects are presented once, twice, 5, 10, and 25 times. After these presentations, the objects are shown again one at a time, along with objects that the person never saw in the prior series. The participants' affective disposition to these stimuli is then recorded. Of course, the objects are always counterbalanced, such that the same object was frequent for some participants and infrequent for others. In one of the first studies, we presented Chinese ideographs, some frequently, some infrequently, some never, all at optimal durations, with good illumination, and at a comfortable distance. Participants were subsequently asked whether these ideographs represented something "good" or something "bad." Figure 2.1 shows that the frequently presented ideographs, independently of which ones they were (because they were counterbalanced with frequency), were liked better than the infrequent ones.

If the experiment is replicated using, say, Turkish-like nonsense words or photographs of students from a yearbook, the same results are obtained, as can be seen from Figure 2.2.

And the relationship between the frequency of exposure and positive affect for the stimuli exposed is systematically logarithmic. Figure 2.3 shows that the relationship between frequency of exposure and affect ratings is linear when plotted on a log scale. The early encounters matter most.

Everyday effects of repeated exposure have also been explored in some interesting ways. For example, Mita, Dermer, and Knight (1977) called into their laboratory couples of friends or lovers. They took portrait photographs of each member of the pair. Then they made two prints of each photograph: a regular print, and another one in which the negative was reversed. Thus, the regular photograph displays the image of the participants as other people see them, whereas the reversed print displays the image that the participants see in the mirror. Clearly, the reversed orientation is the most frequent experience of

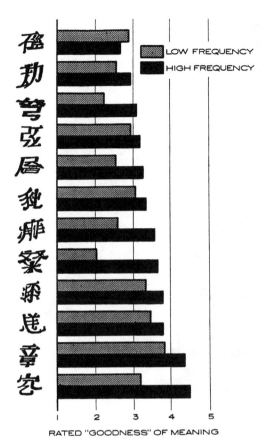

Figure 2.1. The effects of frequency of prior exposure on liking for Chinese ideographs.

one's own face, and the regular photograph is the vastly more frequent experience of a friend or lover. (We do, on some occasions, see our friends in a mirror.) The participants were asked which of the two photographs they preferred. The results were quite clear. The reversed photograph of oneself was clearly preferred to the regular photograph and the regular photograph of one's friend or lover was clearly preferred to the reversed photograph.

In many cases, the paradigm of *imprinting* cannot be distinguished from mere exposure research. Typical in this category of work is an experiment by Taylor and Sluckin with chicks (1964). They raised newly hatched chicks under three conditions: with a conspecific peer, alone, or with a matchbox. The researchers then observed the chicks'

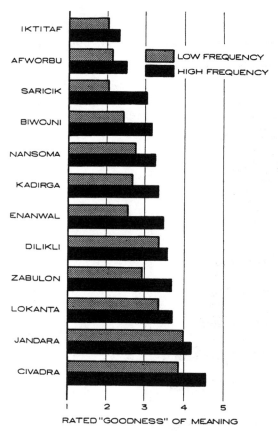

Figure 2.2. The effects of frequency of prior exposure on liking for nonsense words.

preferences. The chicks were placed in a choice situation, an arena containing three pie-shaped segments that could be approached: One contained a same-age chick (but not the one they lived with), another segment contained a matchbox, and the third segment was empty. The chicks chose the pie segment that most resembled their immediate past experience. Most significantly, they clearly preferred the matchbox over a conspecific when their early exposure was to a matchbox (see Fig. 2.4).

The generality and robustness of the phenomenon is in fact remarkable. Here is an extreme example. In another experiment on the effects of exposure, Cross, Halcomb, and Matter (1967) exposed rats to two types of music for a period of 4 weeks. Some heard Mozart, others

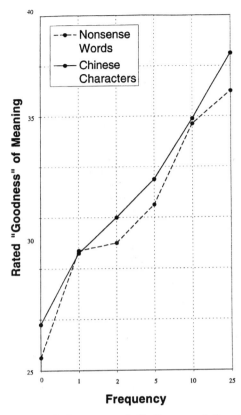

Figure 2.3. Average rated affective connotation of nonsense words and Chinese-like characters as a function of frequency of prior exposure. (From Zajonc, 1968.)

heard Schoenberg, and the least fortunate control group was deprived of this rich experience altogether. After this heavy dose of culture, all groups were tested in a chamber with a suspended floor that was hinged in the middle. Microswitches installed under each side of the floor could activate Channel 1 or Channel 2 of a tape recorder. Channel 1 played Mozart, Channel 2 Schoenberg. They were not the same compositions the rats had heard previously. While in training, the rats heard *Eine Kleine Nachtmusik* and the *Trumpet Concerto*, whereas the test featured the *Jupiter Symphony* and other compositions not heard before. If the training presented the animals with Schoenberg's *Pierrot Lunaire*, the test piece was *Verklärte Nacht* or *Chamber Symphony No. 1*. There is no doubt from Figure 2.5 that the rats preferred to hear the music that became familiar to them. It is also of passing interest that

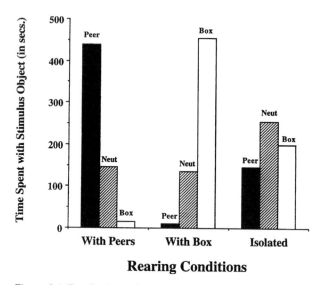

Figure 2.4. Familiarity with stimuli influences preferences: Imprinting or exposure effects? (From Taylor & Sluckin, 1964.)

12-tone music is not as attractive to rats as Mozart: The results for the familiarized music in the experimental groups and in the control group showed a greater preference for Mozart. An important aspect of the mere exposure studies, in the case of human participants, is that they have no idea that their feelings have changed. They do not know that objects repeatedly presented to them are now more attractive to them. We have always asked our participants why they liked or disliked the objects we showed them. Out of the hundreds of participants we have tested, perhaps one or two have ever said that the feeling of familiarity was a factor in their preferences. Most said that they liked the ideograph because it was symmetrical, for example (or complex, or rounded, or stable), or because it reminded them of a landscape, or a particular sculpture. Even when participants were told that some stimuli were shown more frequently than others and they were asked why they liked one stimulus better than another, they decidedly ignored any explanation having to do with familiarity or frequency of experience. They insisted that they would never be influenced by sheer familiarity in making an esthetic judgment.

It would seem obvious that the frequently exposed stimuli would be liked better. Or should they be liked less? Because, after all, "familiarity breeds contempt"? Titchener (1910) agreed with the findings

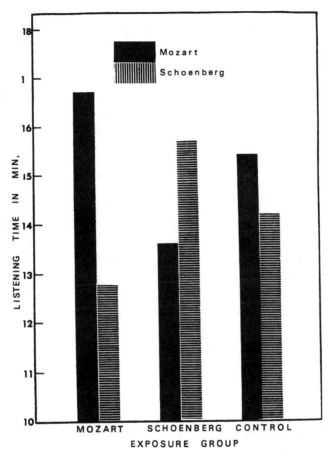

Figure 2.5. Musical preferences of rats reared with music by Mozart, of rats reared with music by Schoenberg, and of rats without musical background. (From Cross, Halcomb, & Matter, 1967.)

cited above. He spoke of the warm glow of recognition. One sees something, one recognizes it as something from one's past, and as a result the person feels "one with it," united with it, drawn to it. Titchener's foremost example was our experience of music. One hears a piece of music. When it is familiar, one can successfully predict the development, the next few bars, hum along with it, and there is as a result a pleasure of recognition.

All subsequent research, however, has demonstrated that Titchener was quite wrong and that recognition itself, or the subjective impression of recognition, cannot explain the exposure effect. In a typical mere exposure experiment, Matlin (1970) asked participants not only whether they liked the given objects, after exposing them, but outright how familiar they were. She found clear evidence that subjective judgments of familiarity mattered little. What really mattered was the objective history of exposures. In another experiment, Wilson (1979), using auditory stimuli to examine the role of recognition and familiarity, also found that preferences for often presented stimuli can be established in the absence of subjective familiarity or objective recognition memory (Fig. 2.6).

Exposure Effects in the Absence of Awareness

If preferences can be established in the absence of participants' recognition of the stimuli previously exposed, the role of awareness in the mere exposure effect becomes critical. The possibility must therefore be entertained that under some, perhaps most, conditions, mere exposure effects are not conscious, are not the outcome of a cognitive computation, and are not the result of a subjective feeling of familiarity. In short, they may occur unconsciously.

The role of awareness in exposure effects was studied more closely in another experiment (Kunst-Wilson & Zajonc, 1980). Instead of examining the differences in exposure effects between optimally pre-

Objective familiarity	Subjective familiarity			
	"OLD"	"NEW"	Mean	Δ
OLD	3.51	3.85	3.66	
				.63
NEW	3.03	3.02	3.03	
MEAN	3.29	3.40		
Δ		-.11		

Figure 2.6. Average stimulus affect ratings as a function of objective familiarity (OLD–NEW and subjective familiarity ("OLD"–"NEW"). (From Wilson, 1979: Experiment II.)

sented stimuli that were or were not recognized, we created conditions of stimulus exposure that made it impossible for participants to become aware of exposures altogether. The polygons used as stimuli were each presented three times without a mask for a duration of 1 msec in a randomized order. After the exposure phase, a pair of polygons was presented for a substantial duration: 2 sec. One of these polygons had been shown previously and the other was entirely new. There were two conditions, counterbalanced for order. In both conditions, the participants made two sets of forced choices, one requiring them to identify the stimulus they preferred and another to identify the stimulus that was presented previously. In one condition, preference judgments were made first and recognition memory judgments second; in the other condition, the order was reversed. The results showed that even without conscious recognition of the old stimuli (the success of the recognition memory responses was at chance level), objectively old stimuli were preferred to the new ones (Fig. 2.7).

Even under these minimal exposure conditions a typical exposure

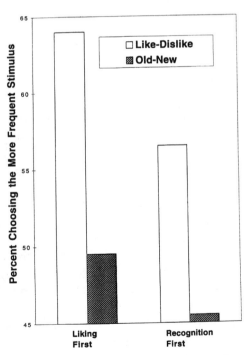

Figure 2.7. Previous exposure determines subsequent preferences for stimuli. (From Kunst-Wilson & Zajonc, 1980.)

effect was obtained – an effect of an experience so minimal that no awareness could have been involved. Thus, preferences can be built up without participants' awareness of the sources of these preferences. The experiment also demonstrated that a subjective impression of familiarity does not mediate the exposure effect. It is the objective history of stimulus exposure, the objective history of the participants' past experience, that constitutes the critical factor in the exposure effect. In other words, these data show that an affective reaction is possible without much participation of conscious cognitive processes. This experiment produced another interesting result. Preference judgments were made faster than recognition memory judgments. And participants had more confidence in these judgments than in other judgments they made, such as old-new judgments or judgments of how complex the polygons were. Since then, the result that preference judgments established by repeated exposure can be obtained in the absence of recognition has been replicated many times (see Bornstein, 1989).

The Kunst-Wilson/Zajonc experiment suggested the possibility that affect and cognition may not be one complex process but two distinct ones, that although they interact constantly in everyday life, perhaps in principle there exist two basic processes – processes that it may be possible to separate (Zajonc, 1980). As already noted, no direct neuroanatomic or neurophysiological evidence was available at that time to support the idea that we have two separate systems here, affect and cognition. But such evidence was eventually found, and it is now a widely accepted fact that affect and cognition are functionally and anatomically distinct processes (Damasio, 1994). LeDoux (1995) has perhaps provided the most convincing research on the question. The older work on the Klüver-Bucy syndrome, and the work by Mishkin (1978) on the connections between the amygdala, the hippocampus, and the neocortex converge to show the independence of affect and cognition. The amygdala-thalamus pathway is apparently only one synapse in length, whereas the hippocampus is separated from the thalamus by several synapses. This configuration allows a response in the amygdala to occur 40 msec faster than in the hippocampus (LeDoux, 1986). Zola-Morgan and his colleages (1991) performed bilateral amygdalectomies on some monkeys and tested them for reactions to emotional stimulation. The animals did not respond appropriately, as can be seen from Figure 2.8. But they were able to engage in complex cognitive tasks, such as learning and recall, matching to sample, and

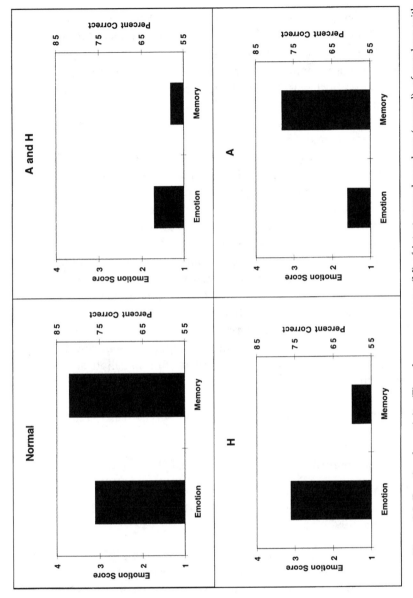

Figure 2.8. Emotional reactivity (E) and memory scores (M) of intact normal monkeys (normal), of monkeys with amygdalae removed (A), of monkeys with hippocampi removed (H), and of monkeys with both amygdalae and hippocampi removed (A and H). (From Zola-Morgan, Squire, Alvarez-Royo, & Clower, 1991.)

discrimination. Another group of monkeys had their hippocampi removed. These monkeys, in turn, were emotionally intact. But they had great difficulty on the cognitive tasks.

The anatomical separation of preference and recognition specific to the exposure effect was clearly demonstrated in a recent experiment by Elliott and Dolan (1998) of the Royal Free Hospital in London. They replicated the Kunst-Wilson/Zajonc study and collected positron Emission Tomography (PET) scans while participants were making preference and recognition judgments. Their data revealed a clear exposure effect in the absence of recognition. They discovered, moreover, that the two processes – recall and preferences – are localized in separate regions of the brain. Memory judgments showed activation in the left frontopolar cortex and the parietal areas, whereas preference judgments based on frequency of exposure showed right lateral frontal activation. As in our experiments, the presentations were degraded to prevent recognition. The participants could not distinguish between novel stimuli and stimuli that were presented on 10 successive occasions. Nor did the participants have any subjective impressions of familiarity for stimuli previously presented. Yet there was distinctive activation in the right hippocampal gyrus during the recognition test, especially for the unfamiliar stimuli. Elliott and Dolan speculate that this activation may reflect some form of retrieval effort, albeit unsuccessful, that was not active when preference judgments were made. Here, the medial frontal region was active.

The Affect-Cognition Distinction Specified

If affect and emotions are distinct from cognition, what is the nature of the difference between them? Several differences have been identified (Zajonc, 1997):

1. There is an infinite number of distinct cognitions. The number of distinct emotions is rather small in comparison.
2. We speak of basic emotions. But what are basic cognitions?
3. Cognitions can be evaluated for their correctness. Individuals can be asked to compare the sizes of a turkey and a hummingbird, and the accuracy of their estimates can be evaluated. But we can also ask the same individuals which of the two birds they find more attractive. These latter judgments cannot be tested for their accuracy or validity.

4. Cognitions are always *about* something. They have a referent, an address; they stand for something. They are representations of some aspect of reality or imagination. Emotions, too, are object-oriented, but neither are they about something nor do they stand for something else outside of themselves. They are not representations of reality – they are reality. Moreover, some emotions have no referent at all. Free-floating anxiety is an example of an emotion without a referent. In contrast, there is no such thing as a free-floating cognition.

5. Emotions often precipitate action, sometimes very drastic and dangerous action. Anger will evoke antagonistic, sometimes quite violent, reactions and fear will instigate flight or panic. In contrast, cognitions of themselves are incapable of triggering an instrumental process, unless they first generate an emotion that mobilizes a motivational state capable of recruiting action.

6. We share many of our emotions with the lower animals. But our mental lives, our cognitive processes, are light-years apart from those of even the great apes.

7. Emotional expressions seem to be universal across cultures. Cognitions, and certainly their communication through language, are diverse in many respects.

8. We admire mathematical prodigies, mnemonists, geniuses – in short, "cognitive virtuosos." But there are no "emotional prodigies." We speak of an "intellectual giant," but what might an "emotional giant" be?

If we can accept these differences between affect and cognition, it is easier to accept the proposition that they are independent processes. Of course, in everyday life they interact constantly and one seldom occurs without the other. But the proposition I offer here – that they are conceptually, anatomically, and dynamically independent processes – is that they are so in principle.

The Consequences of Affect Inaccessible to Awareness

Given the properties of nonconscious, unaddressed affect, what are its consequences? What happens when we induce nonconscious affect? Nonconscious affect has been recognized in clinical psychology in the form of the phenomenon of free-floating anxiety. Free-floating anxiety is a state – a feeling – a mood, in which the person has no idea of the origin of the feeling. It is a sort of fear, but the person does not know what he or she is afraid of, and has no idea of how to escape it. It is diffuse and nonspecific. If all nonconscious affect has this quality of being diffuse, unaddressed, and undedicated, then this affect should have properties that conscious affect would not have.

The differences between cognition and emotion are even more pronounced when we compare cognition and nonconscious affect. For example, because it is undedicated and unreferenced, such affect should spill onto almost any stimuli that are currently present – stimuli totally unrelated to the individual's condition at the moment. If the person is unable to specify either the origin or the target of affect he or she is experiencing, then this affect can attach itself to anything that is present at the moment. It should be possible for this affect to suffuse any stimulus that happens to be around. Stimuli that have no connection with its origin can thus become targets of nonconscious affect.

Can affective changes be induced without a subject's awareness? Murphy and Zajonc (1987) explored this question using the experimental paradigm of affective priming. We picked the face to work with as a stimulus, believing that the human face is just the kind of stimulus that can exert strong but unconscious affective influences. It is quite likely that the face is a very special stimulus. There are structures in the brain that, when damaged, produce prosopagnosia – the inability to recognize faces. Also, Perret, Rolls, and Caan (1982) found cells in the temporal sulcus of the monkey that respond to faces and only to faces. These cells respond mainly to faces in the frontal orientation. There are other cells that fire only to faces shown in profile. Because facial expressions are so critical, an appropriate emotional reaction might be expected to the various emotional expressions. In fact, Dimberg (1982) has shown photographs of smiling and frowning faces while measuring participants' myographic responses in the corrugator and the zygomatic muscles. He found clear evidence of corresponding muscular reactions to photographs of faces. Smiles produced zygomatic activity and suppressed corrugator, whereas frowns enhanced corrugator activity while suppressing the zygomatic muscles.

Because of the strong power of the face as an interpersonal stimulus, the person might respond positively to a smiling face even without having full visual access – even when presented in visual periphery. We took advantage of these special affective properties of the face to obtain affective influences without awareness. We also made use of the priming method. In the priming method, thus far employed principally in semantic priming, and used mainly at optimal viewing conditions, two stimuli are shown in close succession. The subject is required to respond only to the second stimulus. Suppose there are two words in succession, say, DOCTOR and APPLE. On some trials, the second stimulus may simply be a random string of letters. The participant is asked whether the second is a word or not. The results of semantic priming show that the first word can influence the response to the second. If the second word is NURSE and not APPLE, for example, the participant's lexical decision is quicker. On some occasions, semantic primes are given at degraded viewing conditions. Here, priming effects are also obtained, but they are weaker.

In our own experiment, we also employed priming, but we did not prime meaning. We primed emotions; hence, we used the term *affective priming*. Since the early experiment by Murphy and Zajonc (1987), a considerable number of other studies have successfully induced nonconscious affect (Barchas & Perlaki, 1986; Bonnano & Stilling, 1986; Bornstein, 1989; Bornstein, Leone, & Galley, 1987; Kunst-Wilson & Zajonc, 1980; Mandler, Nakamura, & Van Zandt, 1987; Murphy & Zajonc, 1993; Murphy, Monahan, & Zajonc, 1995; Seamon, Brody, & Kauff, 1983a, 1983b; Seamon, Marsh, & Brody, 1989). All participants were shown Chinese ideographs for a duration of 2 sec. In all cases they were asked how much they liked each of them, or sometimes whether the ideograph represented something that was GOOD or something that was BAD. These ideographs were affectively primed – that is, they were preceded – by smiling or frowning faces, either for 4 msec or for a full second. There were 45 trials altogether with two controls: no primes at all or neutral primes, that is, random polygons. However, the crucial ones were 20 trials interspersed over the entire series. On 10 of these trials a smiling face preceded each of 10 ideographs (different face for each ideograph), and on the other 10 a frowning face preceded each of the 10 ideographs.[1] In the two sets of trials the ideographs were the same. So when we compare the liking for ideographs that followed smiling and frowning primes we are comparing liking for the same ideographs judged by the same participants. The results were quite clear. Figure 2.9 shows those conditions in which the priming stimulus was presented at subliminal or supraliminal levels.

There is a clear difference between the liking of the Chinese ideo-

MEAN LIKING RATINGS

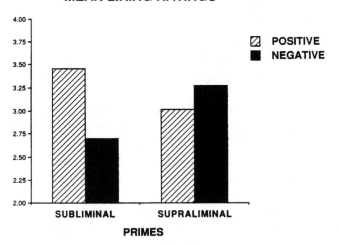

Figure 2.9. Liking ratings following subliminally and supraliminally presented positive and negative primes. (From Murphy & Zajonc, 1993.)

graphs when they were preceded by a smiling prime and when they were preceded by a frowning prime. Recall that identical ideographs, primed once positively and once negatively, were presented to the same participants. Because the faces were presented at suboptimal viewing levels, no participant became aware that anything preceded the ideographs. Yet their ratings of these ideographs showed a clear effect derived entirely from the suboptimal affective stimuli. So there is an affective reaction without awareness.

But we are still a few steps away from understanding how all these things happen. How can mere exposure, or priming, make people change their preference for such objects as polygons, ideographs, or nonsense words, especially when the participant has no conscious access to these stimuli or is unaware of their influence? One way of thinking about the results was proposed to me by Norbert Schwarz, who suggested that affect might well serve as a source of information about the individual's own state (see Schwarz & Clore, 1983). This idea is supported by studies in which people are asked about their well-being under two conditions. In one case, respondents are made aware of the weather and in the other they are not. They are simply asked if it is raining outside, or if the sun is shining. When the person is made aware of the weather, and the weather happens to be nice, then the ratings of well-being are lower than when the weather is bad.

The result is taken to mean that the participants read their total feelings and that they distribute all the influence over all the possible causes: their actual well-being, the weather, their recent successes, or quarrels. Thus, when asked about affect of a particular kind or of a particular source, a person will discount affect that derives from sources other than those that constitute the focus of the question. If it is impossible, under the given conditions, to attribute one's "gut feeling" to anything else, then all the affect felt will combine to mistakenly reflect the totality of affect that the person feels about the object in question – in the case of the Schwarz-Clore experiment, his or her own well-being. So, under ambiguous circumstances such as those in which affective priming occurs subliminally, there is a chance of misattribution. Forgas (1995) has written a very cogent article showing that this sort of discounting indeed occurs, but it occurs under some very special and perhaps infrequent conditions.

Winkielman, Zajonc, and Schwarz (1997) carried out a study that derived from the affect-as-information theory. We more or less replicated the Murphy-Zajonc experiment, adding to it manipulations that would allow the participants to discount in various ways the gut feeling they were experiencing as a result of affective priming. Essentially, we tried to determine if misattribution would occur and if affective priming would thereby be obliterated when participants were made aware of the source of their affective reactions. The manipulation consisted of comparing five groups. In the case of one group, we simply replicated the conditions of the Murphy-Zajonc study – same stimuli (i.e., Chinese ideographs), same primes (i.e., smiling and frowning faces), and same presentation intervals (i.e., 4 msec with a mask). The other four groups received a warning that the ideograph would be preceded by another brief presentation. In the nonspecific treatment, the participants were told only that something would be shown just before the ideograph. In the positive expectation treatment, they were told that a slide of a smiling face would be presented. In the negative expectation treatment, the participants were told that a frowning face would be presented. And in the positive or negative expectation treatment, the participants were alerted to the fact that *either* a smiling *or* a frowning face would precede the ideograph. The experiment was replicated using affect-inducing music.

The overall results did not reveal a discounting process of any sort, and the effects were the same as in the Murphy-Zajonc experiment. Moreover, no discounting was obtained even when the participants were told that the prior presentation might have positive effects on their judgments. The induced expectations could not obliterate the priming effect.

We now know that affect can be induced without a participant's awareness – just by showing a degraded stimulus a few times. In the priming experiments, we were also able to induce affect without awareness, but here the induction was such that it spilled onto unrelated stimuli. A smiling face caused a Chinese ideograph to be attractive. A frowning face caused it to be unattractive. This suggests that nonconscious affect must be quite subtle and diffuse. It cannot be terribly well articulated or else the participants would be able to discover its origin and therefore appraise it, a condition under which Forgas's (1995) Affect Infusion Model (p. 45) would predict discounting.

The effects of exposure are also not accessible to the person's awareness, as we have seen. The next question, then, is whether the nature of affect induced by mere exposure is similar to that elicited by affective priming. We examined this question in a series of experiments that compared optimal and suboptimal priming (Murphy, Monahan, & Zajonc, 1995). If nonconscious affect is generally diffuse, as it is in free-floating anxiety, for example, it should be possible to combine affect from two sources into one reaction. Moreover, if the two sources of affect are both nonconscious, and therefore of the same quality – gross and diffuse – then the effects should combine.

The Murphy-Monahan-Zajonc experiment simply combined the priming paradigm used by Murphy and Zajonc (1987, 1993) and the subliminal exposure effect used by Kunst-Wilson and Zajonc (1980). The procedure consisted of varying the exposure frequency of Chinese ideographs, presented subliminally, and then having participants judge these ideographs, and others not previously presented, under three conditions. Some ideographs were presented once, some three times, and some were not presented at all. After these presentations, the participants were asked about their liking for these ideographs, but just before the slide of the ideograph appeared for judgment, there was a subliminal presentation of a face. The face was neutral, smiling, or frowning. The participants were asked to judge the ideographs for attractiveness. Figure 2.10 presents the results of the condition in which both the exposure manipulation and affective priming were at suboptimal viewing levels.

The slopes of the graph show that the exposure effect induced at

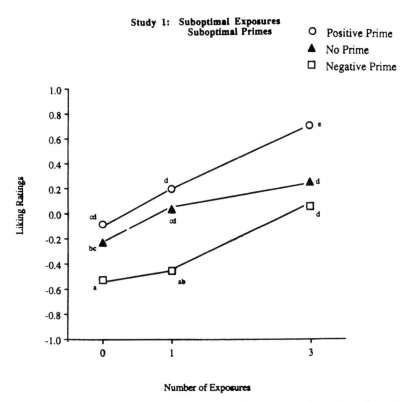

Figure 2.10. Liking ratings as a function of exposure and priming effects. (From Monahan, Murphy, & Zajonc, 1995.)

levels below awareness were replicated. It is possible then to make people like something just by exposing them to it even at levels at which they have no conscious access to the stimuli. Interestingly the difference between 0 and 1 exposures is significant in two cases. This means that sometimes one exposure alone is sufficient to alter a person's preference for an innocuous object. The differences in the intercepts, on the other hand, replicate the nonconscious affective priming effect. Positive faces enhance the liking ratings, whereas negative faces depress it. The curves are parallel and there is no interaction, which means that the influences of the two sources of affect are indeed additive.

The nature of nonconscious affect is now somewhat better understood. The differences between the properties of nonconscious and conscious affect might best be represented by a metaphor that highlights the contrast with cognition, especially conscious cognition. Cognitions are like antigens. They are dedicated. They must address themselves to something specific. They all have their own referents. They must be *about* something. And they can be attached only to entities that have a specifiable quality; they are referent-specific. There is no such thing as a free-floating cognition. But nonconscious affect is quite different. It is more like moisture, it is like odor, like heat. It can disperse, displace, scatter, permeate, float, combine, fuse, blend, spill over, and become attached to any stimulus, even one totally unrelated to its origins. We saw that affect produced by priming Chinese ideographs with a slide of a smiling or frowning face, shown under degraded conditions, made the ideograph more or less attractive. There was then, so to speak, an infusion of affect from the face onto the ideograph. Note that I am not speaking of all affect; I am speaking mainly about nonconscious affect, although some conscious affect may under some circumstances – mainly somewhat pathological – act that way too.

The quality of nonconscious affect that is generated from repeated exposure was also investigated further to see just how diffuse it might be (Monahan, Murphy, & Zajonc, 1999). The question was whether, under the paradigm of mere exposure experiments, the very aspect of repetition, even if it is not accessible to the individual's awareness, can in itself have an affective influence – one that is unconnected to the stimuli that are presented but derives entirely from the fact that they were repeated and as such generated an agreeable mood. To determine the nature of this affect, we showed two groups of participants Chinese ideographs under different conditions. We showed one group 5 ideographs presented subliminally 5 times in random order. We showed the other group 25 ideographs, presented once each. We then asked the participants to rate for liking the ideographs presented, similar ideographs that were not presented, and entirely new stimuli previously not exposed at all, namely, random polygons. The experiment was replicated with polygons serving as target stimuli and ideographs as the novel stimuli.

The results show that stimuli unrelated to the prior experience were rated more positively when they were preceded by an experience of repeated exposures of unrelated and distinct stimuli. It would appear, then, that repetition of experience, even when not accessible to awareness, constitutes a positive hedonic event.

In a final experiment, we simply wanted to know whether the participants' own mood changes when they experience repeated exposures to anything, that is, whether their general hedonic tone is somehow made more positive. So we repeated the previous procedure – that is, 5 stimuli each subliminally exposed 5 times, or 25 stimuli each subliminally exposed once. But now we asked the participants about their mood state. There was a clear evidence of increase in positive mood state as a result of just repeating the exposure of the same stimulus.

These results, it seems, cannot be easily explained by some form of perceptual fluency effect (e.g., Jacoby, 1983) because no recognition measures are taken from the participants and the test questions expose nothing of the previous experience – only a face that varies from neutral to smiling. But it is clear that repetition of an experience can in itself change specific and nonspecific affect in a positive direction.

In summary, the following conclusions might now be drawn from the foregoing discussion:

1. Repeated stimulus exposures result in the growth of positive affect toward that stimulus, even when the stimulus is not accessible to awareness.
2. Under some conditions, especially under degraded stimulus access, affective ratings of stimuli are better indicators of the individual's past experience with these stimuli than recognition memory.
3. Nonconscious affect can be gross and diffuse. It is undedicated and unaddressed. It has a weak attachment to its referent. In contrast, cognition, both conscious and nonconscious, is specific, dedicated, addressed, and referenced.
4. Because of these properties, nonconscious affect can become attached to any stimulus, even an irrelevant one, and it can combine additively with affect from other sources.
5. These findings, together with the recent neuroanatomical evidence, agree with the proposition that affect may function independently of cognition.

If it is the case that under some conditions – conditions that occur quite frequently in everyday life – affective responses are often reliable indicators of the person's past experience, the challenge for psychology, for a postcognitive psychology, is to unite cognitive theory with emotion theory. In practice, this means that we need to start to collect affective reactions as we collect cognitive judgments, even though we are primarily interested in cognitive outcomes, and to collect cognitive judgments even if we are primarily interested in affective ones.

Note

1. Other methods of inducing nonconscious affect were also successfully employed by the Michigan Group (Edwards, 1990; Kitayama, 1991; Niedenthal, 1990).

References

Aristotle. (1991). *The art of rhetoric.* Translated by H. C. Lawson-Tancred. London: Penguin.

Barchas, P. R., & Perlaki, K. M. (1986). Processing preconsciously acquired information measured in hemispheric asymmetry and selection accuracy. *Behavioral Neuroscience, 100,* 343–349.

Bonnano, G. A., & Stilling, N. A. (1986). Preference, familiarity, and recognition after repeated brief exposure to random geometric shapes. *American Journal of Psychology, 99,* 403–415.

Bornstein, R. F. (1989). Exposure and affect: Overview and meta-analysis of research, 1968–1987. *Psychological Bulletin, 106,* 265–289.

Bornstein, R. F., Leone, D. R., & Galley, D. J. (1987). The generalizability of subliminal mere exposure effects: Influence of stimuli perceived without awareness on social behavior. *Journal of Personality and Social Behavior, 53,* 1070–1079.

Cross, H., Halcomb, A., & Matter, C. G. (1967). Imprinting or exposure learning in rats given early auditory stimulation. *Psychonomic Science, 7,* 233–234.

Damasio, A. R. (1994). *Descartes' error: Emotion, reason, and the human brain.* New York: Putnam.

Dimberg, V. (1982). Facial reactions to facial expressions. *Psychophysiology, 19,* 643–647.

Edwards, K. (1990). The interplay of affect and cognition in attitude formation and change. *Journal of Personality and Social Psychology, 59,* 202–216.

Elliott, R., & Dolan, R. J. (1998). Neural response during preference and memory judgments for subliminally presented stimuli: A functional neuroimaging study. *Journal of Neuroscience, 18,* 4697–4704.

Forgas, J. P. (1995). Mood and judgment: The affect infusion model (AIM). *Psychological Bulletin, 117,* 39–66.

Harrison, A. A. (1977). Mere exposure. In L. Berkowitz (Ed.), *Advances in experimental social psychology* (Vol. 10, pp. 610–646). New York: Academic Press.

Jacoby, L. L. (1983). Perceptual enhancement: Persistent effects of experience. *Journal of Experimental Psychology: Learning, Memory and Cognition, 9,* 21–38.

Kitayama, S. (1991). Impairment of perception by positive and negative affect. *Cognition and Emotion, 5,* 255–274.

Kunst-Wilson, W. R., & Zajonc, R. B. (1980). Affective discrimination of stimuli that cannot be recognized. *Science, 207,* 557–558.

Lazarus, R. S. (1982). Thoughts on the relations between emotion and cognition. *American Psychologist, 37,* 1019–1024.

Lazarus, R. S. (1991). Cognition and motivation in emotion. *American Psychologist, 46,* 352–367.

Le Bon, G. (1995). *The Crowd.* New Brunswick, NJ: Transaction Publishers.

LeDoux, J. E. (1986). Sensory systems and emotion. *Integrative Psychiatry, 4,* 237–248.

LeDoux, J. E. (1995). Emotions: clues from the brain. *Annual Review of Psychology, 46,* 209–235.

Mandler, G., Nakamura, Y., & VanZandt, B. J. S. (1987). Nonspecific effects of exposure on stimuli that cannot be recognized. *Journal of Experimental Psychology: Learning, Memory, and Cognition, 13,* 646–648.

Matlin, M. W. (1970). Response competition as a mediating factor in the frequency-affect relationship. *Journal of Personality and Social Psychology, 16,* 536–552.

Mishkin, M. (1978). Memory in monkeys severely impaired by combined but not separate removal of amygdala and hippocampus. *Nature, 273,* 297–298.

Mita, T. H., Dermer, M., & Knight, J. (1977). Reversed facial images and the mere exposure hypothesis. *Journal of Personality and Social Psychology, 35,* 597–601.

Monahan, J. L., Murphy, S. T., & Zajonc, R. B. (1999). *Mere exposure, novel stimuli and mood: Is the positive affect generated by exposure specific, general, or diffuse?* Unpublished manuscript.

Murphy, S. T., Monahan, J. L., & Zajonc, R. B. (1995). Additivity of nonconscious affect: Combined effects of priming and exposure. *Journal of Personality and Social Psychology, 69,* 589–602.

Murphy, S. T., & Zajonc, R. B. (1987, August–September). *Affect and awareness: Comparisons of subliminal and supraliminal affective priming.* Paper presented at the 95th Annual Convention of the American Psychological Association, New York.

Murphy, S. T., & Zajonc, R. B. (1993). Affect, cognition, and awareness: Affective priming with suboptimal and optimal stimulus. *Journal of Personality and Social Psychology, 64,* 723–739.

Niedenthal, P. M. (1990). Implicit perception of affective information. *Journal of Experimental Social Psychology, 26,* 505–527.

Perrett, D. I., Rolls, E. T., & Caan, W. (1982). Visual neurons responsive to faces in the monkey temporal cortex. *Experimental Brain Research, 47,* 329–342

Rajecki, D. W. (1972). *Effects of prenatal exposure to auditory and visual stimuli on social responses in chicks.* Unpublished doctoral dissertation, University of Michigan, Ann Arbor.

Schwarz, N., & Clore, G. L. (1983). Mood, misattribution, and judgments of well-being: Informative and directive functions of affective states. *Journal of Personality and Social Psychology, 45,* 513–523.

Seamon, J. G., Brody, N., & Kauff, D. M. (1983a). Affective discrimination of stimuli that are not recognized: Effects of shadowing, masking, and cerebral laterality. *Journal of Experimental Psychology: Learning, Memory, and Cognition, 9,* 544–555.

Seamon, J. G., Brody, N., & Kauff, D. M. (1983b). Affective discrimination of stimuli that are not recognized: II. Effect of delay between study and test. *Bulletin of Psychonomic Society, 21,* 187–189.

Seamon, J. G., Marsh, R. L., & Brody, N. (1989). Critical importance of exposure duration for affective discrimination of stimuli that cannot be recognized. *Journal of Experimental Psychology, Learning, Memory, and Cognition, 10,* 465–469.

Smith, P. B., & Bond, M. B. (1993). *Social psychology across cultures.* New York: Harvester Wheatsheaf.

Taylor, K. F., & Sluckin, W. (1964). Flocking in domestic chicks. *Nature, 201,* 108–109.

Titchener, E. B. (1910). *A textbook of psychology.* New York: Macmillan.

Wilson, W. R. (1979). Feeling more than we can know: Exposure effects without learning. *Journal of Personality and Social Psychology, 37,* 811–821.

Winkielman, P., Zajonc, R. B., & Schwarz, N. (1997). Subliminal affective priming resists attributional intervention. *Cognition and Emotion, 11,* 433–465.

Zajonc, R. B. (1968). Attitudinal effects of mere exposure. *Journal of Personality and Social Psychology 9,* 1–27.

Zajonc, R. B. (1980). Feeling and thinking: Preferences need no inferences. *American Psychologist, 35,* 151–175.

Zajonc, R. B. (1997). Emotions. In D. Gilbert, S. T. Fiske, & G. Lindzey (Eds.), *Handbook of Social Psychology* (4th ed., pp. 591–632). New York: McGraw-Hill.

Zola-Morgan, S., Squire, L. R., Alvarez-Royo, P., & Clower, R. P. (1991). Independence of memory functions and emotional behavior: Separate contributions of the hippocampal formation and the amygdala. *Hippocampus, 1,* 207–220.

3. Challenge and Threat Appraisals

The Role of Affective Cues

JIM BLASCOVICH AND WENDY BERRY MENDES

Introduction

In their well-known debate that took place nearly two decades ago, Zajonc (1981, 1984) and Lazarus (1981, 1984) discussed the primacy of affect versus cognition. These arguments foreshadowed a continuing lack of integration between purely affective and cognitive mechanisms and processes in social psychological theories on a wide range of topics (e.g., coping, persuasion, prejudice, motivation).

Until recently, our own theoretical perspective on challenge and threat (e.g., Blascovich, 1992; Blascovich & Tomaka, 1996) had much in common with Lazarian appraisal theory emphasizing (albeit not exclusively) the operation of usually conscious cognitive processes. However, recently we have become convinced that affective cues influence the experience of challenge and threat not only indirectly, via their influence on cognitive processes (see Smith and Kirby, this volume), but also directly and noncognitively in ways quite compatible with Zajonc's arguments and evidence (see Zajonc, this volume), as well as those of LeDoux (1996).

This chapter represents our initial attempt to integrate purely affective and cognitive processes into our biopsychosocial model of challenge and threat. We present our current theorizing on the appraisal component of our more general biopsychosocial model of challenge and threat (cf. Blascovich & Tomaka, 1996; Blascovich, 1992), and we

This research was supported in part by National Science Foundation grant SBR9596222 to Jim Blascovich and a National Research Service grant MH12013-01 to Wendy Mendes.

Correspondence concerning this chapter should be addressed to Jim Blascovich, Department of Psychology, University of California, Santa Barbara, Santa Barbara, CA 93106-9660. Electronic mail may be sent to Jim Blascovich at blascovi@psych.ucsb.edu.

briefly review our research validating the cardiovascular indexes of challenge and threat that we have developed. We then turn to the role of affective stimuli on challenge and threat appraisal processes and discuss research suggestive of that role. The first order of priority, however, is to define what we mean by *challenge* and *threat*.

Challenge and Threat

For us, challenge and threat represent person/situation-evoked motivational states that include affective (or emotional), cognitive, and physiological components. To consider these solely as emotional, cognitive, or physiological states undermines their richness and intricacy. Thus, challenge and threat represent the complex and likely simultaneous interplay of affective, cognitive, and physiological processes. Affectively, they involve positive and negative feelings and emotions; cognitively they form what Lazarus (1991) termed "core relational themes"; and physiologically they relate at least loosely to approach/avoidance or appetitive/aversive states.

As elucidated more fully in the next section, challenge occurs when the individual experiences sufficient or nearly sufficient resources to meet situational demands. Threat occurs when the individual experiences insufficient resources to meet situational demands. Because of the idiosyncratic nature of these reactions one individual may experience challenge in a particular situation (e.g., a final exam, a championship tennis match), whereas another may experience threat. Furthermore, the same individual may experience challenge in a particular type of situation at one time (e.g., taking a first exam in a course) but threat at another time (e.g., taking a second exam).

We have limited the context of our theoretical and empirical work nearly exclusively to nonmetabolically demanding performance situations, that is, those situations high in psychological demands relative to physical demands (but see Rousselle, Blascovich, & Kelsey, 1995; Blascovich et al., 1992). Furthermore, within the category of nonmetabolically demanding situations, we have limited ourselves to those involving active performance (e.g., speech giving, verbal and mathematical problem solving, game playing) rather than passive performance (e.g., viewing a scary film, listening to rousing music). We do not mean to imply that our work is irrelevant either to metabolically demanding or to passive performance situations, only that we limit its generalizability at present to the nonmetabolically demanding, active performance context. We believe that such contexts abound in everyday life (including home, work, and recreational contexts) and provide an important opportunity to better understand and explain the interplay of affective and cognitive processes.

The Biopsychosocial Model of Challenge and Threat

Our biopsychosocial model of challenge and threat rests on the *identity thesis*. Psychophysiologists and other neuroscientists embrace this thesis, the fundamental assumption of which is in sharp contrast to Descartes's notion of mind/body dualism that all psychological phenomena are embodied (Cacioppo & Tassinary, 1990). Paying more than lip service to the identity thesis, psychophysiologists, including social psychophysiologists, seek answers to questions generated from psychological theory, in part, by pursuing, developing, and validating physiological indexes of psychological constructs. Investigators have used physiological indexes to assess a plethora of psychological processes and constructs, including affective, cognitive, and motivational ones (Blascovich, in press).

Our own investigation of what we term "challenge" and "threat" has relied heavily on cardiovascular response patterns indicative of these states. We believe that these indexes enable us to identify challenge and threat *in vivo* and thus make it possible to examine the influence of psychological and social factors on challenge and threat experiences.

We describe our full arousal-regulation model elsewhere (Blascovich & Tomaka, 1996). Here we focus on the key initial process in our model (depicted in Figure 3.1), the situation-physiological response component.[1]

Performance Situations

The challenge and threat process begins in a situation in which a person expects to perform. For challenge and threat processes to commence, the person must perceive the performance situation as *goal-relevant* and *evaluative*. Specifically, the individual must believe that adequate performance is necessary to his or her continued well-being or growth. The individual must also believe that he or she will undergo evaluation in this situation, either by others or by oneself, on some important self-relevant domain. Academic examinations for col-

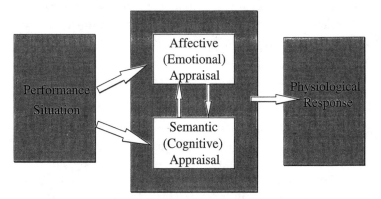

Figure 3.1. Situation-physiological response component.

lege students, lectures for college professors, and counseling sessions for clinicians provide examples of such performance situations.

Though *performance* required by the situation on the part of the actor may take either an *active* or *passive* form, or both, we focus on the former, as just mentioned. Active performance requires instrumental cognitive responses in the individual. Without these responses, the performance aspects of the situation (e.g., giving a speech, taking an exam, playing a game) cease, and the nature of the situation changes radically. Though not instrumental to task continuation, active performance situations generally also include emotional responses (e.g., anxiety, confidence) and behavioral responses (e.g., vocalizations, muscle movement). In contrast, passive performance may include responses noninstrumental to task continuation. These may be cognitive responses (e.g., mentally distracting oneself while watching a scary film), behavioral responses (e.g., closing one's eyes), and emotional ones (e.g., fear).

Finally, the situation may be metabolically (e.g., require large muscle movements) or nonmetabolically demanding. We have focused on nonmetabolically demanding performance situations largely because the expected cardiovascular responses differ under metabolically demanding and nondemanding situations.

Appraisal

Our recent model specified *cognitive* appraisal as the initial mediator in the challenge and threat process. In our previous theoretical statements (e.g., Blascovich & Tomaka, 1996), we posited a fairly simple cognitive appraisal process consisting of "primary" appraisals (of situational demands) and "secondary" appraisals (of the individual's resources). This simple model served us well initially. However, it has become apparent that the cognitive appraisal rubric does not capture the nature of appraisal processes fully. Here we expand and reframe these earlier notions.

Demand Appraisal. The appraisal process consists of the interplay between demand and resource appraisals. Demand appraisals involve the perception or assessment of danger, uncertainty, and required effort inherent in the situation. At this time, we choose not to specify an exact calculus for demand appraisals using these dimensions. They may be additive. They may be interactive or synergistic. Or, perceptions of high demand on any one of these dimensions may trigger high overall demand appraisals. Perceptual cues associated with danger, uncertainty, and required effort undoubtedly contribute to demand appraisals.

Resource appraisals involve the perception or assessment of knowledge and skills relevant to situational performance. Again, we cannot specify an exact calculus for resource appraisals. They may be additive, synergistic, or such that appraisal high on one dimension triggers high overall resource appraisals. Perceptual cues associated with knowledge and skills undoubtedly contribute to resource appraisals.

As stated earlier, *challenge* occurs when the individual experiences sufficient or nearly sufficient resources to meet situational demands. For example, playing chess against an opponent perceived as worse or slightly better than oneself results in a state of challenge. Threat occurs when the individual experiences insufficient resources to meet situational demands. In the chess example, playing against a player who is clearly superior to oneself results in a state of threat. The cases of extremely high levels of resources compared to demands or extremely high demands compared to resources are likely to make the situation nonevaluative for the performer. Hence, challenge and threat states do not occur (e.g., when playing chess against an inexperienced young child, playing chess against Bobby Fisher).

Apart from their substance, appraisals vary on at least two important psychological dimensions: self-consciousness and consciousness. Neither demand nor resource appraisal need be self-conscious. Individuals may make conscious appraisals without being aware that they are engaging in an appraisal process. The poker player, for example, may weigh or compare various strategies consciously without being aware that she or he has engaged in such a comparison process. More important, neither demand nor resource appraisals need even be conscious. The individual may make nonconscious demand or resource appraisals, or both, arriving at a state of challenge or threat without any awareness of the appraisals themselves. Conscious and nonconscious appraisals may occur in parallel. The more conscious the appraisal, the more elaborate and time consuming the process. However, even conscious appraisals such as those in familiar motivated performance situations can be quite fast.

In addition, appraisals may involve affective (i.e., feeling) processes, cognitive (i.e., semantic) processes, or both. Early and continuing work by Zajonc and his colleagues (see Zajonc, this volume) clearly demonstrates that affective processing can occur independently of cognitive processing. Recent work by LeDoux (1996) confirms and extends Zajonc's notions in this regard. LeDoux suggests that affective and cognitive processing systems, though independent, may actually communicate with one another. Figure 3.1 illustrates the appraisal link in the situation-physiological response component of our model to incorporate the conscious and nonconscious, affective and cognitive processing possibilities described here. In our view, nonconscious appraisals may be reflexive or learned.

Finally, we must note the iterative nature of the appraisal process. Before and during actual task performance, individuals continuously reappraise the situation. What may begin as a threatening situation for an individual may become less threatening or even challenging, and vice versa. For example, a student may be more threatened by some questions on an exam than others. A lecturer may become more challenged by positive audience feedback. Neither the situation nor the individual remain perfectly static during performance situation episodes. Both act upon the other, and external events may intervene.

Physiological Responses

Cardiovascular. Among physiological systems, the cardiovascular system appears particularly attuned to challenge and threat. Whether this specific "tuning" resulted evolutionarily from some sort of adaptive advantage inherent to early development of the "visceral" brain (i.e., midbrain and the medial cortex) and its role in "fight or flight" responses, though interesting, remains incidental to our arguments here.

We have devoted much work to the delineation of cardiovascular response patterns evoked during goal-relevant, active performance situations. Drawing on the early psychophysiological theorizing of Paul Obrist (1981) and the more recent theorizing of Richard Dienstbier (1989), we have developed indexes of challenge and threat on the basis of patterns of autonomically and endocrinologically controlled cardiovascular responses.

Accordingly, increased activity of the sympathetic-adreno-medullary (SAM) axis marks the challenge pattern. Specifically, sympathetic neural stimulation of the myocardium occurs, thereby enhancing cardiac performance. Such enhanced cardiac performance occurs by means of sympathetically enhanced ventricular contractility, thereby increasing stroke volume, which together with increased heart rate enhances cardiac output. At the same time, adrenal medullary release of epinephrine causes vasodilation in the large skeletal muscle beds and bronchi, which results in a general decline in systemic vascular resistance. This pattern generates relatively unchanged hemodynamic (i.e., blood pressure) responses. As Figure 3.2 shows, the challenge pattern (represented by the white bars) is characterized by

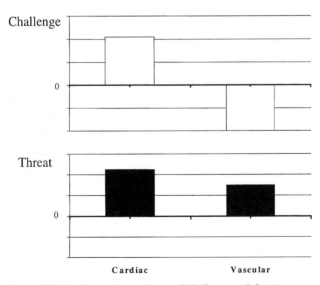

Figure 3.2. Cardiovascular patterns of challenge and threat.

increases in cardiac activity coupled with decreases in peripheral resistance, or vasodilation. This pattern mimics cardiovascular performance during aerobic exercise and represents the efficient mobilization of energy for coping.

Increased activity of the SAM axis together with increased activity of the pituitary-adrenal-cortical (PAC) axis marks the threat pattern. This PAC activity serves to inhibit the SAM-generated release of epinephrine from the adrenal medulla. Consequently, contractility and stroke volume, heart rate, and cardiac output increase, but without accompanying decreases in systemic vascular resistance (i.e., vasodilation). Rather, vasomotor tone does not change and may even increase slightly. This pattern results in relatively large increases in hemodynamic responses (i.e., blood pressure). In Figure 3.2 the threat pattern (represented by the black bars) is characterized by increases in cardiac activity coupled with no change or increases in peripheral resistance, or vasoconstriction.

Expressive. To the extent that appraisals resulting in challenge and threat carry hedonic tone, we expect activation of expressive physiological responses sensitive to affect. Prototypically, somatic responses constitute such expressive physiological responses, particularly facial somatic activity (Blascovich, in press). Thus, we expect greater activity in the region of the corrugator supercilii muscles (brow) region during threat than during challenge and greater activity in the region of the zygomaticus major muscles (cheek) during challenge than during threat.[2]

Physiological versus Subjective Responses. We take the position that physiological, particularly cardiovascular, responses to appraisal outcomes provide relatively unambiguous evidence of challenge and threat states within the individual. These responses provide continuous, on-line information in this regard and sensitivity to changes in appraisal over time.

Whether or not individuals can veridically articulate their appraisals during (or after) a performance situation depends on the degree to which they are conscious of the appraisal process, the extent to which such appraisal processing occurs consciously, and the extent to which self-presentation concerns predominate. Much more room for error exists when one tries to capture appraisals via self-report than physiologically, though such reports can provide important information to investigators, and we must sometimes still rely on them for our purposes.

Research Validating Cardiovascular Indexes of Challenge and Threat

As just mentioned, we devoted much of the early empirical work on our model to the validation of cardiovascular response patterns as indexes of challenge and threat appraisals. Toward this end, we conducted three types of studies: free appraisal, manipulated appraisal, and manipulated physiology studies.

Free Appraisal Studies. In three separate studies (reported in Tomaka, Blascovich, Kelsey, & Leitten, 1993), we created nonmetabolically demanding active performance situations. We believe that participants perceived these situation as goal-relevant and evaluative in large part because they were "psychology experiments" (cf. Rosenberg, 1965). We used verbal arithmetic operations (i.e., serial subtraction) as the actual performance tasks in the psychology experiment situation.

We assessed baseline cardiovascular responses before participants received task instructions, after task instructions, and throughout task performances. After the instructions but before commencement of the tasks, we assessed participants' self-reported demand and resource appraisals for the upcoming task. From these, we calculated the relationship between these two assessments (i.e., demand in relation to resources). Following the tasks, we assessed self-reported post-task stress ratings. We also recorded performance data on the math tasks themselves.

We obtained the expected results in all three studies.[3] Physiologically, the patterns of cardiovascular responses associated with challenge (resources > demands) and threat (demands > resources) were as follows (see also Figure 3.3): Challenged participants exhibited increased cardiac performance coupled with reduced total peripheral resistance (i.e., vasodilation), while threatened participants exhibited increased cardiac performance coupled with slightly increased total peripheral resistance (i.e., vasoconstriction). Not surprisingly, as a consequence of these patterns threatened participants exhibited higher levels of blood pressure (i.e., mean arterial pressure). Subjective post hoc reports of stress during task performance indicated greater stress

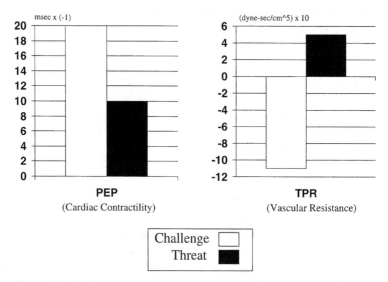

Figure 3.3. Cardiac and vascular patterns (adapted from Tomaka, Blascovich, Kelsey, & Leitten, 1993).

for threatened as opposed to challenged participants. Finally, challenged participants outperformed threatened participants not only in attempted subtractions but also in accurate subtractions.

Manipulated Appraisal Studies. Though our free appraisal studies strongly suggested the validity of the predicted challenge and threat cardiovascular patterns, these correlational studies relied heavily on the self-selection of participants into challenge and threat groups. In a subsequent experiment (reported in Tomaka, Blascovich, Kibler, & Ernst, 1997) in which we used the same basic performance situation as in the free appraisal studies, we manipulated challenge and threat experimentally via instructional set and paralanguage (i.e., tone). Participants randomly assigned to the threat condition heard audiotaped instructions emphasizing the mandatory nature of task performance and the intention of the investigators to evaluate the participants' performance. Participants randomly assigned to the challenge condition heard audiotaped instructions, including a request that they try their best and to think of the task as one to be met and overcome.

The manipulation produced the expected appraisal patterns: Participants in the threat condition reported the task as more demanding and their resources as less demanding than participants in the challenge condition. Cardiovascular patterns demonstrated the predicted threat and challenge patterns (see Figure 3.4). These experimental data provide more powerful support for the validity of our cardiovascular indexes.

Manipulated Physiology Studies. We conducted one additional set of experiments to further validate the challenge and threat patterns. We wanted to determine whether the physiological patterns indexed appraisal or vice versa. Perhaps we had it backwards. By peripheralist reasoning, appraisal should follow from and index the physiological patterns. Accordingly, we attempted to manipulate independently the physiological patterns to see if appraisals followed from the patterns.

In one study, we manipulated the patterns via aerobic exercise (moderate versus rest). Moderate aerobic exercise produces a pattern of cardiovascular response very similar to our challenge pattern. In another, we manipulated the patterns via external pressor (cold vs. warm). Immersion of a hand or foot in nearly freezing water produces a pattern of cardiovascular response similar to our threat pattern, while immersion in warm water produces a pattern similar to our challenge pattern. In both studies, the cardiovascular manipulations preceded and continued during performance task instructions, self-

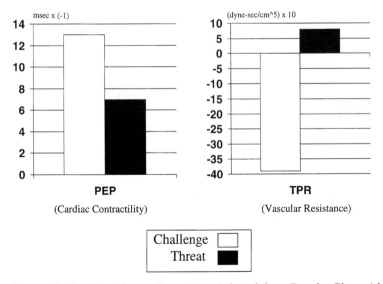

Figure 3.4. Cardiac and vascular patterns (adapted from Tomaka, Blascovich, Kibler, & Ernst, 1997).

reported demand and resource appraisals, and the first two minutes of task performance. Though the cardiovascular manipulations had the desired effects, appraisals did not differ as a function of cardiovascular pattern in either study. Hence they added further, albeit null, evidence to support our cardiovascular indexes of challenge and threat.

The Role of Affective Cues on Challenge and Threat Appraisal Processes

Sometimes by design, sometimes inadvertently, we have employed specific affective stimuli or cues in our manipulations of intrapersonal (e.g., dispositions, attitudes) and interpersonal factors (e.g., presence of others, race, ethnicity) thought to influence the appraisal process. We have performed manipulations using vocal tone, music, and pain. We have included sensory objects potentially laden with affective meaning for participants in our performance situations including attitudinal objects, pets, and physical stigma.

In reviewing and reframing our work in order to consider the role of affective cues in the appraisal process, we have discovered a remarkable consistency in the likely impact of affective cues on appraisals, cues that we (and appraisers) cannot reasonably and rationally relate to the objective performance requirements of participants' tasks. We believe that our work and that of others (LeDoux, 1996) suggests that such cues may lead to challenge or threat appraisals via affective processing or appraisal sometimes independently of, and sometimes together with, cognitive processing or appraisal. Furthermore, affective cues appear to play a role in both demand and resource appraisals.

Typology of Affective Cues

Note that when we speak of affective cues, we mean sensory objects in the situation that may elicit affective responses or meaning. These include animate and inanimate objects, sounds, smells, and touches: for example, a good friend, a doll, a gift, a special song, a room, perfume, a touch on the wrist. We explicitly exclude ongoing or ambient mood from this discussion, though we certainly believe that mood can have important effects on appraisals in performance situations (see Ernst, 1995), both demand appraisals (e.g., depressed individuals may perceive the effort required by a task as relatively high) and resource appraisals (e.g., elated individuals may perceive great confidence for task performance). We acknowledge that affective cues may trigger mood processes that can influence appraisals, but our focus here is more on the acute and direct effects of the cues themselves.

Conscious versus Nonconscious. Sensory objects may elicit both conscious and nonconscious affective processes in the individual. As affective cues, certain sensory objects have affective or emotional meaning for the individual. Though this meaning can certainly reach consciousness, it often fails to do so. However, the failure to reach awareness does not preclude psychological and behavioral effects of affective cues, as Zajonc (this volume) has shown.

Support for both conscious and nonconscious processing of emotion stems from work by neuroscientists and comparative psychologists. The neural systems perspective includes both conscious and nonconscious emotional responses mediated by different neural networks originating in the amygdala (LeDoux, 1995). Defensive responses can elicit both nonconscious and conscious emotional responses.

Learned versus Nonlearned. Whether or not cues elicit conscious or nonconscious meaning, affective or emotional meaning imputed to sensory objects (i.e., affective cues) may be learned or innate. No one would argue against the notion that individuals learn the affective or emotional meaning of many objects throughout their lives. Furthermore, few would argue that such learning can take place via semantic and associative processes. The argument that specific sensory cues can elicit nonlearned or innate affective or emotional meaning is somewhat controversial, but suggestive theoretical arguments and empirical evidence exist. For example, evolutionists argue that our own and other species have attached affective meaning to sensory objects (e.g., snakes) that have or have had significance for survival. Jungians describe such objects as archetypes that exist in the collective unconscious.

Certain categories of sensory stimuli appear to elicit affective-type responses, thereby implying the automaticity of at least some affective meaning. Psychophysiologists know quite well that sudden, intense stimuli elicit defensive responses reflexively. Lang, Bradley, and Cuthbert (1990) have theorized and demonstrated convincingly that hedonically toned reflexes such as startle eyeblinks are facilitated or inhibited by affective cues.

More directly, researchers have demonstrated that both visual and auditory objects elicit inborn affective meaning. Infants prefer graphic oval-shaped representations of faces over graphic face-shaped representations incorporating all the same facial features (e.g., nose, lips, eyes), but with such features arranged randomly (Fantz, 1958, 1961). Similarly, infants prefer rhythmic heartbeat sounds to nonrhythmic ones (Salk, 1973). And affective meanings can become automatic through associative learning processes. Whether or not affective meaning evoked by sensory cues is learned or innate poses little problem for our conception of the appraisal processes. Either type can affect appraisals, though one would expect innate affective cues to be much more resistant to modification than learned ones.

Demand Appraisal

Required Effort. Recall that, according to our model, demand appraisals involve assessments of required effort, danger, and uncertainty. Regarding required effort, our current theorizing suggests that affective cues play little role in its assessment. Instead, we believe that perceived task difficulty and task length in large part determine required effort, at least with regard to the inherent performance requirements of active tasks. However, we remain open to evidence that affective cues play a role in the assessment of required effort.

Danger. Affective cues certainly appear to play a role in danger appraisals. We learn the affective meaning of some such cues. Within cultures and subcultures, we may share affective meaning associated with them. Some types of affective cues appear more obvious than others in this regard. For example, a lone customer sporting a skull and cross-bones tattoo and wearing the colors of a motorcycle gang on a black leather vest may well signal danger to a lone clerk in a convenience store. This would make the customer transaction more threatening to the clerk. Conversely a lone customer wearing a police uniform and badge may well signal safety to the same clerk. This would make the transaction more challenging.[4] Other types of learned affective cues appear more subtle but have the same effects. Thus, to a hearing person, a hostile voice or one with a certain accent may cause threat or challenge appraisal as a function of prior learning of associated affective meaning.

Innate cues should operate similarly. For example, a multiple comparison task or a dissection task involving snakes may prove more threatening than tasks involving butterflies. Indeed, that such danger appraisal occurs forms part and parcel of the evolutionary argument underlying the existence of nonlearned cues.

Uncertainty. Affective cues may play an even larger role in the assessment of situational and task uncertainty. Individuals generally prefer familiar objects, which Zajonc (this volume) has shown to reduce situational uncertainty. For example, the child's security blanket or the child's (or adult's) teddy bear can make even a novel performance environment less uncertain. Absence of familiar objects increases situational uncertainty. If one subscribes to attachment theory (Bowlby, 1988), the secure attachment figure (i.e., the secure base) represents the ultimate affective cue in this regard. Likewise, familiar objects can reduce task uncertainty. For monolingual English speakers, purely spatial manipulations of Chinese ideographs or Russian words composed of letters from the Cyrillic alphabet may engender more uncertainty than spatial manipulations of English words composed of letters from our own alphabet.

Resource Appraisal

The extent to which affective cues affect resource appraisals may at first appear less clear-cut than the extent to which they affect demand appraisals. However, we can make a case for such a role. Certain sensory objects can serve as affect-laden symbols associated with resources or their absence. Objects that form the basis for superstitions provide some good examples. Hence, talismans and good luck charms may cause resource appraisals of confidence or even invincibility while their absence may cause more negative resource appraisals, as in the case of the baseball pitcher who continues to wear the same socks or underwear in each game of winning streak. The resource superstitions behind other objects may not appear so obvious, as in the case of the surgeon who cannot operate well without listening to music, the symphony conductor who cannot direct the orchestra well without a specific baton, the author who cannot write without holding a cigarette, or the woman who cannot flirt without wearing makeup.

Additional Considerations

Finally, we must add a couple of points. First, affective cues may play multiple roles in the appraisal process, both within and between the demand and resource appraisal categories. For example, the presence of a pet dog in a performance situation may decrease danger appraisal, increase situational familiarity (thereby decreasing uncertainty appraisal), and serve as a good luck charm (thereby increasing resource appraisal). A hostile vocal warning by an instructor in an academic testing situation may increase danger appraisal, decrease situational familiarity, and decrease resource appraisal.

Second, many sensory cues carry both affective and semantic meaning, though one or the other may dominate. Thus, in addition to engendering appraisals involving affective meaning, even primarily affective cues may influence cognitive appraisals involving semantic meaning. For example, consider the hostile warning example discussed previously. In addition to a feeling of danger, the vocal (i.e., affective tone) of the warning may cause students to believe that the instructor will grade the exams very strictly, allow them no extra time to complete the exam, and so on. The customer wearing the tattoo and motorcycle gang colors may evoke semantic meanings of danger in addition to fear.

Similarly, cues or information such as specific instructional sets that we expect would clearly influence conscious semantic or cognitive appraisal often, if not always, carry some affective properties directly (e.g., we may not like the content of the instructions). In addition, extrasemantic properties (often nonverbal) usually accompany semantic information (e.g., vocal tone). These extrasemantic properties can serve as affective cues themselves.

Research

As mentioned earlier, we have employed affective cues in many of our experiments. These cues generally accompanied more semantically meaningful information, but not always. We believe that much of this research supports the roles of affective cues in appraisals delineated in this discussion. Though we cannot unambiguously categorize these studies in terms of the various subtypes of demand and resource appraisals involved, themselves admittedly fuzzy constructs, we believe the data resulting from these studies speak to issues regarding the role of affective cues in challenge and threat appraisals.

Demand Appraisal: Danger and Vocal Tone. Recall the manipulated appraisal study described previously (reported in Tomaka, Blascovich, Kibler, & Ernst, 1997) to validate our cardiovascular indexes. In that study we manipulated appraisal via instructional set. Our audiotaped "threat" instructions differed from our "challenge" instructions somewhat in content. But they also clearly differed in affective tone such that our "experimenter" delivered the threat instructional set in a staccato and stern tone while he delivered the challenge set in a much more pleasant way. As mentioned, the "manipulation" worked. Threat patterns of cardiovascular response resulted from threat instructions and challenge patterns from challenge instructions. In retrospect, however, we doubt it would have worked without the difference in affective vocal tone.[5]

Demand Appraisal: Danger and Pain. Recall also the studies in which we independently manipulated cardiovascular patterns mimicking the challenge and threat patterns and found that such manipulations did not lead to differences in appraisal. When we manipulated the cardiovascular patterns via cold and warm pressor, we included both pressor conditions in part to control for the participants' perceived pain. We did not want to confound the physiological patterns with different levels of pain. However, we did find within-condition differences in pain perceptions, with high- and low-pain perceivers in each group. As reported by Tomaka et al. (1997), pain across both conditions was related to challenge and threat appraisals such that high-pain perceivers had more threatening appraisals than low pain perceivers.

More interesting still were the effects of pain perceptions on cardiovascular patterns of participants in the cold pressor condition. As Figure 3.5 shows, these participants did not differ during the first minute of the 3-minute cold pressor task in vascular tone. High-pain participants exhibited increased vasoconstriction, low-pain participants exhibited decreasing vasoconstriction, so much so that actual vasodilation occurred and overcame the well-documented vasoconstrictive response to the cold pressor during the actual cold pressor experience. These data (and Figure 3.5) also reveal that the trends in vasoconstriction and vasodilation continue during task performance

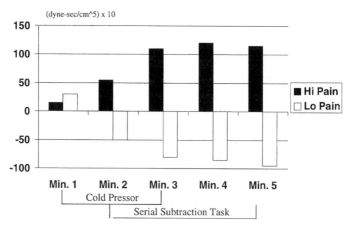

Figure 3.5. Vascular responses as a function of pain (adapted from Tomaka, Blascovich, Kibler, & Ernst, 1997).

after the cold pressor stimulation ceases, but before the performance task ends. These data support not only the notion of affect danger appraisal but also our contention that the pituitary-adrenal-cortical (PAC) axis, which responds to harm and potential harm (Mason, 1975), contributes to the threat pattern.

Demand Appraisal: Danger and Physical Stigma. In a recent exploratory study (Mendes, Hunter, Lickel, & Blascovich, 1998), we set out to test the effects of a partner's physical stigma on challenge and threat during a cooperative interaction. Using female confederates, we randomly assigned our female participants to one of two conditions: stigmatized other or nonstigmatized other. For the stigmatized other condition, confederates bore a large port wine facial birthmark. For the nonstigmatized other condition, confederates bore no birthmark. We kept confederates from knowing whether or not they bore the physical stigma. After introducing the confederate as the other participant and after the confederate and participant exchanged some structured information about themselves,[6] each returned to their own physiological recording rooms. We then informed real participants that they would play a cooperative word-finding game with the other participant via computer and intercom while we assessed their physiological responses. Significant differences in cardiovascular patterns were found, such that participants in the stigmatized other condition exhibited the threat pattern and participants in the nonstigmatized other condition exhibited challenge.

We think it quite possible that physical stigmas such as facial birthmarks evoke danger appraisals. Indeed, such bodily disfigurements may evoke some sort of nonconscious existential terror or threat to observers. Individuals avoid stigmatized others in part because they bring to mind their own frailty and mortality (Goffman, 1963). Note that individuals often become scared or frightened at the sight of someone wearing a costume mask mimicking facial disfigurement, but not when a mask appears friendly, such as one showing a beloved public character. Facial and other physical stigmas are also likely to increase uncertainty appraisals in addition to danger appraisals.

Demand Appraisal: Uncertainty and Pet Dogs. A few years ago (Allen, Blascovich, Tomaka, & Kelsey, 1991), we observed the effects of the presence of pet dogs on cardiovascular responses during an active performance situation. We asked middle-aged female dog owners, recruited from responses to a newspaper ad, to perform a serial subtraction task. We assigned the women to one of three conditions: alone, in the presence of their pet dog, or in the presence of the best, female human friend.

Participants in the presence of their pet dog exhibited little or no increases in blood pressure during the task (consistent with our later defined challenge pattern). Participants in the alone condition exhibited significant increases in blood pressure (consistent with threat). Participants in the friend condition exhibited even greater increases in blood pressure (consistent with high threat). We believe that the pet dogs, among other things, contributed to decreased uncertainty appraisals, creating sort of a "safe haven" in an attachment sense (Bowlby, 1988). On the other hand, human friends probably increased the evaluation apprehension of participants.

Demand Appraisal: Uncertainty and Ethnicity/Status Pairings. In another recent exploratory study (Lickel et al., 1998), we followed the same procedures as the facial stigma study described previously. Instead of manipulating physical stigma, however, we employed female confederates so that we could manipulate ethnicity (Latina vs. Anglo). We crossed the ethnicity manipulation with a status (high vs. low) manipulation by means of the demographic information exchanged by confederates and female participants when they met. Significant differences in cardiovascular response patterns emerged such that during the cooperative work-finding task Anglo participants exhibited challenge when their partners' status appeared stereotypically consistent with their ethnicity (high-status Anglos and low-status Latinas) but threat when their partners' status appeared stereotypically inconsistent with their ethnicity (high status Latinas and low-status Anglos). We contend that the more surprising pairings of ethnicity and status contributed to high uncertainty appraisal. Though we had no data, we would not be surprised if prejudice moderated these effects.

Demand Appraisal: Uncertainty and Familiar versus Novel Attitude Objects. In another study (reported in Blascovich et al., 1993), we tested the cardiovascular functionality of attitudes in potentially stressful decision-making situations. In the first phase of this study, all participants viewed and repeatedly rehearsed attitudes (i.e., like/dislike ratings) toward a randomly selected set of 15 novel abstract paintings.

In the second phase, participants viewed short presentations of pairs of paintings and indicated which painting in each pair they preferred while we recorded cardiovascular responses. Participants had two seconds to view the pair of paintings and indicate their preferences. We randomly assigned participants to one of two conditions during the second phase. In one condition, we drew the painting pairs from the set toward which they had rehearsed attitudes. In the second, we drew the painting pairs from a totally novel set.

As expected, participants in the novel painting condition exhibited threat patterns whereas participants in the familiar painting condition exhibited challenge patterns. In retrospect, we believe this study provides an interesting test of the affect-uncertainty appraisal connection because we manipulated familiarity by incorporating affective cues (i.e., paintings) in the actual performance task.

Resource Appraisal: Skills, Abilities, and Music. Another of our studies (Allen & Blascovich, 1994) suggests that affective cues can increase resource appraisals. In this study, we recruited approximately 50 surgeons to participate in an experiment on music and active performance. All of the surgeons listened to music while performing surgery (a not uncommon practice). Using a within-participant design, all surgeons in our study performed a serial subtraction task while listening to their self-selected music (the same as the music they listened to during surgery), another subtraction task while listening to a control musical selection (Pachelbel's *Canon in D*), and another with no music. We completely counterbalanced order.

Surgeons listening to their own music showed little or no increases in blood pressure during the task (consistent with our challenge pattern). Surgeons in the control music condition showed significant increases in blood pressure (consistent with threat). Surgeons in the no music condition showed even greater increases in blood pressure (consistent with high threat).[7] Though the surgeons' own music quite possibly also affected uncertainty demand appraisals, we believe it contributed to resource appraisals based on the association of these musical selections with perceived positive performance on another task (i.e., surgery). Surgeons who played music during surgery typically report they do so because of its affective properties. In addition, although the type of music differed substantially across surgeons, most of them reported playing the same music, or at least selections from a small set across surgeries. This finding makes our contention of their association of music with positive performance more tenable.

Other Research. Other investigators have also conducted research, albeit nonphysiological research, into the mediating role of affective cues in performance situations. For example, Isen and her colleagues have demonstrated that positive affect can have substantial influence on social interactions and thought processes (for a review, see Isen, 1987). Positive affect induced by relatively small manipulations, such as receiving a bag of candy, a coin, or a small gift, demonstrably increases creative problem solving and facilitates retrieval of positive material from memory. We contend that these "tokens" serve as affective cues that facilitate problem solving, either by decreasing the demand appraisals, especially danger appraisals, or by increasing resource appraisals, or both. The well-established link between positive cues and positive affect appears likely in the findings of other researchers who contend that positive affect has positive effects on cognition (Bryan, Mathur, Sullivan, & Pukys, 1995; Deldin & Levin, 1986; Teasdale & Fogarty, 1979; see also chapters by Eich & Macaulay, Forgas, and Martin, this volume).

Summary

We have sought here to address the role of affective cues in challenge and threat appraisal processes. We believe that appraisals, specifically the relationship between demand and resource appraisals, mediate the link between performance situations and physiological responses. Furthermore, we have argued that these component appraisals may involve both affective and cognitive appraisals with and without awareness or consciousness, and they may utilize both affective and semantic or cognitive cues. We contend that affective cues may affect demand appraisals of danger and uncertainty and resource appraisals of skills and abilities. Our review of research employing cardiovascular indexes of challenge and threat is supportive of our notions regarding affective cues and appraisals. As always, more definitive research is needed to fully test our notion, research that we hope is forthcoming.

Notes

1. We do not mean to suggest affective cues play no role in the remaining components of our model. They do. However, space limitations preclude this additional discussion here.
2. We base this contention on the expressive role of facial expressions rather than a causal or social communications role.
3. We used the full set of cardiac and vascular measures only in the last two of the three studies reported in this chapter. However, the first study that included cardiac measures did not deviate from the predicted pattern in terms of those cardiac measures.
4. Of course, in different contexts (e.g., a Halloween party, an illegal casino), the valence of the cues of the others (i.e., the motorcycle gang member, the police officer) may differ from the illustrations portrayed here.
5. Indeed, our own "lab lore" indicates the necessity of such tone to elicit challenge and threat responses.
6. The exchanged information included instant photographs, demographic background, and extracurricular activities.
7. Anecdotal information received from the surgeons in this study indicated that they listened to music to feel good and to avoid distraction.

References

Allen, K. M., & Blascovich, J. (1994). Effects of music on cardiovascular reactivity among surgeons. *Journal of American Medical Association, 272*, 882–884.
Allen, K. M., Blascovich, J., Tomaka, J., & Kelsey, R. M. (1991). Presence of

human friends and pet dogs as moderators of autonomic responses to stress in women. *Journal of Personality and Social Psychology, 61*, 582–589.

Blascovich, J. (1992). A biopsychosocial approach to arousal regulation. Special Issue: Social psychophysiology. *Journal of Social and Clinical Psychology, 11*, 213–237.

Blascovich, J. (in press). Using physiological indexes of psychological processes in social psychological research. In C. M. Judd & H. Reis (Eds.), *Handbook of advanced research methods in social psychology*. London: Cambridge University Press.

Blascovich, J., Brennan, K., Tomaka, J., Kelsey, R. M., and others. (1992). Affect intensity and cardiac arousal. *Journal of Personality and Social Psychology, 63*, 164–174.

Blascovich, J., Ernst, J. M., Tomaka, J., Kelsey, R. M., Salomon, K. A., & Fazio, R. H. (1993). Attitude accessibility as a moderator of autonomic reactivity during decision making. *Journal of Personality and Social Psychology, 64*, 165–176.

Blascovich, J., & Tomaka, J. (1996). The Biopsychosocial model of arousal regulation. *Advances in Experimental Social Psychology, 28*, 1–51.

Bowlby, J. (1988). *A secure base: Parent–child attachment and healthy human development*. New York: Basic Books.

Bryan, T., Mathur, S. R., Sullivan, K., & Pukys, K. (1995). The impact of induced positive affect on incarcerated males' learning. *Behavioral Disorders, 20*, 204–211.

Cacioppo, J. T., & Tassinary, L. G. (Eds.). (1990). *Principles of psychophysiology: Physical, social, and inferential elements*. New York: Cambridge University Press.

Deldin, P. J., & Levin, I. P. (1986). The effect of mood induction in a risky decision-making task. *Bulletin of the Psychonomic Society, 24*, 4–6.

Dienstbier, R. A. (1989). Arousal and physiological toughness: Implications for mental and physical health. *Psychological Review, 96*, 84–100.

Ernst, J. (1995). The effect of mood on cognitive appraisal. Unpublished doctoral dissertation. State University of New York at Buffalo.

Fantz, R. L. (1958). Pattern vision in young infants. *Psychological Record, 8*, 43–47.

Fantz, R. L. (1961). The origin of form perception. *Scientific American, 204*, 66–72.

Goffman, E. (1963). *Stigma: Notes on the management of spoiled identity*. Englewood Cliffs, NJ: Prentice-Hall.

Isen, A. M. (1987). Positive affect, cognitive processes, and social behavior. In L. Berkowitz, (Ed.), *Advances in Experimental Social Psychology* (Vol. 20, pp. 203–252). San Diego, CA: Academic Press.

Lang, P. J., Bradley, M. M., & Cuthbert, B. N. (1990). Emotion, attention, and the startle reflex. *Psychological Review, 97*, 377–395.

Lazarus, R. S. (1981). A cognitivist's reply to Zajonc on emotion and cognition. *American Psychologist, 36*, 222–223.

Lazarus, R. S. (1984). On the primacy of cognition. *American Psychologist, 39*, 124–129.

Lazarus, R. S. (1991). *Emotion and adaptation.* New York: Oxford University Press.

LeDoux, J. E. (1995). Emotion: Clues from the brain. *Annual Review of Psychology, 46,* 209–235.

LeDoux, J. E. (1996). *The emotional brain: The mysterious underpinnings of emotional life.* New York: Simon & Schuster.

Lickel, B., Mendes, W. B., Hunter, S., Blascovich, J., Watson, J., Gonzalves, M., & Ramon, C. (1998, May). *Cardiovascular reactivity during interpersonal interactions.* Poster presented at the annual meeting of the American Psychological Society, Washington, DC.

Mason, J. W. (1975). A historical view of the stress field. *Journal of Human Stress, 1,* 6–12.

Mendes, W. B., Hunter, S., Lickel, B., & Blascovich, J. (1998, May). *Cardiovascular reactivity during interactions with stigmatized others.* Poster presented at the annual meeting of the American Psychological Society, Washington, DC.

Obrist, P. A. (1981). *Cardiovascular psychophysiology: A perspective.* New York: Plenum.

Rosenberg, M. J. (1965). When dissonance fails: On eliminating evaluation apprehension from attitude measurement. *Journal of Personality and Social Psychology, 1,* 28–42.

Rousselle, J. G., Blascovich, J., Kelsey, R. M. (1995). Cardiorespiratory responses under combined psychological and exercise stress. *International Journal of Psychophysiology, 20,* 49–58.

Salk, L. (1973). The role of the heartbeat in the relations between mother and infant. *Scientific American, 228,* 24–29.

Teasdale, J. D., & Fogarty, S. J. (1979). Differential effects of induced mood on retrieval of pleasant and unpleasant events from episodic memory. *Journal of Abnormal Psychology, 88,* 248–257.

Tomaka, J., Blascovich, J., Kelsey, R. M., & Leitten, C. L. (1993). Subjective, physiological, and behavioral effects of threat and challenge appraisal. *Journal of Personality and Social Psychology, 18,* 616–624.

Tomaka, J., Blascovich, J., Kibler, J., & Ernst, J. M. (1997). Cognitive and physiological antecedents of threat and challenge appraisal. *Journal of Personality and Social Psychology, 73,* 63–72.

Zajonc, R. B. (1981). A one-factor mind about mind and emotion. *American Psychologist, 36,* 102–103.

Zajonc, R. B. (1984). On the primacy of affect. *American Psychologist, 39,* 117–123.

4. Consequences Require Antecedents

Toward a Process Model of Emotion Elicitation

CRAIG A. SMITH AND LESLIE D. KIRBY

Introduction

Humans are multipurpose beings functioning in an uncertain world. We are often faced with complex situations in which we are striving to achieve multiple goals simultaneously. Although most of the stimuli with which we are confronted are not matters of life and death, our response repertoire must enable us to deal with such extreme circumstances as well as with more mundane ones. Emotions prepare and motivate people to respond to situations, allowing them to respond adaptively to the complex world in which they must survive and reproduce (see, e.g., Darwin, 1872/1965).

Emotions have not always been perceived in this way (see Calhoun & Solomon, 1994; and Forgas, this volume, for an overview of the history of perceptions of emotions). To many philosophers emotions represent an interruption to an otherwise logical (and preferred) mode of being. In psychology, following the seminal work of William James and Walter Cannon, behaviorism essentially prohibited the study of emotion – at least as a psychological, as opposed to a behavioral, event. After a long period of neglect, the past two decades have

We thank Laura Griner, Heather Scott, and Carien van Reekum for their theoretical contributions to the development of the model described in this chapter. We also thank Carien van Reekum, Joseph Forgas, and the participants of the First Sydney Symposium of Social Psychology, held at the University of New South Wales in Sydney, Australia, March 14–18, 1998, for their helpful comments on an earlier version of this manuscript. Finally, thanks to Reid Fontaine and Lawrence Contratti for helping us to polish the final version.

Correspondence concerning this chapter should be directed to Craig A. Smith, Department of Psychology and Human Development, Box 512 Peabody, Vanderbilt University, Nashville, TN 37212, USA; or electronically to craig.a.smith@vanderbilt.edu.

witnessed a virtual explosion of research on affective phenomena, especially on the interrelations between emotion and cognition. Much of this work has examined the influence of moods and emotions on a variety of cognitive processes, including perception (e.g., Niedenthal, Setterlund, & Jones, 1994), attention (e.g., Derryberry & Tucker, 1994), memory (e.g., Bower, 1981, Eich, 1995, this volume; Forgas & Bower, 1987), and complex social judgments (e.g., Clore, Schwarz, & Conway, 1994; Fiedler, Asbeck, & Nickel, 1991), including judgments of personal well-being (Schwarz & Clore, 1983).

Although this work has revealed a great deal about the influence of emotion on how people reason, remember, and make decisions, it has virtually ignored the nature of the emotions themselves and how they are generated. It is vital, however, that we now develop clear and accurate models concerning the elicitation of emotion and its antecedents. The development of such models should allow us to predict and understand when, under what conditions, and by whom, different emotions are likely to be experienced. Without this type of understanding, the value of the knowledge we've gained regarding the effects of emotion on cognition is necessarily limited. Although we may be able to predict specific effects on cognition given the experience of a particular emotion or set of emotions, we have no way of predicting whether or when such emotions will arise.

How emotions are elicited has been the province of a distinct line of research, commonly referred to as the *appraisal* approach to emotion (but see also, Izard, 1977; Tomkins, 1962; Zajonc, 1980; this volume for rather different accounts of emotion elicitation). The focus of this approach has been to explicitly model how emotions are produced. As this chapter explains, research within this tradition has highlighted the cognitive antecedents responsible for the elicitation of emotion. Largely successful attempts have been made to develop and test precise models describing the specific cognitions that elicit and differentiate a broad range of emotional experience (e.g., Frijda, 1986; Roseman, 1984; Scherer, 1984; Smith & Ellsworth, 1985; Smith & Lazarus, 1990; Smith & Kirby, 1998).

Unfortunately, there has been little cross-fertilization between the appraisal-based study of emotional antecedents and the work examining the cognitive consequences of emotion (but see Keltner, Ellsworth, & Edwards, 1993, for a notable exception). The present chapter attempts to bridge the gap between these two research areas. Our focus is on appraisal theory, but we attempt to consider this theory in a way that highlights the relevance of the two research areas to each other. Specifically, we advance a process-oriented model of emotion elicitation that we believe should be of interest to those studying the effects of emotion on cognition and other psychological processes. In doing so, we also illustrate how appraisal theory can benefit from previous findings regarding the influence of mood and emotion on cognition.

First, we review the major postulates and assumptions of appraisal theory, and discuss the types of appraisal models that have been developed and tested to date. We argue that although such models have been quite successful in delineating the structural relations between certain cognitions and the experience of specific emotions, they have been virtually silent as to the mechanisms by which these cognitions are generated. We then make the case as to why it is important that the existing *structural models* be supplemented with explicit *process models*, and we discuss some of the constraints such models should be designed to meet. Next we provide a sketch of one such process model that we have been developing with our colleagues (e.g., Smith, Griner, Kirby, & Scott, 1996). We discuss the major assumptions underlying this model and illustrate how it can account for some important psychological phenomena, including ones that are often considered problematic for appraisal theory. Finally, we discuss the major areas in which we believe the process model needs to be further developed, and consider how these efforts might be facilitated by drawing upon the insights gained by studying the influence of mood and emotion on cognition.

The Current Status of Appraisal Theory

Appraisal theory is somewhat unique among contemporary theories of emotion in that it attempts to offer a comprehensive view of how emotions are generated. The emotional reactions themselves are commonly conceptualized as having multiple response components, including a distinctive subjective feeling state; an organized pattern of skeletomuscular, autonomic, and endocrine activity; and a felt urge to respond to the situation in a particular way, often referred to as an "action tendency" or "mode of action readiness" (Ekman, 1984; Frijda, 1986; Izard, 1977; Plutchik, 1980; Scherer, 1984; Smith & Lazarus, 1990; Tomkins, 1980). These multicomponent reactions are said to arise under conditions that, to the individual, represent potential benefits or harm. They are believed to serve both social-communicative and self-regulatory functions (e.g., Lazarus, 1968; Scherer, 1984; Smith, 1989; Smith & Lazarus, 1990). First, through their observable expressions (e.g., facial activity, vocal tone, posture), emotions can communicate important information to others in the social environment regarding the person's emotional state and likely behaviors (Scherer, 1984; Smith, 1989). Second, through their subjective feeling states, the emotions serve as salient and compelling signals to the individual that he or she is in a situation having important adaptational implications. These signals are hypothesized to be supported by accompanying patterns of physiological activity and felt action tendencies that serve to motivate and physically prepare the individual to contend with the signaled implications (e.g., Lazarus, 1991; Scherer, 1984; Smith & Lazarus, 1990; see also Blascovich & Mendes, this volume).

A key question raised by this view of emotion is how do the emotions come to be elicited under appropriate environmental conditions? Simple stimulus-based models have proved untenable, given that different individuals often respond to highly similar situations with very different emotional reactions, and, even more important, the same individual often reacts differently to the same situation across multiple occasions (Ekman, 1984; Frijda, 1986; Smith & Pope, 1992). Thus, rather than being fixed responses to specific patterns of stimulation, emotional reactions appear to be highly context-sensitive and take into account not only the environmental circumstances confronting an individual, but also numerous properties of the individual, including his or her personal needs, goals, desires, abilities, and beliefs (Lazarus, 1991; Kirby & Smith, 1998; Smith & Lazarus, 1990; Smith & Pope, 1992). The appraisal approach to emotion grew out of attempts to explain how emotions might be elicited within this high degree of context specificity.

A central postulate of virtually all appraisal theories is that, rather than being a response to one's objective circumstances, the emotion is a response to an evaluation, or appraisal, of what those circumstances imply for personal well-being. Emotions probably evolved out of the same basic approach/avoid dichotomy that produces drives and reflexes (Cannon, 1929; cf. Smith & Lazarus, 1990); however, emotions evolved as meaning-based phenomena. So, although an emotion is an acute response to an acute stimulus, it is not the stimulus itself that triggers the emotion, but instead what that stimulus implies for the personal goals of the individual, given that individual's beliefs, expectations, and abilities. In a way, an emotion can still best be viewed as a reflex, but it is a reflexive response to an appraised meaning, rather than to an objective pattern of stimulation (Smith & Lazarus, 1990). An important corollary of this postulate is that each emotion is elicited by its own characteristic appraisal and that different emotions are associated with different appraisals (cf. Roseman, 1984; Scherer, 1984; Smith & Ellsworth, 1985; Smith & Lazarus, 1990).

In recent efforts to test appraisal theory, an initial task adopted by several theorists has been to develop explicit models that attempt to describe the specific appraisals responsible for eliciting each of a broad range of emotions. Several such models have been proposed (e.g., Roseman, 1984, 1991; Scherer, 1984; Smith & Ellsworth, 1985; Smith & Lazarus, 1990), and a large body of research designed to test these models has been highly supportive of them. In particular, many studies have now asked subjects to report on both their appraisals and a wide array of emotions across a variety of contexts, including diverse retrospectively remembered experiences (Ellsworth & Smith, 1988a, 1988b; Frijda, Kuipers, & ter Schure, 1989; Scherer, 1997; Smith & Ellsworth, 1985), hypothetical vignettes (e.g., Roseman, 1991; Smith & Lazarus, 1993), and even ongoing meaningful experiences (e.g., Griner & Smith, 1997; Kirby & Smith, 1998; Smith & Ellsworth, 1987; Smith & Kirby, 1998). Each of these studies has found not only that the experiences of different emotions are reliably and systematically associated with different appraisals, but also that the specific relations observed between the appraisals and the emotions are by and large in line with the models being investigated (for a discussion of some of the limitations of this work, see Lazarus & Smith, 1988; Parkinson, 1997; Parkinson & Manstead, 1992, 1993).

Although these models differ in their details, at a general level, they share important similarities. First, there is considerable agreement as to the types of cognitions that differentiate among various emotions. For instance, each model includes an evaluation of the degree to which one's circumstances are consistent with, or conducive to, achieving one's goals. This evaluation is important in differentiating so-called positive emotions, such as happiness and pride, from so-called negative or stress-related ones, such as anger, guilt, fear, and sadness. Each model includes additional evaluations concerning such things as who or what is responsible for the situation, and whether and to what degree the individual is able to cope with the situation, each of which further differentiates among the various emotions. For example, both anger and guilt arise in situations appraised as undesirable; however, which emotion is experienced depends on an additional appraisal of responsibility or blame, since in anger someone else is blamed, whereas in guilt one blames oneself. Fear also involves an evaluation of the situation as undesirable but is differentiated by an appraisal along a different dimension, namely, uncertainty as to whether one can cope with or adjust to the undesirable aspects of the situation. Thus, through the use of a relatively small number of appraisal components, or dimensions, these models allow for the differentiation of emotional experience into discrete emotional states (e.g., Izard, 1977; Tomkins, 1962) in a way that goes well beyond the approach/avoidance dichotomy inherent in many two-dimensional accounts of emotion (e.g., Watson & Tellegen, 1985).

Beyond the similarities in the appraisals proposed to be associated with the various emotions, each of the appraisal models cited above also shares the property that it is almost exclusively concerned with the *contents* of the cognitions responsible for eliciting the various emotions and is silent as to the *processes* that produce those cognitions. Thus, the existing models are predominantly *structural* ones that delineate the relations between specific appraisals and the experience of specific emotions. What is currently missing is a *process model* that delineates the cognitive processes by which those appraisals are produced. As we argue below, we believe it is important to supplement the existing structural models with process-oriented ones.

The Need for Process Models

It is important to develop explicit process-oriented models of emotion-eliciting appraisals for at least two reasons. First, at a pragmatic level, appraisal theorists' ideas about the appraisal process tend to be misunderstood. Individual components of appraisal have been traditionally described in abstract, conceptual terms, often represented as a series of questions that need to be evaluated (e.g., Roseman, 1984; Scherer, 1984; Smith & Ellsworth, 1985; Smith & Lazarus, 1990). Perhaps because of this, there has been a tendency by nonappraisal theorists to assume that the appraisals claimed to underlie emotion must be made consciously, rationally, and in a verbally mediated fashion. If appraisal is conceptualized solely in this manner, severe theoretical difficulties arise. For instance, dependence on a slow, rational, deliberative appraisal process flies in the face of observations that emotions can be elicited very quickly, often with a minimum of cognitive effort, and sometimes with little or no awareness of the nature of the emo-tion-eliciting stimulus (e.g., Izard, 1993; Zajonc, 1980). To the extent that appraisals are by necessity verbally mediated, it also seems diffi-cult to apply one's appraisal-based theory to either preverbal infants or nonhuman vertebrates, as many appraisal theorists would like to do (e.g., Arnold, 1960; Lazarus, 1991; Smith & Lazarus, 1990; Scherer, 1984).

Appraisal theorists have been cognizant of these difficulties, and to our knowledge none has claimed that appraisal should be performed consciously or that the information evaluated in appraisal should be represented verbally. To the contrary, beginning with Magda Arnold (1960), for whom appraisal was "direct, immediate, [and] intuitive" (p. 173), most appraisal theorists have explicitly maintained that ap-praisal can occur automatically and outside of focal awareness (e.g., Lazarus, 1968; Smith & Lazarus, 1990; Leventhal & Scherer, 1987). However, with few exceptions (e.g., Lazarus, 1991, ch. 4; Leventhal & Scherer, 1987; Robinson, in press), little attention has been devoted to backing up these claims with an explicit process model of appraisal that would explain how appraisals can occur in this manner. In the absence of such a model, theorists' claims regarding the potential automaticity of appraisal may not have been fully appreciated.

Moreover, a careful consideration of the self-regulatory functions commonly proposed to be served by emotion further highlights the necessity of developing a viable model in which appraisals can be made automatically and outside of focal awareness. In particular, a number of appraisal theorists have begun to discuss a role for emotion in attention regulation that would seem to demand such a model (e.g., Frijda & Swagerman, 1987; Lazarus, 1991; Scherer, 1984; Smith & Lazarus, 1990). Much of this discussion appears closely related to Simon's (1966) analysis of emotion as an "interrupt" mechanism.

Working from an artificial intelligence perspective, Simon (1966) argued that any autonomous being or device that needed to be able to service multiple, potentially competing goals under uncertain, po-tentially changing conditions would require a mechanism for detect-ing changes in the environment that required shifting one's activities and/or reprioritizing one's goals. He further asserted that, in humans, emotion represents such a mechanism; in particular, emotion repre-sents an "interrupt" mechanism that monitors the environment for goal-relevant conditions and evaluates the urgency of addressing those conditions, once detected. When conditions of sufficient urgency are detected, this mechanism interrupts one's ongoing activities and pushes one to address the newly detected, urgent conditions. Thus, in Simon's (1966) view, emotions represent a system that enables individuals to function flexibly in a complex and uncertain environment.

Similarly, views of the self-regulatory functions served by emotions are evident in a number of contemporary theories (e.g., Frijda & Swagerman, 1987; Lazarus, 1991; Scherer, 1984; Smith & Lazarus, 1990). However, these views go beyond Simon's in a variety of respects. For one thing, rather than serving merely as an interrupt signal indicating the appearance of goal-relevant events that require a switch of attention and a reprioritization of goals, emotions are further conceptualized as monitoring and providing feedback regarding one's progress in achieving current goals. Thus, positive emotions can signal that good progress is being made and/or that the goal has been achieved, whereas negative emotions can signal that things are not going well for some reason. In addition, these signals appear to be rich in the information they provide (in other words, they offer considerably more information than merely that something important is happening, or even whether that thing is good or bad). Given that each distinct emotion results from a distinct appraisal, the subjective feeling state associated with each emotion carries considerable information about the appraised situation that elicited it. For example, the feeling of anger carries the information that one is in an undesirable situation and that someone else is responsible for this circumstance, although the angry feeling itself does not indicate who that someone else might be. Further, as discussed earlier, the emotion provides physiological preparation and motivational guidance for how the person might contend with the situation. For instance, the feelings of anger are accompanied by a strong urge to lash out at the person or thing responsible for the anger-inducing situation in order to make it stop doing whatever it is that brought on the anger. Combining these considerations, we propose that emotion can be profitably conceptualized as a sophisticated *well-being monitor and guidance system* that serves both attention-regulatory and motivational functions.

The idea that emotion serves both attentional and motivational functions places competing constraints on the properties that a model of the appraisal process should exhibit. First, to the extent that an important function of emotion is attention regulation, it stands to reason that the eliciting mechanism cannot be too dependent on processes requiring focal attention. If a mechanism designed to shift focal attention to significant conditions in the environment itself required focal attention to detect those conditions, inherently it could not function well because it would only be able to call attention to conditions to which focal attention was already devoted. Instead, a more diffuse detection mechanism is required that is capable of monitoring for and responding to significant conditions without placing heavy demands on the person's attentional capacities. In opposition to this constraint, however, the motivational, coping-preparatory functions served by emotion push for the emotion signal to be as information-rich as possible. The more information regarding the nature of the emotion-eliciting circumstances that the emotion signal can carry, the more useful that signal can be in both alerting the person to those circumstances, and preparing the person to contend with them.

The puzzle, then, is to articulate a model of the appraisal process that can explain the production of the information-rich, motivating signals that discrete emotions represent without placing undue demands on the person's limited attentional capacities. Our progress in developing such a model (e.g., Smith et al., 1996) is described next.

Sketch of a Process Model

We propose that, rather than a single unitary appraisal process, there are multiple appraisal processes that can occur in parallel, and that involve distinct cognitive mechanisms. Furthermore, we highlight two distinct modes of cognitive processing that we believe are especially important for understanding appraisal: *associative processing*, which involves priming and activation of memories and can occur quickly and automatically; and *reasoning*, which involves a more controlled and deliberate thinking process that is more flexible than associative processing but is relatively slow and attention-intensive.

The distinction between these two general modes of cognition is not new. In fact, it is modeled on the distinction between schematic processing and conceptual processing discussed by Leventhal and Scherer (1987).[1] Moreover, this distinction is closely related to similar ideas that have been proposed in the literature. These include the distinction between controlled and automatic processing (Shiffrin & Schneider, 1977), between knowledge by description and knowledge by acquaintance (Buck, 1985), between the experiential system and the rational system (Epstein, 1994), and the distinction between direct access and substantive processing described by Forgas (1995; see also

Forgas, Ch. 11, this volume). Recently, Sloman (1996) has reviewed the evidence in support of at least two basic modes of cognition along the lines we are proposing. We have integrated both of these modes of processing into our model, depicted in Figure 4.1. Three things distinguish this model from previous work. First, it applies the distinction between the two modes of processing to the elicitation of emotional responses. Second, the model applies this distinction in a way that can account explicitly for a number of phenomena that have traditionally been problematic for appraisal theory. And third, it suggests some ways in which the two modes of processing interact in shaping appraisal.

A central feature of this model is the existence of what we call "appraisal detectors." These detectors continuously monitor for, and are responsive to, appraisal information from multiple sources. The appraisal information they detect determines the person's emotional state. Several features of the proposed appraisal detectors are noteworthy. First, they do not actively compute the appraisals, in the sense

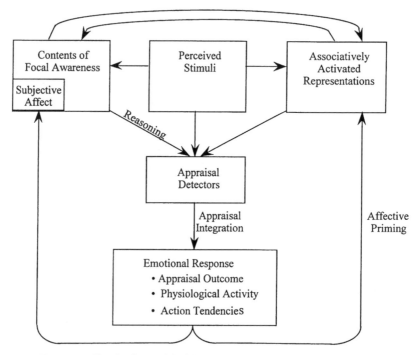

Figure 4.1. Sketch of a model of the appraisal process.

that they perform an active evaluation of the person's relationship to the environment in terms of the various components of appraisal. Instead, they detect the appraisal information that is generated from different modes of processing. This detected information is then combined into an integrated appraisal that initiates processes to generate the various components of the emotional response, including an organized pattern of physiological activity, the action tendency, and the subjective feeling state.

Second, although detailed speculations regarding the neuroanatomy of the appraisal detectors is beyond the scope of both this chapter and our expertise, we believe them to be subcortical and to most likely reside in the limbic system. This speculation is based in large part on the recent work of LeDoux (1986, 1989), who has found the amygdala to be an important site of meaning integration associated with the elicitation of fear in the rat, as well as on the long theoretical and empirical tradition that has posited an important role for the limbic system in generating and organizing emotional reactions (e.g., Mac-Lean, 1973; Papez, 1937).

As depicted in Figure 4.1, the appraisal detectors receive information from three distinct sources. First, some perceptual stimuli, such as pain sensations, looming objects, and possibly even certain facial expressions (e.g., Ohman, 1986), may be preset to carry certain appraisal meanings that can be detected directly. For instance, all else being equal, painful sensations are inherently motivationally incongruent, or undesirable. This suggestion that perceptual information can directly result in an emotional reaction is in line with the proposals of Leventhal and Scherer (1987), who propose a third level of processing – the perceptual-motor level – to accompany their distinction between schematic and conceptual processing. It is hypothesized, however, that most of the information processed by the appraisal detectors is generated through either associative processing or reasoning.

As mentioned, associative processing is a fast, automatic, memory-based mode of processing that involves priming and spreading activation (Bargh, 1989; Bower, 1981). Perceptual or conceptual similarities with one's current circumstances or associations with other memories that are already activated cause memories of prior experiences to become activated quickly, automatically, in parallel, outside of focal awareness, and with a minimum use of attentional resources. As these memories are activated, any appraisal meanings associated with them are also activated, and when these meanings are activated to a sufficient degree, they can be recognized by the appraisal detectors and influence the person's emotional state. Note in passing that a number of the techniques used to induce mood, including music (e.g., Niedenthal, Halberstadt, & Setterlund, 1997) and other priming techniques, appear to utilize the type of associative processing we are describing here.

We make several assumptions about associative processing here. First, we assume that anything that can be represented in memory – ranging from concrete representations of physical sensations, sounds, smells, tastes, and images to representations of highly abstract concepts – is subject to this form of processing. That is, cues that can activate appraisal-laden memories include not only concrete stimuli, such as sensations, images, and sounds, but also highly conceptual stimuli, such as abstract ideas or the appraisal meanings themselves. Second, we assume that through principles of priming and spreading activation, full-blown appraisals associated with prior experiences can be activated quickly and automatically. Thus, highly differentiated emotional reactions can be elicited almost instantaneously. Third, an especially important assumption related to the attention-regulatory functions we ascribe to emotion is that the activation threshold at which appraisal information becomes available to the appraisal detectors is somewhat less than the threshold at which the appraisal information and its associated memories become accessible to focal awareness and/or working memory. Through this assumption it becomes possible that adaptationally relevant circumstances in one's environment, of which one is focally unaware, can activate memories and produce an emotional reaction such that the first conscious indication to the person that he or she might be in an adaptationally relevant situation is the perception of the subjective feeling state associated with the associatively elicited emotional reaction. Finally, we assume that the processes of memory activation, priming, and spreading activation occur continuously and automatically, just as the appraisal detectors continuously monitor for activated appraisal information. Thus, the person can be characterized as continuously appraising his or her circumstances for their implications for well-being, albeit not in a conscious, attention-intensive manner. In sum, the activation of appraisal information through associative processing provides the emotion system with the diffuse, non-attention-intensive elicitation mechanism demanded by the attention-regulatory functions believed to be served by emotion.

In contrast to associative processing, reasoning is a relatively slow, controlled process that is effortful, requires considerable attention and focal awareness, and is by and large verbally mediated. Moreover, whereas associative processing is passive in the way that appraisal information is made available to the appraisal detectors (i.e., appraisal information that happens to be sufficiently activated becomes available for detection), reasoning is a much more constructive process, whereby the contents of focal awareness are actively operated on and transformed to produce the appraisal meanings. In other words, what we are calling reasoning corresponds closely to the active posing and evaluating of appraisal questions that have sometimes been incorrectly assumed to encompass all of appraisal. In Figure 4.1, we have labeled the arrow from focal awareness as "reasoning" to reflect the fact that reasoning involves the active generation of appraisal information for the appraisal detectors.

Because reasoning is active and highly resource-intensive, it comes at a price. In addition, this mode of processing is somewhat limited in the forms of information that it can access. In contrast to associative processing, which can operate on any form of information stored in memory, only information that has been semantically encoded in some way is readily accessible to reasoning (Anderson, 1983; Paivio, 1971; Polyani, 1962). That is, sensations, images, sounds, and the like are relatively inaccessible to reasoning unless and until they have been associated with some sort of semantic meaning. Hence, although associative processing has access to all of the information to which the reasoning process has access, the reverse is not true.

Despite these limitations, reasoning is extremely important in that it enables the emotion system to utilize the full power of our highly developed and abstract thinking processes. Emotion-eliciting situations can be thoroughly analyzed and their meanings reappraised (Lazarus, 1968, 1991). Thus, initial associatively elicited appraisals that might not fully fit the current circumstances can be modified to provide a more appropriate evaluation and emotional response. New connections can be forged between one's present circumstances and potentially related previous experiences. It is even possible that appraisal meanings associated with previous experiences in memory can be reevaluated and changed. In addition, the "cognitive work" represented by reasoning – the results of the interpretation and reinterpretation of the emotion-eliciting situation – can be stored in memory as part of the emotion-eliciting event and thus become available for subsequent associative processing. This last fact is vital, in that it provides a mechanism by which the emotion system can "learn" and, through associative processing, can quickly and automatically produce the highly differentiated, information-rich signals that the motivational functions believed to be served by emotion seem to require.

Finally, as depicted in Figure 4.1, the emotional response resulting from the appraisals produced through both associative processing and reasoning feeds back to influence both of these processes, albeit in different ways. For associative processing, the various components of the emotional response, the appraisal outcome itself, the physiological activities, and the felt action tendencies can all serve as cues to prime memories associated with similar emotional reactions in the past. To the extent that these newly activated memories correspond sufficiently to the person's current circumstances, they can further intensify the developing emotional response. In addition, when this developing emotional response becomes sufficiently intense, it intrudes into focal awareness, making the person subjectively aware that he or she is emotionally aroused. It is this representation of the emotion in subjective awareness that serves the crucial motivational signaling functions that we have ascribed to emotion.

The Unfolding of an Emotional Reaction

At this point it is probably useful to provide a relatively concrete example of how we view these two modes of processing as contributing to an emotional experience. Consider the following situation: You are attending a conference in an unfamiliar city. It is late in the afternoon and you and a colleague are walking around town intensely discussing the implications of an intriguing presentation you both have just heard. The two of you are so engrossed in conversation that you are not paying close attention to where you are going. This continues for a while, until, suddenly, you realize that you are feeling rather anxious. Looking around, you quickly realize why: You have wandered off the beaten path, it is starting to get dark, the buildings around you look run down, and seedy-looking characters are wandering about. You stop your conversation to point out the situation to your companion, and the two of you turn around and head back to the touristic part of town without incident.

According to the model we have outlined, what has happened in this situation is this: As you and your colleague were walking along, you were so engrossed in your conversation that the accumulating cues to danger in your situation did not register in focal awareness. However, they were perceived to a degree sufficient to activate appraisals of danger and threat associated with these cues in memory. As these appraisal meanings became increasingly activated, they were picked up by the appraisal detectors, which set into motion processes generating the anxiety reaction that results from these appraisals. When this reaction became sufficiently intense, it intruded into your focal awareness, alerting you, effectively for the first time, that you were in a potentially dangerous situation. This enabled you to consciously size up the situation and to take appropriate action to avoid the potential danger that you had associatively detected.

What the Model Can Do

Combining the above example with the more general description of the model underlying it, it should be evident that the combination of both associative processing and reasoning appraisal generation provides for an extremely powerful and adaptive emotion system. Working together, these two modes of appraisal allow emotion to function as a sophisticated well-being monitor and guidance system that is fast, flexible, and highly "intelligent." That is, the system is able to take advantage of what a person learns through his or her life experiences in a way that allows even associatively elicited appraisals to be highly customized, and to combine key aspects of the situational context with key properties of the individual, such as his or her needs, goals, beliefs, and expectations. Within the context of an ongoing emotional encounter, the power and flexibility of reasoning allows one to perform the sophisticated relational analysis that underlies highly context-specific appraisals. Once this analysis has been performed, however, to the degree that it is associated with appropriate situational cues in memory, these highly individualized, context-specific appraisals can be quickly and automatically elicited through associative processing.

Clearly, the model we have presented goes well beyond a rather simple theory stating that "what you think determines what you feel," as has sometimes been suggested of appraisal theory. Hence, our model can readily account for a number of phenomena that have been considered problematic for cognitive theories of emotion in general, and appraisal theory in particular. First, it should be evident that associative processing provides a mechanism by which full-blown, highly differentiated emotional reactions can be elicited, quickly, automatically, outside of focal awareness, and with a seeming minimum of cognitive activity, in line with Zajonc's (1980) influential observations.

Second, it is possible to reconcile facial feedback phenomena – whereby posing the facial expression characteristic of a particular emotion can influence one's subjective feeling state in line with the expressed emotion (e.g., Larsen, Kasimatis, & Frey, 1992; Lanzetta, Cartwright-Smith, & Kleck, 1976; Strack, Martin, & Stepper, 1988) – with an appraisal account of emotion elicitation. Representations of facial expressions associated with particular emotions are likely to be linked with memories of experiences of those emotions, as are the relevant appraisal meanings. For example, when one assumes an angry facial expression, regardless of current mood state, memories of other times when one has displayed this expression become associatively activated. Not coincidentally, these memories are likely to involve other times when one was angry and thus to have associated with them the appraisals that elicit anger. In this way, angry sentiments become primed and can have an impact on one's current mood.

Because associative processing occurs automatically and outside of focal awareness, it is quite possible for emotions to emerge into conscious awareness unbidden, unwanted, and outside of the person's control. Moreover, because it is the integrated appraisal information from the appraisal detectors that determines one's emotional state, rather than either associatively based or reasoning-based appraisal information directly, a person can be in a strong emotional state because of associative activation of the relevant appraisals even as the person actively denies the basis of the appraisal. For instance, it is quite possible to experience intense anger at someone for a perceived offense even as one works strenuously to convince oneself that "it just doesn't matter," or that the person was perfectly justified to do whatever had elicited the anger.

Pushed to the extreme, the possibility that the appraisal meanings produced by associative processing versus reasoning can be quite different allows appraisal theory to handle the phenomenon of repression. Here, an individual may give many expressive and behavioral signs of being in a clear emotional state, yet with all sincerity vehemently deny that this is the case (e.g., Weinberger, 1990). To account for this phenomenon, one need only assume that the threshold at which an associatively based emotional reaction presents itself into consciousness is somewhat higher in repressors than in other individuals. In this case, the appraisals generated associatively produce an emotional reaction, including physiological and expressive changes, in the normal fashion, yet the feeling state itself often fails to serve its signaling function because it is not strong enough to be subjectively detected.

Finally, and more generally, the potential decoupling of associative and reasoning-based appraisal meanings may provide an integrative account of emotional misattribution phenomena (e.g., Schachter & Singer, 1962; Schwarz & Clore, 1983; Zillman, 1978). Although under many conditions the appraisal meaning to be derived from a given set of circumstances is likely to be sufficiently clear for both modes of processing to generate similar appraisals (as was the case in the anxiety example mentioned earlier), under certain circumstances associative processing and reasoning may lead to very different appraisal outcomes. This is because the two types of processing are especially sensitive to different types of information. In particular, associative processing is sensitive to sensory and other perceptual information that often may not be semantically encoded and thus is largely unavailable to reasoning. Conversely, the abstract thinking abilities inherent in reasoning allow this mode of processing to make novel connections between one's current circumstances and one's prior experiences, theories, and expectations, which until they have been made and stored in memory would necessarily be inaccessible to associative processing. Thus, subtle, nonobvious factors, hidden from focal attention, can effectively elicit a particular emotional reaction through associative processing, but these factors might be missed by the reasoning process, which, instead, arrives at a more "obvious" (but incorrect) interpretation of one's situation and the resulting emotional reaction.

Issues Requiring Development

As the preceding examples suggest, the model we have proposed derives much of its power from the operation of two distinct modes of cognition, which have rather different properties but operate in parallel. Importantly, associative processing and reasoning do not operate independently of one another but interact in significant ways. Our model now needs to be further developed so as to articulate more clearly not only the respective properties, strengths, and weaknesses of these two modes of cognition, but also the many ways in which these two modes of processing systematically interact.

For example, we have already explained that an important proposed function of reasoning is to define, shape, and sometimes alter the appraisal meanings associated with memories that will become available for subsequent associative processing. However, we believe the two modes of processing influence each other in more subtle ways as well. For instance, concepts and appraisal meanings primed through associative activation are likely to be more accessible to focal awareness and the reasoning processes than they might otherwise be (e.g., Bargh, 1989). This situation is represented in Figure 4.1 by the arrow from the associatively activated representations to the contents of focal awareness. In a similar manner, because of residual activation (Bargh, 1989), concepts that have been activated through reasoning are likely to be especially accessible to subsequent associative processing, which is reflected in Figure 4.1 by the arrow between the two boxes facing the other way. That is, fewer situational cues are required to activate an appraisal when its associated memories have been recently activated through reasoning processes. This possibility would seem to be an especially important one to investigate. Not only does it suggest a reason why there is a tendency to appraise subsequent events in line with one's current emotional state (e.g., Keltner et al., 1993), but it also potentially represents an indirect method of exerting some control over the results of one's associative processing.

In the efforts to more fully articulate the nature of the two modes of processing and their interactions, we believe that drawing on the insights gained through the study of the role of emotion in social judgment will prove to be extremely helpful. For example, in our conceptualization, the Affect Infusion Model (AIM) proposed by Forgas (1995) and the mood-as-information models advanced by Schwarz, Clore, and their colleagues (e.g., Clore & Parrott, 1994; Martin, Ward, Achee, & Wyer, 1993; Schwarz, 1990; Schwarz & Clore, 1988) represent efforts to describe the ways in which the information carried by the subjective feeling state, which is often initially evoked primarily through associative processing, influences subsequent cognitive processing and behavior. These efforts indicate a great deal about how the information carried by the subjective emotion signal influences subsequent reasoning, as is the case when it leads to congruent reasoning that will intensify the emotional reaction (e.g., Eich, 1995), or when it is discounted (Schwarz & Clore, 1983), perhaps sometimes to the point of producing paradoxical effects (e.g., Berkowitz, Jaffee, Jo, & Troccoli, this volume). In addition, some of these theories, such as the AIM (Forgas, 1995), also consider how, through priming and spreading activation, the emotion signal itself can further systematically influence subsequent associative processing (e.g., Bower, 1981; Forgas & Bower, 1987).

The methodological techniques developed in these research programs should prove useful in empirically testing the process model. The initial steps in that testing should be, first, to document that information from both types of processing influences the emotional response and, second, to begin documenting the specific ways in which appraisal information from both types of processing are combined and integrated in shaping the emotional response. Addressing these issues will require considerable experimental control over the contents and operation of the two modes of processing. Guidelines on how to exercise this control are readily available from the work on the effects of emotion on cognition. For example, the use of previously established priming techniques should prove useful in manipulating the contents of associative processing, whereas the careful use of instructions may help to determine not only the contents of appraisal-related reasoning, but also whether this resource-intensive form of processing even occurs (e.g., Berkowitz et al., this volume; Forgas, 1995; Schwarz & Clore, 1983).

In sum, the model we have outlined in this chapter is clearly a work in progress. We have laid out most, if not all, of the major components, discussed how these pieces are likely go together, and illustrated some of the promise of this model. However, many aspects of this model, particularly the ways in which reasoning and associative processing interact in the generation of emotion, require further theoretical development, and the model has yet to be empirically tested in any significant way. As our model is further developed and tested, we expect that advances in its development will not only contribute to our understanding of the role of cognition in eliciting emotions, but also improve our understanding of the broader, multidirectional interactions between cognition and emotion.

Note

1. In fact, we originally considered adopting Leventhal and Scherer's (1987) terminology rather than introducing our own. We opted against this, however, for two reasons. First, as discussed by Leventhal and Scherer (1987), in addition to the differences in the cognitive processes, the distinction between schematic and conceptual processing involves differences in the types of information that can be operated on by each type of process. Conceptual processing is limited to the processing of "conceptual" (i.e., semantically encoded) information, whereas schematic processing is limited to information that has been "schematically" encoded. Although the range of information encompassed by schematic encoding is not fully defined, the processing of abstract information appears to be clearly precluded. As will become apparent in our discussion, although we largely agree that the information accessible to conceptual or reasoning processes is limited to semantically encoded, or "conceptual," information, we do not agree that there are limits to the types of information that can be processed through the more automatic mode. Instead, we believe that anything that can be represented in memory is potentially accessible to associative, or automatic processing. Second, the term "schematic" tends to imply that this form of processing necessarily involves the activation of "schemas," or already organized knowledge structures. This assumption is too restrictive. We prefer the term "associative" because it is less restrictive and encompasses the processes of priming and of spreading activation that can operate on items associated in memory for any of a number of reasons that need not include being part of an organized schema (cf. Berkowitz, 1993).

References

Anderson, J. R. (1983). *The architecture of cognition*. Cambridge, MA: Harvard University Press.

Arnold, M. B. (1960). *Emotion and personality*. New York: Columbia University Press.

Bargh, J. A. (1989). Conditional automaticity: Varieties of automatic influence in social perception and cognition. In J. S. Uleman & J. A. Bargh (Eds.), *Unintended thought* (pp. 3–51). New York: Guilford Press.

Berkowitz, L. (1993). Toward a general theory of anger and emotional aggression. In T. K. Srull & R. S. Wyer (Eds.), *Advances in social cognition* (Vol. 6, pp. 1–46). Hillsdale, NJ: Erlbaum.

Bower, G. H. (1981). Mood and memory. *American Psychologist, 36*, 129–148.

Buck, R. (1985). Prime theory: An integrated view of motivation and emotion. *Psychological Review, 92*, 389–413.

Calhoun, C., & Solomon, R. C. (1994). *What is an emotion? Classical readings in philosophical psychology*. Oxford: Oxford University Press.

Cannon, W. B. (1929). *Bodily changes in pain, hunger, fear, and rage* (2nd ed.). New York: Appleton-Century.

Clore, G. L., & Parrot, G. (1994). Cognitive feelings and metacognitive judgements. *European Journal of Social Psychology, 24,* 101–116.

Clore, G. L., Schwarz, N., & Conway, M. (1994). Affective causes and consequences of social information processing. In R. S. Wyer & T. K. Srull (Eds.), *Handbook of social cognition* (2nd ed., Vol. 1, pp. 323–419). Hillsdale, NJ: Erlbaum.

Darwin, C. (1965). *The expression of the emotions in man and animals.* Chicago: University of Chicago Press. (Original work published in 1872)

Derryberry, D., & Tucker, D. M. (1994). Motivating the focus of attention. In P. M. Niedenthal & S. Kitayama (Eds.), *The heart's eye: Emotional influences in perception and attention* (pp. 167–196). New York: Academic Press.

Eich, E. (1995). Searching for mood dependent memory. *Psychological Science, 6,* 67–75.

Ekman, P. (1984). Expression and the nature of emotion. In K. R. Scherer & P. Ekman (Eds.), *Approaches to emotion* (pp. 329–343). Hillsdale, NJ: Erlbaum.

Ellsworth, P. C., & Smith, C. A. (1988a). From appraisal to emotion: Differences among unpleasant feelings. *Motivation and Emotion, 12,* 271–302.

Ellsworth, P. C., & Smith, C. A. (1988b). Shades of joy: Patterns of appraisal differentiating pleasant emotions. *Cognition and Emotion, 2,* 301–331.

Epstein, S. (1994). Integration of the cognitive and the psychodynamic unconscious. *American Psychologist, 49,* 709–724.

Fiedler, K., Asbeck, J., & Nickel, S. (1991). Mood and constructive memory effects on social judgement. *Cognition and Emotion, 5,* 363–378.

Forgas, J. P. (1995). Mood and judgement: The affect infusion model (AIM). *Psychological Bulletin, 117,* 39–66.

Forgas, J. P., & Bower, G. H. (1987). Mood effects on person perception judgements. *Journal of Personality and Social Psychology, 53,* 53–60.

Frijda, N. H. (1986). *The emotions.* New York: Cambridge University Press.

Frijda, N. H., Kuipers, P., & ter Schure, E. (1989). Relations among emotion, appraisal, and emotional action readiness. *Journal of Personality and Social Psychology, 57,* 212–228.

Frijda, N. H., & Swagerman, J. (1987). Can computers feel? Theory and design of an emotional system. *Cognition and Emotion, 1,* 235–257.

Griner, L. A., & Smith, C. A. (1997). Contributions of motivational orientation to appraisal and emotion. Manuscript submitted for publication. Vanderbilt University.

Izard, C. E. (1977). *Human emotions.* New York: Plenum.

Izard, C. E. (1993). Four systems for emotion activation: Cognitive and noncognitive processes. *Psychological Review, 100,* 68–90.

Keltner, D., Ellsworth, P. C., & Edwards, K. (1993). Beyond simple pessimism: Effects of sadness and anger on social perception. *Journal of Personality and Social Psychology, 64,* 740–752.

Kirby, L. D., & Smith, C. A. (1998). Hidden costs of competence: Performance orientation and sex as moderators of emotional, physiological, and behavioral responses to a stressful task. Manuscript submitted for publication. Vanderbilt University.

Lanzetta, J. T., Cartwright-Smith, J., & Kleck, R. E. (1976). Effects of nonverbal dissimulation on emotional experience and autonomic arousal. *Journal of Personality and Social Psychology, 33,* 354–370.

Larsen, R. J., Kasimatis, M., & Frey, K. (1992). Facilitating the furrowed brow: An unobtrusive test of the facial feedback hypothesis applied to unpleasant affect. *Cognition and Emotion, 6,* 321–338.

Lazarus, R. S. (1968). Emotions and adaptation: Conceptual and empirical relations. Paper presented at the Nebraska Symposium on Motivation, Lincoln.

Lazarus, R. S. (1991). *Emotion and adaptation.* New York: Oxford University Press.

Lazarus, R. S., & Smith, C. A. (1988). Knowledge and appraisal in the cognition-emotion relationship. *Cognition and Emotion, 2,* 281–300.

LeDoux, J. E. (1986). Sensory systems and emotion: A model of affective processing. *Integrative Psychiatry, 4,* 237–248.

LeDoux, J. E. (1989). The neurobiology of emotion. In J. E. LeDoux & W. Hirst (Eds.), *Mind and brain: Dialogues in cognitive neuroscience* (pp. 301–354). Cambridge: Cambridge University Press.

Leventhal, H., & Scherer, K. R. (1987). The relationship of emotion to cognition: A functional approach to a semantic controversy. *Cognition and Emotion, 1,* 3–28.

MacLean, P. D. (1973). *A triune concept of the brain and behaviour.* Toronto: University of Toronto Press.

Martin, L. L., Ward, D. W., Achee, J. W., & Wyer, R. S. (1993). Mood as input: People have to interpret the motivational implications of their moods. *Journal of Personality and Social Psychology, 64,* 317–326.

Niedenthal, P. M., Halberstadt, J. B., & Setterlund, M. B. (1997). Being happy and seeing "happy": Emotional state mediates visual word recognition. *Cognition and Emotion, 11,* 403–432.

Niedenthal, P. M., Setterlund, M. B., & Jones, D. E. (1994). Emotional organization of perceptual memory. In P. M. Niedenthal & S. Kitayama (Eds.), *The heart's eye: Emotional influences in perception and attention* (pp. 87–113). New York: Academic Press.

Ohman, A. (1986). Face the beast and fear the face: Animal and social fears as prototypes for evolutionary analyses of emotion. *Psychophysiology, 23,* 123–145.

Paivio, A. (1971). *Imagery and verbal processes.* New York: Holt, Rinehart, and Winston.

Papez, J. W. (1937). A proposed mechanism of emotion. *Archives of Neurology and Psychiatry, 38,* 725–743.

Parkinson, B. (1997). Untangling the appraisal-emotion connection. *Personality and Social Psychology Review, 1,* 62–79.

Parkinson, B., & Manstead, A. S. R. (1992). Appraisal as a cause of emotion. In M. S. Clark (Ed.), *Review of personality and social psychology: Vol 13. Emotion* (pp. 122–149). Newbury Park, CA: Sage.

Parkinson, B., & Manstead, A. S. R. (1993). Making sense of emotions in stories and social life. *Cognition and Emotion, 7,* 295–323.

Plutchik, R. (1980). *Emotion: A psychoevolutionary synthesis.* New York: Harper & Row.

Polyani, M. (1962). *Personal knowledge: Towards a post-critical philosophy.* Chicago: University of Chicago Press.

Robinson, M. D. (in press). Running from William James' bear: A review of preattentive mechanisms and their contributions to emotional experience. *Cognition and Emotion, 12,* 667–696.

Roseman, I. J. (1984). Cognitive determinants of emotion: A structural theory. In P. Shaver (Ed.), *Review of personality and social psychology: Vol. 5. Emotions, relationships, and health* (pp. 11–36). Beverly Hills, CA: Sage.

Roseman, I. J. (1991). Appraisal determinants of discrete emotions. *Cognition and Emotion, 5,* 161–200.

Schachter, S., & Singer, J. E. (1962). Cognitive, social, and physiological determinants of emotional state. *Psychological Review, 69,* 379–399.

Scherer, K. R. (1984). On the nature and function of emotion: A component process approach. In K. R. Scherer & P. Ekman (Eds.), *Approaches to emotion* (pp. 293–317). Hillsdale, NJ: Erlbaum.

Scherer, K. R. (1997). Profiles of emotion-antecedent appraisal: Testing theoretical predictions across cultures. *Cognition and Emotion, 11,* 113–150.

Schwarz, N. (1990). Feelings as information: Informational and motivational functions of affective states. In E. T. Higgins & R. Sorrentino (Eds.), *Handbook of motivation and cognition: Foundations of social behavior* (Vol. 2, pp. 527–561). New York: Guilford Press.

Schwarz, N., & Clore, G. L. (1983). Mood, misattribution and judgements of well-being: Informative and directive functions of affective states. *Journal of Personality and Social Psychology, 45,* 513–523.

Schwarz, N., & Clore, G. L. (1988). How do I feel about it? The informative function of affective states. In K. Fiedler & J. P. Forgas (Eds.), *Affect, cognition, and social behavior* (pp. 44–62). Gottingen, Germany: Hogrefe.

Shiffrin, R. M., & Schneider, W. (1977). Controlled and automatic human information processing: II. Perceptual learning, automatic attending, and a general theory. *Psychological Review, 84,* 127–190.

Simon, H. A. (1966). Motivational and emotional controls of cognition. *Psychological Review, 74,* 29–39.

Sloman, S. A. (1996). The empirical case for two systems of reasoning. *Psychological Bulletin, 119,* 3–22.

Smith, C. A. (1989). Dimensions of appraisal and physiological response in emotion. *Journal of Personality and Social Psychology, 56,* 339–353.

Smith, C. A., & Ellsworth, P. C. (1985). Patterns of cognitive appraisal in emotion. *Journal of Personality and Social Psychology, 48,* 813–838.

Smith, C. A., & Ellsworth, P. C. (1987). Patterns of appraisal and emotion related to taking an exam. *Journal of Personality and Social Psychology, 52,* 475–488.

Smith, C. A., Griner, L. A., Kirby, L. D., & Scott, H. S. (1996). Toward a process model of appraisal in emotion. *Proceedings of the Ninth Conference of the*

International Society for Research on Emotions (pp. 101–105), Abstract. International Society for Research on Emotions, Toronto.

Smith, C. A., & Kirby, L. D. (1998). *The person and situation in transaction: Antecedents of appraisal and emotion.* Manuscript submitted for publication.

Smith, C. A., & Lazarus, R. S. (1990). Emotion and adaptation. In L. A. Pervin (Ed.), *Handbook of personality: Theory and research* (pp. 609–637). New York: Guilford Press.

Smith, C. A., & Lazarus, R. S. (1993). Appraisal components, core relational themes, and the emotions. *Cognition and Emotion, 7,* 233–269.

Smith, C. A., & Pope, L. K. (1992). Appraisal and emotion: The interactional contributions of dispositional and situational factors. In M. S. Clark (Ed.), *Review of Personality and Social Psychology: Vol. 14. Emotion and Social Behavior* (pp. 32–62). Newbury Park, CA: Sage.

Strack, F., Martin, L. L., & Stepper, S. (1988). Inhibiting and facilitating conditions of the human smile: A nonobtrusive test of the facial feedback hypothesis. *Journal of Personality and Social Psychology, 54,* 768–777.

Tomkins, S. S. (1962). *Affect, imagery, consciousness: Vol. 1. The positive affects.* New York: Springer.

Tomkins, S. S. (1980). Affect as amplification: Some modifications in theory. In R. Plutchik & H. Kellerman (Eds.), *Emotion: Theory, research, and experience: Vol. 1. Theories of emotion* (pp. 141–164). New York: Academic Press.

Watson, D., & Tellegen, A. (1985). Toward a consensual structure of mood. *Psychological Bulletin, 98,* 219–235.

Weinberger, D. A. (1990). The construct validity of the repressive coping style. In J. L. Singer (Ed.), *Repression and dissociation: Implications for personality theory, psychopathology, and health* (pp. 337–386). Chicago: University of Chicago Press.

Zajonc, R. B. (1980). Feeling and thinking: Preferences need no inferences. *American Psychologist, 35,* 151–175.

Zillman, D. (1978). Attribution and misattribution of excitatory reactions. In J. H. Harvey, W. Ickes, & R. F. Kidd (Eds.), *New directions in attribution research* (Vol. 2, pp. 335–368). Hillsdale, NJ: Erlbaum.

PART II

The Informational Role of Affect

5. Fundamental Factors in Mood-Dependent Memory

ERIC EICH AND DAWN MACAULAY

Introduction

Are events that have been encoded in a certain state of affect or mood more retrievable in the same state than in a different one? Stated more succinctly, is memory mood dependent?

In principle, the answer is plainly "yes" on two accounts. In the first place, the cognitive literature is replete with theories that suggest memory *should* be mood dependent; examples include such classic contributions as McGeogh's (1942) interference theory of forgetting and Miller's (1950) drive-as-stimulus hypothesis, as well as such contemporary innovations as Bower's (1981) network theory of emotions and Tulving's (1983) encoding specificity principle. By the same token, the clinical literature contains numerous conjectures implicating mood-dependent memory (MDM) as a causal factor in the memory deficits displayed by patients with alcoholic blackout, chronic depression, traumatic amnesia, multiple personality, and other psychiatric disorders (see Goodwin, 1974; Ludwig, 1984; Reus, Weingartner, & Post, 1979; Schacter & Kihlstrom, 1989).

In practice, however, the answer is a much more guarded "maybe." Over the past 20 years, many studies have sought to demonstrate MDM using a variety of memory materials, encoding tasks, retrieval measures, retention intervals, and mood-modification techniques (for

Preparation of this chapter was aided by grants to Eric Eich from the (American) National Institute of Mental Health (R01-MH48502) and the (Canadian) Natural Sciences and Engineering Research Council (37335).

Correspondence concerning this work should be addressed to Eric Eich, Department of Psychology, University of British Columbia, Vancouver, British Columbia, Canada V6T 1Z4. E-mail: EE@CORTEX.PSYCH.UBC.CA.

reviews, see Bower, 1992; Eich, 1995a; Kenealy, 1997). The fact that these studies have failed about as often as they have succeeded raises a new question: Even if mood dependence is not the powerful and prevalent effect many cognitivists and clinicians once thought it was, might MDM nevertheless emerge in a clear and consistent manner under certain limited conditions? In order to answer this question, we focus on three factors that appear fundamental to the occurrence of mood dependence – one concerned with the nature of the subjects' encoding and retrieval tasks, another with qualities of the moods they experience while performing these tasks, and the last with character-istics of the subjects themselves.

Task Factors

Intuitively, it is plausible to assume that how strongly memory is mood dependent will depend on how the to-be-remembered or target events are encoded. To clarify, consider two hypothetical cases related by Eich, Macaulay, and Ryan (1994). In Scenario 1:

> Two individuals – one happy, one sad – are shown, say, a *rose* and are asked to identify and describe what they see. Both individuals are apt to say much the same thing and to encode the *rose* event in much the same manner. After all, and with all due respect to Gertrude Stein, a rose is a rose is a rose, regardless of whether it is seen through a happy or sad eye. The implication, then, is that the manner in which the perceivers encode the *rose* event will be largely, if not entirely, unrelated to their mood. If true, then when retrieval of the event is later assessed via nominally noncued or "spontaneous" recall, it should make little if any difference whether or not the subjects are in the same mood they had experienced earlier. In short, memory for the *rose* event will proba-bly not appear to be mood dependent under these circumstances.
>
> Now imagine a different situation [Scenario 2]. Instead of identifying and describing the rose, the subjects are asked to recall an episode, from any time in their personal past, that the object calls to mind. Rather than involving the relatively automatic or data-driven perception of an exter-nal stimulus, the task now requires the subjects to engage in internal mental processes such as reasoning, reflection, and cotemporal thought, "the sort of elaborative and associative processes that augment, bridge, or embellish ongoing perceptual experience but that are not necessarily part of the veridical representation of perceptual experience" (Johnson & Raye, 1981, p. 70). Furthermore, even though the stimulus object is itself affectively neutral, the autobiographical memories it triggers are apt to be strongly influenced by the subjects' mood. Thus, for example, whereas the happy subject may recollect receiving a dozen roses from a

secret admirer, the sad subject may remember the flowers that adorned his father's coffin. In effect, then the *rose* event becomes closely associated with or deeply colored by the subject's mood, thereby making mood a potentially potent cue for retrieving the event. Thus, when later asked to spontaneously recall the gist of the episode they had recounted earlier, the subjects should be more likely to remember having related a vignette involving roses if they are in the same mood they had experienced earlier. In this situation, then, memory for the *rose* event should appear to be mood dependent.

These armchair conjectures concur with the results of actual research. Many of the earliest experiments on MDM used a simple list-learning paradigm analogous to the situation envisioned in Scenario 1, in which subjects memorized unrelated words while they were in a particular mood: typically either happiness or sadness, induced via hypnotic suggestions, guided imagery, mood-appropriate music, or some other means. As Bower (1992) has observed, the assumption was that the words would become associated, by virtue of temporal contiguity, to the subjects' current mood, as well as to the list context; hence, reinstatement of the same mood would be expected to enhance performance on a later test of word retention. Though a few list-learning experiments found MDM, several others showed no sign whatsoever of the phenomenon (see Blaney, 1986; Bower, 1987). Worse, attempts to replicate positive results seldom prevailed, even when undertaken by the same investigator using similar materials, tasks, and mood-modification techniques (see Bower & Mayer, 1989).

Unlike list-learning experiments, studies involving autobiographical memory – including those modeled after Scenario 2 – have revealed robust and reliable evidence of mood dependence (see Bower, 1992; Eich, 1995a; Fiedler, 1990; Forgas, 1993). An example is the second of three studies reported by Eich et al. (1994). During the encoding session of this study, university undergraduates were asked to recollect or generate 16 specific, real-life events, each of which was called to mind by a common-noun probe (e.g., *rose*). After recounting the particulars of a given event (what happened, when, and who was involved), subjects rated its original emotional valence – that is, whether the event was a positive, neutral, or negative experience when it occurred. Half of the subjects completed the task of autobiographical event generation while they were feeling happy (H) and half did so while sad (S), moods that had been induced through a combination of music and ideation.

During the retrieval session, held 2 days after encoding, subjects were asked to recall – in any order, and without benefit of any observable reminders or cues – the gist of as many of their previously generated events as possible, preferably by recalling their precise corresponding probes. Subjects undertook this test of event free recall either in the same mood in which they had generated the events or in the alternative affective state, thus creating two conditions in which encoding and retrieval moods matched (H/H and S/S) and two in which they mismatched (H/S and S/H).

Results of the encoding session showed that, on average, subjects generated more positive events (11.1 vs. 6.7), fewer negative events (3.3 vs. 6.8), and about the same, small number of neutral events (1.2 vs. 2.0) when they were in a happy rather than a sad mood. This pattern replicates earlier experiments (e.g., Clark & Teasdale, 1982; Snyder & White, 1982), and it provides evidence of mood-*congruent* memory: the "enhanced encoding and/or retrieval of material the affective valence of which is congruent with ongoing mood" (Blaney, 1986, p. 229).

Results of the retrieval session provided evidence of mood-*dependent* memory. Compared with subjects whose encoding and retrieval moods matched, those whose moods mismatched recalled, on average, a smaller percentage of their previously generated positive events (26% vs. 37%), neutral events (17% vs. 32%), and negative events (27% vs. 37%).

This effect does not appear to be a fluke: the same advantage was seen in two other studies using moods instilled via music and thought (Experiments 1 and 3 in Eich et al., 1994), as well as in three separate studies in which the subjects' affective states were altered by changing their physical surroundings (Eich, 1995b). Moreover, similar results were obtained in a recent investigation of patients who cycled rapidly – and spontaneously – between states of mania or hypomania and depression (Eich, Macaulay, & Lam, 1997). Thus, it seems that autobiographical event generation, when combined with event free recall, constitutes a useful tool for exploring mood-dependent effects under both laboratory and clinical conditions, and that these effects emerge in conjunction with either exogenous (experimentally engendered) or endogenous (naturally occurring) shifts in affective state.

We started this discussion of task factors by stating our intuitions about the circumstances under which MDM would or would not be expected to occur. Though the results reviewed thus far fit our intuitions, the former are by no means "explained" by the latter. We can, however, point to two recent theoretical developments that provide a clearer and greater understanding of why mood dependence sometimes comes, sometimes goes.

One of these developments is the *affect infusion model* (AIM), which Forgas (1995) has advanced as a comprehensive account of the role of mood states in social judgments. Affect infusion may be defined as "the process whereby affectively loaded information exerts an influence on and becomes incorporated into the judgmental process, entering into the judge's deliberations and eventually coloring the judgmental outcome" (Forgas, 1995, p. 39). For present purposes, the crucial feature of AIM is its claim that

> affect infusion is most likely to occur in the course of constructive processing that involves the substantial transformation rather than the mere reproduction of existing cognitive representations; such processing requires a relatively open information search strategy and a significant degree of generative elaboration of the available stimulus details. This definition seems broadly consistent with the weight of recent evidence suggesting that affect "will influence cognitive processes to the extent that the cognitive task involves the active generation of new information as opposed to the passive conservation of information given" [Fiedler, 1990, pp. 2–3]. (Forgas, 1995, pp. 39–40).

Though AIM is chiefly concerned with mood congruence, it is relevant to mood dependence as well. Compared with the rote memorization of unrelated words, the task of recollecting and recounting real-life events would seem to place a greater premium on active, substantive processing and thereby promote a higher degree of affect infusion. Thus, AIM agrees with the fact that list-learning experiments often fail to find mood dependence, whereas studies involving autobiographical memory usually succeed.

Further, AIM suggests a number of interesting possibilities for future MDM research. Suppose that happy and sad subjects read about and form impressions of named individuals, some of whom appear quite normal and some who seem rather strange. AIM predicts that "atypical, unusual, or complex targets should selectively recruit longer and more substantive processing strategies, and correspondingly greater affect infusion effects" (Forgas, this volume). Accordingly, strange people should be evaluated more positively by happy than by sad subjects, whereas normal individuals should be perceived similarly – a deduction that has been verified in several studies (see Forgas, 1992).

Now suppose that the subjects are later asked to freely recall, by name, all of the people they can, and that testing takes place either in the same mood they had experienced earlier or in the alternative affect. The prediction is that, compared with their mismatched mood counterparts, subjects tested under matched mood conditions will recall more of the strange people, but an equivalent number of the normal individuals. More generally, it is conceivable that mood dependence, like mood congruence, is magnified by the encoding and retrieval of atypical targets, for the reasons given by AIM. Similarly, it may be that judgments about the self, in contrast to others, are more conducive to demonstrating MDM, as people tend to process self-relevant information in a more extensive and elaborate manner (see Forgas, 1995; Sedikides, 1995). Just how real or remote these possibilities are remains to be seen.

The second theoretical development relates to Bower's (1981; Bower & Cohen, 1982) network model of emotions, which has been revised in light of recent MDM research (Bower, 1992; Bower & Forgas, in press). A key aspect of the new model is the idea, derived from Thorndike (1932), that in order for subjects to associate a target event with their current mood, contiguity alone between the mood and the event may not be sufficient. Rather, it may be necessary for subjects to perceive the event as enabling or causing their mood, for only then will a change in mood cause that event to be forgotten.

To elaborate, consider first the conventional list-learning paradigm, alluded to earlier. According to Bower and Forgas (in press, p. 12), this paradigm is ill-suited to demonstrating mood dependence, because it

> arranges only contiguity, not causal belonging, between presentation of the to-be-learned material and emotional arousal. Typically, the mood is induced minutes before presentation of the learning material, and the mood serves only as the prevailing background; hence, the temporal relations are not synchronized to persuade subjects to attribute their emotional feelings to the material they are studying. Thus, contiguity, without causal belonging, produces only weak associations at best. (p. 12)

In contrast, the model allows for strong mood-dependent effects to emerge in studies of autobiographical memory, such as those reported by Eich et al. (1994). With regard to Figure 5.1, which shows a fragment of a hypothetical associative structure surrounding the concept *lake*, Bower and Forgas (in press, p. 13) propose the following:

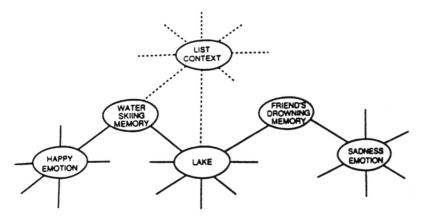

Figure 5.1. Part of the associative network representing the concept *lake*. Source: Bower & Forgas (in press).

Suppose in one of Eich's experiments, the subject has been induced to feel happy and is asked to recall an incident from her life suggested by the target word *lake*. This concept has many associations including several autobiographic memories, a happy one describing a pleasantly thrilling water-skiing episode, and a sad one recounting an episode of a friend drowning in a lake. These event-memories are connected to the emotions the events caused. When feeling happy and presented with the list cue, lake, the subject is likely (by summation of activation) to come up with the water-skiing memory. Upon retrieving [this] memory, the subject also associates the list-context to the water-skiing memory and to the word *lake* which evoked it. These newly formed list associations, depicted by dashed lines [in Figure 5.1], are formed by virtue of the subject attributing causal belonging of the word-and-memory to the experimenter's presentation of the item within the list.

These contextual associations are called upon later when the subject is asked to free recall the prompting words (or the memories prompted by them) when induced into the same mood or a different one. If the subject is happy at the time of recall testing, the water-skiing memory would be advantaged because it would receive the summation of activation from the happy-mood node and the list context, thus raising it above a recall level. On the other hand, if the subject's mood at recall were shifted to sadness, that node has no connection to the water-skiing memory that was aroused during list input, so that her recall of *lake* in this case would rely exclusively upon the association to lake of the overloaded, list-context node in the figure.

Thus, the revised network model, like the AIM, makes a clear case for choosing autobiographical memory over list learning as a means of demonstrating mood dependence.

Also, both theories accommodate an important qualification, which is that MDM is more apt to occur when retention is tested in the absence than in the presence of specific, tangible reminders or cues (see Bower, 1981; Eich, 1989). Thus, free recall is a much more sensitive measure of mood dependence than are either cued recall or recognition memory. According to the network model, "recognition memory for whether the word *lake* appeared in the list [of probes for autobiographical event generation] simply requires retrieval of the *lake*-to-list association; that association is not heavily overloaded at the list node, so its retrieval is not aided by reinstatement of the [event generation] mood" (Bower & Forgas, in press, p. 13). According to AIM, recognition memory entails *direct access thinking* – Forgas's (1995) term for cognitive processing that is simpler, more automatic, and less emotionally suffused than that required for free recall (similar ideas are suggested by Bless and by Fiedler, this volume).

In terms of their overall explanatory power, however, the AIM may have an edge over the revised network model on two accounts. First, though several studies have sought, without success, to demonstrate mood-dependent recognition, most have used simple, concrete, and easily codable stimuli (such as common words or pictures of ordinary objects) as the target items. However, the elusive effect was revealed in a recent study (Eich et al., 1997) in which bipolar patients were tested for their ability to recognize abstract, inchoate Rorschach-like inkblots, the sort of complex and unusual stimuli that AIM suggests should be highly infused with affect.

Second, although the network model speaks to *explicit* measures of MDM (e.g., free recall vs. recognition memory), it is silent on whether or not *implicit* indices of retention should show mood dependence. AIM, however, suggests that implicit tests may indeed be sensitive to MDM, provided that the tests call upon substantive, open-ended thinking and admit a wide range of possible responses (i.e., conceptually driven tests, such as free association and category-instance generation, as opposed to data-driven tests, such as perceptual identification and word-fragment completion; see Roediger, 1990; Roediger & McDermott, 1993). To date, only a handful of studies of implicit mood dependence have been reported, but their results are generally consistent with this reasoning (see Eich, Macaulay, Loewenstein, & Dihle, 1997; Kihlstrom, Eich, Sandbrand, & Tobias, 1998; Macaulay, Ryan, & Eich, 1993; Nissen, Ross, Willingham, MacKenzie, & Schacter, 1988; Tobias, Kihlstrom, & Schacter, 1992).

To draw this discussion of task factors to a close, we wish to return to the question posed at the chapter's outset: Even if MDM is not, as was once commonly believed, a powerful and prevalent effect, might it nevertheless emerge in a clear and consistent manner under certain limited conditions? We are sure that the answer is "yes," though we are not altogether sure why. One promising idea is that the higher the level of affect infusion achieved at encoding *and* at retrieval, the higher the likelihood of detecting mood dependence. This idea accords well with what is now known about mood dependence, and – more important – it has numerous testable implications (including those identified earlier) that are well worth pursuing.

Mood Factors

Up to now, our discussion has focused on factors that determine the sensitivity of an encoding or a retrieval task to the detection of mood-dependent effects. It stands to reason, however, that no matter how sensitive these tasks may be, the odds of demonstrating MDM are slim in the absence of an effective manipulation of mood. So, what makes a mood manipulation effective?

One consideration is mood strength. By definition, mood dependence demands a statistically significant loss of memory when target events are encoded in one mood and retrieved in another. It is doubtful whether anything less than a substantial shift in mood, between the occasions of event encoding and event retrieval, could produce such an impairment. Indeed, the results of an MDM meta-analysis by Ucros (1989) revealed that the greater the difference in moods – depression versus elation, for example, as opposed to depression versus a neutral affect – the greater the mood-dependent effect. Bower (1992) has argued a similar point, proposing that MDM reflects a failure of information acquired in one state to generalize to the other, and that generalization is more apt to fail the more dissimilar the two moods are.

No less important than the strength of the moods is their stability over time and across tasks. In terms of demonstrating MDM, it does no good to engender a mood that evaporates as soon as the subject is given something to do, such as memorize a list of words or recall a previously studied story. It is possible that some studies failed to find MDM simply because they relied on moods that were potent initially, but that paled rapidly (see Eich & Metcalfe, 1989).

One practical means of inducing a mood – either happy (H) or sad (S) – that is stable as well as strong is the *continuous music technique* (CMT). By this technique, subjects are asked to contemplate elating or depressing thoughts while they listen to various selections of sprightly or somber classical music (for a detailed account of the CMT, see Eich et al., 1994; for an insightful analysis of mood/music interactions, see Balch & Lewis, 1996). The music plays softly in the background throughout testing – hence *continuous* music technique.

Periodically, subjects mark a copy of the *affect grid*, drawn in Figure 5.2, to indicate their current levels of pleasure/displeasure and arousal/sleepiness, the two bipolar dimensions underlying the circumplex model of mood developed by Russell (1980; Russell, Weiss, & Mendelsohn, 1989). The columns of the grid connote a mood that, reading from left to right, is extremely unpleasant (scored as −4), very unpleasant (−3), moderately unpleasant (−2), slightly unpleasant (−1), neutral (0), slightly pleasant (1), moderately pleasant (2), very pleasant (3), and extremely pleasant (4). In contrast, the rows represent varying degrees of arousal, ranging from extremely high arousal (4) at the top through neutral (0) in the middle to extremely low arousal at the bottom (−4).

A key aspect of the CMT is that subjects are not allowed to begin their initial cognitive task until they have attained a critical level of mood: typically, very or extremely pleasant in the case of H-mood induction; very or extremely unpleasant in the case of S-mood induc-

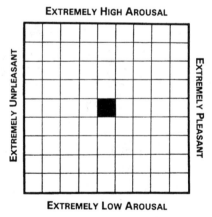

Figure 5.2. The affect grid used to assess current levels of pleasure and arousal. Source: Russell, Weiss, and Mendelsohn (1989).

tion. In principle, subjects can satisfy the pleasantness criterion without regard to their concurrent level of arousal. In practice, however, ratings of pleasure are correlated (around $r = .50$ in most studies) with those of arousal, meaning that H-mood subjects *usually* feel more active or alert than do their S-mood counterparts. The emphasis on "usually" will be explained shortly.

Understandably, subjects are not told in advance about the pleasure criteria, and, as one might expect, they vary widely in how long it takes them to reach the critical levels of mood. Thus, the CMT does not allocate to every subject the same, fixed amount of time for mood induction – the common practice in prior research on MDM, and one that virtually guarantees substantial differences among subjects in their postinduction levels of mood. Rather, the CMT takes an idiographic approach to mood induction, affording each individual ample time (typically 40–60 minutes, depending on the expected length of cognitive testing) to achieve a predetermined degree of pleasure or displeasure at his or her own pace. Though the CMT can be time-consuming, it instills moods that not only start out strong but stay that way over time and across tasks (for supporting data, see Eich et al., 1994, Tables 1 & 2).

In our most recent studies of MDM, we asked subjects to candidly assess (postexperimentally) whether the CMT technique created an authentic change in their mood. Nearly 90% of the participants in these studies rated the technique as being at least moderately effective in this regard (i.e., a rating of 5 or higher on a 0–10 mood genuineness scale), indicating a high degree of affective realism. Moreover, those who felt most genuinely "moved" tended to show the strongest mood-dependent effects (for pertinent correlational evidence, see Eich, 1995a). Thus, it seems that the odds of demonstrating MDM are improved by instilling affective states that have three important properties: strength, stability, and sincerity.

To introduce a fourth important property, recall from earlier discussion of the continuous music technique and the affect grid that ratings of pleasure are correlated with those of arousal, so that subjects induced to feel happy usually report higher levels of arousal than do their sad-mood peers. Nevertheless, when the affect-grid data derived from a typical CMT study are checked closely, it becomes clear that although all subjects assigned to the mismatched mood conditions (H/S and S/H) show a substantial shift in pleasure between the encoding and retrieval sessions (as is required by the CMT), only some show a sizable change in arousal as well. This being so, it is meaningful to ask: Is memory more impaired by a shift along both the pleasure and arousal dimensions of mood than by a shift in pleasure alone?

Apropos of this question, Eich and Metcalfe (1989) and Eich et al. (1994) reported a total of seven studies in which subjects generated materials (during the encoding session) that later served as targets in surprise tests of free recall (during the retrieval session). Participants in each study were separated into three groups, reflecting different degrees of pleasure/arousal change between the encoding and retrieval sessions. Representatives of the Small/Small group, who were drawn solely from the matched mood conditions (H/H and S/S), displayed little or no disparity between sessions in their ratings of either pleasure or arousal. In contrast, the Large/Small group consisted of subjects, selected from the mismatched conditions H/S and S/H, who reported large differences in pleasure but little difference in arousal. Mismatched mood subjects who experienced marked changes in both pleasure and arousal formed the Large/Large group.

Analysis of the recall data revealed that, in six of the seven studies, the Small/Small group significantly outscored the Large/Large group, while subjects in the Large/Small category performed at a level that fell between these extremes. This pattern of results provides correlational evidence that memory is more impaired by a two-dimensional (pleasure plus arousal) than by a one-dimensional (pleasure only) alteration in affective state.

Would the same pattern emerge when dimensional shifts between encoding and retrieval moods are manipulated experimentally? In search of an answer, a new study is under way that involves tasks similar to those used by Eich et al. (1994, Experiment 2). Thus, during the encoding session of the ongoing study, subjects are presented with *rose* and other common nouns as probes for generating specific events from any time in their personal past. Subjects describe each event in detail and rate its original emotional valence (i.e., positive, neutral, or negative). Two days later, during the retrieval session, subjects try to freely recall the gist of as many of their previously generated events as possible.

Superimposed on these procedures is a 4 × 4 design, such that every subject advances to either the event-generation or the event-recall task once he or she has achieved a critical level of one of four moods: happy (H), sad (S), calm (C), or anxious (A). Operationally, the critical level of happiness is defined by a rating, made by the subject on the affect grid, of 2 or higher on both dimensions – that is, moderately to extremely pleasant feelings in tandem with moderately to extremely high arousal. Sadness, in contrast, corresponds to a rating of −2 or lower on both dimensions – that is, moderately to extremely unpleasant feelings coupled with moderately to extremely low arousal. A pleasure rating of 2 or higher, plus an arousal rating of −2 or lower, defines calmness, whereas anxiety is identified with a maximum pleasure rating of −2 coupled with a minimum arousal rating of 2.

As in our earlier MDM experiments, subjects in the current study (a) provide a baseline rating of pleasure and arousal at the outset of each session, (b) mark a fresh copy of affect grid every few minutes until they have reached the requisite level of mood (either H, S, C, or A), (c) indicate how pleasant and aroused they feel immediately following event generation and event recall, and (d) rate, on a 0–10 mood genuineness scale, the authenticity of the feelings they had experienced while performing each task. Also adhering to standard practice, subjects are not told that the start of either task is contingent on their reaching a critical level of mood; this contingency is kept confidential because we do not want the subjects to try to rush matters by rating their current levels of pleasure and arousal as being more extreme than they actually are.

To aid in the development of a particular mood, the experimenter instructs the subjects to imagine a particular scenario, such as playing a rousing game of volleyball with their friends (in the H-mood condition) or lounging in a cozy bed on a Sunday morning (in the C-mood condition). All the while, and throughout the rest of the session, various selections of mood-appropriate music play softly in the background. Subjects assigned to any one of the four matched mood conditions (H/H, S/S, C/C, or A/A) visualize different scenarios and listen to different musical selections during the encoding and retrieval sessions.

To date, usable data have been collected from 123 UBC undergraduates; a final sample size of 256 (or 16 subjects per cell) will be sought. All 123 subjects claimed to have experienced a moderately to extremely realistic mood during both the event-generation and event-recall tasks (i.e., ratings of 5 or higher on the 0–10 mood genuineness scale). In addition, none of the 123 subjects suffered a "mood reversal." For instance, no subject who was suitably anxious at the start of either event generation or event recall – "suitably" meaning a pleasure rating of −2 or lower and a concurrent arousal rating of 2 or higher – wound up at the end of the task with a pleasure rating of 1 or higher or an arousal rating of −1 or lower. Similarly, upon completing a given task, no happy-mood subject reported less than a neutral level of either pleasure or arousal. The absence of mood reversals ensures a certain degree of mood stability, and, as was noted earlier, mood stability enhances the prospects of demonstrating MDM.

Results obtained thus far from the encoding session show that whereas happy subjects generate about four times more positive than negative events, sad subjects generate roughly equal numbers of each type. These results reflect mood congruence, and they resemble the pattern seen in the methodologically similar study by Eich et al. (1994, Experiment 2). Interestingly, the present results go beyond prior research in that they reveal a close correspondence between the memorial consequences of calmness and happiness, on the one hand, and between anxiety and sadness, on the other; specifically, the ratio of positive-to-negative events generated is about 4:1 for both calm and happy subjects, and 1:1 for both anxious and sad subjects. Thus, the likelihood that, say, *rose* will call to mind a positive emotional experience from the personal past appears to depend more on how pleasant one feels, rather than on how aroused.

Table 5.1 displays the mean percentage of total events recalled (i.e., positive, neutral, and negative events averaged together) in the 16 combinations of encoding/retrieval moods. Two points merit comment in connection with these data, the first of which relates to the question of chief concern in this on-going study: Is memory more impaired by a two- than by a one-dimensional shift in mood?

To help answer this question, we reformatted the data in Table 5.1 to reveal how total-event recall varies as a function of four levels of pleasure/arousal change (see Table 5.2). Three of these levels – Small/Small, Large/Small, and Large/Large – are akin to the eponymous groups described earlier, except that now these levels are operationalized before rather than after the fact. The fourth level of pleasure/arousal change – Small/Large – is unique to the present study because, in all of our prior MDM work, we endeavored to experimentally manipulate only the subjects' level of pleasure, and not their level of arousal.

Analysis of the data in Table 5.2 shows that subjects who experience a small change in both pleasure and arousal recall a greater percentage of their previously generated events than do subjects who incur a

Table 5.1. *Total Event Recall as a Function of Encoding and Retrieval Moods* *(percentage)*

Encoding Mood	Retrieval Mood			
	Happy	*Calm*	*Sad*	*Anxious*
Happy	57	53	52	52
Calm	55	57	48	52
Sad	54	60	67	61
Anxious	55	36	44	60

Table 5.2. *Total Event Recall as a Function of* *Pleasure/Arousal Change*

Pleasure/Arousal Change	Total Event Recall (%)
Small/small [H/H, C/C, S/S, A/A]	59
Small/large [H/C, C/H, S/A, A/S]	54
Large/small [H/A, A/H, C/S, S/C]	54
Large/large [H/S, S/H, C/A, A/C]	50

Note: Brackets enclose contributing encoding/retrieval moods (H = happy, C = calm, S = sad, A = anxious).

large change in both pleasure and arousal (means of 59% and 50%, respectively; $F(1/67) = 6.95$, $p = .01$). For subjects in either the Small/ Large or Large/Small categories of pleasure/arousal change, the level of event recall is not only the same (54%), but also falls midway between the other two conditions. Though these results should be taken with a large grain of salt, since the study is only about half-completed, the overall pattern that has developed to date suggests that shift along both the pleasure and arousal dimensions of mood impairs memory more than does a shift along either dimension alone.

It will be interesting to see whether this pattern maintains as more data are added.

To illustrate the second point of interest, we rearranged the data in Table 5.1 to show how the relative advantage in recall of matched over mismatched moods varies as a function of encoding mood (see Table 5.3). Referring to the first line of data in Table 5.3, 57% of the events generated in a happy encoding mood are later recalled in a happy retrieval mood, whereas 53% of these events are recalled in states of calmness, sadness, or anxiety (averaged together). Thus, for H-generated events, recall performance in the matched mood condition (H/H) exceeds average recall in the mismatched conditions (H/C, H/S, and H/A) by 8%. The rest of Table 5.3 shows that the relative advantage in recall of matched over mismatched moods rises steadily as one moves from C-generated events (10%) through S-generated events (18%) to A-generated events (30%).

Assume – pending additional data – that this pattern of results is real. We think that the answer lies in the idea of distinctiveness, a concept that gained currency during the heyday of levels-of-processing research (see Lockhart & Craik, 1990). Here, we add a new

Table 5.3. *Total Event Recall under Matched and Mismatched Encoding/Retrieval Moods, and Relative Advantage of the Former over the Latter, as a Function of Encoding Mood (percentage)*

| Encoding Mood | Encoding/Retrieval Moods | | Relative Advantage |
	Matched	*Mismatched*	
Happy	57 [H/H]	53 [H/C, H/S, H/A]	8
Calm	57 [C/C]	52 [C/S, C/A, C/H]	10
Sad	67 [S/S]	57 [S/A, S/H, S/C]	18
Anxious	60 [A/A]	46 [A/H, A/C, A/S]	30

Note: Brackets enclose contributing encoding/retrieval moods (H = happy, C = calm, S = sad, A = anxious).

twist to the meaning of distinctiveness and use it to refer to the salience of the affective context in which subjects generate autobiographical events.

To clarify, consider first the fact that the typical subject arrives at the lab feeling pretty good: the average baseline rating of pleasure is 1.3 (between slightly and moderately pleasant), and the average baseline rating of arousal is 0.3 (between neutral and slightly high arousal). Thus, if by random assignment the subject is slated to generate autobiographical events in a happy mood (operationally defined as a moderate to extreme level of pleasure combined with a moderate to extreme degree of high arousal), he or she is already well on the way to achieving that mood. Indeed, 32% (14/44) of the H-encoding subjects are, figuratively speaking, in the "happiness zone" (i.e, the top right quadrant of the affect grid diagrammed in Figure 5.1) before H-mood induction even begins. Analogously, 29% (8/28) of C-encoding subjects are in the calmness zone (the bottom right quadrant of the affect grid) prior to C-mood induction. Among subjects scheduled to generate events in a sad mood, only 12% (3/25) are already in the sadness zone (the bottom left quadrant) before S-mood induction is initiated. Among A-encoding subjects, the figure is even lower: Only 4% (1/26) report feeling at least slightly aroused and slightly unpleasant immediately before A-mood induction.

The aforementioned percentages provide an estimate of *affective distance*, how far (in affect-grid space) a subject must go to get to the critical level of a given mood, in relation to where he or she started (as indicated by the subject's encoding-session baseline ratings of pleasure and arousal). Ranked from largest to smallest affective distance, the order of the four encoding moods is A > S > C > H, the same order in which these moods line up in terms of the relative advantage in event recall of matched over mismatched mood conditions.

Though this correspondence may merely be a coincidence, an alternative hypothesis is available. Specifically, assume that (a) the salience or distinctiveness of a mood increases with its affective distance; (b) events are more closely connected to, or deeply colored by, moods that are high rather than low in distinctiveness; and (c) the closer the event/mood connection, the more retrieval depends on reinstatement of the original encoding mood. Under these assumptions, it is understandable why the advantage in recall of matched over mismatched encoding/retrieval conditions is largest for events generated in the most distinctive mood of anxiety, and smallest for events generated in the least distinctive mood of happiness. Though this reasoning admittedly rests on as-yet unproven assumptions, it provides a serviceable starting point for future empirical research and theoretical analysis.

Subject Factors

We conclude this chapter by briefly considering two issues concerned with the role of subject factors in MDM. Discussion will necessarily be brief, because even though it is possible – indeed probable – that individual differences play a pivotal part in mood dependence, to date their contribution has been completely overlooked.

The first issue relates to the work of the renowned drama director, Constantin Stanislavski. In *An actor prepares*, Stanislavski (1946) argued that for acting to be truthful and convincing, performers must do more that merely create the external signs of emotion. Rather, they must be moved emotionally, for only through their own inner feelings can actors project themselves into a character or situation. This led Stanislavski to develop a variety of acting techniques or exercises, and he recommended that performers practice these exercises repeatedly so as to stimulate the growth of their imagination, enhance their ability to identify with the emotional experiences of others, and learn how to use their own "emotion memory" for dramatic effect.

These exercises form an integral part of *method acting*, a system that is taught today in the theater departments of most major universities. In the UBC Department of Theater, for instance, students seeking a Bachelor of Fine Arts degree in acting are required to take at least seven full-year (26-week) courses that include instruction in the Stanislavski method, in addition to other systems of acting. Thus, by their third or fourth year in the acting stream, these students have acquired a good deal of specialized knowledge about how to develop and control their emotions. Moreover, these students are adept at experiencing emotions at a level of intensity and with a degree of consistency that few people unpracticed in the art of method acting can match. Given that strong, stable, and sincere moods are critical for demonstrating mood-dependent effects in memory, as was suggested earlier, then method actors should show these effects in spades. We plan to put this idea to a formal test in the near future.

The preceding paragraph highlighted the possibility that certain individuals, by virtue of their special talents and training, may have a particular propensity for showing MDM. It seems plausible to assume, however, that this propensity also varies among people at large, and that individual differences in personality may be associated with individual differences in MDM.

Though we are unaware of any published research on personality correlates of mood dependence, several studies have investigated individual differences in mood congruence (see Bower & Forgas, in press; Mayer & Salovey, 1988; Rhodewalt, Strube, & Wysocki, 1988; Smith & Petty, 1995). These studies suggest that mood-congruent effects are relatively small, even nonexistent, in people who score high on standardized scales of self-esteem, need for approval, and Type-A personality. As Bower and Forgas (in press, p. 59) have remarked, high scores on these scales "probably indicate a habitual tendency to approach certain cognitive tasks from a motivated perspective, which should reduce affect infusion effects." Assuming that affect infusion is as important to mood dependence as it is to mood congruence, individuals high in self-esteem, need for approval, Type-A personality, and perhaps other traits (such as the ability to regulate negative emotional states) should seem to be impervious to mood dependence. Tests of this assumption may aid our understanding of fundamental factors that determine MDM and provide new insights into the intricate relations among mood, memory, and personality.

References

Balch, W. R., & Lewis, B. S. (1996). Music-dependent memory: The roles of tempo change and mood mediation. *Journal of Experimental Psychology: Learning, Memory, and Cognition, 22,* 1354–1363.

Blaney, P. H. (1986). Affect and memory: A review. *Psychological Bulletin, 99,* 229–246.

Bower, G. H. (1981). Mood and memory. *American Psychologist, 36,* 129–148.

Bower, G. H. (1987). Commentary on mood and memory. *Behavior Research and Therapy, 25,* 443–455.

Bower, G. H. (1992). How might emotions affect learning? In S.-A. Christianson (Ed.), *Handbook of emotion and memory* (pp. 3–31). Hillsdale, NJ: Erlbaum.

Bower, G. H., & Cohen, P. R. (1982). Emotional influences in memory and thinking: Data and theory. In M. S. Clark & S. T. Fiske (Eds.), *Affect and cognition* (pp. 291–331). Hillsdale, NJ: Erlbaum.

Bower, G. H., & Forgas, J. P. (in press). Affect, memory, and social cognition. In E. Eich, J. F. Kihlstrom, G. H. Bower, J. P. Forgas, & P. M. Niedenthal (Eds.), *Counterpoints: Cognition and emotion* (pp. 2–89). New York: Oxford.

Bower, G. H., & Mayer, J. D. (1989). In search of mood-dependent retrieval. *Journal of Social Behavior and Personality, 4,* 121–156.

Clark, D. M., & Teasdale, J. D. (1982). Diurnal variation in clinical depression and accessibility of memories of positive and negative experiences. *Journal of Abnormal Psychology, 91,* 87–95.

Eich, E. (1989). Theoretical issues in state dependent memory. In H. L. Roediger & F. I. M. Craik (Eds.), *Varieties of memory and consciousness: Essays in honour of Endel Tulving* (pp. 331–354). Hillsdale, NJ: Erlbaum.

Eich, E. (1995a). Searching for mood dependent memory. *Psychological Science, 6,* 67–75.

Eich, E. (1995b). Mood as a mediator of place dependent memory. *Journal of Experimental Psychology: General, 124,* 293–308.

Eich, E., Macaulay, D., & Lam, R. W. (1997). Mania, depression, and mood dependent memory. *Cognition and Emotion, 11,* 607–618.

Eich, E., Macaulay, D., Loewenstein, R. J., & Dihle, P. H. (1997). Memory, amnesia, and dissociative identity disorder. *Psychological Science, 8,* 417–422.

Eich, E., Macaulay, D., & Ryan, L. (1994). Mood dependent memory for events of the personal past. *Journal of Experimental Psychology: General, 123,* 201–215.

Eich, E., & Metcalfe, J. (1989). Mood dependent memory for internal versus external events. *Journal of Experimental Psychology: Learning, Memory, and Cognition, 15,* 443–455.

Fiedler, K. (1990). Mood-dependent selectivity in social cognition. In W. Stroebe & M. Hewstone (Eds.), *European review of social psychology* (Vol. 1, pp. 1–32). Chichester, England: Wiley.

Forgas, J. P. (1992). On bad mood and peculiar people: Affect and person typicality in impression formation. *Journal of Personality and Social Psychology, 62,* 863–875.

Forgas, J. P. (1993). On making sense of odd couples: Mood effects on the perception of mismatched relationships. *Personality and Social Psychology Bulletin, 19,* 59–71.

Forgas, J. P. (1995). Mood and judgment: The Affect Infusion Model (AIM). *Psychological Bulletin, 117,* 39–66.

Goodwin, D. W. (1974). Alcoholic blackout and state-dependent learning. *Federation Proceedings, 33,* 1833–1835.

Johnson, M. K., & Raye, C. L. (1981). Reality monitoring. *Psychological Review, 88,* 67–85.

Kenealy, P. M. (1997). Mood-state-dependent retrieval: The effects of induced mood on memory reconsidered. *Quarterly Journal of Experimental Psychology, 50A,* 290–317.

Kihlstrom, J. F., Eich, E., Sandbrand, D., & Tobias, B. A. (1998). Emotion and memory: Implications for self-report. In A. Stone & J. Turkkan (Eds.), *The science of self-report: Implications for research and practice* (pp. 221–253). Mahwah, NJ: Erlbaum.

Lockhart, R. S., & Craik, F. I. M. (1990). Levels of processing: A retrospective commentary on a framework for memory research. *Canadian Journal of Psychology, 44,* 87–112.

Ludwig, A. M. (1984). Intoxication and sobriety: Implications for the understanding of multiple personality. *Psychiatric Clinics of North America, 7,* 161–169.

Macaulay, D., Ryan, L., & Eich, E. (1993). Mood dependence in implicit and explicit memory. In P. Graf & M. E. J. Masson (Eds.), *Implicit memory: New directions in cognition, development, and neuropsychology* (pp. 75–94). Hillsdale, NJ: Erlbaum.

McGeoch, J. A. (1942). *The psychology of human learning.* New York: Longmans, Green.

Mayer, J. D., & Salovey, P. (1988). Personality moderates the interaction of mood and cognition. In K. Fiedler & J. Forgas (Eds.), *Affect, cognition and social behavior* (pp. 87–99). Gottingen, Germany: Hogrefe.

Miller, N. E. (1950). Learnable drives and rewards. In S. S. Stevens (Ed.), *Handbook of experimental psychology* (pp. 435–472). New York: Wiley.

Nissen, M. J., Ross, J. L., Willingham, D. B., MacKenzie, T. B., & Schacter, D. L. (1988). Memory and awareness in a patient with multiple personality disorder. *Brain and Cognition, 8,* 21–38.

Reus, V. I., Weingartner, H., & Post, R. M. (1979). Clinical implications of state-dependent learning. *American Journal of Psychiatry, 136,* 927–931.

Rhodewalt, F., Strube, M. J., & Wysocki, J. (1988). The Type A behaviour pattern, induced mood, and the illusion of control. *European Journal of Personality, 2,* 231–237.

Roediger, H. L. (1990). Implicit memory: Retention without remembering. *American Psychologist, 45,* 1043–1056.

Roediger, H. L., & McDermott, K. B. (1993). Implicit memory in normal human subjects. In F. Boller & J. Grafman (Eds.), *Handbook of neuropsychology* (Vol. 8, pp. 63–131). Amsterdam: Elsevier.

Russell, J. A. (1980). A circumplex model of affect. *Journal of Personality and Social Psychology, 39,* 1161–1178.

Russell, J. A., Weiss, A., & Mendelsohn, G. A. (1989). Affect grid: A single-item scale of pleasure and arousal. *Journal of Personality and Social Psychology, 57,* 493–502.

Schacter, D. L., & Kihlstrom, J. F. (1989). Functional amnesia. In F. Boller & J. Grafman (Eds.), *Handbook of neuropsychology* (Vol. 3, pp. 209–230). New York: Elsevier.

Sedikides, C. (1995). Central and peripheral self-conceptions are differentially influenced by mood: Tests of the differential sensitivity hypothesis. *Journal of Personality and Social Psychology, 69,* 759–777.

Smith, S. M., & Petty, R. E. (1995). Personality moderators of mood congruency effects on cognition: The role of self-esteem and negative mood regulation. *Journal of Personality and Social Psychology, 68,* 1092–1107.

Snyder, M., & White, P. (1982). Moods and memories: Elation, depression, and the remembering of the events of one's life. *Journal of Personality, 50,* 149–167.

Stanislavski, C. (1946). *An actor prepares.* New York: Theatre Arts.

Thorndike, E. L. (1932). *The fundamentals of learning.* New York: Teachers College.

Tobias, B. A., Kihlstrom, J. F., & Schacter, D. L. (1992). Emotion and implicit memory. In S.-A. Christianson (Ed.), *Handbook of emotion and memory* (pp. 67–92). Hillsdale, NJ: Erlbaum.

Tulving, E. (1983). *Elements of episodic memory.* Oxford: Oxford University Press.

Ucros, C. G. (1989). Mood state-dependent memory: A meta-analysis. *Cognition & Emotion, 3,* 139–167.

6. On the Correction of Feeling-Induced Judgmental Biases

LEONARD BERKOWITZ, SARA JAFFEE, EUNKYUNG JO, AND BARTHOLOMEU T. TROCCOLI

Theoretical Background

The theorizing behind the studies reported in this chapter began several years ago, during investigations into the determinants of affective aggression. That work led to a cognitive-neoassociationistic analysis of the automatic influences operating on the instigation to aggression (e.g., Berkowitz, 1990, 1993). In the spirit of Forgas's (1995a; also this volume) multiprocess affect infusion model of the conditions under which feelings shape judgments, the cognitive-neoassociationistic formulation held that several psychological processes determined the strength of people's urge to assault an available target when they were affectively aroused.

In this formulation, summarized in Figure 6.1, aversive situations that produce fairly intense negative affect, especially the feelings experienced as strong distress, give rise automatically to two or more sets, or syndromes, of feelings, expressive-motor reactions, thoughts, and memories.[1] One of these syndromes is linked to aggression – that is, to the inclination to attack someone (preferably but not only the perceived source of the displeasure) – whereas the reactions in the other syndrome have to do with the urge to escape or to avoid the aversive situation. Taken together, the reactions in the aggression-related syndrome are experienced as "anger," and those in the escape/avoidance syndrome are consciously registered as "fear." From this perspective, a decidedly unpleasant occurrence produces both "fight" and "flight" tendencies, not one or the other. A host of factors – some

Correspondence about this work should be addressed to Leonard Berkowitz, Department of Psychology, University of Wisconsin-Madison, Madison, WI USA.

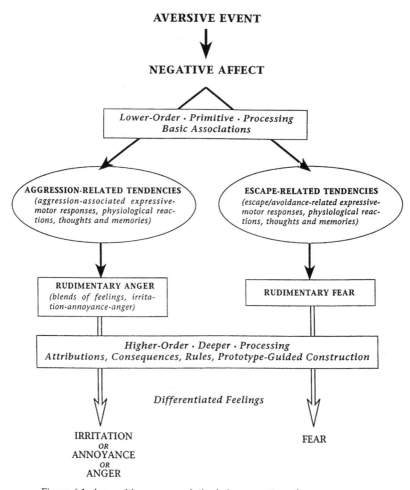

Figure 6.1. A cognitive-neoassociationistic conception of anger.

genetically based, others learned, and still others situational – determine which of these inclinations is dominant at any one time.

These initial reactions to aversive events theoretically are governed primarily by associative processes, so are in accord with Bargh's (1997) discussion of "the automaticity of everyday life" and the Greenwald et al. (this volume) "unified theory of attitudes, stereotypes, and the self-concept." Berkowitz (1990, 1993) contends that a good many aggression-related ideas and actions emerge automatically in response to an associatively linked stimulus situation. But, consistent with a growing number of other theoretical formulations, this model also contends that the initial automatic reactions can be regulated by higher-order cognitive processes. As the distressed, suffering people think more about their feelings and what is happening, the cognitive processes that are activated can now suppress or intensify, and/or enrich and further differentiate, the first relatively primitive reactions. It is at this more cognitive stage that attributions and appraisals enter to influence what the afflicted persons think, do, and say about what happened. In other words, as Martin (this volume) accurately points out, Berkowitz essentially believes that many (but not all) affectively generated reactions are first automatic and then, very soon afterward, are controlled by cognitive processes (see also Smith & Kirby, this volume).

Although this theorizing recognized that aggression-related ideas and actions could be affected in important ways by analytic thinking, most of the studies conducted in our laboratory focused on the first part of the conjectured sequence: the relatively automatic elicitation of hostile thoughts and aggressive inclinations by fairly intense negative affect. With a few exceptions, these experiments, as well as other investigations conducted by other researchers (e.g., Anderson, 1989; Anderson, Deuser, & DeNeve, 1995), often led to supportive findings (see Berkowitz, 1990, 1993). Also attesting to the usefulness of this conception, Berkowitz (1989) reformulated the classic frustration-aggression hypothesis by proposing that frustrations (i.e., blockages preventing the expected attainment of a desired goal) evoke an instigation to aggression only to the degree that they are decidedly unpleasant. It is this experienced displeasure that generates the aggression-related thoughts and motor reactions, not the thwarting per se.

Nevertheless, as was just noted, our experiments did not all have the predicted outcomes. Indeed, in some cases we even obtained a puzzling result: The participants exposed to a decidedly aversive physical condition were *more favorable* to the available target than were their counterparts exposed to a more pleasant situation. Intrigued by these unexpected findings, we looked more closely into what might have led to them.

Relationships with Research into Mood Congruency

The major dependent measures in the later Wisconsin experiments were primarily judgmental indices requiring the participants to evaluate a stranger. We had originally thought of these studies somewhat narrowly as investigations of negative affect-instigated hostile/aggressive ideas. However, it now became obvious that they could also be considered from the perspective of the social psychological research into the impact of feelings on cognitions, and more specifically, the research asking how affect influences judgments. Looked at in this light, we had essentially expected a mood congruence, believing that the induced negative affect would lead to negative assessments of the target.

Given Berkowitz's attachment to neoassociationistic theorizing, we were particularly drawn to Bower's (1981, 1991) associative network analysis of mood effects. Bower's conception, like ours, envisioned relatively passive effects of one's feelings on the ideas that subsequently come to mind. The affect presumably automatically primes semantically associated ideas, ideas having the same valence as the affect, so that these are then apt to shape the evaluation of the available target (see Bower, 1991).[2]

As this network model predicts, people's feelings often influence their judgments in the direction of greater congruence with their existing affect (Bower, 1991; Forgas, 1995a; Matt, Vazquez, & Campbell, 1992; Mayer, Gaschke, Braverman, & Evans, 1992).[3] This feeling-induced judgmental change is sometimes termed an *assimilation effect*. As research has accumulated, it has also become clear that this affective congruence is not always seen. And more surprisingly, in many of these instances there seems to be a contrast-like effect in which the judgment shifts away from the mood's hedonic nature. Thus, in several studies those persons made to feel bad tended to evaluate the judgmental target *more favorably* than did their counterparts who were in a good mood (e.g., Berkowitz & Troccoli, 1990; Martin, Seta, & Crelia, 1990; Parrott & Sabini, 1990; Strack, 1992). These results reflect more than the absence of an affective congruence in judgments; a psychological mechanism evidently had intervened to produce the opposite effect.

Following the spirit of the multiprocess conceptions of affective influences, such as the affect infusion model and the cognitive-neoassociationistic analysis of affective aggression, we believe these seemingly anomalous findings do not invalidate the associative network theory. Instead, they suggest that additional processes might operate to control what judgments are made, perhaps very soon after the initial automatic priming occurs. Our attention therefore turned to the possible nature of these "additional" processes. We were particularly interested in the factors that might produce the frequently observed affective asymmetry, or contrast effect, in which unpleasant feelings lead to more favorable judgments than do pleasant feelings.

Accounting for the Contrast Effect

Social psychologists have offered a variety of explanations for this affective incongruence in judgments (see Wegener & Petty, 1995, 1997), such as Martin's set/reset model (Martin et al., 1990), the Schwarz and Bless (1992) inclusion/exclusion analysis, the mental contamination account formulated by Wilson and Brekke (1994), and the flexible correction model advanced by Wegener and Petty (1997). All of these formulations basically propose that the contrast effect arises when people are aware that their feelings might bias their assessment of the target and that, in attempting to counter this possible distortion, they make an overcorrection. However, the schemes differ as to just how this overcorrection comes about. The first two formulations just cited resemble what Wegener and Petty (1997) termed *partialling models*. They hold that when people in an affective state believe their feelings are not relevant for the judgmental task and try to reach a judgment unbiased by their feelings, they will "exclude" or "partial out" of their consideration those elements in their thoughts that they think are due to their feelings. In doing this, however, they are apt to rule out of consideration some ideas that are activated by the judgmental target as well as by their affect, so that, in essence, too much is partialled out. Also, as Wegener and Petty noted, both the set/reset and inclusion/exclusion analyses assume that the feeling's influence is ordinarily toward affective congruence and that mental effort is required for the partialling operation (see, e.g., Martin et al., 1990).

Of course, the partialling accounts implicitly assume that people's beliefs about feeling effects determine what cognitive elements they exclude from their consideration in forming their assessments of the target. However, the Wilson-Brekke (1994) and Wegener-Petty (1997) models emphasize more explicitly that the judgmental correction is guided by people's lay theories about the direction and magnitude of the possible distorting influence. Applying these latter, relatively far-ranging analyses to the specific problem of mood effects, the formulations would say that the individuals in an affective state correct for the way they believe their feelings might bias their evaluations of some target when they are (a) aware of their feelings and (b) motivated to arrive at an accurate assessment. The overcorrection presumably arises because most people's ideas of how their feelings might influence their judgments exaggerates the degree of this affective influence.[4]

These latter two analyses of affective incongruence were especially appealing because their reference to the role of lay theories of mood effects clearly identifies a plausible intervening mechanism. Wegener and Petty have evidence that judgmental corrections can be steered by the individual's theory regarding the direction and magnitude of the biasing influence (see Wegener & Petty, 1997, p. 171). The present discussion will be guided by these theoretical schemes, especially by the Wegener-Petty conception.

Consistent with the Wegener-Petty flexible correction model, the research findings summarized here suggest that a number of conditions cause evaluations to be influenced in an affectively incongruent manner (i.e., the contrast effect). At these times, it is as if the research participants had overcorrected for the possible distorting influence of their feelings. Our results demonstrate that this apparent overcorrection can occur reliably under certain conditions, and, in accord with the flexible correction conception, that it is especially likely to arise when those making the judgment (a) are highly conscious of their affective state at the time, (b) want to arrive at an accurate evaluation, and (c) are mentally active.

Demonstrations of the Overcorrection Effect

The Initial Wisconsin Findings

Findings published by Berkowitz and Troccoli (1990) illustrate how awareness of one's feelings can lead to this overcorrection. In their second experiment, half of the female participants experienced fairly substantial muscular discomfort as they held their nondominant arm out unsupported for 6 minutes (High Discomfort), whereas the other women rested their arm comfortably on the table beside them for the same period of time (Low Discomfort).[5] At the same time, all the participants listened to a tape-recorded autobiographical statement supposedly made by a woman student as part of her application for a job at the university. When the statement ended, half of the people at both discomfort levels rated their feelings (Feelings Attention condition), but the remaining women were given a distracting word association task (Distracted condition). When these experimental manipulations were completed, everyone responded to a questionnaire, first indicating their impressions of the job applicant's personality on an adjective checklist, and then rating how unpleasant their arms had felt during the experiment.

A multiple regression analysis of the women's impressions of the job applicant revealed that their prior degree of attention to their feelings had interacted with the level of their felt displeasure to influence their judgments. As shown in Figure 6.2, which summarizes this interaction, those people whose attention had been diverted from their feelings displayed the usual affective congruence: The worse they felt, the greater the number of bad qualities they attributed to the job applicant. This result is in line with those analyses of mood effects, such as the set/reset and inclusion/exclusion formulations, that assume affective congruence is the default effect in the influence of feelings on judgments. The finding is also relevant to Forgas's (1995a) affect infusion model. It could be that the congruence was produced by what Forgas termed heuristic processing, but it also appears that the cognitively active, substantive processing is not necessary for congruent affect infusion to occur.

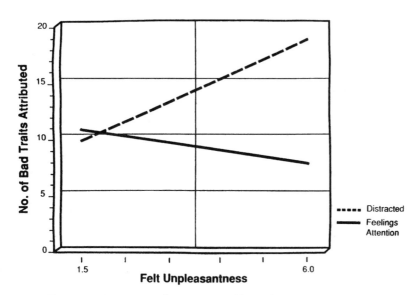

Figure 6.2. Interaction of participants' felt unpleasantness and the direction of their attention on their target judgment, calculated from regression analysis.

More significantly here, Figure 6.2 also shows there was an affective asymmetry when the participants were made highly aware of their feelings. In this case, the greater their discomfort, the fewer the bad traits they said the applicant possessed.[6]

Accounting for the Results

The original Berkowitz and Troccoli (1990) interpretation of these re-sults emphasized the role of the women's awareness of their affective state. We hypothesized that under the novel circumstances of the experimental situation this awareness stimulated the participants to think about their feelings – what they were experiencing and why. Because of their high level of cognitive activity, they presumably paid more attention to situational cues indicating the most appropriate judgment in that setting and expressed an evaluation in accord with these cues.

Although it is now clear that this interpretation is at best seriously incomplete, principally in that it omitted consideration of influences such as the participants' own beliefs about feeling effects, it is consistent with several theoretical analyses in cognitive psychology, as well as with other research findings regarding the regulation of feeling effects. A number of cognitive theorists (e.g., Posner, 1982; Shiffrin & Schneider, 1977) have argued that automatic reactions, responses that unfold relatively quickly in an effortless and passive manner, often can be regulated, at least to some extent, by directing attention to them. Thus, Norman and Shallice (1986, p. 8) spoke of a "supervisory attentional system" and proposed that this attention-activated higher-level control is particularly likely to arise when errors are detected, or planning has to be done, or "if the situation is novel, or temptation must be overcome." From this perspective, the automatic tendency toward affective congruence was regulated and overcome by an atten-tion-activated supervisory system. McFarland and Buehler (1997) have postulated such a supervisory system, at least implicitly, in contend-ing that people in a negative mood are particularly likely to have affectively incongruent, positive memories when they are highly con-scious of, and acknowledge, their unpleasant feelings. The person's clear recognition of his or her bad mood presumably is the first step in regulating the ill effects of negative feelings. McFarland and Bueh-ler (1997, p. 201) showed that "those individuals who are most atten-tive to and aware of their feeling states . . . [are] best able to invoke strategies designed ιo regulate their emotions." Note that the Berkowitz and Troccoli (1990) interpretation has a family resemblance to Strack's (1992) analysis of affective incongruence, which also stressed the part played by one's direction of attention. Where Strack proposed that attention given to the *judgmental task* facilitates the bias correction, however, the 1990 account maintained that attention to *one's feelings* initiates the adjustment.

At first glance, these results and the theorizing just spelled out seem to differ from the findings obtained in studies based on self-awareness theory (Duval & Wicklund, 1972) and Tesser's (1978) notion of thought-generated attitude polarization. Both of these models suggest that attention to one's feelings tends to heighten the consistency between these feelings and subsequent behavior, whereas the feeling-directed attention in the Berkowitz-Troccoli research lessened the consistency between affect and subsequent evaluations. Nevertheless, as Berkowitz and Troccoli (1990) pointed out, their findings can easily be reconciled with these other theoretical accounts. The persons in the self-awareness theory experiments typically began the experimental session with an *established* attitude or feelings toward the target and probably felt committed to this attitude/feeling. Therefore, they presumably believed it was easier to modify what they did in the given situation than to alter their attitude. In the Berkowitz-Troccoli research, by contrast, the suffering participants had not started out with a particular attitude toward the target, were not committed to a negative assessment of that person, and may even have believed it was not proper to be harsh to the target. It was therefore relatively easy for them to modify the evaluation they expressed.

We now suggest, with Wegener and Petty (1997), that when the women in the Berkowitz-Troccoli (1990) experiment had become highly conscious of their unpleasant feelings, they had also realized that their discomfort might unduly bias their judgment. Presumably exaggerating the magnitude of this possible distortion, they overcorrected for it in their expressed assessment.

Extending the Phenomenon: Overcorrecting for Facial Effects

Other findings obtained in our laboratory testify to the pervasiveness of this apparent overcorrection and also suggest that this effect can arise even when the feelings are created in a subtle and not-too-obvious manner. Employing the unobtrusive Strack, Martin, and Stepper (1988) facial manipulation procedure, Berkowitz and Jo had half of their women participants smile by asking them to hold a pen in their mouths in a particular way, whereas the others were led to frown by having them bite on tissue paper. After the requisite expression was adopted, our standard direction-of-attention variation was established. Still holding their mouths in the specified position, the participants then read the brief autobiographical statement supposedly made by the job applicant, and, also as is standard in our research program, responded to the final questionnaire, in which they indicated their impression of the job applicant on the adjective checklist and also rated their feelings.

Analysis of these latter ratings showed that the participants' facial expression had affected the level of their experienced anger; in the Distracted condition especially, those making the frown reported feeling reliably angrier than their counterparts who had adopted the smiling expression. More important, the multiple regression analysis of the women's judgments of the applicant demonstrated that these angry feelings had interacted with the experimental treatments in affecting their assessments. Since this interaction was readily interpretable only for those who had been led to frown (that is, when the facial expression was psychologically consistent with the feelings), Figure 6.3 summarizes the relationships among the variables only in this latter condition.[7]

Here, too, we see that when the women were distracted, the number of negative traits they assigned to the applicant was directly related to the level of their self-rated anger. Again, the figure also shows the affective incongruence in the case of those made to attend to their feelings; the angrier they had rated themselves, the fewer the number of bad qualities and the greater the number of favorable traits that they attributed to the target. In sum, being aware of their anger, these latter people had evidently also overcorrected for the possible distorting influence of their negative feelings.

Note that these results might help account for at least some of the cases (e.g., Tourangeau & Ellsworth, 1979) in which manipulated facial expressions failed to alter the participants' mood. The people in these studies could have been emotionally affected. However, they conceivably could have believed the activated feelings were not warranted in the situation confronting them. In being highly conscious of these feelings, they might then have attempted to regulate the expression of these feelings.

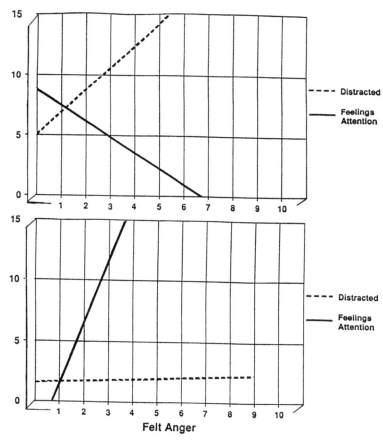

Figure 6.3. Interaction of felt anger and attention direction on target judgments in frown condition, calculated from regression analyses. Top figure: number of negative traits assigned; bottom figure: number of positive traits assigned.

Evidence of Overcorrection

Although we and other researchers have spoken of the observed affective incongruence (or asymmetry or contrast effect) as an indication of an overcorrection for a feeling-induced bias, there has been little evidence so far that the people displaying this effect actually tried to correct for their supposedly erroneous inclination. Indications that this does indeed occur can be found in the Berkowitz and Troccoli (1990) research cited earlier.

Recall that in this study, as in the other Wisconsin experiments reported here, the participants were supposedly judging a job applicant. In this particular investigation, however, before the people gave their impressions of the applicant they were informed that an expert selection committee had unanimously either approved or disapproved of her. This information could have served as a standard indicating generally the "right" opinion of the applicant.

If we assume that affective congruence is the default when people assess an ambiguous target, as seems to be the case (Matt et al., 1992; Mayer et al., 1992), those who were feeling bad at the time because of their great muscular discomfort were inclined to be unfavorable to the applicant. Then, when they heard the selection committee's "expert" evaluation, participants who were told the experts had rejected the applicant learned that their negative inclination was generally consistent with the judges' view. On the other hand, the people informed that the applicant had been approved by the committee found that their discomfort-induced negative attitude was inconsistent with the expert opinion and could well be wrong. If there is any overcorrection effect, it should be displayed by these latter persons – to the extent that they were aware of their negative disposition and were motivated to be accurate.

Figure 6.4, summarizing the impressions of the job applicant expressed under High Discomfort, supports this expectation. The top line shows that those women led to be highly aware of their negative feelings and who learned their disposition was inconsistent with the committee evaluation attributed the fewest negative qualities to the applicant. But, more to the point, suppose we use the scores in the Low Discomfort condition for each of these groups as a baseline: the level to be expected in each group if there is no negative inclination toward the applicant. Scores lower than this baseline might then signify an over-

| | Feelings Attention | | Distracted | |
	Consistent	Inconsistent	Consistent	Inconsistent
Number of negative adjectives	12.6	3.3	17.8	9.0
Difference From Same Low Discomfort Condition	−0.9	−5.9	3.1	1.0

Figure 6.4. Evaluations of job applicant under high discomfort as affected by attention direction and consistency of inclination with the judgments of others. Participants in the "Feelings Attention" – "Inconsistent" condition show the lowest number of negative judgments, and the greatest overcorrection compared to the "No Discomfort" baseline condition. From Berkowitz and Troccoli (1990).

correction. We can see in the second line that those who had been made aware of their great discomfort and whose negative inclination was inconsistent with the "proper" assessment were well below the baseline level for their group. Instead of merely taking up the expected level, they evidently overcorrected and were relatively favorable to the applicant. If we can generalize from this result, it would appear that an overcorrection might take place when people having negative feelings express views that are much less unfavorable than the judgment exhibited by an affectively congruent comparison group.

Conditions Promoting the Overcorrection Effect

Motivation to Be Accurate

Since this kind of overcorrection happens fairly often, as Wegener and Petty (1997) have noted and as the Wisconsin research has also found, it is essential to identify the conditions under which the phenomenon is particularly likely to occur. Obviously, according to both the Wegener-Petty and Wilson-Brekke models, people seek to counter whatever situationally induced biases they believe they possess when they are motivated to arrive at a correct judgment of the target. Adding to evidence reported by Wegener and Petty, research conducted by Ahn Shin-Ho in Korea supports this fundamental assumption (personal communication).

Ahn induced either a positive or negative mood in his female participants by placing them in either a pleasant or decidedly unpleasant room. One condition cross-cutting this variation was as follows: Nothing was said about the room influencing the women's feelings (low source salience), while the experimenter told the others that the room could have affected their mood at that time (high source salience). In line with the Schwarz and Clore (1983) mood-as-information conception, the room-produced feelings had an affectively congruent effect on the participants' subsequent judgments when they had not been alerted to the cause of these feelings. But of greater interest to us here, in one of the High Source Salient treatments, the experimenter went on to say that the participants should not let their mood affect their answers to the questions asked of them. Even though this admonition to be accurate said nothing about how much of a distorting influence might be exerted by their feelings, when the participants in this particular condition later rated how satisfied they were with their lives, they apparently overcorrected for the possible impact of their mood on their judgments. Thus, those made to feel bad typically said they were happier about their lives than did the other women in this condition who had been placed in a good mood. (Wegener and Petty [1997, p. 168] have reported similar findings.)

Accuracy Motivation and Cognitive Activity

A Wisconsin experiment by Jaffee and Berkowitz (1996) points more clearly to the role of accuracy motivation in producing the over-correction effect but goes further in suggesting that this effect is facil-itated by a high level of cognitive activity. Modifying an experimental paradigm that had been devised by Forgas (1995b), researchers in this study showed female participants placed in either a happy or sad mood two pairs of photographs. Each pair consisted of a picture of a man and a picture of a woman, with each pair said to be a romantic couple. As in Forgas's research, the physical attractiveness of the pho-tographed persons' was varied: For half of the participants, the couple members were matched in that both were either very good looking or both were somewhat less attractive (the so-called typical couples). The remaining participants were shown mismatched persons, with one member of each pair, either the man or the woman, being better looking than the other (these are termed the atypical couples). All of the participants were then asked to rate the general likability of the photographed people. In half of the cases they were urged to be accurate in their assessments, whereas the others were essentially in-formed that the investigation was only a pilot study.

In employing this basic procedure, Forgas (1995b) found that his participants took longer to evaluate the atypical, mismatched couples than the typical, matched ones, as if the former's unusual nature had prompted greater cognitive activity. In turn, this heightened thought evidently facilitated what Forgas terms an *affect infusion*, so that there was also greater affective congruence in the likability ratings of the atypical as opposed to the typical couples. The Jaffee and Berkowitz results were somewhat more complicated, even though we used the same likability measures. On timing our participants, we found a greater response latency for the atypical couples than for the typical ones only when the participants had been asked to be accurate in their judgments. It could be that in this study the couples' unusual nature led to the presumed increased cognitive activity only under accuracy motivation. Furthermore, in this experiment the heightened thought led to the incongruent overcorrection effect rather than to a greater affect infusion (i.e., affective congruence).

This mental activity–engendered overcorrection was found in two ways. On one hand, there was a significant mood by typicality interaction in the women's rating of the supposed couples' likability. Their induced mood had not influenced these ratings when they were judging the typical couples. On the other hand, if they had been asked to evaluate the unusual, atypical couples, those who were feeling sad at the time rated the couples as more likable than did the people who were in a good mood.

Closer inspection of these ratings indicated that this apparent overcorrection was most pronounced when the women were asked to be as accurate as possible, although the interaction with accuracy motivation was not statistically significant. However, we did obtain the expected significant interaction of mood by typicality by accuracy motivation in the participants' evaluations of the likability of the two male targets. (There was not such a significant interaction in the judgments of the female targets, apparently because the women participants in our investigation were fairly restrained in their assessments of the females.) As can be seen in Figure 6.5, there was an affective congruence – but only when the women had judged the typical couples. Whether asked to be accurate or not, the people in this condition who had been placed in a happy mood rated the men more favorably than did those made to be sad. Since these women had made their judgments of the ordinary couples relatively quickly, it could be that they had not thought much about these evaluations. In other words, they evidently engaged in a heuristic processing in which their mood had a direct and congruent influence on their assessments.

Those seeing the unusual atypical couples took longer to formulate their opinions, presumably reflecting their higher level of mental activity, and this cognitive activity apparently facilitated the overcorrection effect. In this condition, as shown in Figure 6.5, the happy people actually rated the targets *less* favorably than did their sadder counterparts, but this difference was statistically significant only for those trying to be accurate in their judgments. In thinking about the unusual couples, those who were concerned about making accurate evaluations evidently tried especially hard to overcome the biasing influence of their feelings.[8]

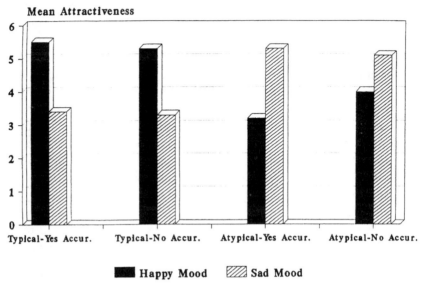

Mean Attractiveness

Typical-Yes Accur.   Typical-No Accur.   Atypical-Yes Accur.   Atypical-No Accur.

■ Happy Mood   ▨ Sad Mood

Figure 6.5. General attractiveness of male member of couples as affected by participants' mood, their accuracy motivation, and couple typicality. Data from Jaffee and Berkowitz (1996).

Discussion

Although the reported results are consistent with the set/reset and inclusion/exclusion analyses of affective incongruence, we believe that at least some of the findings are best explained by the Wegener-Petty flexible correction model of the overcorrection effect. Recall that when the participants in the Berkowitz and Troccoli (1990) experiment received information suggesting that their negative inclination to the target might well be wrong, those made to be greatly aware of their discomfort were the ones who most went out of their way not to say anything bad about the target person. Given an indication of the correct assessment, they apparently overcorrected for their discomfort-produced negative bias, and to such an extent that they actually were more favorable to the target than were their counterparts who were in a neutral mood. (The set/reset and inclusion/exclusion models do not explicitly recognize that an available standard identifying what is the appropriate judgment would have such an effect.) Although we have no direct evidence as to precisely when the participants made this overcorrection, these findings suggest that it came about after the women had become aware of their inclination to judge the target unfavorably.

However, our research lacks direct evidence for two fundamental assumptions in the Wegener-Petty analysis: that the participants in these experiments had actually employed their belief regarding how feelings influence judgments when they made their judgments, and that the overcorrection resulted because this lay belief essentially held that feelings would have a substantial impact on evaluations. Wegener and Petty (1997, p. 171) demonstrated that their subjects' previously measured theories of how a particular judgmental context would bias their ratings correctly predicted the direction and magnitude of the subsequent overcorrection. The "more negative (or less positive) a person's theory of how the context might bias his or her perceptions of the target, the more positive (or less negative) . . . the person's shift in target ratings" (p. 171). But feelings were not the source of the possible bias in the Wegener-Petty experiment, and it would be nice to have the same kind of evidence for feeling effects.

Common sense and everyday experience suggest that there probably is a widespread recognition that one's existing feelings can distort judgments. However, common sense does not tell us what people believe is the magnitude of this possible bias. Their lay theorizing might exaggerate the size of this distortion. Gilbert and Wilson (this volume) have proposed that many persons overestimate the duration of their affective reactions to a variety of aversive events, perhaps because they fail to recognize the operation of feeling "ameliorative" processes. They might also overestimate the intensity and duration of their affective reactions.

Yet another question has to do with the hedonic nature of the judgment-biasing source. Most of the findings reported here (with the exception of those involving the judgment of the male targets in the Jaffee-Berkowitz experiment; see note 9) had to do with negative affect, and one might ask whether there would be the same effects when positive feelings are involved. The flexible correction model and the research cited by Wegener and Petty both indicate that the answer should be "yes." Theoretically, as long as we think that our feeling can distort our judgment, whether this experience is pleasant or unpleasant, we should attempt to correct for this possible bias if we want to be accurate in our assessment. However, negative affect might be more likely to produce an overcorrection than positive feelings would because the negative feelings are more apt to generate a high level of cognitive activity. Schwarz and Bless (1992) held that negative affect is especially likely to promote analytic thinking because such feelings signal that the surrounding situation is problematic and that ways must be found to cope with the difficulties. As our research indicates, this active analytic thinking could facilitate the overcorrection process. Moreover, according to several studies (Wood, Saltzberg, & Goldsamt, 1990; Sedikides, 1992), unpleasant feelings often lead to inward-directed attention. As a consequence, there could be a greater awareness of the negative affect, and thus a relatively stronger activation of the "supervisory executive system" that produces the judgmental overcorrection.

Yet another problem arises from the difference between our findings and the results obtained by Forgas (1995b) in conceptually similar experiments. In our investigation, the participants evaluating the atypical couples displayed the overcorrection effect in their judgments, whereas Forgas's participants in the same condition exhibited a relatively strong affective congruence (or affect infusion). The likeliest reason for this difference, it seems to us, is accuracy motivation. Perhaps because more of our participants had a relatively high level of evaluation apprehension, a greater proportion of the Wisconsin subjects might have sought to be careful and thoughtful in making their ratings. Since feeling awareness is evidently necessary for this correction process, it is also possible that the Australian participants were somewhat less conscious of their affective state than were our people.

Having emphasized the part played by feelings-directed attention in moderating affective reactions, we should remind the reader of the importance of accuracy motivation. People do not always want to arrive at objective judgments of the targets they are assessing. They might be so intensely disturbed (or unhappy or angry) that affectively congruent negative ideas activated by their strong feelings completely overcome any inclinations they might otherwise have to be fair and objective in their evaluations. Indeed, lacking the desire to be accurate, their attention to their strong negative feelings may even heighten the judgment-distorting influence.

Notes

1. To employ the Blascovich and Mendes (this volume) terminology, these aversive conditions probably can be regarded as threatening rather than challenging in nature. For Blascovich and Mendes, threatening situations are those in which the demands placed on persons are seen as much greater

than the resources they believe are available to them. However, we suggest that the displeasure evoked by the threat, rather than the threat appraisal as such, may well be the root of the behavioral and physiological reactions observed by Blascovich and Mendes. A number of the factors that produced the threat-linked cardiovascular patterns in the Blascovich and Mendes research, such as physical pain and the sight of a partner's ugly facial birthmark, are similar to factors that heightened aggressive inclinations in our Wisconsin research (cf. Berkowitz, 1993). We argue that it was the felt distress created by these factors that led to the threat reactions including the aggressive tendencies.

It should be clear by now that the cognitive-neoassociationistic conception is eclectic with regard to the role of cognitions in the creation of anger, and possibly other emotional states as well. Although it recognizes the important part played by appraisals and attributions, it also holds that anger (including annoyance and irritation) can be elicited automatically, with little cognitive involvement, by strong negative affect, as well as by situational stimuli linked to previously encountered unpleasant occurrences and/or to aggression (see Berkowitz, 1993).

2. Bower's network formulation differs from Forgas's affect infusion model (AIM) in an important way. Where AIM proposes that active, substantive processing is necessary for affect infusion to lead to mood congruency in judgments, Bower's conception, in maintaining that affect primes semantically related ideas in an automatic, "bottom-up" manner, holds that this substantive processing can *facilitate* the occurrence of mood congruency (as long as opposing ideas are not activated) but is not necessary for this congruency to arise.

3. The evidence pointing to mood-state dependent memory, particularly the findings obtained in Eich's (this volume) impressive research program, also support the associative network formulation. One can regard mood-state dependent memory as a relatively weak context effect; the memories brought to mind by the mood apparently can easily be masked or suppressed by other memories evoked by stronger situational cues.

4. The affect infusion model would say that the participants had engaged in motivated processing when they attempted to correct for a possible affect-induced judgmental bias. Up to the time of his 1995 presentation of this formulation, however, Forgas's discussion of motivated processing emphasized only that this processing would minimize or even eliminate affective congruence in judgments. Nothing was said about how it could lead to a contrast effect.

5. Since the source of the participants' discomfort was always very clear in these Wisconsin experiments, it is decidedly improbable that the participants had misattributed their negative affect to the judgmental target. The mood as information formulation is therefore inapplicable as an explanation of the mood congruency we obtained.

We should also note that all the experiments in this series employed only female participants. This was because we had recruited only women undergraduate assistants to run these studies. Our standard practice was to have participants of the same gender as the experimenters in order to minimize possible artifacts such as a male participant's desire to please the woman experimenter.

6. There is good reason to believe the negative slope indicated in Figure 6.2 for the Feelings Attention condition is reliable. In the analysis of variance of the scores in the four conditions of the Discomfort Level by Attention Direction design, the mean number of bad adjectives attributed to the target in the High Discomfort – Feelings Attention group (M = 8.1) is significantly lower (by a planned comparison) than the mean number assigned to the target in the Low Discomfort – Feelings Attention group (M = 11.3). Figure 6.4 indicates that the overcorrection is especially strong when the participants had evidence that their initial inclinations might be wrong or inappropriate.

7. Inspection of the relationships revealed by the multiple regression analysis showed that it was difficult to come up with a plausible explanation of how the smile facial expression had interacted with whatever psychologically inconsistent negative feelings the participants possessed when they made their judgments. We therefore focused only on the more easily explained results for the people induced to frown.

8. Interestingly, in this study it evidently was the *happy* participants shown the atypical couples who "leaned over backwards" to correct for the influence of their feelings when they were asked to be accurate. The mean liking rating in the Atypical Couples – Happy Mood – Accuracy Instruction group (M = 3.2) was significantly lower than the means in each of the other groups.

References

Anderson, C. A. (1989). Temperature and aggression: The ubiquitous effects of heat on the occurrence of human violence. *Psychological Bulletin, 106,* 74–96.

Anderson, C. A., Deuser, W. E., & DeNeve, K. M. (1995). Hot temperatures, hostile affect, hostile cognition, and arousal: Tests of a general model of affective aggression. *Personality and Social Psychology Bulletin, 21,* 434–448.

Bargh, J. A. (1997). The automaticity of everyday life. In R. S. Wyer, Jr. (Ed.), *Advances in social cognition* (Vol. 10, pp. 1–61). Mahwah, NJ: Erlbaum.

Berkowitz, L. (1989). The frustration-aggression hypothesis: Examination and reformulation. *Psychological Bulletin, 106,* 59–73.

Berkowitz, L. (1990). On the formation and regulation of anger and aggression: A cognitive-neoassociationistic analysis. *American Psychologist, 45,* 494–503.

Berkowitz, L. (1993). *Aggression: Its causes and consequences.* New York: McGraw-Hill.

Berkowitz, L., & Troccoli, B. T. (1990). Feelings, direction of attention, and expressed evaluations of others. *Cognition and Emotion, 4,* 305–325.

Bower, G. H. (1981). Mood and memory. *American Psychologist, 36,* 129–148.

Bower, G. H. (1991). Mood congruity of social judgments. In J. P. Forgas (Ed.),

Emotion and social judgments (pp. 31–53). New York: Oxford University Press.

Duval, S., & Wicklund, R. A. (1972). *A theory of objective self-awareness.* New York: Academic Press.

Forgas, J. P. (1995a). Mood and judgment: The affect infusion model (AIM). *Psychological Bulletin, 117,* 39–66.

Forgas, J. P. (1995b). Strange couples: Mood effects on judgments and memory about prototypical and atypical relationships. *Personality and Social Psychology Bulletin, 21,* 747–765.

Jaffee, S., & Berkowitz, L. (1996). *Influences affecting the overcorrection for one's mood-induced judgmental bias.* Unpublished manuscript. University of Wisconsin-Madison.

Martin, L. L., Seta, J. J., & Crelia, R. A. (1990). Assimilation and contrast as a function of people's willingness and ability to expend effort in forming an impression. *Journal of Personality and Social Psychology, 59,* 27–37.

Matt, G. E., Vazquez, C., & Campbell, W. K. (1992). Mood-congruent recall of affectively toned stimuli: A meta-analytic review. *Clinical Psychology Review, 12,* 227–255.

Mayer, J. D., Gaschke, Y. N., Braverman, D. L., & Evans, T. W. (1992). Mood-congruent judgment is a general effect. *Journal of Personality and Social Psychology, 63,* 119–132.

McFarland, C., & Buehler, R. (1997). Negative affective states and the motivated retrieval of positive life events: The role of affect acknowledgment. *Journal of Personality and Social Psychology, 73,* 200–214.

Norman, D. A., & Shallice, T. (1986). Attention to action: Willed and automatic control of behavior. In: R. J. Davidson, G. E. Schwartz, & D. Shapiro (Eds.) *Consciousness and Self-regulation* (Vol 4, pp. 1–18). New York: Plenum.

Parrott, W. G., & Sabini, J. (1990). Mood and memory under natural conditions: Evidence for mood incongruent recall. *Journal of Personality and Social Psychology, 59,* 321–336.

Posner, M. I. (1982). Cumulative development of attentional theory. *American Psychologist, 37,* 168–179.

Schwarz, N., & Bless, H. (1992). Constructing reality and its alternatives: An inclusion/exclusion model of assimilation and contrast effects in social judgment. In L. L. Martin & A. Tesser (Eds.), *The construction of social judgments* (pp. 217–245). Hillsdale, NJ: Erlbaum.

Schwarz, N., & Clore, G. L. (1983). Mood, misattribution, and judgments of well-being: Informative and directive functions of affective states. *Journal of Personality and Social Psychology, 45,* 513–523.

Sedikides, C. (1992). Mood as a determinant of attentional focus. *Cognition and Emotion, 6,* 129–148.

Shiffrin, R. M., & Schneider, W. (1977). Controlled and automatic human information processing. II. Perceptual learning, automatic attending, and a general theory. *Psychological Review, 84,* 127–190.

Strack, F. (1992). The different routes to social judgments: Experiential versus informational strategies. In L. L. Martin & A. Tesser (Eds.), *The construction of social judgment.* Hillsdale, NJ: Erlbaum.

Strack, F., Martin, L. L., & Stepper, S. (1988). Inhibiting and facilitating conditions of the human smile: A nonobtrusive test of the facial feedback hypothesis. *Journal of Personality and Social Psychology, 54,* 768–777.

Tesser, A. (1978). Self-generated attitude change. In L. Berkowitz (Ed.), *Advances in experimental social psychology* (Vol. 11, pp. 289–338). New York: Academic Press.

Tourangeau, R., & Ellsworth, P. C. (1979). The role of facial response in the experience of emotion. *Journal of Personality and Social Psychology, 37,* 1519–1531.

Wegener, D. T., & Petty, R. E. (1995). Flexible correction processes in social judgment: The role of naive theories in corrections for perceived bias. *Journal of Personality and Social Psychology, 68,* 36–51.

Wegener, D. T., & Petty, R. E. (1997). The flexible correction model: The role of naive theories of bias in bias correction. In M. Zanna (Ed.), *Advances in experimental social psychology* (Vol. 29, pp. 141–208). San Diego, CA: Academic Press.

Wilson, T. D., & Brekke, N. (1994). Mental contamination and mental correction: Unwanted influences on judgments and evaluations. *Psychological Bulletin, 116,* 117–142.

Wood, J. V., Saltzberg, J. A., & Goldsamt, L. A. (1990). Does affect induce self-focused attention? *Journal of Personality and Social Psychology, 58,* 899–908.

7. Moods Do Not Convey Information

Moods in Context Do

LEONARD L. MARTIN

Perhaps the first thing a person notices when reviewing the research on moods is its diversity. Even a quick glance through the chapters of this book can give one a feel for the wide range of approaches developed to explain the multiple effects of mood. Different theoretical models focus on different phenomena, propose different mediating processes and moderating variables, and, on occasion, generate contradictory predictions. Despite the almost bewildering diversity in the area, some common themes can be extracted. In this chapter, I focus on four. Specifically, I discuss four assumptions that seem to be underlying most current research on mood effects. After that, I suggest that these assumptions may actually be inhibiting rather than facilitating a more complete understanding of mood, and I propose a new way of looking at mood effects. In doing this, I outline the mood-as-input model (e.g., Martin, Abend, Sedikides, & Green, 1997; Martin, Achee, Ward, & Harlow, 1993; Martin & Davies, 1998; Martin & Stoner, 1996; Martin, Ward, Achee, & Wyer, 1993) and the research that has been generated by that model. Finally, I consider the connections between the mood-as-input work and the research discussed in other chapters in this volume.

The Commonalities Behind the Diversity

A review of the theoretical models that explain mood effects reveals that they have at least four assumptions in common. Although each

Correspondence concerning this work should be addressed to Leonard L. Martin, Department of Psychology, University of Georgia, Athens, GA 30602. E-mail: LLMartin@arches.uga.edu.

assumption by itself may not be particularly significant, when taken together, they provide a clear picture of the way researchers are conceptualizing moods.

1. Inherent relations. Most models assume that there are inherent relations between specific moods and specific effects. For example, it has generally been assumed that, relative to positive moods, negative moods lead to greater recall of negative material, more unfavorable evaluations, more systematic, but less flexible, less creative processing, and a strong motivation to eliminate the mood.

2. Contextual interference. Even models that assume inherent links between moods and their effects do not predict that these relations will always be seen. Nevertheless, the relations are typically construed as basic in the sense that they *will* be seen unless some outside, overriding factor intervenes. For example, some models (Berkowitz et al., this volume; Forgas, 1995, this volume; Mayer, Gaschke, Braverman, & Evans, 1992) assume that mood-congruent evaluations occur unless individuals engage in effortful processing to override the more basic congruence effect. Other models assume that mood-congruent evaluations occur unless individuals attribute their moods to something other than the target of their evaluation (Schwarz & Clore, 1988) or engage in processing (e.g., recall of a previously stored judgment) that bypasses their use of their moods in the judgment (Fiedler, this volume; Forgas, this volume). The models suggest that if individuals use their moods in their judgments and if there are no interfering processes, the result will be a mood-congruent evaluation.

3. Hedonism. Most models also include, in one form or another, the assumption that individuals are highly motivated to attain or maintain positive moods while being highly motivated to avoid or eliminate negative moods. Although some models allow for conditions under which individuals do not act hedonistically, the models construe these conditions as special circumstances in which the more basic hedonistic motive has been overridden by a goal that happened, at that particular time in that particular circumstance, to be stronger than the hedonistic motive (e.g., Bless, Bohner, Schwarz, & Strack, 1990).

4. Moods do things to people. The fourth commonality deals with the way in which mood effects are described. This may be merely a stylistic feature, but it may also reflect a more substantive view of mood. Not uncommon in the literature are sentences of the sort "negative moods lead participants to . . ." or "positive moods resulted in greater activation of. . . ." Such phrasing gives the impression that moods do things to people, rather than the other way around. In other words, individuals appear to be little more than the place in which moods have their effects.

In this chapter, I explore the possibility that each of these assumptions may be more constricting than helpful. Specifically, there are reasons to believe that, contrary to the four assumptions just described; (1) there are no inherent relations between the valence of one's mood and one's tendencies in memory, evaluation, or processing (2) the evaluative and motivational implications of moods are naturally different in different contexts such that no special interfering or overriding processes are needed to account for the context-dependent nature of mood effects; (3) people are motivated to attain positive outcomes, not positive moods (and sometimes a positive outcome can be signaled by a negative mood); and (4) the processes by which moods cause their effects are more sophisticated than the simple associative mechanisms depicted in most models. Taken together, these four alternate assumptions point the way to a quite different view of mood, in which moods are analogous to the number six (or any other number for that matter). They provide some context-invariant information (e.g., a whole number between five and seven), but they have no evaluative or motivational implications until we know the context in which they occur (e.g., six rejections vs. six publications). Thus, experiencing a positive mood at a wedding does not convey the same evaluative and motivational implications as experiencing a positive mood at a funeral.

In the next section, I describe how this alternate conceptualization of mood works within the mood-as-input model. In the remainder of the chapter, I discuss research related to that model, and show how the model accounts for the effects of mood on evaluation and on processing motivation without recourse to inherent relations, overriding processes, or hedonistic motivations. Finally, I discuss the connections between this work and several other lines of research discussed in this volume.

The Mood-as-Input Model

The mood-as-input model (e.g., Martin, Achee, et al., 1993; Martin & Davies, 1998; Martin & Stoner, 1996; Martin, Ward, et al., 1993; Martin et al., 1997) begins with the null hypothesis that there are no inherent relations between the valence of one's mood and one's tendencies in recall, evaluation, processing, or self-regulation. Instead, the model assumes that the effect of any given mood depends on the context in which the mood is experienced. This is the case because, according to the mood-as-input model, moods convey their evaluative and motivational implications by serving as information in a configural processing system. This means that people consider simultaneously not only how they feel but also the context in which they experience those feelings.

To illustrate the context-dependent nature of mood effects reflected in the mood-as-input model, suppose you are with your loved one at the airport and you feel sad. What are the implications of these sad feelings? It depends. If you are feeling sad because your loved one is leaving on a trip, you may interpret your sadness as a sign that you care deeply about the person. If, on the other hand, you are feeling sad because your loved one is returning from a trip, you may interpret your sadness as a sign that you prefer your freedom to the relationship. Thus, the informative properties of the mood change with the context. In one context, a negative mood signals a strong interpersonal relationship; in another context, it signals a weak interpersonal relationship.

More generally, the mood-as-input model assumes that moods convey their evaluative and motivational implications through a sort of self-perception process. According to self-perception theory (Bem, 1965), individuals draw inferences about themselves by observing their overt behavior and the context in which that behavior occurs. According to the mood-as-input model, individuals can draw inferences about themselves by observing their feelings and the context in which these feelings occur. Although this self-perception view of mood is related to the view adopted by the mood-as-information model (Schwarz & Clore, 1983, 1988), the two models differ in important ways. First, the mood-as-information model takes the context of one's mood into consideration only by allowing for the discounting of one's mood to salient nontarget causes. By comparison, the mood-as-input model takes a configural view of context. In this way, the meaning of a mood experience, not just its relevance, can change in different contexts. Second, the mood-as-information model assumes that there are inherent relations between the valence of one's mood and one's tendencies in evaluation, processing, and self-regulation. The mood-as-input model does not. And third, according to the mood-as-input model, it is the implications of one's mood, not the simple valence, that influences behavior. This means that in some contexts the implications of experiencing a negative mood can be positive, whereas the implications of experiencing a positive mood can be negative. This hypothesis does not follow from the mood-as-information depiction of mood as a bottom-line evaluation in a "How do I feel about it?" heuristic (e.g., Schwarz & Clore, 1988).

In the following sections, I consider in more detail how the mood-as-input model addresses the effects of moods on evaluation and processing, and how it does so without recourse to assumed inherent relations or interfering processes.

Mood Configurality and Evaluations

The first point to make about the mood-as-input approach is that under it one's mood is not synonymous with one's evaluation. Whether a positive or a negative mood leads to a favorable or an unfavorable evaluation depends on the meaning of one's mood in the context of the particular judgment. The question is, "What determines the meaning of one's mood in different contexts?" To answer this question, we have to consider more generally how individuals go about making evaluations. The mood-as-input model assumes that individuals make evaluations by assessing the status of the target in relation to some criterion (or criteria). How, for example, would one go about answering the question, "Are you happy with your life as a whole?" One would first have to know the features that constitute a good life. Then, one would have to know the features of one's life, and finally, the extent to which these two sets of features overlap. Research by Ross, Eyman, and Kishchuk (1986) has shown that in assessing their happiness, individuals often consider their past accomplishments, their likelihood of attaining their goals in the future, their standing in relation to others, and how they feel at the moment. Furthermore, individuals believe that a good life is one in which they have accomplished some things in the past, have future hopes, compare favorably to others, and experience good feelings. So, how do individuals know if they are happy with their lives as a whole? If their lives contain some past accomplishments, future hopes, favorable comparisons, and good feelings, then individuals are likely to evaluate their lives favorably. If their lives do not contain these features, then individuals are likely to evaluate their lives unfavorably (Ross, Eyman, & Kishchuk, 1986; Schwarz & Strack, 1991).

As this example shows, individuals can use both descriptive features and subjective experiences as evidence that a target has matched a criterion. One's life is evaluated favorably not only if one has past accomplishments, for example, but also if one experiences positive feelings. It is this feeling-based aspect of the feature-matching process that is at the heart of the mood-as-input model. The model assumes that individuals can use their feelings (along with other features) as input to assess the extent to which a target matches the criterion in relation to which it is being evaluated. More specifically, the mood-as-input model assumes that moods influence evaluations by serving as input to a "What would I feel if . . . ?" question. It is as though individuals ask themselves (not necessarily explicitly or verbally), "How do my feelings compare with what I would be feeling if the target I am evaluating fulfilled the role for which I am evaluating it?" (e.g., a good life, an emotional person). Favorable evaluations arise to the extent that the person's feelings (positive or negative) are congruent with what would be expected if the target had fulfilled a desirable (e.g., more emotionally responsive) role, whereas negative evaluations arise to the extent that the person's feelings are congruent with what would be expected if the target had fulfilled an undesirable (e.g., too emotional) role.

This "How would I feel if . . . ?" process is analogous to a process proposed by Higgins and Rholes (1976; see also Wyer, 1970) to account for the impressions people form on the basis of trait and role information. According to Higgins and Rholes (1976), when people are exposed to a verbal description composed of a role and a descriptor (e.g., mean mother), people call to mind stored information about the target to which the description as a whole refers. Then, they use this information to make a configural judgment involving (1) assessment of the social value of the role (i.e., mother) and (2) assessment of the extent to which the descriptor (i.e., mean) allows the target to fulfill its expected role (i.e., the role of mothers is to be kind rather than mean). In this way, a kind mother would be evaluated more favorably than a mean mother because it is the role of mothers to be kind. By the same reasoning, though, a mean army drill instructor would be evaluated more favorably than a kind army drill instructor because the role of army drill instructors is to be mean.

According to the mood-as-input model, moods are functionally equivalent to the descriptor in the role fulfillment process. Mood-congruent evaluations arise when positive feelings indicate that the target is fulfilling a desirable role (e.g., a happy life), whereas mood-incongruent evaluations arise when negative feelings indicate that the target is fulfilling a desirable role (e.g., empathizing with a sad friend). From this perspective, mood-congruent evaluations are not any more basic than mood-incongruent evaluations. Both arise from the same mechanism. But if this is so, why have mood-congruent evaluations predominated in the literature? One reason is that the conditions in previous studies have been those in which positive moods signaled the fulfillment of a desirable role. Consider the studies in which participants have been asked to rate their satisfaction with their life as a whole (Schwarz & Clore, 1983). Presumably, most people want a happy rather than an unhappy life. If so, how would a person feel if his or her life were fulfilling its role? The person would feel happy. It is not surprising, therefore, that people in positive moods report greater life satisfaction than people in negative moods.

A similar point can be made with regard to studies in which participants were asked to evaluate their progress toward their goals (Cervone, Kopp, Schaumann, & Scott, 1994), decisions they have made (Isen, 1993), their household products (Isen, Shalker, Clark, & Karp, 1978), or their liking for a target person (Sinclair, 1988). In each case, a positive mood signals the fulfillment of a desirable role. People typically strive to attain positively valenced goals, make decisions they hope will lead to favorable outcomes, buy products they hope will work satisfactorily, and like pleasant as opposed to unpleasant people. This means that in each of these studies there was a tacit association between positive mood and role fulfillment. It is not surprising, therefore, that in each study participants in positive moods rendered more favorable evaluations than participants in negative moods. According to the mood-as-input model, such mood congruence is neither inevitable nor more basic than mood incongruence. Under conditions in which a negative mood signals fulfillment of a desirable role, people in negative moods will make the more favorable evaluations. Evidence for this hypothesis has been obtained in a number of studies.

In one study, Martin et al. (1997) reversed the typical finding that people in positive moods render more favorable evaluations of themselves than people in negative moods (Sedikides, 1992). Although in many cases negative moods imply that one possesses a negative trait (e.g., unhealthy, unintelligent), this is not an inherent relation. Empathy, for example, is a positive trait, that, by definition, a person has if he or she feels what another person is feeling. So, if individuals feel sad after reading about another person's misfortune, they should rate themselves favorably in terms of empathy – more favorably than individuals who feel happy after reading about another's misfortune. Martin et al. (1997) tested this hypothesis by placing participants in either a happy or a sad mood and having the participants read a story that either had a positive outcome or a negative outcome. After reading the story, participants rated themselves in terms of traits such as understanding, compassionate, and empathetic (which reduced to a single empathy scale).

According to the mood-as-input model, participants might use their moods to assess the extent of their empathy. If so, participants who read the story with the positive outcome should rate themselves more favorably in terms of empathy when they have previously seen the happy rather than the sad videos (i.e., when they were happy), but participants who read the story with the negative outcome should rate themselves more favorably in terms of empathy when they have seen the sad rather than the happy video (i.e., when they were sad). This crossover interaction was in fact obtained. The most favorable self-ratings occurred when participants in positive moods read a story with a happy ending and participants in negative moods read a story with a sad ending. The least favorable self-ratings were seen among participants whose moods did not match the tone of the story. There was no main effect for the valence of the participants' moods in this study. Thus, the favorableness of the ratings was determined, not simply by the valence of the participants' moods, but by the extent to which the participants' moods matched what would be expected (positive or negative) if the participants were in fact empathetic. In this study, we obtained the typical mood congruent effect in one set of conditions, and a mood incongruent effect under another set of conditions, and both outcomes were easily interpretable in terms of role fulfillment. There was no need to assume that one outcome was basic, whereas the other reflected the operation of an interfering process.

Green, Sedikides, and Martin (1997) provided additional evidence for the role fulfillment hypothesis using another rating for which negative moods signal fulfillment. Green et al. placed participants in positive, negative, or mixed (saw positive and negative videos) moods and asked these participants to indicate how deep, reflective, and thoughtful they were. Obviously, no one wants to think of themselves as shallow as opposed to deep, vacuous as opposed to reflective, or mindless as opposed to thoughtful. So, a simple mood-congruence hypothesis would lead us to expect that participants in positive moods would rate themselves more favorably (i.e., deeper) in terms of these traits than participants in negative moods. Pilot testing revealed, however, that participants believed that being deep, reflective, and thoughtful was signaled by a negative rather than a positive mood. So, a role fulfillment mechanism would predict the opposite of the mood-congruence hypothesis. The results supported the role fulfillment mechanism. Sad participants rated themselves the most deep, thoughtful, and reflective, followed by the participants in mixed moods, with participants in positive moods rating themselves the least thoughtful, reflective, and deep. These results show that positive moods are not inherently associated with more favorable evaluations. They lead to such evaluations only to the extent that they signal role fulfillment. When negative moods signal fulfillment, these moods lead to the more favorable evaluations.

Evidence of Mood Configurality in Processing

In addition to influencing evaluations, moods have also been shown to influence the extent to which individuals process information. The typical finding has been that individuals in negative moods process more extensively than individuals in positive moods (Mackie & Worth, 1989; Schwarz & Bless, 1991). Not surprisingly, the mood-as-input model leads us to believe that there is nothing in positive and negative moods that leads inherently to these outcomes. Either a positive or a negative mood can lead to systematic or heuristic processing.

How does the mood-as-input model account for the contextually dependent effects of mood on processing? It does so in essentially the same way that it addressed the effects of mood on evaluation. It assumes that moods serve as input to a configural evaluative system. Specifically, the model assumes that in determining the extent to which they will process information, individuals evaluate their processing (e.g., Chaiken, Liberman, & Eagley, 1989). If they feel confident that heuristic processing can provide them with an acceptable (e.g., valid) outcome, then individuals engage in heuristic processing. If they do not feel confident with heuristic processing, then individuals increase the extent of their processing (i.e., they engage in systematic processing). What determines an individuals's confidence? It is determined, at least in part, by the individual's mood and the context in which that mood occurs. The context in this case is a stop-rule.

If individuals process according to an "enough" rule, then they essentially process until they have a "yes" answer to the question, "Have I processed enough to accomplish my goal (e.g., understanding a persuasive message)?" With this stop-rule, a "yes" answer can be provided by a positive mood, whereas a "no" answer can be provided by a negative mood. This is because positive moods can signal progress toward one's goals, whereas negative moods can signal retreat from one's goals (Carver & Scheier, 1990; Cervone et al., 1994). So, when individuals operate under an "enough" rule, those in positive moods are likely to process less extensively than those in negative moods (the typical finding in the literature). When individuals are more intrinsically oriented, however, their stop-rule is essentially "Am I enjoying this task?" In this case, a positive mood signals enjoyment, whereas a negative mood signals lack of enjoyment (Hirt, Melton, McDonald, & Harackiewicz, 1996; Sansone & Harackiewicz, 1996). Hence, when individuals operate under an "enjoy" rule, those in a positive mood are likely to process more extensively than those in a negative mood (the opposite of the typical finding in the literature).

A variety of investigators have demonstrated that different stop-rules can flip the effects of moods on processing in the ways just described (see Hirt et al., 1996; Martin, Ward, et al., 1993; Sanna, Turley, & Mark, 1996). Perhaps even more interesting is the strong version of the mood-as-input model. If the model is correct, not only should the direction of mood effects be context dependent, but mood should exert no effect whatsoever on motivation to process unless individuals interpret their moods in light of their stop-rules. This is because, from the mood-as-input perspective, moods are like the number six. They have no evaluative or motivational implications until they have been instantiated in a given context (six acceptances vs. six rejections).

This strong version of the mood-as-input hypothesis can be contrasted with the view of mood and processing that currently predominates in the field. According to that view, different moods produce specific motivational effects unless these effects are overridden by some outside factor (e.g., Schwarz & Bless, 1991; Mackie & Worth, 1989). To distinguish the two views more concisely, we can say that the dominant view is that contextual factors are responsible for *eliminating* the inherent motivational effects of moods, whereas the input view is that contextual factors are responsible for *creating* whatever motivational effects of moods might be seen. These two views make diametrically opposed predictions of what would happen in the complete absence of contextual constraints. The inherent motivation view would lead us to believe that individuals in positive moods would process less extensively than individuals in negative moods because the default effects would be free to manifest themselves. The mood-as-input view would lead us to believe that there would be no differences in the processing of individuals in positive and negative moods because there would be no context to suggest a motivationally relevant interpretation of the mood.

Unfortunately for the mood-as-input model, a quick review of the literature seems to favor the inherent motivation view. Most of the published studies did not include explicit manipulations of stop-rules, yet in those studies participants in negative moods processed more extensively than participants in positive moods (e.g., Bless et al., 1990; Mackie & Worth, 1989; Sinclair & Mark, 1995). According to the mood-as-input model, this could not have occurred unless there were cues in the experimental setting that induced participants to adopt an "enough" rule. So, the absence of explicit manipulations of stop-rules in these studies is problematic for the mood-as-input hypothesis that moods have no default motivational implications.

On the other hand, the mood-as-input view could be bolstered if it were found that there had indeed been subtle motivational cues in the settings of the earlier studies. Suppose, for example, that the target tasks had been inherently unpleasant (cf. Smith & Shaffer, 1991). In that case, participants might have performed the tasks only as much as they felt they had to, even in the absence of an explicit "enough" manipulation. This would lead participants in negative moods to process more extensively than those in positive moods. To find out if this might have been the case, Martin and Crepaz (1998) described some tasks used in earlier mood and processing studies to a group of participants and asked these participants to indicate the extent to which, if they performed each task, it would be because they wanted to (enjoy) or because they had to (enough). The results revealed a collection of tasks associated with an "enough" rule. Specifically, participants indicated that they would generate the names of birds (Martin, Ward et al., 1993), read an essay about acid rain (Mackie & Worth, 1989), read an essay about a comprehensive final exam (Bless et al., 1990), and estimate the correlation in scatter plots (Sinclair & Mark, 1995) only to the extent that they had to. In other words, the tasks used in earlier mood and processing studies were ones that induced participants to adopt an "enough" rule. It is not surprising, therefore, that in these studies participants in negative moods processed more extensively than participants in positive moods.

If the results of the previous studies were really a function of stop-rules being implicitly elicited by the target tasks, it should be possible to eliminate the previously obtained effects simply by having participants perform a task free of motivational implications. Fortunately, in rating the tasks used in the earlier research, our pilot participants showed us such a task. These participants rated the impression formation task used by Martin, Ward et al. (1993, Experiment 1) about midway between the enjoy and the enough ends of the scale. This task, unlike those used in most mood and processing research, is not likely to elicit an "enough" stop-rule in the participants (nor an "enjoy" rule for that matter). So, if the mood-as-input model is correct, when participants rate a task that is free of motivational implications, participants in positive and negative moods should not differ in the extent of their processing.

Martin and Crepaz (1998, Experiment 1) tested this hypothesis by placing participants in either a positive or negative mood and then having them perform the motivationally neutral impression formation task from Martin, Ward et al. Specifically, after watching either happy or sad videos, participants were provided with a stack of cards with one behavior described on each card. They were asked to read the cards and to form an impression of the person who had ostensibly performed the behaviors. The participants were told, however, that they did not have to read all of the cards and that there was no right or wrong time to stop. Subsequent to these general instructions, different participants read more specific instructions that provided them with different stop-rules. Those in the "enough" condition read: "You can stop whenever you feel that you have enough information on which to base an impression." Those in the "enjoy" condition read: "You can stop whenever you feel that you no longer enjoy reading the cards." Those in the no-stop-rule condition read simply: "You do not need to read all of the cards. You can stop when you are ready to stop. There is no right or wrong time."

If the mood-as-input model is correct, participants in a negative mood would have read more behaviors than participants in a positive mood when provided with the "enough" stop-rule, but the reverse would have occurred when participants were provided with the "enjoy" stop-rule. When participants were told merely to "stop when you are ready," mood would have had no effect on processing. All three of these predictions were confirmed. Participants given the "enough" stop-rule read more cards when they were in negative compared with positive moods, whereas participants given the "enjoy" stop-rule read more cards when they were in positive compared with negative moods. When participants were told to stop whenever they felt like it, mood did not influence the number of cards they read. Thus, in this one study, we obtained all possible effects of mood on processing and all three effects are explicable in terms of the mood-as-input model.

Consistent with that model's view of moods as analogous to the number six, participants' moods influenced the extent of participants' processing only when participants could interpret their moods in a motivationally relevant way (e.g., as a stop-rule). When participants performed a motivationally neutral task in a motivationally neutral context, their moods did not influence the extent of their processing. These results suggest that the reason prior studies found that participants in negative moods processed more extensively than participants in positive moods is that the tasks used in those studies induced participants to adopt an "enough" rule. In rating the tasks used in those studies, our pilot participants indicated that they would perform those tasks only as much as they had to. One general implication of these findings is that future research will have to be careful about specifying the stop-rules conveyed (perhaps implicitly) by their tasks and settings. Researchers cannot make claims about the basic or default effects of moods until they know how participants are interpreting their moods.

Input or Override?

Although the Martin and Crepaz results provide strong support for the mood-as-input model, one might ask whether their results in any way challenge the assumption that there are inherent relations between certain moods and certain forms of processing? Consider that even the models that assume inherent relations do not assume that these relations will always be seen. Sometimes, an interfering process overrides the default effect and keeps it from being manifested. Are there reasons to favor the input hypothesis over the inherent-override hypothesis as an explanation of the Martin and Crepaz data? Yes, there are.

First, the input hypothesis is supported by the fact that none of the factors assumed to be important for overriding the default effects were varied in our experiment. These included awareness of the predispositions (Berkowitz, 1993), mood repair concerns (Joseph, Singer, & Salvey, 1996), extra processing time (Mackie & Worth, 1989), and competing goals (Schwarz & Bless, 1991).

Second, there was nothing in the manipulations that in any way induced or compelled participants to perform in ways contrary to their motivational predispositions. It was not as though the participants in positive moods wanted to process shallowly, for example, but were instructed to process systematically anyway (see Bless et al., 1990). The instructions for all participants made it clear that there was no right or wrong time for them to stop. It was up to them. They could stop when they felt they had done enough, they no longer enjoyed the task, or they were ready to stop. In other words, the experimenter did not tell the participants to continue or to stop; their moods in relation to their stop-rule did.

Third, when participants were instructed merely to stop when they were ready (i.e., the no stop-rule condition), their moods did not influence the extent of their processing. One would think that it would be precisely under such conditions of no constraint that the inherent processing motivations would manifest themselves. Yet, it was precisely under these conditions that no effects were seen. So, quite apart from interfering with or overriding any default effects, the stop-rules were actually responsible for creating the mood effects.

Problematic Implications?

Our results (see also Martin & Davies, 1998; Martin & Stoner, 1996) suggest that moods have their effects on evaluation and on processing motivation as part of a stimulus configuration. Individuals do not ask merely, "How do I feel?" They ask, "What is the meaning of my feelings in this context?" Because of this, moods can naturally have different evaluative and motivational implications in different contexts. Unfortunately, if we take seriously the hypothesis that mood effects are highly dependent on context, we are forced to confront some possibly sticky issues. If mood effects really change from context to context, for example, can we ever predict the effects of any given mood, and if we cannot, will it be possible to disconfirm the mood-as-input model? A second concern relates to the complexity of the processes that presumably mediate the mood-as-input effects. Most models rely upon some form of simple associative process to account for mood effects. Proponents of these models might wonder if we really need to assume all of the extra processing that seems to be involved in the mood-as-input model. A third consideration is whether the seemingly complex processes depicted in the mood-as-input model are compatible with a functional, evolutionary view of mood. Some theorists (e.g., Zajonc, this volume) have suggested that affective reactions are the product of a primitive evolutionarily adaptive approach-avoidance mechanism that resides in subcortical regions of the brain. How can we reconcile this view of affect as simple and basic with the seemingly complex, high-order processes depicted in the mood-as-input model? I will address each of these concerns in turn.

Can the Model Predict?

If moods really mean different things for different people performing different tasks in different contexts, how can we ever predict the effect of mood on performance? We do so by taking into consideration not only the valence of the mood but the context in which that mood occurs. Thus far, we have relied on the role fulfillment process (Higgins & Rholes, 1976; Wyer, 1970) to do this. Once we know which mood signals fulfillment of what role, we can make predictions as strong as any mood model. In the Green et al. (1997) study discussed previously, we asked participants which valence of mood signaled being deep and which signaled being shallow. On the basis of these ratings, we were able to predict that participants in negative moods would rate themselves more favorably on the deep/shallow dimension than participants in positive moods. These predictions were supported. Had they not been supported, the mood-as-input model would have been disconfirmed.

Similarly, the findings that a positive mood can signal approach to a goal whereas a negative mood can signal retreat (Carver & Scheier, 1990; Hsee & Abelson, 1991; Martin, Ward et al., 1993) led to the prediction that a positive mood would induce less processing than a negative mood when participants were performing according to an "enough" rule (e.g., Have I met my goal?). In addition, on the basis of the findings that a positive mood can signal task enjoyment whereas a negative mood can signal lack of enjoyment (Hirt et al., 1996; Sansone & Harackiewicz, 1996), Martin, Ward et al. (1993) also predicted that a positive mood would induce greater processing than a negative mood when participants were performing according to an "enjoy" rule. Both of these predictions were supported. Had they not been, the mood-as-input model would have been disconfirmed. In short, the mood-as-input model makes predictions as clearly as any model of mood, and, therefore, it stands just as much a chance of being disconfirmed.

Too Complex?

According to most models, moods exert their influence through some sort of passive associative process. According to the mood-as-input model, moods exert their influence when individuals consider not only their moods, but also some target information and some context information, and do all of this concurrently. Does Occam's razor compel us to accept the simple associative models over the seemingly more complicated mood-as-input model? No, it does not. There are two reasons for this. First, the mood-as-input model accounts for a full range of effects with one simple set of assumptions. For example, it uses the same role fulfillment mechanism to account for mood-congruent evaluations, mood-incongruent evaluations, and no effect of mood on evaluations. By comparison, to account for these same three effects, the associative models need to resort to outside, interfering factors (e.g., attributions, correction processes, contrast effects, mood repair strategies). What this means is that when one considers each model's ability to account for a range of phenomena, it is actually the mood-as-input model that is the more parsimonious one.

Second, the processes spelled out in the mood-as-input model are not complex. There is a great deal of evidence from a wide range of areas indicating not only that individuals engage in configural processing but that they do so quickly, effortlessly, and efficiently. It is a natural way to process information. Evidence for this assertion can be seen not only in the early work on perceptual Gestalts (e.g., Wertheimer, 1923) but also in the more recent work in parallel distributed processing (e.g., Seidenberg, 1993). There is also evidence of configural processing in predictive learning (Williams, Sagness, & McPhee, 1994), judgment of the value of outcomes (Birnbaum, Coffey, Millers, &

Weiss, 1992), preferences for different gambles (Birnbaum, Thompson, & Bean, 1997), memory (Dosher & Rosedale, 1997), discrimination and classification (Kimchi, 1994), evaluation of faces (Sergent, 1984), and impression formation (Asch, 1946; Higgins & Rholes, 1976; Wyer, 1970).

Particularly compelling examples of configural processing can be seen in research on word recognition. Jacewicz (1979), for example, asked participants to determine whether or not a letter had been present in a tachistoscopically exposed word. He found that participants identified the target letter faster if it was clearly sounded in the word (g in the word tiger) than if it was not (g in the word right). These results suggest that participants first recognized the word as a whole, then transformed the word from a visual to an acoustic code, and only then analyzed its component letters.

The mood-as-input model suggests that moods are processed in an analogous holistic way. People do not consider each piece of target, context, and mood information separately and then combine them into an overall judgment. Rather, people evaluate them configurally, as a pattern, asking, in essence, "What is the meaning of my current feelings given the judgment I am making?" This view of mood is compatible with the kind of processing individuals have been shown to do easily and efficiently in a wide range of areas.

Is Configural Responding Evolutionarily Basic?

Even if we accept the evidence that individuals often engage in configural processing and that such processing can be quicker and more efficient than piecemeal processing, do we have any reason to believe that configural responding is adaptive and basic in an evolutionary sense? Does it not make more sense to assume that organisms have very simple, initial approach-avoidance tendencies and that configural processing comes later in the stream and involves higher-order brain structures (e.g., Zajonc, this volume)? No, it does not. Why should evolution be restricted to using simple, primitive mechanisms to help organisms adapt? Consider a simple fight-or-flight decision. To make the appropriate decision, an organism needs to know not only the markings that distinguish a predator from a nonpredator, but also whether that predator is advancing or retreating, and how fast. Moreover, the organism needs to know (among other things) how far away the predator is, whether there are any barriers between itself and the predator, whether there are any means of escape at hand, and, if so, which of these might be preferable. Presumably, organisms that could take this and other relevant information into consideration quickly, reliably, and efficiently would have a clear adaptive advantage over organisms that merely possessed simple approach-avoidance reflexes.

Additional reasons to believe that configural responding is evolutionarily basic can be seen in the repeated demonstrations of this responding across the phylogenetic spectrum. Configural responding has been found in monkeys (Delgado, 1983; Gaffan & Harrison, 1993), rats (Capaldi, 1985), pigeons (Pearce & Wilson, 1990), frogs and toads (Ingle, 1983), lizards (Hertz, Huey, & Nevo, 1982), salamanders (Roth, 1987), and even insects (Rilling, Mittelstaedt, & Roeder, 1959). When Prete (1990) measured the visual configurations that release predatory behaviors in the praying mantis, he found that a mantis does not respond merely to the length, the thickness, or the direction of movement of a potential prey. It responds to all three simultaneously. Specifically, a mantis is likely to attack an approaching lure if that lure is 10 mm thick and 3–55 mm long. It is not likely to attack a lure in this same size range, however, if that lure is moved orthogonally to the mantis. On the other hand, an orthogonally moving lure does elicit predatory behavior if the lure is only 3 mm thick. What these results show is that even a creature as simple as a praying mantis does not respond merely to length, thickness, or movement, but it responds to the configuration of all three. Prete (1990) speculated that these visual configurations might influence mantis predatory behavior by way of the retinal ganglion cells and the assembly of feature-detectors to which the ganglion cells project.

Obviously, there are many differences between the kind of configural processing depicted in the mood-as-input model and that observed in lower organisms. I am not suggesting that the processes are the same. The point of discussing the research on lower organisms is to make it clear that when configural responding is important to the adaptiveness of an organism, evolution finds a way to build it in – even if the organism involved does not possess a brain in the true sense of the word, as is the case with insects. There, evolution may build configural sensitivity into the retinal ganglia (Prete, 1990). What reason is there, therefore, to assume that the supremely more sophisticated human organism is not capable of fast, efficient configural processing?

Not only do we know that configural responding is present across the phylogenetic spectrum, but we are also beginning to learn which brain mechanisms govern configural responding in organisms such as rats and monkeys. Configural responding in these organisms entails significant participation of the hippocampus (e.g., Gaffan & Harrison, 1993; Rudy & Sutherland, 1995; Whishaw & Tomie, 1991). This finding is consistent with the mood-as-input conjecture that configural responding need not involve lengthy, effortful processing in higher-order brain structures. This finding is also consistent with LeDoux's (1994, p. 53) observation that "the emotional significance of a stimulus is determined not only by the sound itself but by the environment in which it occurs. Rats must therefore learn not only that a sound or visual cue is dangerous, but under what conditions it is so." Ironically, LeDoux's work has often been cited as support for a simple fight or flight view of affect (Zajonc, this volume). What his work, like that of others (Delgado, 1983), actually shows is that organisms such as rats and monkeys are sensitive to the context in which an emotional event takes place and that aspects of this context are processed in subcortical structures of the brain (i.e., amygdala, hippocampus).

In sum, there is no reason to believe that the configural processing depicted in the mood-as-input model involves conscious, deliberate, time-consuming processing in higher-order brain structures. In fact, everything in evolution theory, and a wealth of evidence from research on lower organisms, leads us to the opposite conclusion. Configural responding is basic, adaptive, widespread, and efficient.

Implications for Other Research in This Volume

According to Berkowitz (this volume), being in a mood leads automatically to the activation of memories congruent with the valence of that mood. These memories, in turn, automatically become the basis for mood-congruent predispositions. These predispositions are not expressed, however, when individuals become highly aware of the mood influence and are both willing and able to devote considerable cognitive effort to inhibiting the predisposition. There is certainly nothing in the mood-as-input view that argues against this view of mood effects. On the other hand, the mood-as-input view does raise the possibility that mood-incongruent activities may occur without awareness and effort. In fact, according to the mood-as-input model, both mood-congruent and mood-incongruent activities can arise from the same role fulfillment process.

To place the two theoretical models together, one might speculate that different moods naturally give rise to different predispositions in different contexts, but once these predispositions have been instantiated in a given context, individuals may realize that expressing these predispositions would be undesirable. If so, it will be at this point that they would engage in the effortful correction suggested by Berkowitz. So, it is quite possible that people suppress mood-induced predispositions by means of effortful, high-order correction processes, but this possibility is not at all incompatible with the possibility that the initial predispositions are context dependent, and that they arise from fast, nonconscious, configural responding.

According to Bless, people in positive moods are more likely than those in negative moods to rely on general knowledge structures when processing information. These predictions are based on two assumptions: (1) bottom-up processing is more likely in problematic situations, whereas top-down processing is more likely in nonproblematic situations; and (2) a person's mood can inform him or her about the extent to which the current situation is problematic. Although mood-as-input research does not address the first assumption, it does address the second. Specifically, it suggests that moods do not convey evaluative or motivational implications that are context invariant. In some contexts, it is possible for a negative mood to signal that the environment is nonproblematic, and for a positive mood to signal that the environment is problematic. Consider a person who is feeling happy after hearing of a tragedy involving a close friend. The positive mood is inappropriate under these circumstances and may induce the person to engage in detailed analysis of himself and/or the situation to find out why he or she is feeling happy when he or she should be feeling concerned. More generally, problematic situations may be more likely than nonproblematic situations to elicit bottom-up processing, but negative moods are not necessarily more likely than positive moods to inform a person that the situation is problematic. As a result, there should be no inherent relation between the valence of one's mood and one's tendency to engage in top-down versus bottom-up processing.

Although the Fiedler (this volume) and the Forgas (1995; this volume) models differ in a number of respects, they do share at least one feature that distinguishes them from most other models: their strong emphasis on moderating factors. According to Fiedler, moods are likely to influence evaluations only when processing of the target information involves some cognitive construction. Moods will not influence evaluations when processing of the target information is merely reproductive (e.g., cued recall). Similarly, Forgas (1995) has suggested that moods will not infuse into judgments when individuals have a specific processing objective or when they access a previously stored judgment. There is nothing in the mood-as-input model that qualifies either of these sets of assumptions. In fact, the work of Fiedler and of Forgas points to conditions under which predictions from the mood-as-input model are not likely to hold. After all, there can be no mood-as-input effects if people do not use their moods as input.

What the mood-as-input model contributes to the views of Fiedler and Forgas, on the other hand, is the configural nature of mood. Note that both Fiedler and Forgas assume inherent relations between specific moods and specific effects. When mood infuses into a judgment, the effect is mood-congruent evaluation, and the only way to keep a mood-congruent evaluation from happening is to keep people from incorporating their moods into their judgments. In the mood-as-input view, on the other hand, mood-incongruent evaluations can occur even when people incorporate their moods into their judgments.

According to Zajonc, emotional reactions can be engendered with little to no involvement of cognitive processes. The mood-as-input model depicts mood effects as involving a consideration of (1) one's own feelings, (2) some target features, (3) various criteria, and (4) the relations among these. Oddly enough, these two views are not nearly as incompatible as they may at first seem. As noted earlier, the configural processing assumed in the mood-as-input model is not the conscious, linear, rational, effortful, time-consuming kind of processing to which Zajonc refers when he uses the word "cognitive." There is evidence of configural responding across the phylogenetic spectrum, and this responding seems to involve subcortical structures. So, both the Zajonc model and the mood-as-information model agree that affect is generated and/or processed in large part by unconscious, evolutionarily basic structures. The models differ, however, in the capabilities they assign to these structures. According to Zajonc, initial affective processing involves no more than very crude approach-avoidance tendencies. According to the mood-as-input model, such processing is more adaptive as it takes into consideration information such as the status of the organism, features of a potential predator, and features of the context (cf. Delgado, 1983; Hertz et al., 1982). The latter view is clearly more adaptive from an evolutionary standpoint, and it also provides a better fit with the observations of configural responding across the phylogenetic spectrum.

Summary and Conclusions

In sum, the bulk of the evidence suggests that humans have the ability to process information, including moods, configurally, and that simple hedonistic and associationistic assumptions fail to capture the full richness of the human information processing system. A strong argument can be made, therefore, that it is time to move beyond simple hedonistic and associationistic assumptions to theoretical models that do not underestimate the sophistication of the human organism.

References

Asch, S. E. (1946). Forming impressions of personality. *Journal of Abnormal and Social Psychology, 67*, 258–290.

Bem, D. (1965). An experimental analysis of self-persuasion. *Journal of Experimental Social Psychology, 1*, 199–218.

Berkowitz, L. (1993). Towards a general theory of anger and emotional aggression: Implications of the cognitive-neoassociationistic perspective for the analysis of anger and other emotions. In R. S. Wyer, Jr., & T. K. Srull (Eds.), *Advances in social cognition* (Vol. 6, pp. 1–46). Hillsdale, NJ: Erlbaum.

Birnbaum, M. H., Coffey, G., Millers, B. A., & Weiss, R. (1992). Utility measurement: Configural-weight theory and the judge's point of view. *Journal of Experimental Psychology: Human Perception and Performance, 18*, 331–346.

Birnbaum, M. H., Thompson, L. A., & Bean, D. J. (1997). Testing interval independence versus configural weighting using judgments of strength of preference. *Journal of Experimental Psychology: Human Perception and Performance, 23*, 939–947.

Bless, H., Bohner, G., Schwarz, N., & Strack, F. (1990). Mood and persuasion: A cognitive response analysis. *Personality and Social Psychology, 16*, 331–345.

Capaldi, E. J. (1985). Anticipation and remote associations: A configural approach. *Journal of Experimental Psychology: Learning, Memory, and Cognition, 11*, 444–449.

Carver, C. S., & Scheier, M. F. (1990). Origins and functions of positive and negative affect: A control-process view. *Psychological Review, 97*, 19–35.

Cervone, D., Kopp, D. A., Schaumann, L., & Scott, W. D. (1994). Mood, self-efficacy, and performance standards: Lower moods induce higher standards for performance. *Journal of Personality and Social Psychology, 67*, 499–512.

Chaiken, S., Liberman, A., & Eagley, A. H. (1989). Heuristic and systematic processing within and beyond the persuasion context. In J. S. Uleman & J. A. Bargh (Eds.), *Unintended thought* (pp. 212–252). New York: Guilford Press.

Delgado, J. M. R. (1983). Dominance, hierarchy, and brain stimulation. *The Behavioral and Brain Sciences, 2,* 334–335.

Dosher, B. A., & Rosedale, G. S. (1997). Configural processing in memory retrieval: Multiple cues and ensemble representations. *Cognitive Psychology, 33,* 209–265.

Forgas, J. P. (1995). Mood and judgment: The Affect Infusion Model. (AIM). *Psychological Bulletin, 117,* 39–66.

Gaffan, D., & Harrison, S. (1993). Role of the dorsal prestriate cortex in visuospatial configural discrimination by monkeys. *Behavioural Brain Research, 56,* 119–125.

Green, J. D., Sedikides, C., & Martin, L. L. (1997). Unpublished data. University of North Carolina at Chapel Hill.

Hertz, P. E., Huey, R. B., & Nevo, E. (1982). Fight versus flight: Body temperature influences defensive responses of lizards. *Animal Behavior, 30,* 676–679.

Higgins, E. T., & Rholes, W. S. (1976). Impression formation and role fulfillment: A "holistic reference" approach. *Journal of Experimental Social Psychology, 12,* 422–435.

Hirt, E. R., Melton, R. J., McDonald, H. E., & Harackiewicz, J. M. (1996). Processing goals, task interest, and the mood-performance relationship: A mediational analysis. *Journal of Personality and Social Psychology, 71,* 245–261.

Hsee, C. K., & Abelson, R. P. (1991). Velocity relation: Satisfaction as a function of the first derivative of outcome over time. *Journal of Personality and Social Psychology, 60,* 341–347.

Ingle, D. (1983). Brain mechanisms of visual localization by frogs and toads. In J. P. Ewert, R. R. Capranica, & D. J. Ingle (Eds.), *Advances in vertebrates neuroethology* (pp. 177–226). New York: Plenum.

Isen, A. M. (1993). Positive affect and decision making. In M. Lewis & J. Haviland (Eds.), *Handbook of emotions* (pp. 261–277). New York: Guilford Press.

Isen, A. M., Shalker, T. E., Clark, M. S., & Karp, L. (1978). Affect, accessibility of material in memory, and behavior: A cognitive loop? *Journal of Personality and Social Psychology, 36,* 1–12.

Jacewicz, M. M. (1979). Word context effects on letter recognition. *Perceptual and Motor Skills, 48,* 935–942.

Joseph, B. R., Singer, J. A., & Salovey, P. (1996). Mood regulation and memory: Repairing sad moods with happy memories. *Cognition and Emotion, 10,* 437–444.

Kimchi, R. (1994). The role of holistic/configural properties versus global properties in visual form perception. *Perception, 23,* 489–504.

LeDoux, J. E. (1994). Emotion, memory, and the brain. *Scientific American, 270,* 50–57.

Mackie, D. M., & Worth, L. T. (1989). Processing deficits and the mediation of positive affect in persuasion. *Journal of Personality and Social Psychology*, *57*, 1–14.

Martin, L. L., Abend, T., Sedikides, C., & Green, J. D. (1997). How would it feel if . . . ? Mood as input to a role fulfillment evaluation process. *Journal of Personality and Social Psychology, 73*, 242–253.

Martin, L. L., Achee, J. W., Ward, D. W., & Harlow, T. F. (1993). The role of cognition and effort in the use of emotions to guide behavior. In R. S. Wyer & T. K. Srull (Eds.), *Advances in social cognition* (Vol. 6, pp. 147–157). Hillsdale, NJ: Erlbaum.

Martin, L. L., & Crepaz, N. (1998). Unpublished data. University of Georgia.

Martin, L. L., & Davies, B. (1998). Beyond hedonism and associationism: A mood as input look at the role of mood in evaluation, processing, and self-regulation. *Motivation and Emotions, 11*, 33–51.

Martin, L. L., & Stoner, P. (1996). Mood as input: What people think about how they feel determines how they think. In L. L. Martin & A. Tesser (Eds.), *Striving and feeling: Interactions between goals, affect, and self-regulation* (pp. 279–301). Hillsdale, NJ: Erlbaum.

Martin, L. L., Ward, D. W., Achee, J. W., & Wyer, R. S. (1993). Mood as input: People have to interpret the motivational implications of their moods. *Journal of Personality and Social Psychology, 64*, 317–326.

Mayer, J. D., Gaschke, Y. N., Braverman, D. L., & Evans, T. (1992). Mood-congruent judgment is a general effect. *Journal of Personality and Social Psychology, 63*, 119–132.

Pearce, J. M., & Wilson, P. N. (1990). Configural associations in discrimination learning. *Journal of Experimental Psychology: Animal Behavior Processes, 16*, 250–261.

Prete, F. R. (1990). Configural prey recognition by the praying mantis, *Sphodromantis lineola* (Burr.): Effects of size and direction of movement. *Brain, Behavior, and Evolution, 36*, 300–306.

Rilling, S. H., Mittelstaedt, K. D., & Roeder, K. D. (1959). Prey recognition in the praying mantis. *Behaviour, 14*, 164–184.

Ross, M., Eyman, A., & Kishchuk, N. (1986). Determinants of subjective well-being. In J. M. Olson, C. P. Herman, & M. Zanna (Eds.), *Relative deprivation and social comparison* (pp. 79–93). Hillsdale, NJ: Erlbaum.

Roth, G. (1987). *Visual behaviour in salamanders*. New York: Springer.

Rudy, J. W., & Sutherland, R. J. (1995). Configural association theory and the hippocampal formation: An appraisal and reconfiguration. *Hippocampus, 5*, 375–389.

Sanna, C. J., Turley, K. J., & Mark, M. M. (1996). Expected evaluation, goals, and performance: Mood as input. *Personality and Social Psychology Bulletin, 22*, 323–335.

Sansone, C., & Harackiewicz, H. M. (1996). "I don't feel like it": The function of interest in self-regulation. In L. L. Martin & A. Tesser (Eds)., *Striving and feeling: Interactions among goals, affect, and self-regulation* (pp. 203–228). Mahwah, NJ: Erlbaum.

Schwarz, N., & Bless, H. (1991). Happy and mindless, but sad and smart? The impact of affective states on analytic reasoning. In J. Forgas (Ed.), *Emotion and social judgments* (pp. 55–71). London: Pergamon Press.

Schwarz, N., & Clore, G. L. (1983). Mood, misattribution, and judgements of well-being: Informative and directive functions of affective states. *Journal of Personality and Social Psychology, 45,* 513–523.

Schwarz, N., & Clore, G. L. (1988). How do I feel about it? The information function of affective states. In K. Fiedler & J. Forgas (Eds.), *Affect, cognition and social behavior* (pp. 44–62). Lewinston, NY: C. J. Hogrefe.

Schwarz, S., & Strack, F. (1991). Evaluating one's life: A judgment model of subjective well-being. In F. Strack, M. Argyle, & N. Schwarz (Eds.), *Subjective well-being* (pp. 27–47). London: Pergamon Press.

Sedikides, C. (1992). Changes in the valence of the self as a function of mood. In M. S. Clark (Ed.), *Review of personality and social psychology* (Vol. 14, pp. 271–311). Newbury Park, CA: Sage Publications.

Seidenberg, M. S. (1993). Connectionist models and cognitive theory. *Psychological Science, 4,* 228–235.

Sergent, J. (1984). An investigation into component and configural processes underlying face perception. *British Journal of Psychology, 75,* 221–242.

Sinclair, R. C. (1988). Mood, categorization breadth, and performance appraisal: The effects of order of information acquistion and affective state on halo, accuracy, information retrieval, and evaluations. *Organizational Behavior and Human Decision Processes, 42,* 22–46.

Sinclair, R. C., & Mark, M. M. (1995). The effects of mood state on judgmental accuracy: Processing strategy as a mechanism. *Cognition and Emotion, 9,* 417–438.

Smith, S. M., & Shaffer, D. R. (1991). The effects of good moods on systematic processing: "Willing but not able, or able but not willing?" *Motivation and Emotion, 15,* 243–279.

Wertheimer, M. (1923). Untersuchungen zur Lehre von der Gestalt, II. *Psychologische Forschung, 4,* 301–350.

Whishaw, I. Q., & Tomie, J. (1991). Acquisition and retention by hippocampal rats of simple, conditional, and configural tasks using tactile and olfactory cues: Implications for hippocampal function. *Behavioral Neuroscience, 105,* 787–797.

Williams, D. A., Sagness, K. E., & McPhee, J. E. (1994). Configural and elemental strategies in predictive learning. *Journal of Experimental Psychology: Learning, Memory, & Cognition, 20,* 694–709.

Wyer, R. S. (1970). The prediction of evaluations of social role occupants as a function of the favorableness, relevance and probability associated with attributes of these occupants. *Sociometry, 33,* 79–96.

8. Miswanting

Some Problems in the Forecasting of Future Affective States

DANIEL T. GILBERT AND TIMOTHY D. WILSON

> "It would not be better if things happened to men just as they want."
>
> Heraclitus, *Fragments* (500 B.C.)

Introduction

Like and *want* are among the first things children learn to say, and once they learn to say them, they never stop. Liking has to do with how a thing makes us feel, and wanting is, simply enough, a prediction of liking. When we say, "I like this doughnut," we are letting others know that the doughnut currently under consumption is making us feel a bit better than before. When we say, "I want a doughnut," we are making an abbreviated statement whose extended translation is something like, "Right now I'm not feeling quite as good as I might be, and I think fried dough will fix that." Statements about wanting tend to be statements about those things that we believe will influence our sense of well-being, satisfaction, happiness, and contentment. Hence, when we say we want something, we are more or less promising that we will like it when we get it.

But promises are easier to make than to keep, and sometimes we get what we say we want and feel entirely unhappy about it. We order a cheeseburger only to find that it looks and smells precisely as

The writing of this chapter was supported by research grant RO1-MH56075 from the National Institute of Mental Health to Daniel T. Gilbert and Timothy D. Wilson. We thank Joe Forgas for his insightful comments on an earlier version of this chapter, and the other authors in this volume for helpful discussions of these issues.

Correspondence concerning this work should be addressed to Daniel T. Gilbert, Department of Psychology, Harvard University, William James Hall, Cambridge, MA 02138. E-mail: dtg@wjh.harvard.edu.

cheeseburgers always look and smell, and despite that fact, we have absolutely no interest in eating it. We are perplexed and embarrassed by such mistakes and can only offer cunning explanations such as, "I guess I didn't really want a cheeseburger after all." Dining companions often consider such accounts inadequate. "If you didn't *want* the damned thing, then why did you *get* it?" they may ask, at which point we are usually forced to admit the truth, which is that we just do not know. We only know that it looks exactly like what we said we wanted, we are not going to eat it, and the waiter is not amused.

Although we tend to think of unhappiness as something that happens to us when we do not get what we want, much unhappiness is actually of the cheeseburger variety and has less to do with not getting what we want, and more to do with not wanting what we like. When wanting and liking are uncoordinated in this way we may say that a person has *miswanted*. The word sounds odd at first, but if wanting is indeed a prediction of liking, then it, like any prediction, can be wrong. When the things we want to happen do not improve our happiness, and when the things we want not to happen do, it seems fair to say that we have wanted badly. Why should this happen to people as clever and handsome as us?

The Fundamentals of Miswanting

In a perfect world, wanting would cause trying, trying would cause getting, getting would cause liking, and this chapter would be missing all the words. Ours is apparently not such a place. How is it possible to get what we want and yet not like what we get? At least three problems bedevil our attempts to want well.

Imagining the Wrong Event

The fundamental problem, of course, is that the events we imagine when we are in the midst of a really good want are not precisely the events we experience when we are at the tail end of a really disappointing get. For instance, most of us are skeptical when we hear movie stars describe how relentless adoration can be a source of suffering, or when terminally ill patients insist that a dreaded disease has given their lives deeper meaning. We feel certain that we would be delighted in the first instance and devastated in the second because most of us have no idea what stardom or terminal illness actually entail. When we think of "adoring fans," we tend to envision a cheering throng of admirers calling us back for an encore performance rather than a slightly demented autograph hound peeping through our bedroom window at midnight. When we think of "terminal illness," we tend to envision ourselves wasting away in a hospital bed, connected to machines by plugs and tubes, rather than planting flowers in the hospice garden, surrounded by those we love. Terminal illness is not an event, but a class of events, and each member of the class unfolds in a different way. How much we like an event depends mightily on the details of its unfolding. When the imagined cheeseburger (a half-pound of prime aged beef) is not the experienced cheeseburger (three ounces of rubbery soy), it seems inevitable that our wanting and our liking will be poorly matched.

Given how varied a class of events can be, we might expect people prudently to refrain from directing their wants toward classes ("I don't know if I want a cheeseburger") and direct them instead toward particular, well-understood members of the class ("However, I know I don't want *that* cheeseburger"). Research suggests that people are not always so prudent, and that when asked to make predictions about future events, they tend to imagine a particular event while making little provision for the possibility that the particular event they are imagining may not necessarily be the particular event they will be experiencing (Dunning, Griffin, Milojkovic, & Ross, 1990; Griffin, Dunning, & Ross, 1990; Griffin & Ross, 1991; Lord, Lepper, & Mackie, 1984; Robinson, Keltner, Ward, & Ross, 1995). When our spouse asks us to attend "a party" on Friday night, we instantly imagine a particular kind of party (e.g., a cocktail party in the penthouse of a downtown hotel with waiters in black ties carrying silver trays of hors d'oeuvres past a slightly bored harpist) and then estimate our reaction to that imagined event (e.g., yawn). We generally fail to consider how many different members constitute the class (e.g., birthday parties, orgies, wakes) and how different our reactions would be to each. So we tell our spouse that we would rather skip the party, our spouse naturally drags us along anyhow, and we have a truly marvelous time. Why? Because the party involves cheap beer and hula hoops rather than classical music and seaweed crackers. It is precisely our style, and we like what we previously did not want because the event we experienced (and liked) was not the event we imagined (and wanted to avoid).

Using the Wrong Theory

If imagining the wrong event were the sole cause of miswanting, then we would only miswant objects and experiences when the details of their unfolding were unknown to us. The fact is, people often want – and then fail to like – objects and experiences whose details they know quite well. Even when we know precisely the kind of party our spouse is hauling us to, or precisely the kind of cheeseburger this particular restaurant serves, we may still be surprised to find that we enjoy it a great deal more or less than we had anticipated. For example, Read and Loewenstein (1995) asked subjects to plan a menu by deciding which of several snacks they would eat when they returned to the laboratory on each of three consecutive Mondays (cf. Simonson 1990). Subjects tended to order a mixed plate that included instances of their favorite snack ("I'll have a Snickers bar on the first two Mondays"), as well as instances of their next favorite ("And tortilla chips on the third Monday"). Alas, when it actually came time to eat the snacks, subjects were not so pleased on the day when they arrived at the laboratory only to find themselves faced with a snack that was . . . well, not their favorite. Their disappointment was perfectly under-standable. We *should* be disappointed when we do not get what we like most, and the only thing that seems hard to understand is why subjects wanted something that they knew perfectly well they did not like perfectly well?

Apparently, subjects in this study believed that variety is the spice of life – and in this case, they were wrong (cf. Kahneman & Snell, 1992). A Snickers with every meal is indeed a dull prospect for any-one, but a Snickers once a week is just about right. As such, Snickers-lovers are made *less* happy – and not *more* happy – when their weekly Snickers is replaced by a less desirable treat. Because subjects in this study had erroneous theories about their own need for variety over time, they miswanted tortilla chips when they planned their menu. The moral of this ripping yarn about snack foods is that even when people have a perfect idea of what an event will entail (i.e., tortilla chips are deep-fried corn pancakes covered with salt – period), they may still have imperfect ideas about themselves and thus may make imperfect predictions about how they will react to the event. People who can imagine sun, surf, sand, and daiquiris in exquisite detail may still be surprised when their desert island vacation turns out to be a bust – not because they imagined *this* island and ended up on *that* one, but simply because they did not realize how much they require daily structure, intellectual stimulation, or regular infusions of Pop Tarts. Highbrows fall asleep at the ballet, pacifists find themselves strangely excited by a glimpse of world class wrestling, and tough guys in leather jackets are occasionally caught making clucking sounds by the duck pond. To the extent that we have incorrect theories about who we are, we may also have incorrect beliefs about what we will like.

Misinterpreting Feelings

If we could imagine events exactly as they were actually to unfold, and if we had complete and accurate knowledge of our relevant tastes and attitudes, could we necessarily avoid miswanting? Unfortunately not. When we imagine a future event, we normally have an affective reaction to its mental representation (imagining one's spouse happily entwined with the mail carrier usually illustrates this fact convincingly), and we naturally take this affective reaction to the mental representation of the event as a proxy for the affective reaction we might have to the event itself. If the mere thought of a mate's infidelity makes us feel slightly nauseous, then we have every reason to suppose that the real thing would end in an upchuck. Our affective reactions to imaginary events are, in a sense, experiential previews of our affective reactions to the events themselves, and they figure prominently in our predictions of future liking. Few of us need to consult a cookbook to know that we should avoid any event involving liver and maple syrup. That funny feeling right *here* is information enough (see Forgas, 1995; Schwarz & Clore, 1983; Schwarz, 1990).

Wantings, then, are based on three ingredients: the particular details that we imagine when we consider a future event, our beliefs about the ways in which people like us are likely to react to such events, and the "gut reactions" we experience when we imagine the event. Just as the first two of these ingredients can lead us to miswant, so too can the third. How so? The crux of the problem is that the feelings we experience when we imagine a future event are not necessarily or solely caused by that act of imagination. We may feel enormously excited when we contemplate spending next Sunday at the circus, and thus we may drop buckets of money on ringside tickets without realizing that the good news we received about our aging uncle's miraculous recovery from psoriasis just moments before we purchased our ticket has contaminated our affective reaction to the thought of dancing elephants (Wilson & Brekke, 1994). Come Sunday, we may find ourselves bored to tears beneath the big top, wondering why we paid good money to see a herd of clowns in a little car. Our miswanting in this case would not have been a result of having imagined the wrong event ("Oh, I was thinking of a flea circus") nor of having had a false conception of ourselves ("Why did I think I liked men in floppy shoes?"). Rather, we would have miswanted because when we initially thought about the circus we felt excited, and we took that fact as information about the circus rather than as information about Uncle Frank's remission. Feelings do not say where they came from, and thus it is all too easy for us to attribute them to the wrong source.

Experimental demonstrations of this home truth abound. People may mistakenly believe that their lives are empty when, in fact, their gloomy mood is a consequence of rain (Schwarz & Clore, 1983); they may mistakenly believe that a person is attractive when, in fact, their pounding pulse is being caused by the swaying of a suspension bridge (Dutton & Aron, 1974); and so on. Because we cannot always tell if the feelings we are having as we imagine an event are being caused solely by that imagining, we may use these feelings as proxies for future liking, and hence, miswant.

Thinking and Feeling

We ordinarily experience both thoughts and feelings when we imagine a future event, and these influence our wantings to different extents, under different circumstances, and with different results. Sometimes, our affective reactions to an imagined event provide an excellent basis for wanting, but our cognitive reactions muck things up. This seems to be what happened when Wilson et al. (1993) offered college students a reproduction of an impressionist painting or a poster of a cat with a humorous caption. Before making their choices, some students were asked to think about why they liked or disliked each poster ("deep thinkers") and others were not ("shallow thinkers"). When the experimenters phoned the students later and asked how much they liked their new *objet d'art*, the deep thinkers were the least satisfied. Presumably, the shallow thinkers used their current affective reaction as the basis for their decision and ended up liking the posters they had chosen. Deep thinkers, on the other hand, had some badly mistaken theories about their own aesthetic preferences ("Now that I think about it, the olive green in the Monet is rather drab, whereas the cat poster is bright and cheery"), and when they allowed these cognitive reactions to overrule their affective reactions, they inevitably miswanted.

At other times, however, our cognitive reactions can provide an excellent basis for our wantings, and our affective reactions may lead us astray. For example, Gilbert, Gill, and Wilson (1998) asked shoppers at a grocery store to write down all the items they had come to buy, and allowed some shoppers to retain that list. Next, they asked some shoppers to eat a quarter pound of blueberry muffins before entering the store. As shoppers exited the store, the experimenters examined their cash register receipts. When shoppers were deprived of their shopping lists, those who had eaten blueberry muffins bought fewer unwanted items than did those who had not eaten any muffins. Presumably, when these listless shoppers encountered items in the store, they had more positive affective reactions to the items when they were unfed ("The marshmallow cookies look so delicious!") than they did when they were well-fed ("I never want to eat again") and thus were more inclined to buy items that they had not intended to buy. Shoppers who had their lists in hand, however, were unaffected by the blueberry muffins, and bought no more unwanted items when they were unfed than when they were well-fed. These listful shoppers surely had the same affective reactions as did their listless counterparts, but because they had in hand a copy of *A Theory About What I Will Want in the Future* (aka a grocery list), they were able to avoid basing their choices on their affective reactions and thus they were able to avoid miswanting.

It seems, then, that feelings sometimes serve us better than theories, and theories sometimes serve us better than feelings. Alas, sometimes neither serves us well at all. Gilbert et al. (1998) asked college students to predict how much they would enjoy eating a bite of spaghetti the next morning or the next evening. Some of the students were hungry when they made these predictions, others were not. Some students were allowed to think deeply about their predictions, and others were distracted while they made their predictions. When the students were distracted, they relied on their gut feelings to make their predictions, and thus the hungriest students naturally predicted that they would like spaghetti more the next day than did the less hungry students.

Notably, the time of day at which the spaghetti was to be eaten made no difference to them at all. When students were allowed to think deeply, however, they relied on their theories to make their predictions, and thus they predicted that they would enjoy spaghetti (which is generally considered a more appropriate dinner than breakfast) more the next evening than they would the next morning. Notably, the students' current hunger made no difference to them at all. Finally, when students were actually brought to the laboratory in the morning or evening and given a bite of spaghetti, neither the extent of their hunger the day before nor the time of day at which the spaghetti was eaten had a measurable influence on their enjoyment of the food. In other words, students relied on their cognitive reactions when they could, their affective reactions otherwise, and in this instance, neither of these reactions to the imagined event enabled them to want correctly.

Miswanting Over Time

What do spaghetti, cheeseburgers, marshmallow cookies, tortilla chips, and Snickers bars have in common? They are objects that can be wanted today and liked tomorrow, but once that liking occurs, they quickly become a trivial bit of personal history that only our thighs remember. Each of these objects can be experienced, but none of these experiences has enduring emotional consequences, and thus none provides an opportunity for us to think about how people might want or miswant in the long run. When we want a bite of pecan pie or a warm shower or a sexy kiss, it is not because we think these things will change us in some significant way, but because we think they will be perfectly lovely for as long as they last. On the other hand, when we want a promotion or a wedding or a college degree, it is not so much because we believe these things will improve our lives at the moment we attain them, but because we think they will provide emotional rewards that will persist long enough to repay the effort we spent in their pursuit. Significant events are supposed to have significant emotional consequences, and the duration of these consequences matters a lot.

If it is difficult to know whether we will be happy 15 minutes after eating a bite of spaghetti, it is all the more difficult to know whether we will be happy 15 months after a divorce or 15 years after a marriage. Gilbert, Pinel, Wilson, Blumberg, and Wheatley (1998) have suggested that people tend to overestimate the duration of their emotional reactions to future events – especially negative events – and that this can lead them to miswant in the long term. For example, Gilbert et al. (1998) asked assistant professors to predict how happy they would be in general a few years after achieving or failing to achieve tenure at their current university, and they also measured the general happiness of those former assistant professors who had or had not achieved tenure at the same institution. Although assistant professors believed that the tenure decision would dramatically influence their general happiness for many years to come (and hence desperately wanted tenure), the former assistant professors who had not achieved tenure were no less happy than the former assistant professors who had. Similarly, Gilbert et al. (1998) asked voters in a gubernatorial election to predict how happy they would generally be a month after an election. Voters believed that they would be significantly happier a month after the election if their candidate won than if their candidate lost. As it turned out, a month after the election, the losers and winners were just as happy as they had been before the election (see Brickman, Coates, & Janoff-Bulman, 1978; Taylor, 1983; 1996; Wortman & Silver, 1989).

Do not misunderstand: Those assistant professors who were promoted and those voters whose candidate triumphed were surely happier about the event, and were surely happier for some time after the event, than were those who lost their jobs or who backed the incumbent governor, who lost hers. But after just a little while – a much littler while than the assistant professors and voters had themselves predicted – the emotional traces of these events had evaporated (see Suh, Diener, & Fujita, 1996). What might cause people to overestimate the enduring emotional impact of such events?

Focalism: The Invisible Future

When asked how we might feel a year after losing our left hand, we tend to imagine the immediate emotional impact of this calamity ("No more clapping, no more shoe tying – I'd be sad"). What we do *not* do is go on to calculate the impact of the dental appointments, foreign films, job promotions, freak snowstorms, and Snickers bars that will inevitably fill the year that follows our unhanding. Rather, we naturally focus on the event whose emotional impact we are trying to gauge and then make some provision for the passage of time ("I guess a year later I'd be a little less sad"). But how we will feel in general a year after losing a hand, and how we will feel *about* losing a hand a year after the loss, are not the same thing. Predicting the latter may be relatively simple, but predicting the former requires that we estimate the combined impact of the focal event and all the nonfocal events that follow it. Put another way, our general happiness some time after an event is influenced by just two things: (a) the event, and (b) everything else. If we estimate that happiness by considering only the event, then we are ignoring some of the most powerful determinants of our future well-being (see Loewenstein & Schkade, in press; Schkade & Kahneman, 1997).

Wilson, Wheatley, Meyers, Gilbert, and Axsom (1998) demonstrated how focalism (the failure to consider the consequences of nonfocal events when making predictions about the ultimate affective impact of focal events) can give rise to the durability bias and hence promote miswanting. College students were asked to predict their happiness the day after their football team won or lost an important game. Some students were also asked to complete a "future diary" in which they listed the events that they thought would occur in the 3 days after the game. Those students who completed the diary, and who were thus most likely to consider the impact of future nonfocal events when making their predictions, made less extreme predictions about their general happiness – predictions that turned out to be more accurate when their overall happiness was measured the day after the game.

It seems that merely considering the emotional impact of an event can lead us to overestimate that impact, simply because we do not also consider other impactful events as well. Focalism is an especially vexing problem because avoiding it seems to require that we do the impossible, namely, consider the impact of *every* event before estimating the impact of *any* event. If we think of happiness as a general state that is determined by innumerable events, it does indeed seem likely that no single event will have the power to influence our general happiness for very long. Indeed, those events that seem to make a big difference (e.g., moving to a new country) tend to be those that give rise to many other events, which suggests that the ramifications of an event – that is, the sheer number of experiences it alters – may be the best predictor of its ultimate emotional impact. Although few parents would believe it, the death of a spouse may have more impact than the death of a child, simply because the former produces more changes in one's life than does the latter (see Lehman et al., 1993). In any case, it seems quite clear that focusing on an event can cause us to overestimate the duration of its influence on our happiness, and, hence, to miswant.

Immune Neglect: The Invisible Shield

Many shrewd observers of the human condition have remarked on people's extraordinary ability to change the way they feel simply by changing the way they think. When circumstances threaten our psychological well-being, we execute an assortment of cognitive strategies, tactics, and maneuvers that are designed to prevent, limit, or repair the damage (e.g., Festinger, 1957; Freud, 1937; Steele, 1988; Taylor & Brown, 1988; Vaillant, 1993; Westen, 1994). These maneuvers usually have two properties. First, they work like a charm, enabling all of us to be well above average in all the ways that count. Second and more important, we tend not to know we are executing them, and what looks like rationalization to the giggling onlooker feels very much like rational reasoning to us. Taken together, the mechanisms that protect the sources of our psychological well-being (e.g., our sense of competence, integrity, and worth) in the face of assault constitute a psychological immune system that seems to be both powerful and invisible to the person it serves.

If our happiness is, in fact, defended by an invisible shield, then it is easy to see why we overestimate our vulnerability to the slings and arrows of outrageous fortune. Recall that voters in the Gilbert et al. (1988) study overestimated the duration of their emotional reactions to their candidate's electoral triumph or defeat. Interestingly, voters in that study were also asked to predict how their opinions of the candidates would change once one was elected, and their answers may tell us something about why they overestimated the durability of their emotions. Although voters flatly denied that the outcome of the election would change their opinions of the candidates by even a hair, a month after the election, those voters whose candidate had lost had experienced an unforeseen transformation: Although the new governor had yet to take office, had yet to perform an official act, and had yet to make a substantive speech, those who had voted against him had a significantly higher opinion of him than they had had a month earlier. It seems that those voters overestimated the duration of their disappointment because they did not realize that once they were stuck with a governor whom they had not wanted, their psychological immune systems would help them locate 16 new reasons to like him anyway.

Gilbert et al. (1998) provided direct experimental evidence of immune neglect: the tendency for people to fail to consider how readily their psychological immune systems will vitiate their despair. Students were given the opportunity to apply for an exciting and lucrative position as an ice-cream taster in a model business. The application process included answering several questions before a video camera while judges watched from another room. The situation was arranged such that if students were rejected, their psychological immune systems would have much more work to do in one condition than the other. Specifically, students in the "difficult rationalization" condition were shown a number of highly relevant questions and were told that while answering these questions they would be observed by a panel of judges, who would then vote on the student's appropriateness for the job. Unless the judges unanimously disapproved of the student, he or she would be offered the job. In the "easy rationalization" condition, students were shown a number of largely irrelevant questions and were told that while answering these questions they would be observed by a single judge who would solely determine whether or not they were offered the job. Students in each condition predicted how they would feel if they were rejected, and how they would feel 10 minutes later. All participants then answered the relevant or irrelevant questions before the video camera and were promptly rejected. Their happiness was measured immediately following the rejection and then again 10 minutes later.

As the top part of Figure 8.1 shows, the students believed they would be much less happy immediately following rejection than they actually turned out to be. But as the bottom part of Figure 8.1 shows, the more interesting effect occurred 10 minutes later. Not only were all the students happier than they expected to be 10 minutes after being rejected, but they were happier when they had been rejected by a solo judge who had heard them answer irrelevant questions than when they had been rejected by a panel of judges who had heard them answer irrelevant questions. This difference reveals the work of the psychological immune system, which should have found it easier to heal the wounds of rejection in the easy rationalization condition ("One guy doesn't think I'm competent. So what? Maybe I look like his ex-roommate, or maybe he's biased against Southerners, or maybe

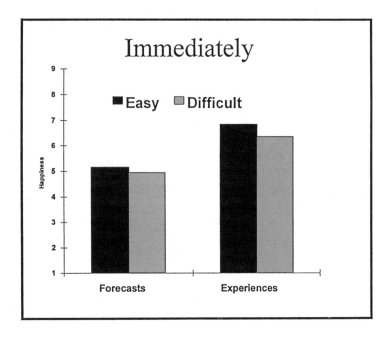

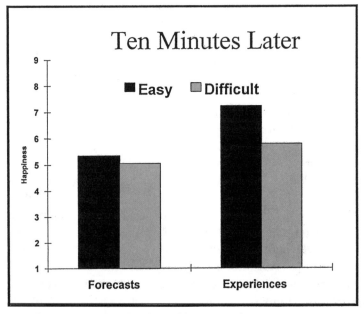

Figure 8.1. Predicted and actual happiness after rejection.

he just didn't have enough information to go on") than in the difficult rationalization condition ("An entire group of judges agreed on the basis of adequate information that I'm not smart enough to taste ice cream? Yikes!"). The important point is that the students did not *anticipate* this difference, which suggests that when they looked into their emotional futures, they saw only the pain of rejection. What they did not consider was the ease or difficulty with which their psychological immune systems would dispatch their malaise.

Immune neglect can have important interpersonal consequences too. For example, few of us would expect to come undone if an irritated motorist shouted a few choice words about our parentage as we crossed against the light, but we might well expect to be shocked and dismayed if a good friend did the same. We expect an insulting remark from a stranger to be less painful than an insulting remark from a friend, and thus we might naturally expect the former to have less enduring emotional consequences than the latter. Gilbert and Lieberman (1998) asked pairs of college students to evaluate each other's personalities on the basis of brief autobiographies in which they had explicitly been asked to describe some embarrassing incidents. Some students were told that they would work together as a team later in the experiment ("partners") and others were told that they would never meet ("strangers"). The students were asked to predict how they would feel a few minutes after finding out that the other student had read their autobiography and given them a very negative evaluation, and indeed, they predicted that they would feel worse if the negative evaluation came from their partner than from a stranger. In fact, the students were considerably *happier* after receiving a negative evaluation from their partner than a from a stranger, and they even forgave their partners more readily than they forgave strangers. Why should this have happened?

Once again, the invisibility of the psychological immune system seems to explain these paradoxical results. Most of us find it rather uncomfortable to interact with people we do not like, and so we are highly motivated to like those with whom we must interact (Darley & Berscheid, 1967). Our psychological immune systems work much harder to help us find ways to forgive our partner's transgressions ("My partner probably didn't realize that the embarrassing incident I wrote about in my autobiography was a unique occurrence, and now that I think of it, I'd probably have made the same negative evaluation myself if I were in the same position") than to forgive the transgressions of strangers. The insulted students' psychological immune systems did what they were designed to do by enabling them to feel happy about working with someone who had evaluated them negatively. What is interesting, of course, is that the students were unable to predict this outcome just 10 minutes before it happened. Like most of us, they blithely predicted that a big pain would last longer than a little one, unaware that big pains often evoke remedies that little pains do not. Broken legs hurt so much that they cry out to be fixed, whereas trick knees are often allowed to go on hurting for a lifetime.

Immune neglect can cause us to miswant by causing us to fear and avoid outcomes that will not, in the long run, hinder our happiness. But one ironic consequence of the failure to anticipate the operation of the psychological immune system is that we may inadvertently do things that impair its operation, thereby undermining our own hidden talent for happiness. For example, if given the opportunity to shop at a store that allows customers to return merchandise for any reason and another store at which all sales are final, most of us would patronize the first rather than the second – and we might even be willing to pay a bit more just so we could have the luxury of changing our minds later on. We firmly believe that bridges ought to be there for crossing and recrossing, and our aversion to burning them is probably wise in many respects. But if keeping one's options open is wise in many respects, it is not wise in all respects, because open options have the unfortunate consequence of paralyzing the psychological immune system. As dissonance theorists have long noted, it is the firm commitment to a single course of action that most effectively triggers attempts to justify it.

Gilbert and Jenkins (1998) gave college students a short course in black-and-white photography. The students took photographs of their favorite people and places on campus and were then taught how to develop their photographs. After students had printed their two favorite photographs, they were asked to donate one of them to the experimenter's "photography project." Some students were told that the donated photograph would be mailed to England that evening, whereas others were told that the photograph would not be mailed for 5 days. Students in this latter condition were told that if they changed their minds about which photograph to keep after they made the donation, they could swap the chosen for the donated photograph anytime before it was mailed. When the students' happiness with their photographs was measured 2 days later, those whose decisions were reversible did not like the chosen photograph as much as did those students whose decisions were irreversible. This makes sense inasmuch as these students were probably still in the process of deciding which photograph they would keep, and thus they did not yet have a final outcome with which their psychological immune systems could help them feel happy. But interestingly, 9 days later, the irreversible deciders were *still* happier with their photographs than were the reversible deciders – despite the fact that the reversible deciders' "swapping opportunity" had expired days ago and their unchosen photograph was irrevocably winging its way across the Atlantic. It seems that merely having had a brief opportunity to change their minds prevented reversible deciders from *ever* exercising their hidden talent for happiness.

All of this work on immune neglect leads to one conclusion: Our tendency to neglect the operation of the immune system when anticipating the future can have unhappy consequences. We often want one thing so much more than another that we willingly incur enormous costs in our attempts to avoid the unwanted event. We may spend little time with our children and neglect our hobbies while putting in long hours at the office because we are convinced that keeping our current job will be better than being forced to find a new one. What we fail to realize is that while the thing we wanted to experience is in some ways better than the thing we wanted to avoid, it is probably worse in others, and should we fail to achieve what we wanted, our psychological immune systems will quickly help us locate the ways in which the thing we got was better than the thing we were aiming for. As the man who narrowly missed the opportunity to franchise the first McDonalds restaurant (and hence narrowly missed the opportunity to become a billionaire) noted many decades later, "I believe it turned out for the best" (Van Gelder, 1997). If we do indeed have a greater talent for happiness than we recognize, then our ignorance of this talent may cause us to pay a steeper price for future experiences than we should.

Conclusions

The naïve psychology of happiness is simple: We want, we try, we get, we like. And then, with the help of television commercials, we want some more. Wants are underwritten by our beliefs about the relation between getting and liking, and in this sense they are prescriptions for action. They tell us what to do with our time by telling us what to aim for and what to avoid, and we allow ourselves to be steered by them because we trust that they are, by and large, correct. Most of us feel certain that if we could experience all the events and only the events we want to experience, happiness would inevitably follow.

The research discussed in this chapter suggests that there are at least two flaws in the naïve analysis of happiness. First, our wants are, like any other prediction, susceptible to error. We may misconstrue events, misunderstand ourselves, misinterpret our feelings – and any of these mistakes can be a cause of miswanting. In short, things do not always feel the way we expect them to feel. Second, even if we could predict how much we would like an event when it happened, we might still be unable to predict how that event would affect us in the long run. One reason is that our general happiness is influenced by a multitude of events. It is impossible to consider all of these influences every time we consider one of them, of course, but unless we do just that, we have little hope of correctly predicting the future states that are their conjoint products. A second reason why we have trouble predicting the enduring emotional consequences of an event is that liking does not *follow* from getting so much as it *accommodates* it. Although our initial emotional reaction to an event is usually based on those properties of the event that caused us to aim for it or avoid it in the first place, once a particular outcome is achieved, we have an uncanny ability to reconstrue it in terms of its most sanguine properties. Because we do not recognize how easily we can reconstrue events in this way, we anticipate more enduring reactions than we often have.

"In the world there are only two tragedies," wrote Oscar Wilde (1893). "One is not getting what one wants, and the other is getting it." We all chuckle and nod knowingly when we hear this clever quip, but not one of us believes it for a moment. Rather, our chuckling and nodding are licensed by a serene certainty that the things we run after will, in fact, bring us far greater happiness than the things we run from. The research discussed in this chapter does not suggest that all ends are emotionally equivalent or that all desires are misdirected. Rather, it merely suggests that if we could know the future, we still might not know how much we would like it when we got there. The psychological mechanisms that keep us from this knowledge are many, and a better understanding of them seems well worth wanting.

References

Brickman, P., Coates, D., & Janoff-Bulman, R. J. (1978). Lottery winners and accident victims: Is happiness relative? *Journal of Personality and Social Psychology, 36*, 917–927.

Darley, J. M., & Berscheid, E. (1967). Increased liking caused by the anticipation of interpersonal contact. *Human Relations, 10*, 29–40.

Dunning, D., Griffin, D. W., Milojkovic, J., & Ross, L. (1990). The overconfidence effect in social prediction. *Journal of Personality and Social Psychology, 58*, 568–581.

Dutton, D. G., & Aron, A. P. (1974). Some evidence for heightened sexual attraction under conditions of high anxiety. *Journal of Personality and Social Psychology, 30*, 510–517.

Festinger, L. (1957). *A theory of cognitive dissonance.* Stanford, CA: Stanford University Press.

Forgas, J. P. (1995). Mood and judgment: The affect infusion model (AIM). *Psychological Bulletin, 117*, 39–66.

Freud, A. (1937). *The ego and the mechanisms of defense.* London: Hogarth Press.

Gilbert, D. T., Gill, M., & Wilson, T. D. (1998). *How do we know what we will like? The informational basis of affective forecasting.* Unpublished manuscript, Harvard University.

Gilbert, D. T., & Jenkins, J. (1998). *Effects of decision reversibility on satisfaction.* Unpublished data, Harvard University.

Gilbert, D. T., & Lieberman, M. (1998). *Factors influencing forgiveness of an interpersonal transgression.* Unpublished data, Harvard University.

Gilbert, D. T., Pinel, E., Wilson, T. D., Blumberg, S., & Wheatley, T. (1998). Immune neglect: A source of durability bias in affective forecasting. *Journal of Personality and Social Psychology, 75*, 617–638.

Griffin, D. W., Dunning, D., & Ross, L. (1990). The role of construal processes in overconfident predictions about the self and others. *Journal of Personality and Social Psychology, 59*, 1128–1139.

Griffin, D. W., & Ross, L. (1991). Subjective construal, social inference, and human misunderstanding. In M. Zanna (Ed.), *Advances in experimental social psychology* (Vol. 24, pp. 319–356). New York: Academic Press.

Kahneman, D., & Snell, J. (1992). Predicting a change in taste: Do people know what they will like? *Journal of Behavioral Decision Making, 5*, 187–200.

Lehman, D. R., Davis, C. G., Delongis, A., Wortman, C. B., Bluck, S., Mandel, D. R., & Ellard, J. H. (1993). Positive and negative life changes following bereavement and their relations to adjustment. *Journal of Social and Clinical Psychology, 12*, 90–112.

Loewenstein, G., & Schkade, D. (in press). Wouldn't it be nice?: Predicting future feelings. In E. Diener, N. Schwartz, & D. Kahneman (Eds.), *Hedonic psychology: Scientific approaches to enjoyment, suffering, and well-being.* New York: Russell Sage Foundation Press.

Lord, C. G., Lepper, M. R., & Mackie, D. (1984). Attitude prototypes as determinants of attitude-behavior consistency. *Journal of Personality and Social Psychology, 46*, 1254–1266.

196   *D. T. Gilbert and T. D. Wilson*

Read, D., & Loewenstein, G. (1995). Diversification bias: Explaining the discrepancy in variety seeking between combined and separated choices. *Journal of Experimental Psychology: Applied, 1,* 34–49.

Robinson, R. J., Keltner, D., Ward, A., & Ross, L. (1995). Actual versus assumed differences in construal: "Naive realism" in intergroup perception and conflict. *Journal of Personality and Social Psychology, 68,* 404–417.

Schwarz, N. (1990). Feelings as information: Informational and motivational functions of affective states. In E. T. H. R. Sorrentino (Ed.), *Handbook of motivation and cognition: Foundations of social behavior* (Vol. 2, pp. 527–561). New York: Guilford Press.

Schwarz, N., & Clore, G. L. (1983). Mood, misattribution, and judgments of well-being: Informative and directive functions of affective states. *Journal of Personality and Social Psychology, 45,* 513–523.

Schkade, D. A., & Kahneman, D. (1997). *Would you be happy if you lived in California? A focusing illusion in judgments of well-being.* Unpublished manuscript, University of Texas, Austin.

Simonson, I. (1990). The effect of purchase quantity and timing on variety seeking behavior. *Journal of Marketing Research, 32,* 150–162.

Steele, C. M. (1988). The psychology of self-affirmation: Sustaining the integrity of self. In L. Berkowitz (Ed.), *Advances in experimental social psychology* (Vol. 21, pp. 261–302). New York: Academic Press.

Suh, E., Diener, E., & Fujita, F. (1996). Events and subjective well-being: Only recent events matter. *Journal of Personality and Social Psychology, 70,* 1091–1102.

Taylor, S. E. (1983). Adjustment to threatening events: A theory of cognitive adaptation. *American Psychologist, 38,* 1161–1173.

Taylor, S. E., & Brown, J. D. (1988). Illusion and well-being: A social-psychological perspective on mental health. *Psychological Bulletin, 103,* 193–210.

Taylor, S. E., & Armor, D. A. (1996). Positive illusions and coping with adversity. *Journal of Personality, 64,* 873–898.

Vaillant, G. (1993). *The wisdom of the ego.* Cambridge: Harvard University Press.

Van Gelder, L. (1996, January 7). Remembering the road not taken. *The New York Times,* p. F7.

Westen, D. (1994). Toward an integrative model of affect regulation: Applications to social psychological research. *Journal of Personality, 62,* 641–667.

Wilde, O. (1893). *Lady Windermere's fan: A play about a good woman.* London: Mathews & Lane.

Wilson, T. D., & Brekke, N. (1994). Mental contamination and mental correction: Unwanted influences on judgments and evaluations. *Psychological Bulletin, 116,* 117–142.

Wilson, T. D., Lisle, D., Schooler, J., Hodges, S. D., Klaaren, K. J., & LaFleur, S. J. (1993). Introspecting about reasons can reduce post-choice satisfaction. *Personality and Social Psychology Bulletin, 19,* 331–339.

Wilson, T. D., Wheatley, T., Meyers, J., Gilbert, D. T., & Axsom, D. (1998).

Focalism: A source of durability bias in affective forecasting. Unpublished manuscript, University of Virginia.

Wortman, C. B., & Silver, R. C. (1989). The myths of coping with loss. *Journal of Consulting and Clinical Psychology, 57,* 349–357.

PART III

Affect and Information Processing

9. The Interplay of Affect and Cognition

The Mediating Role of General Knowledge Structures

HERBERT BLESS

Introduction

Common knowledge suggests that our judgment and behavior in a social situation is affected by how we feel in that situation. Over the past two decades, psychologists have addressed this interplay of affect and cognition from different perspectives, as seen in the contributions to this volume. Following a period of neglect, with the advent of the information processing paradigm (see Tomkins, 1981; Zajonc, 1980), psychologists' interest in emotional processes was revitalized in the early 1980s (for overviews, see Clore, Schwarz, & Conway, 1994; Forgas, 1991; Fiedler & Forgas, 1988; Isen, 1987; Martin & Clore, in press). The accumulating research convincingly demonstrated that subtle changes in our affective states can have a pronounced impact on what and how we think. Affective states can influence encoding, retrieval, and judgment processes, as well as strategies of information processing (for an integrative discussion of the various issues, see Forgas, 1992, this volume). The present chapter focuses on the latter aspect, that is, affective influences on *how* individuals process social information. In general, the studies addressing this issue suggest that affective states have a pronounced impact on our thinking without disrupting or distracting cognitive processes. Indeed, the impact of affective states on cognitive processes is often conceptualized as highly adaptive (e.g., Frijda, 1988).

In the present paper we emphasize the role of affective states in

The reported research was supported by grants Bl 289/5 from the Deutsche Forschungsgemeinschaft to H. Bless, N. Schwarz, and M. Wänke.

Correspondence should be addressed to Herbert Bless, FB I-Psychologie, Universität Trier, D-54286 Trier, Germany.

interpreting and understanding social situations. The interpretation of a social situation requires individuals to relate the specifics of that situation to their preexisting knowledge. The relative impact of these sources of information depends on whether the individual pursues a bottom-up or top-down strategy of information processing (cf. Fiske & Taylor, 1991; Wyer & Srull, 1989). I propose that the choice of these processing strategies depends in part on the individual's affective state. In general, individuals in happy moods are more likely to rely on general knowledge structures, using a top-down strategy, whereas individuals in sad moods are more likely to rely on the specifics of the present situation, using a bottom-up strategy (see also Fiedler, this volume). In the remainder of this chapter I first present a general framework that conceptualizes the proposed relationship between affect and the use of the general knowledge structures, and subsequently report experimental evidence bearing on this proposal. Finally, I compare the present approach to other conceptualizations of the interplay of affect and cognition.

The Mood-and-General-Knowledge-Structure Assumption

The present model builds partly on our previous theorizing on the informative function on affective states (Schwarz, 1990; Schwarz & Bless, 1991). As in this previous work, we assume that affective states inform the individual about the psychological nature of the current situation (for other accounts emphasizing the informative function of affective states see Frijda, 1988; Jacobsen, 1957; Nowlis & Nowlis, 1956; Pribram, 1970). In line with other theorizing (Frijda, 1988) we assume that individuals usually feel good in situations that are characterized by positive outcomes and/or in situations that do not threaten their current goals. In contrast, individuals usually feel bad in situations that threaten their current goals, either because of negative outcomes or the lack of positive outcomes. If different situations result in different affective states, individuals may consult their affect as a usually valid and quick indicator of the nature of the current psychological situation. Positive affective states may inform the individual that the current situation poses no problem, while negative affective states may signal that the current situation is problematic (for a more detailed discussion, see Schwarz, 1990). Note that the informative function in general tends to be independent of whether the affective state originates from a cognitive appraisal of the situation (see Smith & Kirby, this volume) or not (Zajonc, 1980, this volume). The question is, what happens after the individual receives the signal that the current situation is problematic or benign? The present approach holds that it would be highly adaptive for individuals to differentially rely on their general knowledge structures, in the form of scripts, stereotypes, or other heuristics, depending on the nature of the current psychological situation (Bless, 1997, in press). Specifically, individuals in benign situations may rely on their general knowledge structures, which usually serve them well. In problematic situations – which are usually deviations from normal, routine situations – individuals would be poorly advised to rely on the knowledge they usually apply. Instead, they would do better to focus on the specifics of the current situation. Thus, individuals' current affective state may influence the degree to which they rely on their general knowledge structures, mediated by the impact of affective states on the interpretation of the current situation. Specifically, individuals in positive affective states may feel more confident about relying on activated general knowledge structures that are potentially applicable to the situation, whereas individuals in negative affective states may feel less confident in relying on general knowledge structures and may be more likely to focus on the data at hand. This mood-dependent reliance on general knowledge structures versus the data at hand would direct individuals' attention toward the information that is presumably most useful in the current situation.

Note that this approach departs from previous theorizing. Initially we had argued that the key effect of these different signals is motivational: Individuals in a positive mood see no reason to invest major processing effort, unless this is called for by a current goal (Schwarz, 1990; Schwarz & Bless, 1991; Schwarz, Bless, & Bohner, 1991). In contrast, individuals in a negative mood are motivated to pay attention to the specifics of the situation, which is usually adaptive in addressing problems. Hence, they spontaneously engage in systematic processing. Although the present approach shares the general notion of this previous theorizing that affective states inform the individual about the current situation, it does *not* imply that the motivation to engage in more or less processing is mood dependent. The different implications of the mood-and-general-knowledge account and the motivational account are discussed later in the chapter. At this point it need only be mentioned that although the approaches differ, they are not necessarily incompatible if we assume that rather different implications can result from interpreting the current situation as problematic or benign. Evidence for the diversity of the possible implications has been reported by Martin and his colleagues (Martin, this volume; Martin, Ward, Achee, & Wyer, 1993). The discussion now turns to evidence suggesting that happy individuals are more likely than sad individuals to rely on general knowledge structures in the form of scripts, stereotypes, heuristics, and prior judgments. We will then discuss how the proposed mood-and-general-knowledge assumption and other approaches can account for these differences.

Empirical Evidence

The mood-and-general-knowledge assumption is compatible with much of the available evidence. Across various domains and across various forms of general knowledge structures, happy individuals have been found to be more strongly influenced than sad individuals by stereotypes, scripts, heuristics, and other forms of general knowledge. The first point to consider, then, is the relation between affective states and various forms of general knowledge structures.

Mood and Stereotyping

A number of recent studies have investigated the relation between individuals' affective state and the impact of stereotypes on social judgments. Bodenhausen, Kramer, and Süsser (1994), for example, presented participants in different mood states with descriptions of an alleged student misconduct and asked participants to determine the target's guilt. Participants in a happy mood rated the offender more guilty when he was identified as a member of a group that is stereotypically associated with the described offense than when this was not the case. This impact of the stereotype was not observed for participants in a neutral mood. Similarly, Bodenhausen, Sheppard, and Kramer (1994) observed that sad participants were less affected by an applicable stereotype than neutral-mood participants (for related evidence in the stereotype domain, see also Bless, Schwarz, & Wieland, 1996). Consistent with these findings, Forgas and Fiedler (1996) report that individuals in happy moods are more likely to rely on heuristic group category information in low-relevance intergroup situations.

Edwards and Weary (1993) reported additional converging evidence based on naturally depressed moods. Nondepressed participants were more likely to rely on category membership information than depressed participants, who seemed to engage in a more effortful analysis of the individuating information provided to them. Thus, the available evidence suggests that stereotypes have more impact on individuals in a happy rather than a sad or neutral mood.

Mood and Scripts

Similar conclusions about the relation between a mood and general knowledge structures can be derived from research investigating the relation between affective states and the impact of scripts on information processing (Bless et al., 1996). In a series of studies, different affective states were induced by asking participants to report a happy or sad life-event (Experiment 1) or to watch a happy or a sad movie clip (Experiments 2 and 3). Participants were then provided with information about well-known activities (e.g., "going out for dinner"), for which they were likely to have a well-developed script (Abelson, 1981; Graesser, Gordon, & Sawyer, 1979). Some of this information was script typical ("the hostess placed the menus on the table"), whereas other information was script atypical ("he put away his tennis racket"). After a short delay, participants received a surprise recognition test, assessing their memory for the daily activities information presented to them. This recognition test comprised script typical or script atypical information: Half of the information had actually been presented, and the remaining half was new information. The obtained findings support the assumption that being in a happy mood fosters reliance on general knowledge structures.

Specifically, happy participants were more likely than sad participants to "recognize" statements that were *typical* for the script as having been presented, and this effect was independent of whether the statements were actually presented or not. Presumably, this implies that reliance on a script allows individuals to infer script typical behaviors, and the result, then, is good recognition of typical behaviors that were actually presented, as well as erroneous recognition of script typical behaviors that were not ("intrusion errors"; see Graesser et al., 1979; Snyder & Uranowitz, 1978; cf. Fiske & Taylor, 1991). As expected, these mood effects were not obtained for *atypical* information, which means that this information could not be inferred from the script.[1] Like the studies on mood and stereotyping, these findings suggest that happy moods increase the impact of general knowledge structures on individuals' information processing.

Mood and Heuristics

A considerable amount of research also suggests that *heuristic* processing strategies are more strongly associated with happy rather than sad moods (for an overview, see Clore et al., 1994; Isen, 1987). For example, happy moods seem to increase the likelihood that individuals will rely on an availability heuristic when making frequency judgments (Isen, Means, Patrick, & Nowicki, 1982). Similarly, in the persuasion domain, consistent evidence suggests an increased impact of heuristics under happy moods. Across persuasive messages about a variety of attitudinal issues and across a variety of different mood inductions, happy individuals were more strongly influenced by peripheral cues, while sad individuals attended to the specifics of the situation and were more strongly influenced by the quality of the provided arguments (e.g., Bless, Bohner, Schwarz, & Strack, 1990; Bless, Mackie, & Schwarz, 1992; Mackie & Worth, 1989; Worth & Mackie, 1987; for a review, see Schwarz, Bless, & Bohner, 1991.)[2] As Nisbett and Ross (1980, Chapter 2) note, there is a substantial similarity between heuristics and general knowledge structures, and both can be seen as "general tools" used to go beyond the information given (for an explicit application of this argument to the persuasion domain, see Chen & Chaiken, in press). If, however, we conceptualize heuristic processing strategies as applying general knowledge structures to the task at hand, the observation that being in a happy mood renders the application of these general knowledge structures more likely is quite compatible with happy individuals applying cognitive heuristics more readily.

Mood and Prior Judgments

Prior judgments about similar or related situations can be conceptualized as another form of general knowledge structure. If so, the proposed mood-and-general-knowledge assumption holds that individuals in happy moods should be more likely to rely on prior judgments than individuals in sad moods when required to form a new, but related judgment. Evidence from different domains supports this hypothesis. In the domain of person perception, individuals in an elated mood have been found to be more likely to show halo effects than individuals in a depressed mood, and to be less influenced by detailed person descriptions (for a review, see Sinclair & Mark, 1992). Similarly, Bless and Fiedler (1995) found that specific judgments about a target person were more strongly influenced by preceding general trait judgments about the target when participants were in a happy rather than a neutral or sad mood. In the persuasion domain, when happy participants were asked to report an attitude judgment, they were more likely than sad individuals to rely on a prior global judgment of a persuasive message (Bless et al., 1992). In sum, the reported evidence on stereotypes, scripts, heuristics, and prior judgments is in line with the proposed assumption that happy rather than sad individuals are more likely to rely on general knowledge structures. In the next section, we discuss (a) alternative explanations that may account for these findings, and (b) possibilities to empirically disentangle the various explanations.

Different Explanations for the Impact of Mood on the Use of General Knowledge

Although the reported evidence is in line with the proposed mood-and-general-knowledge assumption, other explanations may also account for the observed findings. Various approaches hold that a happy mood reduces an individual's amount of processing and leads to a greater reliance on heuristics and other forms of general knowledge structures. These accounts incorporate consistent evidence that general knowledge structures allow the individual to reduce the complexity of information processing at different stages, and they often promote a parsimonious and efficient processing (for examples, see Fiske & Taylor, 1991; Markus & Zajonc, 1985; Taylor & Crocker, 1981).

One such argument is that being in a good mood limits processing capacity because of the activation of a large amount of interconnected positive material stored in memory (Isen, 1987; Mackie & Worth, 1989). Hence, individuals in a good mood may default to less taxing strategies and rely more strongly on general knowledge structures that allow a simplified processing. Another account is based on mood maintenance motivation (Isen, 1987; Wegener, Petty, & Smith, 1995) and argues that individuals in happy moods avoid investing cognitive effort in a task unless doing so promises to maintain or enhance their positive mood. Hence, individuals in a good mood may rely on general knowledge structures to avoid more effortful cognitive processing. Third, in our own theorizing based on the affect-as-information hypothesis (Schwarz & Clore, 1983; Schwarz, 1990), we have argued that negative affective cues signal that the environment poses a problem, whereas positive affect signals that the environment is benign. As a result, negative affective cues may motivate detail-oriented, systematic processing, while individuals in positive moods are not motivated to expend cognitive effort unless called for by other goals (for a more detailed discussion, see Schwarz, 1990; Schwarz & Bless, 1991).

Although these three approaches proceed from very different starting points, they share the conclusion that increased reliance on general knowledge structures under happy moods results from the fact that happy moods decrease the amount of information processing. For present purposes, it is not necessary to further differentiate between these three accounts, only to compare their common implications for the mood-and-general-knowledge assumption presented here.

As just mentioned, the alternative accounts share the assumption that happy individuals' reliance on general knowledge structures is a *consequence* of the reduced elaboration of happy-mood subjects, as characterized in Alternative A of Figure 9.1. In contrast, the suggested mood-and-general-knowledge assumption holds that happy individuals' reliance on general knowledge structures is not a consequence but an *antecedent* of simplified processing, as shown in Alternative B of Figure 9.1. Since general knowledge structures often allow efficient and parsimonious processing, happy moods will lead to a more parsimonious processing than sad moods in many situations. Note that this approach does not make any assumptions about mood directly influencing the amount of processing. The seemingly simplified processing is considered a result of the reliance on general knowledge structures.

Obviously, both process assumptions cannot be distinguished by assessing the impact of general knowledge structures per se, because both lead to the prediction that general knowledge structures will have more impact under positive than under negative mood conditions. Thus, the reported evidence per se is not sufficient to differentiate the different alternatives. The two accounts do, however, lead to

Alternative A:

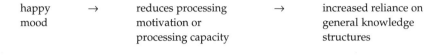

| happy mood | → | reduces processing motivation or processing capacity | → | increased reliance on general knowledge structures |

Alternative B:

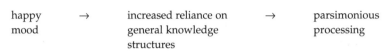

| happy mood | → | increased reliance on general knowledge structures | → | parsimonious processing |

Figure 9.1. Two alternative processes mediating the impact of mood on the use of general knowledge structures.

different additional predictions, which allow empirical testing. One of these predictions pertains to the performance on a secondary task, and a second prediction pertains to the impact of information that is inconsistent with the implications of the general knowledge structure. We address these two possibilities in turn.

Mood and the Secondary Task Paradigm

One way to test the competing accounts just described is to assess the cognitive effort individuals are willing or able to spend in a dual-task paradigm (see Navon & Gopher, 1979). In this paradigm, participants work on two tasks simultaneously, with one often being the primary and the other the secondary task. It is assumed that efficient processing of one task enables individuals to allocate more resources to the other task and therefore to improve performance on that task. Consider what happened when Macrae, Milne, and Bodenhausen (1994) asked participants to form an impression of a person on the basis of a list of trait adjectives. While performing this task, half of the participants were working on a secondary task. Prior activation of a category label resulted in improved recall of adjectives that were consistent with the label but had no impact on the recall of inconsistent or irrelevant adjectives. More important, the activation of the category label resulted in *better* performance on the secondary task. This presumably reflects that the category label allowed access to a general knowledge structure (stereotype), which in turn made it easier for participants to process the stereotype-consistent items, thus enabling them to allocate additional resources to the secondary task.

In our study on mood and scripts (Bless et al., 1996), we applied this dual-processing paradigm. In this study, participants listened to a tape-recorded story about well-known activities (e.g., "going out for dinner"). As discussed earlier, the recognition data suggested that happy individuals are more likely to rely on general knowledge structures for scripts. While encoding the presented information, participants in the reported studies had to work on a secondary task, namely, a concentration test that allowed us to assess how much effort participants were able and willing to allocate to it. The two competing approaches (Alternatives A and B) have different implications with respect to performance on a secondary task in a dual-task paradigm. If happy moods reduce processing motivation or capacity, they should impair performance not only on the primary task, but also on a secondary task. In contrast, a different prediction results from the mood-and-general-knowledge assumption. This account makes no assumption about mood-dependent differences in processing motivation or processing capacity. If happy moods elicit reliance on general knowledge structures pertaining to the primary task, the primary task should be less taxing (e.g., Macrae et al., 1994). In that case, happy participants – who can be assumed to rely on the script, given their recognition data – should have more resources available to allocate to the secondary task, and their performance on the secondary task should improve.

Participants' secondary task performance confirmed the prediction derived from the mood-and-general-knowledge assumption. Most important, happy participants showed *better* performance on the secondary task than either sad or neutral-mood participants. If happy participants' reliance on the script had been due to reduced processing motivation or processing capacity, the respective deficit should also have impaired their secondary task performance, which was not the case. Instead, the findings suggest that happy participants relied more on top-down, script-based processing for the primary task, thus enabling them to allocate additional resources to the secondary task, and thus to improve performance.

Two additional findings further support this conclusion. First, happy participants' secondary task performance depended on the amount of script-inconsistent information presented as part of the primary task. Specifically, increasing the amount of script atypical information decreased happy participants' advantage on the secondary task (Bless et al., 1996, Experiment 3), because increasing the amount of atypical information decreased the resources that could be set free by relying on the script. Second, additional support can be derived from the performance of control group participants who worked on the secondary task as their only task. Under this condition, mood did *not* affect performance, rendering a direct impact of mood on secondary task performance rather unlikely.[3]

In conclusion the recognition data suggest that happy moods increase individuals' reliance on general knowledge structures. Although this general conclusion is consistent with Alternatives A and B, the secondary task performances indicate that increased reliance on general knowledge structures is not *necessarily* caused by deficits in processing motivation or processing capacity, as discussed next.

Mood and the Processing of Stereotype-Inconsistent Information

The reported evidence from the stereotyping domain (Bodenhausen, Kramer, & Süsser, 1994) indicates that happy moods increase the likelihood that individuals will rely on stereotypes when processing information about a specific target person. Again, this finding is compatible with both the mood-and-general-knowledge assumption and with the competing hypothesis that reliance on general knowledge structures results from happy subjects' tendency to simplify processing. The two notions differ, however, with respect to the impact of information that is inconsistent with the implications of the general knowledge structure.

It is well documented that dealing with stereotype-inconsistent information requires considerable cognitive resources (e.g., Macrae, Hewstone, & Griffiths, 1993; Stangor & Duan, 1991; see also Fiske & Taylor, 1991; Srull & Wyer, 1989). If individuals are willing and able to allocate sufficient resources that are necessary for processing the inconsistent information, the inconsistent information should be particularly salient and should receive special weight in judgment formation. Note that if the inconsistent information indeed receives a special weight, the resulting judgments may then appear in contrast to the stereotype that initially guided the processing (Bless, Schwarz, Bodenhausen, & Thiel, 1998; Kunda & Oleson, 1997).

Such an increased impact of stereotype-inconsistent information is more likely according to the mood-and-general-knowledge assumption rather than according to the assumption that happy moods reduce extensive processing, either because of capacity or motivational constraints. The latter assumption would predict that happy individuals may use the stereotype simply as a peripheral cue that simplifies their task. If that is so, judgments should be independent of whether stereotype-consistent or stereotype-inconsistent individuating information is provided. In the case of inconsistent information, happy individuals may either not detect, or may simply ignore, the discrepancy because of their reduced processing motivation or capacity. If we assume that no processing constraints are associated with happy individuals' reliance on general knowledge structures, however, happy individuals should allocate additional resources to the inconsistent information. In turn, stereotype-inconsistent information should receive more weight in judgment formation under happy than under sad moods.

In a series of studies investigating the impact of stereotype-inconsistent information on individuals in different affective states (Bless, Schwarz, & Wieland, 1996), participants in a happy, neutral, or sad mood were provided with the description of a target person. We orthogonally manipulated whether the target was a member of a positively or a negatively evaluated group (category membership information) and whether the target's behaviors were predominantly positive or negative (individuating information).

When the individuating information was *consistent* with the implications of the stereotype, the results replicated previous findings by Bodenhausen, Kramer, and Süsser (1994). Specifically, happy participants provided stereotypical judgments, whereas sad participants did not, since the former relied on the stereotype and the latter on the individuating information. Note that these findings in themselves are compatible with either of the mediating mechanisms of interest. Most important with respect to disentangling the mediating mechanisms, the impact of stereotype-*inconsistent* information was more pronounced when participants were in happy rather than sad moods. For example, happy participants evaluated the target more negatively than sad participants when the target was described as a member of a positive group engaging in negative behaviors.[4]

The observed *increased* impact of stereotype-inconsistent individuating information under happy moods is hardly compatible with the assumption that happy moods cause motivational or capacity deficits, as the impact of the inconsistent information presumably required a considerable amount of resources (Macrae et al., 1993; Stangor & Duan, 1991). Rather, this finding is in line with the mood-and-general-knowledge assumption. According to this account, happy individuals relied on the stereotype without processing deficits causing this reliance. As a consequence, happy individuals elaborated on the inconsistent information resulting in a particular weight of this information.

These findings suggest that happy moods increase individuals' reliance on general knowledge structures. This general conclusion is consistent with the described Alternatives A and B. However, the impact of the inconsistent information – as in the case of the secondary task performances in the script studies reported earlier – indicates that the increased reliance on general knowledge structures is not *necessarily* caused by deficits in processing motivation or processing capacity.

Conclusions and Open Issues

Abundant and consistent evidence across various domains indicates that individuals in happy moods tend to rely on general knowledge structures in the form of stereotypes, scripts, heuristics, or prior judgments. In contrast, judgments of individuals in sad moods more strongly reflect the information that is specific for the individuals' current situation (for an overview, see Clore et al., 1994; Schwarz & Clore, 1996). The proposed mood-as-general-knowledge assumption fits much of the available evidence. Previous theorizing by my colleagues and myself on the informative function of affective states (Schwarz, 1990; Schwarz & Bless, 1991; Schwarz & Clore, 1983) leads us to assume that happy moods inform the individual that the current situation is benign and unproblematic. In contrast, negative affective states provide a signal that the situation poses a problem. Departing from our previous theorizing, we assume that the key effect of these different signals is not (or not only) motivational. We assume that it would be highly adaptive for individuals to rely on their general knowledge structures differentially as a function of the current psychological situation (Bless, 1997, in press). Specifically, individuals in benign situations may rely on their general knowledge structures, which usually serve them well. In contrast, problematic situations are usually deviations from normal, routine situations. Hence, individuals would be poorly advised to rely on the knowledge they usually apply.

To deal with problematic situations successfully, the individual must focus on the specifics of the current situation. Thus, individuals' current affective state may influence the degree to which they rely on their general knowledge structures, mediated by their affective states influencing the interpretation of the current situation. This mood-dependent reliance on general knowledge structures versus the data at hand would direct individuals' attention toward the information that is presumably most useful in the current situations.

This proposed mechanism may serve various adaptive functions. First, because general knowledge structures serve as energy-saving devices (e.g., Macrae et al., 1994; cf. Fiske & Taylor, 1991), they enable the individual to reduce the attention allocated to those aspects of the situation that match the general knowledge structure. The present approach holds that the spared resources are allocated to other aspects of the situation or to other tasks. This "transfer" of resources would be a highly adaptive mechanism as it directs the attention to those aspects in which additional processing is potentially more beneficial and effective. Thus, individuals in positive versus negative affective states are not differentially decreasing their amount of processing but differentially allocating their processing attention.

Second, although general knowledge structures enable the individual to reduce attention to certain aspects they quasi-automatically redirect attention to the data at hand if necessary. Such redirection of attention is required if the information at hand does not match the activated schema. *Because* of the attempt to apply general knowledge structures, schema-inconsistent information will receive additional processing attention (Fiske & Taylor, 1991). In other words, the same process that allows the allocation of resources to other tasks redirects the attention if necessary. An important advantage of this redirection of attention is that the additional attention allocated to inconsistent information is not a function of mood. Once happy individuals rely on a general knowledge structure, the additional processing is a function of the match between the knowledge structure and the information at hand, with the inconsistent information itself triggering the additional processing. Therefore, this mechanism allows for a flexibility in attention to the specifics of a situation without a previous change of individuals' affective states.

Like the mood-and-general-knowledge assumption, other models may also account for much of the evidence. Most directly, the model proposed by Fiedler (this volume) allows for similar predictions. In contrast to Fiedler's and the present account, most other approaches have often attributed the observed differences to happy moods eliciting processing constraints either because of reduced processing motivation (Schwarz, 1990; Schwarz & Bless, 1991; Wegener et al., 1995) or because of reduced processing capacity (Isen, 1987; Mackie & Worth, 1989). According to these accounts, the increased reliance on general knowledge structures is a consequence of individuals' need or willingness to simplify processing.

Although similar predictions can be derived from the two perspectives in many situations, the dual-task paradigm and the presentation of inconsistent information described here allow for the testing of competing hypotheses. Happy individuals' improved performance on the secondary task and their attention to the stereotype-inconsistent information is compatible with the mood-and-general-knowledge assumption. However, these findings are difficult to reconcile with a reduced processing account. Thus, the reported findings suggest that the often observed reliance of happy individuals on stereotypes, scripts, and heuristics is at least partly independent of happy moods causing processing deficits.

Interestingly, the evidence for reduced processing under happy moods due to motivational or capacity constraints seems less conclusive than is often assumed. Most important, rather few attempts have been made to directly assess the assumed mediating variables, namely, motivation and/or capacity. In many cases, the assumed processing deficits of happy individuals are only inferred from their reliance on general knowledge structures. This conclusion seems consistent with numerous studies that demonstrated that deficits in motivation or capacity do indeed elicit heuristic processing (for overviews, see Eagly & Chaiken, 1993; Fiske & Neuberg, 1990; Kruglanski, 1989; Petty & Cacioppo, 1986). However, these deficits may only be sufficient, but *not necessary* conditions for the emergence of heuristic processing (for a more extensive discussion of these aspects, see Bless & Schwarz, in press).

Although the presented data support the proposed model, there are, not surprisingly, a number of limitations and open questions that need to be attended to. These issues bear on the proposed model itself, and on how the model relates to other influences of mood on cognitive processes. First, and perhaps most important, the proposed account needs to further specify how the increased reliance of happy individuals on general knowledge structures is mediated. For example, we assume that happy individuals feel more confident about relying on their prior knowledge structures. Additional evidence supporting the mediating role of confidence seems necessary. More attention also needs to be directed toward obtaining processing measures (processing latencies, recall, etc.) although in many cases even these process measures may not allow us to differentiate between different competing models (for a more extensive discussion of this issue, see Bless & Schwarz, in press).

Second, applying the distinction of necessary versus sufficient conditions to the present account itself, it is important to point out that mood is not the only factor that influences the reliance on general knowledge structures. For example, increased reliance on general knowledge structures can result when individuals' arousal levels are either very low (e.g., Bodenhausen, 1990) or very high (e.g., Kim & Baron, 1988). In that case, the impact of mood valence may be overridden by other factors (for differential effects of sad vs. angry moods, see, e.g., Bodenhausen, Sheppard, & Kramer, 1994).

Third, and relatedly, it is an open question as to what degree individuals can control or influence the described mood effects. For example, it has been observed that the differential reliance on general knowledge structures is attenuated when individuals are highly motivated (Bless et al., 1990; Bodenhausen, Kramer, & Süsser, 1994), or when they misattribute their current mood state to some irrelevant factor (Sinclair, Mark, & Clore, 1994).

Fourth, more attention needs to be directed toward the nature of the affective state itself. Emotional responses are often considered highly contextualized (see Smith & Kirby, this volume), and their exact nature depends on variables that influence the appraisal of the current situation. Hence, it will be important to investigate whether and how variables that influence the appraisal process (see Leary, this volume; Smith & Kirby, this volume) also mediate the described effects on the use of general knowledge structures. In this respect, it would be interesting to see whether differential effects are obtained for situations that are characterized by the presence of positive outcomes versus the lack of negative outcomes (or, vice versa, the lack of positive outcomes vs. the presence of negative outcomes; see also Higgins & Tykocinski, 1992). For example, Blascovich and Mendes (this volume) have shown very different arousal patterns and cognitive consequences, depending on whether an individual perceives a problematic situation as a challenge or as a threat.

Fifth, it would be interesting to investigate the link between prior general knowledge structures and positive feeling states more extensively, particularly whether the relation between positive affective states and general knowledge structures may be bidirectional. For example, the presentation of stimuli that elicit an activation of some prior knowledge (even unconsciously) has been demonstrated to elicit more positive affective reactions than new stimuli (see Zajonc, 1980, this volume). Note that this evidence in combination with the present findings would suggest that although positive affective states may lead to an increased reliance on prior knowledge structures, the activation of prior knowledge structures may also lead to positive affective states.

Finally, it seems important to note that the proposed model does not exclude the possibility that other processes may be operating. It may therefore be the case that individuals base their judgments on a "How-do-I-feel-about-it?" heuristic (Schwarz & Clore, 1988), or that being in a positive or negative affective state increases the availability of mood-congruent material (Bower, 1981; Eich & Macaulay, this volume; Forgas & Bower, 1987). With respect to mood and processing style, other mood-as-information processes as well as motivational mediated processes (Wegener et al., 1995) may influence individuals' processing style (see Schwarz, 1990; Martin, this volume; Martin et al., 1993). Presumably, the notion that multiple processes may be operating – perhaps even co-occurring – is explicitly or implicitly inherent in most models of affective influences on cognitive processes (see Martin & Clore, in press). If so, however, we need general frameworks that allow specific hypotheses to be formulated about which process is most likely in which circumstance (for an integrative approach in this direction, see Forgas, 1992, this volume). Further research evaluating such integrative explanations of affective influences on information processing is necessary to maintain the current high level of interest in the interplay of affective states and cognitive processes.

Notes

1. Note that this differential pattern for typical and atypical information rules out an alternative explanation, based on the possibility that different moods may elicit different response tendencies.
2. Evidence suggesting an increased reliance on a peripheral cue in the form of a consensus cue is reported by Bohner, Crow, Erb, & Schwarz (1993).

3. In addition to bearing on our interpretation of the results obtained under dual-task conditions, this latter finding is itself remarkable. As the secondary task was designed to measure cognitive capacity and processing motivation, the investigation of mood effects on this task is one of the few attempts to directly assess the hypothesis of mood effects on the amount of processing. The absence of any impact is hardly compatible with the notion that happy moods reduce the amount of processing, either because of capacity or motivational deficits (although the latter may be mitigated by the explicit task instructions).

4. Interestingly, the very pronounced impact of stereotype-inconsistent information on happy participants was only observed when the behavioral information was perceived as diagnostic (for more details and a more extended discussion of this aspect, see Bless, Schwarz, & Wieland, 1996, Experiment 2).

References

Abelson, R. P. (1981). The psychological status of the script concept. *American Psychologist, 36*, 715–729.

Bless, H. (1997). *Stimmung und Denken: Ein Modell zum Einfluβ von Stimmungen auf Denkprozesse* [Affect and cognition]. Bern: Huber.

Bless, H. (in press). The relation between mood and the use of general knowledge structures. In L. L. Martin & G. L. Clore (Eds.), *Affective states and cognitive processing.* Hillsdale, NJ: Erlbaum.

Bless, H., Bohner, G., Schwarz, N., & Strack, F. (1990). Mood and persuasion: A cognitive response analysis. *Personality and Social Psychology Bulletin, 16*, 331–345.

Bless, H., Clore, G., Schwarz, N., Golisano, V., Rabe, C., & Wölk, M. (1996). Mood and the use of scripts: Does happy mood make people really mindless? *Journal of Personality and Social Psychology, 71*, 665–679.

Bless, H., & Fiedler, K. (1995). Affective states and the influence of activated general knowledge. *Personality and Social Psychology Bulletin, 21*, 766–778.

Bless, H., Mackie, D. M., & Schwarz, N. (1992). Mood effects on encoding and judgmental processes in persuasion. *Journal of Personality and Social Psychology, 63*, 585–595.

Bless, H., & Schwarz, N. (in press). Sufficient and necessary conditions in dual process models: The case of mood and information processing. In S. Chaiken & Y. Trope (Eds.), *Dual process theories in social psychology.* New York: Guilford Press.

Bless, H., Schwarz, N., Bodenhausen, G. V., & Thiel L. (1998). *Personalized versus generalized benefits of stereotype disconfirmation: Tradeoffs in the evaluation of atypical exemplars and their social groups.* Manuscript under review.

Bless, H., Schwarz, N., & Wieland, R. (1996). Mood and the impact of category membership and individuating information. *European Journal of Social Psychology, 26*, 935–959.

Bodenhausen, G. V. (1990). Stereotypes as judgmental heuristics. Evidence of circadian variations in discrimination. *Psychological Science, 1,* 319–322.

Bodenhausen, G. V., Kramer, G. P. & Süsser, K. (1994). Happiness and stereotypic thinking in social judgment. *Journal of Personality and Social Psychology, 66,* 621–632.

Bodenhausen, G. V., Sheppard, L. A., & Kramer, G. P. (1994). Negative affect and social judgment: The differential impact of anger and sadness. *European Journal of Social Psychology, 24,* 45–62.

Bohner, G., Crow, K., Erb, H.-P., & Schwarz, N. (1993). Affect and persuasion: Mood effects on the processing of message content and context cues. *European Journal of Social Psychology, 22,* 511–530.

Bower, G. H. (1981). Mood and memory. *American Psychologist, 36,* 129–148.

Chen, F., & Chaiken, S. (in press). Heuristic and systematic information processing. In S. Chaiken & Y. Trope (Eds.), *Dual process theories in social psychology.* New York: Guilford Press.

Clore, G. L., Schwarz, N., & Conway, M. (1994). Cognitive causes and consequences of emotion. In R. S. Wyer & T. K. Srull (Eds.), *Handbook of social cognition* (vol. 1, 2nd ed., pp. 323–418). Hillsdale, NJ: Erlbaum.

Eagly, A. H., & Chaiken, S. (1993). *The psychology of attitudes.* Fort Worth: Harcourt, Brace, Jovanovich.

Edwards, J. A., & Weary, G. (1993). Depression and the impression-formation continuum: Piecemeal processing despite the availability of category information. *Journal of Personality and Social Psychology, 64,* 636–645.

Fiedler, K., & Forgas, J. P. (Eds.). (1988). *Affect, cognition, and social behavior.* Toronto: Hogrefe International.

Fiske, S. T., & Neuberg, S. L. (1990). A continuum of impression formation from category-based to individuating processing: Influences of information and motivation on attention and interpretation. In M. P. Zanna (Ed.), *Advances in Experimental Social Psychology,* (Vol. 23, pp. 1–74). Orlando, FL: Academic Press.

Fiske, S. T., & Taylor, S. E. (1991). *Social cognition.* New York: McGraw-Hill.

Forgas, J. P. (Ed.). (1991). *Emotion and social judgements.* Oxford: Pergamon Press.

Forgas, J. P. (1992). Affect in social judgments and decisions: A multi-process model. In M. P. Zanna (Ed.), *Advances in Experimental Social Psychology* (Vol. 25, pp. 227–275). San Diego: Academic Press.

Forgas, J. P., & Bower, G. H. (1987). Mood effects on person-perception judgments. *Journal of Personality and Social Psychology, 53,* 53–60.

Forgas, J. P., & Fiedler, K. (1996). Us and them: Mood effects on intergroup discrimination. *Journal of Personality and Social Psychology, 70,* 28–40.

Frijda, N. H. (1988). The laws of emotion. *American Psychologist, 43,* 349–358.

Graesser, A. C., Gordon, S. E., & Sawyer, J. D. (1979). Memory for typical and atypical actions in scripted activities: Test of a script pointer + tag hypothesis. *Journal of Verbal Learning and Behavior, 18,* 319–332.

Higgins, E. T., & Tykocinski, O. (1992). Self-discrepancies and biographical memory: Personality and cognition at the level of psychological situation. *Personality and Psychology Bulletin, 18,* 527–535.

Isen, A. M. (1987). Positive affect, cognitive processes, and social behavior. In L. Berkowitz (Ed.), *Advances in Experimental Social Psychology* (Vol. 20, pp. 203–253). San Diego: Academic Press.

Isen, A. M., Means, B., Patrick, R., & Nowicki, G. (1982). Some factors influencing decision-making strategy and risk-taking. In M. S. Clark & S. T. Fiske (Eds.), *Affect and cognition: The 17th Annual Carnegie Symposium on Cognition.* (pp. 243–261). Hillsdale, NJ: Erlbaum.

Jacobsen, E. (1957). Normal and pathological moods: Their nature and function. In R. S. Eisler, A. F. Freud, H. Hartman, & E. Kris (Eds.), *The psychoanalytic study of the child* (pp. 73–113). New York: International University Press.

Kim, H.-S., & Baron, R. S. (1988). Exercise and illusory correlation: Does arousal heighten stereotypic processing? *Journal of Experimental Social Psychology, 24,* 366–380.

Kruglanski, A. W. (1989). The psychology of being "right": On the problem of accuracy in social perception and cognition. *Psychological Bulletin, 106,* 395–409.

Kunda, Z., & Oleson, K. C. (1997). When exceptions prove the rule: How extremity of deviance determines the impact of deviant examples on stereotypes. *Journal of Personality and Social Psychology, 72,* 965–979.

Mackie, D. M. & Worth, L. T. (1989). Cognitive deficits and the mediation of positive affect in persuasion. *Journal of Personality and Social Psychology, 57,* 27–40.

Macrae, C. N., Hewstone, M., & Griffiths, R. J. (1993). Processing load and memory for stereotype-based information. *European Journal of Social Psychology, 23,* 77–87.

Macrae, C. N., Milne, A. B., & Bodenhausen, G. V. (1994). Stereotypes as energy-saving devices: A peek inside the toolbox. *Journal of Personality and Social Psychology, 66,* 37–47.

Markus, H., & Zajonc, R. B. (1985). The cognitive perspective in social psychology. In G. Lindzey & E. Aronson (Eds.), *The handbook of social psychology* (3rd ed.) (Vol. 1, pp. 137–230). New York: Random House.

Martin, L. L., & Clore, G. L. (in press). *Affective states and cognitive processing.* Hillsdale, NJ: Erlbaum.

Martin, L. M., Ward, D. W., Achee, J. W., & Wyer, R. S. (1993). Mood as input: People have to interpret the motivational implications of their moods. *Journal of Personality and Social Psychology, 64,* 317–326.

Navon, D., & Gopher, D. (1979). On the economy of human processing system. *Psychological Review, 86,* 214–255.

Nisbett, R., & Ross, L. (1980). *Human inference: Strategies and shortcomings in social judgment.* Englewood Cliffs, NJ: Prentice-Hall.

Nowlis, V., & Nowlis, H. H. (1956). The description and analysis of mood. *Annals of the New York Academy of Sciences, 65,* 345–355.

Petty, R. E., & Cacioppo, J. T. (1986). The elaboration likelihood model of persuasion. In L. Berkowitz (Ed.), *Advances in experimental social psychology* (Vol. 19, pp. 124–203). New York: Academic Press.

Pribram, H. H. (1970). Feelings as monitors. In M. Arnold (Ed.), *Feelings and emotions* (pp. 41–53). New York: Academic Press.

Schwarz, N. (1990). Feelings as information: Informational and motivational functions of affective states. In R. M. Sorrentino & E. T. Higgins (Eds.), *Handbook of motivation and cognition: Foundations of social behavior* (Vol. 2, pp. 527–561). New York: Guilford Press.

Schwarz, N., & Bless, H. (1991). Happy and mindless, but sad and smart? The impact of affective states on analytic reasoning. In J. P. Forgas (Ed.), *Emotion and social judgments* (pp. 55–71). Oxford: Pergamon Press.

Schwarz, N., & Bless, H., & Bohner, G. (1991). Mood and persuasion: Affective states influence the processing of persuasive communications. In M. Zanna (Ed.), *Advances in Experimental Social Psychology* (Vol. 24, pp. 161–197). New York: Academic Press.

Schwarz, N., & Clore, G. L. (1983). Mood, misattribution, and judgments of well-being: Informative and directive functions of affective states. *Journal of Personality and Social Psychology, 45*, 513–523.

Schwarz, N., & Clore, G. L. (1988). How do I feel about it? Informative functions of affective states. In K. Fiedler & J. P. Forgas (Eds.), *Affect, cognition, and social behavior* (pp. 44–62). Toronto: Hogrefe International.

Schwarz, N., & Clore, G. L. (1996). Feelings and phenomenal experiences. In E. T. Higgins & A. Kruglanski (Eds.), *Social psychology: A handbook of basic principles* (pp. 433–465). New York: Guilford.

Sinclair, R. C., & Mark, M. M. (1992). The influence of mood state on judgment and action: Effects on persuasion, categorization, social justice, person perception, and judgmental accuracy. In L. L. Martin & A. Tesser (Eds.), *The construction of social judgment* (pp. 165–193). Hillsdale, NJ: Erlbaum.

Sinclair, R. C., Mark, M. M., & Clore, G. L. (1994). Mood-related persuasion depends on misattributions. *Social Cognition, 12*, 309–326.

Snyder, M., & Uranowitz, S. W. (1978). Reconstructing the past: Some cognitive consequences of person perception. *Journal of Personality and Social Psychology, 36*, 941–950.

Srull, T. K., & Wyer, R. S. (1989). Person memory and judgment. *Psychological Review, 96*, 58–83.

Stangor, C., & Duan, C. (1991). Effects of multiple task demands upon memory for information about social groups. *Journal of Experimental Social Psychology, 27*, 357–378.

Taylor, S. E., & Crocker, J. (1981). Schematic bases of social information processing. In E. T. Higgins, C. P. Herman, and M. P. Zanna (Eds.), *Social cognition: The Ontario symposium on personality and social psychology* (Vol. 1, pp. 89–134). Hillsdale, NJ: Erlbaum.

Tomkins, S. S. (1981). The quest for primary motives: Biography and autobiography of an idea. *Journal of Personality and Social Psychology, 41*, 306–329.

Wegener, D. T., Petty, R. E., & Smith, S. M. (1995). Positive mood can increase or decrease message scrutiny: The hedonic contingency view of mood and message processing. *Journal of Personality and Social Psychology, 69,* 5–15.

Worth, L. T. & Mackie, D. M. (1987). Cognitive mediation of positive affect in persuasion. *Social Cognition, 5,* 76–94.

Wyer, R. S., & Srull, T. (1989). *Memory and cognition in its social context.* Hillsdale, NJ: Erlbaum.

Zajonc, R. B. (1980). Feeling and thinking. Preferences need no inferences. *American Psychologist, 35,* 151–175.

10. Toward an Integrative Account of Affect and Cognition Phenomena Using the BIAS Computer Algorithm

KLAUS FIEDLER

Introduction

The past two decades have witnessed intensive and broad-ranging psychological research on the influence of affective states on cognitive processes. However, in spite of the enormous growth of this research, most findings can be classified as belonging in one of two general categories (Fiedler & Forgas, 1988). In the first category, the emphasis is on the interaction of *emotional states and memory performance*. The common finding is that information which is congruent with the individual's mood state enjoys a memory advantage. The other category is concerned with the *influence of emotional states on cognitive style*. The main message here is that positive mood fosters creative thinking whereas negative mood serves to increase systematic and reliable information processing.

Mood-Congruent Memory

Originally, the notion of mood congruency (Blaney, 1986; Bower, 1981) referred to the memory advantage of stimuli that are evaluatively congruent with the individual's affective state (i.e., better recall of stimuli pleasant in positive mood and unpleasant stimuli in negative mood). However, the concept was then extended to cover mood-congruent effects on social judgments and other memory functions as well (Clore, Schwarz, & Conway, 1994; Forgas, 1995). The general finding there was that an individual's mood state facilitates the pro-

Correspondence about this work should be addressed to Klaus Fiedler, Fachbereich Psychologie, University of Heidelberg, Houptstrasse 47–51, Heidelberg, Germany.

cessing and retrieval of information that is associated with the same valence.

Since the work of Bower (1981), theoretical accounts of mood congruency have been based on the associative network metaphor, whereby moods, like any other concepts, are represented as nodes connected to other nodes. The basic assumption is that the semantic network is organized by similarity such that nodes representing similar concepts are located close to one another whereas distant nodes reflect unrelated or incompatible concepts. Thus, when the node for, say, positive mood is activated, the neighboring nodes for mood-congruent, evaluatively similar stimuli should receive a greater part of the spreading activation than more distant nodes representing incongruent stimuli. This simple and straightforward network metaphor not only provides an elegant account for many research findings but is also in line with traditional conceptions of human memory (Anderson, 1983).

Even though, or exactly because, Bower was so explicit about an underlying psychological process, his model became the target of serious criticism. Several authors have pointed out empirical and theoretical problems with a simple network account of mood congruency (Fiedler, Pampe, & Scherf, 1986; Schwarz & Clore, 1988; Simon, 1982). For instance, the model can hardly explain why free-recall protocols are not ordered by congruency (Fiedler, 1985), or why mood priming may sometimes result in contrast rather than assimilation effects (i.e., opposite, incongruent reactions; see Strack, Schwarz, & Gschneidinger, 1985). Another problem is that mood effects on social judgments are sometimes independent of, and more stable than, mood effects on recall (Mayer & Salovey, 1988; Schwarz & Clore, 1988). Most important, the network model cannot explain the whole second category of findings, regarding mood and cognitive style.

Mood and Cognitive Style

Theoretical accounts of the other class of phenomena, related to mood and cognitive style, have remained much weaker and less clear and as a result have been treated with less scrutiny and more leniency. To summarize some of the most popular theories, the general finding of more creativity in positive mood and more caution and carefulness in negative mood was explained by reference to several processes. For example, it was suggested that the consumption of positive affect occupies cognitive capacity and thereby prevents more systematic, less intuitive processing (Mackie & Worth, 1989). Alternatively, happy people do not want to disturb their elated mood through effortful processing (Isen, 1984). Or, people use mood as information (Schwarz & Clore, 1983, 1988) in that positive mood signals that no cognitive efforts are necessary and stimulus judgments can be benevolent, whereas negative mood signals that stimuli are aversive and effortful coping is needed.

Notwithstanding the plausibility of such capacity-related, motivational, or functional assumptions, the convergent and divergent validity of these notions has remained questionable. Hardly any experiment has ever directly tested the assumption whether less effort is expended in good mood or the functionalist assumption that the typical influence of positive mood on cognitive style serves a mood-conserving and adaptive purpose. In fact, recent research using more appropriate methodologies than previous studies has shown that the intuitive, seemingly unsystematic style of people in a good mood is *not* accompanied by reduced capacity, as evident in increased rather than decreased performance on a secondary task (see Bless et al., 1996). That cognitive styles are employed to conserve one's mood or to reduce the load of exhaustive processing was never proven. And the mood-as-information approach is hard to distinguish from other theories, such as a simple conditioning account. Thus, rather than "informing" the individual that effort is necessary, negative mood may be nothing but a conditioned stimulus that was repeatedly paired in past experience with (dangerous or challenging) situations requiring effortful reactions. Though such a conditioned stimulus may of course be referred to as "information," it is unclear whether "mood as information" as a theoretical construct adds anything beyond the long-known conditioning concept.

Regardless of the vagueness of some conceptions and the lack of theoretical distinctiveness, the proposed explanations of the relation between mood and cognitive style fail to account for the other class of findings. Just as the network model cannot readily explain the influence of affect on cognitive styles, the explanations that have been proposed for the latter phenomena are not well suited to deal with mood-congruent memory. Thus, if positive mood signals that no efforts have to be invested, the question remains, why are pleasant stimuli elaborated, learned, and recalled more effectively than unpleasant stimuli? Moreover, if positive mood led to reduced processing, one would expect an overall advantage of negative over positive mood in memory studies, which is clearly not the case (Bower, 1981; Fiedler, 1990, 1991; Fiedler & Stroehm, 1986; Isen, 1984)

An Integral Account in Terms of Assimilation Versus Accommodation

In this section, an integral account of both empirical paradigms, mood congruency and mood effects on cognitive style, is presented within the framework of a so-called dual-force model (Fiedler, 1990, 1991, 1998). Its basic assumption can be described with reference to Piaget's (1952) famous distinction between two complementary adaptive functions, *accommodation and assimilation*. To accommodate means to be responsive, as reliably as possible, to the affordances of the stimuli impinging on the organism. Thus, as summarized in Figure 10.1, successful accommodation requires us to maximize conservation of stimulus input and to avoid mistakes on stimulus-driven, reproductive tasks. In contrast, assimilation refers to an opposite adaptation function, whereby preexisting knowledge and internalized structures are imposed on the stimulus world. This function is typically needed for productive tasks calling for creativity, active exploration, and the generation of novel information. In a word, accommodation is stimulus-driven, whereas assimilation is knowledge-driven.

The central assumption underlying the dual-force model is that *positive mood facilitates assimilation, whereas negative mood supports the accommodation function*. Thus, negative emotional states are assumed to be associated with a cognitive set to stick to the stimulus facts and to respond reliably to any stimulus input. In contrast, the cognitive set induced by positive states encourages the individual to go beyond the given input and to proceed to new grounds, based on active inferences and trust in his or her internalized cognitive structures. The theory refrains from postulating general differences, as a function of mood, in terms of effort, capacity, or performance level. The crucial assumption is only that different emphasis is given to stimulus-driven (accommodation) and knowledge-driven (assimilation) processes in positive versus negative settings.

This central assumption is not an ad hoc attempt to account for local mood effects but is grounded in more general differences observed for appetitive versus aversive settings (see Figure 10.1). Decades of experimental research in the behaviorist tradition have shown

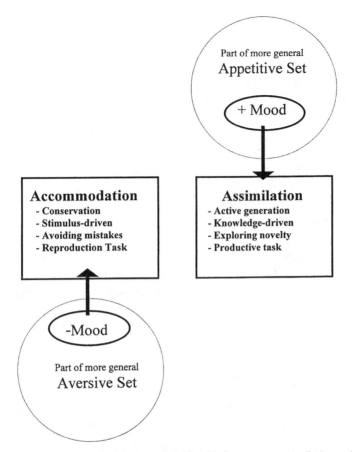

Figure 10.1. The dual-force model: Mood influences on assimilative and accommodative functions.

that performance in appetitive situations is characterized by *exploration*, whereas performance in aversive situations is characterized by successful *avoidance*. Exploration is driven by curiosity, which leads individuals to seek new information, try out new hypotheses, and place relatively little weight on mistakes, risks, and costs. This corresponds neatly to the notion of assimilation and the pattern of results observed in many experiments for the positive-mood condition. Conversely, the key to successful avoidance is to make no mistake and to achieve optimal performance without reinforcement (e.g., the young child must avoid car accidents without ever undergoing the experience). The carefulness and the amount of monitoring that is necessary for such perfect avoidance is descriptive of accommodation as observed under negative mood. Note that the respective learning sets of adaptive behavior do not need genuine emotions to be elicited; similar effects may be obtained by more subtle and transient cues to exploration and avoidance, much below the intensity threshold of experienced moods or emotions (Blascovich and Mendes, this volume; Fiedler, 1991).

The accommodation-assimilation distinction does not refer to two mutually exclusive strategies but to two aspects that are involved, to some degree, in every cognitive operation, just as any thought or utterance has a given and a new aspect (Clark & Haviland, 1977). This is meant as a purely analytical assumption without any loss of generality. In more technical terms, the dual-force model assumes that two components can be distinguished in every cognitive process, namely, *conservation* and *active generation*. The conservation component reflects the necessary fact that, as a premise to all further processing, any input information has to be retained and must not be lost. Thus, the conservation component serves the accommodative, stimulus-driven function in cognitive processes. However, one would not refer to a cognitive "process" unless some new output were actively generated from the stimulus input, on the basis of knowledge-driven, assimilative inferences.

Although both components are in principle involved in any cognitive process, experimental (and natural) tasks differ greatly in the weight they give to conservation versus active generation. If performance on a task requires reliable assessment and sticking to the stimulus details, the emphasis is on the accommodation/conservation component. Conversely, if the task calls for innovations and creative changes of the stimulus input, performance is determined mainly by the assimilation/active generation component. The impact of positive versus negative mood states on cognitive performance should differ markedly between these two types of cognitive tasks.

Applying the Theoretical Model to Empirical Evidence

How can the two major classes of empirical findings be explained within this theoretical framework? With regard to mood effects on cognitive style, it is clear that the basic theoretical assumption immediately accounts for the phenomenon. Numerous studies demonstrate enhanced creative, explorative, generative behavior in positive mood as opposed to careful, error-avoiding, conservative behavior in negative moods (Ellis & Ashbrook, 1988; Fiedler, 1988, 1990; Bless & Fiedler, 1995; Isen, Means, Patrick, & Nowicki, 1982). Inspection of the very tasks that have been shown to gain from negative versus positive mood gives operational meaning to accommodation and assimilation and lends ample support to our basic assumption.

When it comes to explaining mood-congruent memory effects, an important difference between the two process components has to be acknowledged. Although the conservation component is by definition nonselective (i.e., aimed at conserving the valid stimulus input), the second stage of active generation should reflect all selective influences coming from inside the individual, his or her currently active epistemic structures, motivational tendencies, and internal affective states. After all, the essence of the second component is to enrich the stimulus input with assimilative tendencies added by the individual.

Within these two general principles, the dual-force model can account not only for the typical findings in the paradigms of mood congruency and cognitive style but also for several important moderators of mood effects on cognitive performance. Moreover, the model has distinctive implications that can not be derived from other theories of affect and cognition. Since the aim of the present discussion is not to review the literature but to present an algorithmic computer model of the theory, the empirical evidence presented in this section is confined to some of these distinctive, more unusual implications (for more extensive evidence, see Fiedler, 1990, 1991, 1998; Fiedler & Bless, 1998). In particular, the following examples speak to mood influences on the generation effect, higher-order encoding effects, constructive memory and judgment, and constructive recognition tests.

Mood and Memory for Self-Generated Information

One paradigm in experimental memory research that affords a nice operationalization of accommodation versus assimilation is the generation effect (Dosher & Russo, 1976; Fiedler, Lachnit, Fay, & Krug, 1992; Slamecka & Graf, 1978). Some of the stimuli (e.g., the word *happy*) in a list are presented completely and only have to be read, whereas the rest of the stimuli appear as fragments so that the meaning has to be self-generated. Clearly, reading an experimenter-provided word involves less active generation and is more confined to stimulus conservation than inferring the meaning from word fragments. Accordingly, the so-called generation effect – that is, the memory advantage of self-generated over experimenter-provided stimuli – should be stronger in positive than negative mood, owing to the facilitative influence of positive mood on assimilation/active generation. Note that this prediction is derived on theoretical grounds and not with an a priori feeling of what influences mood states could have.

Fiedler et al. (1992) tested this prediction using evaluatively neutral stimulus words. As shown in the left chart of Figure 10.2, there is a strong generation advantage, which is clearly enhanced by positive mood. This lends support to the assumption of enhanced assimilation functions in positive mood. When evaluatively pleasant and unpleasant stimuli are used (as in Fiedler, 1991), the typical three-way interaction in the right chart of Figure 10.2 is observed. It reflects a mood congruency effect that is mainly due to positive mood and self-generated stimuli. This corroborates the assumption that only the generative component, which is supported by positive mood, causes selective processing and mood congruency.

Mood and Higher-Order Encoding

Encoding and organizing stimuli in terms of higher-order units (categories, schemata, scripts) is an important knowledge-driven assimilation function and a key to high memory performance. A positive mood state during encoding should facilitate this process and lead to high performance (when higher-order encoding is possible), compared

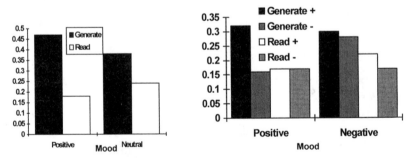

Figure 10.2. Left chart: Positive (as opposed to neutral) mood enhances the recall of self-generated stimuli of neutral valence (from Fiedler et al., 1992). Right chart: Mood congruency is largely due to better recall of pleasant (+) than unpleasant (−) self-generated stimuli under positive mood (from Fiedler, 1991).

with the negative mood condition. For an empirical test (Fiedler, 1991), I used various sets of 10 photographs. While in a positive or negative mood, participants could construct picture stories from subsets of the photos. A mood congruency effect on a subsequent surprise recall test was confined to those stimuli that were actively integrated in the higher-order encoding structures (i.e., the picture stories) but disappeared for pictures that were not included, or assimilated (see Figure 10.3).

Mood and Constructive Memory

As already mentioned, there are conditions leading to better performance under negative than positive mood. This is the case when the task requires careful conservation of stimulus details, or when assimilation leads to erroneous inferences. Some evidence for the latter prediction comes from experiments on constructive memory intrusions. The tendency (mainly in positive mood) to enrich the stimulus input with knowledge-based inferences is a serious source of constructive errors. For example, Fiedler, Asbeck, and Nickel (1991) had their participants verify or falsify various positive and negative attributes of a target person previously described in an ambiguous vignette. When judges were in a good mood, merely thinking about evaluative attributes (e.g., aggressiveness) influenced subsequent judgments (likelihood of attacking others), even when they denied the attitude in question. No such evidence for constructive memory effects on judgment was found for negative mood.

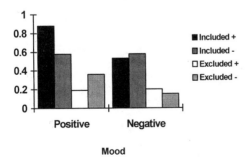

Figure 10.3. Mood congruency is largely due to better recall under positive mood of pleasant (+) than unpleasant (−) stimuli that are assimilated (included) in higher-order encoding units (from Fiedler, 1991).

Constructive Recognition Test

Congruency effects are normally confined to free recall and disappear in recognition tests (Bower, 1981; Fiedler, 1990). As the active process of memory search is cut short and the entire stimulus is presented for recognition, the assimilation component is impoverished. An interesting implication of the present theory is that mood congruency in the recognition paradigm should be possible if only the assimilation component can be enhanced. A more constructive variant of recognition recently developed by Fiedler, Nickel, and Mühlfriedel (1998) starts with a completely masked stimulus, rather than presenting the whole stimulus and merely asking Old or New. The mask disappears gradually, pixel by pixel, in a random fashion, until the full stimulus is visible after several seconds. A semantic cue is given before each trial, inviting active hypothesis testing about the gradually appearing stimulus. The introduction of this inferential component to recognition resulted in the expected mood-congruency effect. Notably, however, this congruency effect was confined to those recognition responses that were made relatively fast, that is, that were based on active inferences rather than mere conservation of stimuli details on slow trials.

An Algorithmic Approach to Understanding the Influence of Affect on Cognition

Suffice it to mention these few distinct and nonobvious inplications of the dual-force model. More systematic overviews can be found elsewhere (Fiedler, 1990, 1991, 1998). The remainder of the chapter is devoted to an attempt to translate the abstract distinction between assimilation and accommodation into an explicit and transparent computer algorithm that can be used to simulate the classical findings and to derive new implications. The advantage of presenting a theory as a computer program is that the predictions can be specified unambiguously, and the theory is less dependent on the theorist's rhetoric than is still often the case in psychology (cf. Ostrom, 1988; Smith, 1996). The present computer model employs a simple connectionist feedforward approach called BIAS (Brunswikian Induction Algorithm for Social Inference; Fiedler, 1996) that was proposed to account for judgments in a probabilistic multiple-cue world.

The BIAS Algorithm

The Brunswikian underpinning of BIAS appears well suited for bridging the representational gap between affect and cognition, that is, between diffuse connotations or feelings and specific denotative meanings. In a Brunswikian framework, most concepts are represented in a similarly diffuse format as affective states. Most meaningful stimulus concepts such as *danger, deception, honesty,* or *attraction* are *distal* in nature and cannot be perceived directly using specialized sense organs but have to be inferred or construed on the basis of multiple *proximal* cues. The validity of individual cues is typically rather low. For example, there is hardly any single cue that unequivocally identifies deception or lying (Fiedler & Walka, 1993; Zuckerman, DePaulo, & Rosenthal, 1981), nor can danger, honesty, and attraction be validly inferred from singular features. Rather, we need multiple, probabilistic cues to infer distal concepts with reasonable validity. For instance, to "perceive" a lie, we need multiple verbal and nonverbal cues such as turning red, disguised smiling, pupil reaction, voice pitch, adapters, and speech hesitations. This reliance on multiple, probabilistic cues that even holds for the psychophysical domain (e.g., depth perception; Brunswik, 1956) has an important theoretical implication for the representation of stimulus information. As a matter of principle, the basic unit of a stimulus is not a scalar (i.e., singular point on a dimension) but a *vector* (point in multidimensional space) describing the *distributed representation* of the distal stimulus across many cues.

This is illustrated in Figure 10.4 with reference to the multicue representation of a vacation experience. For convenience, the vector is structured into several segments of cues that correspond to separable aspects of a stimulus as, in this case, the holiday partner, hedonic valence, or the spatial context. As will become apparent shortly, the valence segment will play an essential role in the affect – cognition interface. It is important to understand that the cue vector describing a distal concept is not constant but changes in a flexible fashion (referred to by Brunswik, 1956, as vicarious functioning or by Wittgenstein, 1953, as familiy resemblence). That is, depending on what cues happen to be available and what values they take, a holiday experience can appear in many different cue patterns. On a different occasion, hedonic pleasure may have come from adventurous sports rather than relaxation, food and eroticism may be absent, and arts or aesthetics may be present. Note also that whole segments may be missing (i.e., the cues of that segment have missing values) as might be the case when we see a holiday photograph without any person reference.

Although the cue values associated with different instances of the vacation concept vary, constant cue patterns are used to describe a *prototype* or an *ideal type* of the concept. A prototype can be conceived as the average of all manifestations of vacation experiences. An ideal type is slightly different, an extreme, superlative example of the category. Many meaningful concepts are cognitively represented by their prototypes, but social concepts may also be represented in terms of ideal types (Barsalou, 1985; Borkenau, 1990).

To illustrate the operation of BIAS using a simple example, imagine that an experimental participant has memory access to 12 vacation items she has experienced. As is evident from Figure 10.5, these 12 episodes (i.e., the 12 column vectors) involve different partners (see upper segment), different degrees of pleasure (middle segment), and different locations or means of accommodation (bottom segment). Even when the references are the same (e.g., the first four stimulus vectors referring to the same vacation partner, A), the respective cue

Cue	Presence (+) / Absence (-)	Segment
Male	+	
Friend	-	**Partner**
Romantic	+	**Reference**
Athletic	+	
Child-age	-	
Relax	+	
Adventure	-	**Hedonic**
Good Food	+	**Valence**
Aesthetics	-	
Erotics	+	
Hotel	+	
Tent	-	**Spatial**
Van	+	**Context**
Flat	-	
Bike	-	

Figure 10.4. Distributed representation of a vacation experience, ordered by three vector segments.

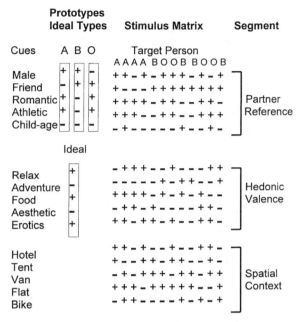

Figure 10.5. Graphical illustration of stimulus vectors arising in a noisy multiple-cue environment. Each column of the stimulus matrix represents one stimulus observation (vacation experience) encompassing three segments, for associated target person (partner), the positive versus negative valence, and the spatial context. Actual stimulus observations are noisy copies of vectors representing partner prototypes (for partner A, B, O in the first segment), or an ideal pattern of positivity (in the second segment).

patterns are not exactly the same, because of forgetting, information loss, or the basic ambiguity of the multiple-cue environment. In spite of this noise in the cue matrix, the stimulus vectors at least resemble (i.e., correlate with) their referents. For instance, the first four stimuli all correlate in the upper segment with the prototype of partner A (in the range of $r = 0.61$ to 0.67). Or, all pleasant vacations correlate, in the middle segment, with the ideal of pleasantness.

Now, consider the process by which an evaluative judgment can be elicited. The task instruction could be to judge one's satisfaction with one particular partner, say, A. This means the participant is to approach the matrix with a prompt vector that has the prototype of the target partner, A, in the upper segment (and neutral or zero values in the other segments). BIAS assesses the similarity of this prompt to every column vector (e.g., in terms of the dot product, or the number of matching minus mismatching features). Each item (column vector) is then weighted by this similarity index so that the resulting weight reflects the degree to which an item is relevant to the prompt. Finally, an aggregate is computed as the horizontal sum of all weighted column vectors, in accordance with the task to judge one's overall satisfaction with A. The judgment outcome (i.e., the overall satisfaction with the target partner) requires a comparison with a criterion. Judged satisfaction is the correlation, within the valence segment, of the aggregate with the ideal type of positive valence.

This example illustrates the basic judgment process. To summarize, a prompt serves to screen memory for relevant information and to weight it accordingly. Then an aggregate is formed and compared with an ideal pattern reflecting the judgment criterion (e.g., the ideal or maximal point on a satisfaction scale). In Figure 10.5, using the partner A prompt yields an aggregate that correlates $+0.40$ with positive valence (in the respective segment). For comparison, the negative correlation for partner B (-0.37) would reflect dissatisfaction.

Introducing Mood into BIAS

Let us now assume the judge is in a positive mood. Within a Brunwikian multiple-cue framework, mood states, like concepts, can be represented as noisy multiple-cue vectors; there is no fundamental difference in representation. Apart from various body cues and internal cues, the distributive representation of positive mood should to some degree overlap with the positive valence segment of stimulus objects. Thus, the cues mediating positive mood and positive stimulus valence are partly the same (see also Niedenthal and Halberstadt, this volume). Now, the prompt that elicits a judgment in positive mood can be assumed to include not only the judgment target but also some cues that reflect the judge's current mood (in the overlapping area of the valence segment). How will the algorithm respond when prompted with this target-mood blend? Obviously, it will give high weights not only to those column vectors that resemble the target but also to those memory entries that share the judge's positive mood. As a consequence, the aggregate will tend to resemble the conjunction of the target and positive valence, and the resulting judgment will be biased toward the ideal of positive valence and thus exhibit mood congruency.

One noteworthy implication of this way of conceiving the interface of subject mood and stimulus valence (as cue overlap) is that so-called mood effects on cognition do not require genuine emotions or mood states. Any other context stimuli that convey the same set of affective valence cues, or just a subset thereof, should be sufficient to produce the typical effect (see Blascovich & Mendes, this volume). Consistent with this notion, there is empirical evidence that in order to increase recall of pleasant and unpleasant words, one does not have to induce enduring emotional states in participants (Fiedler, 1991). Rather, it is sufficient that pictures providing mood-congruent cues are projected on the wall, changing as rapidly as the word stimuli to be learned (e.g., a sunny-beach picture while learning a positive word, or an accident picture while learning a negative word).

Simulating Affect and Cognition Findings within the BIAS Framework

Having introduced the BIAS notation and having depicted the valence segment as an affect–cognition interface, I now describe computer simulations that account for the common findings in affect and cognition. The goal here is to integrate within the same framework both classes of empirical results, mood-congruency and cognitive style.

According to the social judgment context, all simulations use stimulus vectors that include cue segments for the target person, valence (also relevant to mood), and various semantic categories (denoting stereotypes, traits, or context conditions). For example, the stimulus experience of a serious car accident could involve (a) the pattern of an unknown target person in the first segment, (b) the typical pattern of negative valence associated with accidents in the second segment, (c) the stereotype pattern of juvenile drivers in the third segment, (d) the traits (reckless, incautious) associated with this stereotype in the next segment, and (e) the semantic category of severe injuries in the fifth segment. For simplicity, only binary cue values are permitted (patterns of + and −), but the model could use more fine-graded cue values as well.

Influence of Retrieval Mood on Judgment and Inference

The simplest case to start with (that was silently taken for granted in the preceding illustration) is that of retrieval mood influences on social judgment. Assume that no emotion is induced during encoding. As each new stimulus is presented, a column vector is appended to the matrix, including the cue pattern of the stimulus person (if available), valence, and the other meaning aspects in the corresponding segments. Each stimulus vector resembles, but is not identical with, the target in the target segment. In the valence segment, the similarity of each stimulus to ideal valence determines the positivity of a stimulus. Likewise, in the other segments, the resemblance to ideal trait patterns describes the position of the stimulus on semantic dimensions. Some noise or information loss is imposed on the matrix, owing to unreliable perception, lack of attention, forgetting, and less-than-perfect cue validities, by randomly inverting a proportion i of cue values. For the moment, let $i = 0.3$, indicating that 30% of all cue values are inverted. Presenting 15 positive and 15 negative behavior descriptions about the same target person P, then, amounts to accruing 30 matrix columns of which 15 resemble and 15 diverge from the prototypical pattern of positivity in the valence segment.

The mood manipulation is assumed to precede the retrieval and judgment process. To simulate a judgment of person P, the judgment prompt has to include the cue pattern for P plus, in the valence segment, a pattern that reflects the induced mood state. Positive mood is represented by a pattern that overlaps with the ideal type of positive valence, whereas the negative mood pattern overlaps with typical cue values for negative valence. All other segments in the prompt vector remain empty. To repeat the procedure, the prompt is applied to the matrix – in matrix notation, this amounts to premultiplying the transposed vector – and BIAS weights each matrix column by its resemblance (dot product) to the prompt and computes the aggregate across all weighted columns. When the individual is in positive mood (i.e., the prompt overlaps with positive-valence cues) this algorithm will give more weight to positive stimuli than in negative mood. This congruency effect will be reflected in the fact that the positive-mood aggregate will correlate higher with ideal positivity in the valence segment than an aggregate prompted under negative mood.

Specifically, the computer simulation of each judgment was based on a randomly drawn 6-cue pattern to represent the ideal target P, a 10-cue pattern for valence, and random cue values in all other segments to reflect variable stimulus meanings. Fifteen matrix columns were generated for positive valence and 15 matrix columns for negative valence. In each case, the target person pattern was inserted in the first segment, the respective valence pattern in the second segment, and random values in all other segments. The ideal cue pattern from which negative stimuli were generated was not the perfect inverse of ideal positivity, but an imperfect mirror image with 7 out of the 10 valence cues inverted. A proportion of $i = 0.3$ of all cue values was inverted, due to information loss or noise in the probabilistic-cue world. The judgment prompt consisted of the target person prototype in the first segment and a pattern for the mood condition in the valence segment, with null values in all other segments. The pattern for positive (negative) mood consisted of 6 randomly selected cues from the positive (negative) valence ideal, with inverted values on the remaining 4 cues. A mood-valence overlap of only 6 out of 10 (1 above chance) was chosen to demonstrate the sensitivity of the algorithm even to very weak pattern similarity.

One hundred "yoked pairs of participants" were simulated, each based on new randomly chosen patterns denoting the target person and the ideal patterns for valence. Within each yoked pair, one simulated participant was assigned to the positive and negative mood condition. The mean positivity of judgments in the positive-mood group is $r = 0.47$, as compared with a mean evaluative judgment of $r = 0.02$ in the negative-mood condition. This difference is clearly significant in an analysis of variance F-test, $F(1,99) = 115.54$, $p < .001$.

Influence of Encoding Mood on Elaboration

Remember the crucial psychological assumption of the dual-force approach: Elated moods are assumed to facilitate generative inferences, whereas depressed moods are assumed to support conservation of stimulus details. To investigate these assumptions, a more refined picture is needed of the encoding process. Encoding is not merely the passive registration of experimenter-provided stimuli but may be actively enriched by more or less productive encoding inferences. These elaborative inferences can be described as judgments during encoding, much like the judgments simulated in the last section. There is ample evidence that performance will generally increase with the amount of elaborative inferences during encoding (Craik & Tulving, 1975).

How can such active inferences during encoding be implemented in the algorithm? As a matter of rule, encoding elaborations involve knowledge structures residing in long-term memory. That is, stimuli come into contact with schemata, stereotypes, or other semantic categories that mediate the inferences beyond the information given. In simulating this top-down influence, existing knowledge structures are also conceived as a vector reflecting an aggregate of former learning. For example, the knowledge vector in Figure 10.6 reflects a learned stereotype. The first two segments are again reserved for a target person or group and the valence; the third segment contains the stereotype address (e.g., juvenile car drivers), and the fourth and fifth segments represent attributes (recklessness; severe injury) associated with this stereotype. As already said, such a stereotype vector can be understood as a crystallized aggregate of a former stimulus matrix.

Encoding inferences or "internal judgments" are elicited as the knowledge of the stereotype vector is prompted. When a new stimulus is provided that resembles the stereotype within the third segment (juvenile driver), the inference module is activated and the response is a weighted image of the knowledge vector (the activation weight again reflecting the similarity of the prompt). This internal "mini-judgment" (like a weighted aggregate across a single vector) is then

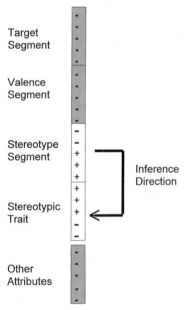

Figure 10.6. Graphical representation of a knowledge vector guiding inferences from stereotype label to associated trait. To the extent that an eliciting prompt matches the pattern of the stereotype label (in the third segment), the inference module responds with a pattern resembling the stereotypical trait (in the fourth segment).

appended (encoded) to the stimulus matrix in much the same way as an original stimulus. In fact, such internally generated stimuli may be stronger than, and may sometimes replace, the raw stimuli. In the present example, prompting the stereotype of juvenile car drivers may enrich the original stimulus input by attributes inferred in the fourth and fifth segment (recklessness; expectation of severe injury).

In this way, encoding elaboration serves to replace missing or noisy segments by systematic idealized knowledge. Two effects of such knowledge-based inference can be distinguished. On the one hand, new attributes can be inferred in a formally empty segment (e.g., the trait "reckless" may be inferred from the juvenile car driver stereotype). On the other hand, incomplete or fragmentary segments may be replaced by more ideal or prototypical information. Thus, although the original may only slightly resemble the stereotype, once the knowledge is activated a more ideal copy of a juvenile car driver can be encoded. Or, an ambivalent, only slightly negative pattern in the valence segment may be replaced by an ambivalent pattern as the stimulus is linked to an evaluatively negative stereotype.

Both types of inference, to attributes in new segments as well as idealized completion of old segments, should be more likely in positive than in negative mood. To simulate this basic assumption, we can assume that in positive mood the similarity threshold for prompting knowledge structures is lower than in negative mood. The other part of the theory, that negative mood supports the conservation of stimulus details, could either mean that inferences are avoided (using a high threshold) or that stimuli are more accurately assessed (using a reduced i parameter for information loss).

In either case, BIAS produces similar predictions. In particular, BIAS can simulate the often-reported finding that stereotyping and other top-down influences increase under positive mood (Forgas, 1992; Forgas & Fiedler, 1996). The literature on affect and social judgment provides strong evidence that both new attribute inferences and idealizing inferences are facilitated under positive mood. On the one hand, the well-known increase of stereotype influence in positive mood pertains to the cross-segmental inference, from a stereotype label to an associated trait or behavior (see Bless, Schwarz, & Kemmelmeier, 1997; Bodenhausen, Kramer, & Süsser, 1994; Forgas, 1992; Forgas & Moylan, 1991). On the other hand, the idealized completion of imperfect vectors plays an essential role in persuasion experiments in which participants in good mood have been shown to differentiate less between strong and weak arguments than participants in bad mood (Bless, Bohner, Schwarz, & Strack, 1990; Mackie & Worth, 1989). Recent findings suggest that people in good mood do not simply lack the capacity or ability to discriminate strong and weak arguments (Bless et al., 1996). Rather, they rely to a greater degree on knowledge-based inferences (Bless & Fiedler, 1995) and presumably turn weak, imperfect stimulus arguments into more complete, idealized patterns.

Impact of Encoding Mood on Social Judgment

Both variants of mood effects on social judgments – pertaining to the common findings in stereotyping and in persuasion research – can be easily simulated. To demonstrate the mood-and-stereotyping effect, a 6-cue pattern is used to represent targets, a 10-cue pattern for valence, 6 cues to represent a stereotype label (e.g., bank teller), and two empty 6-cue segments to denote stereotypic traits (e.g., reliable, cold). One hundred replications of "yoked" cases (one for positive mood and one for negative mood) were again simulated. In each simulation, 15 positive and 15 negative items (valence segment) were paired with the same target person, starting from (randomly selected) prototype patterns for target, valence, and stereotype. Negative valence was not a full inverse of the positive valence ideal but only inverted in 7 cues. As before, positive and negative mood was represented by a pattern that overlapped with the ideal of positive and negative valence in 6 out of 10 cues. The third segment contained the stereotype label (e.g., a cue pattern denoting a bank teller). The last two segments were left open to reflect the absence of explicit information. The information loss parameter was held constant at $i = 0.3$; that is, the influence of negative mood was not simulated through enhanced cue fidelity but only through reduced inferential activities.

During encoding, the positive and negative mood condition within each pair were treated differently. According to the enhanced inference assumption for positive mood, the threshold for invoking the inference module was set at a lower value for positive (dot product > +2 in the stereotype label segment) than negative mood (dot product > +4). Inferences were based on a knowledge vector with the stereotype label in the third segment and ideal trait patterns in segments four and five. The inference module employed the normal BIAS algorithm, using the noisy stereotype label segment of the incoming stimulus as a prompt and producing the idealized pattern of the stereotype vector (weighted by the degree of match) as output, obscured with the normal $i = 0.3$ noise factor. The vectors resulting from inferences (with the inferred traits in segments four and five) were added to the 30 stimulus columns.

After all stimulus items and potential inferences were encoded in this way, the final judgments (using the target as prompt) regarding both stereotype traits were calculated as the correlation, within segments four and five, between the resulting aggregate and the ideal types of the two criterion traits (e.g., reliable and cold). As the upper panel of Table 10.1 reveals, these simulated stereotype judgments are higher for positive mood ($r = 0.73$ and 0.75) than for negative mood ($r = 0.64$ and 0.68). This outcome holds to the same extent for both traits, $F(1,99) = 21.96$, $p < 0.001$. As predicted, the aggregate accrues more information about stereotypical traits under positive than under negative mood.

In this demonstration, it was assumed that stereotypical trait inferences are nonselective; that is, positive mood facilitated the inference of both traits to the same degree. However, it is likely that mood-congruent inferences to positively valued traits are particularly supported under positive mood, according to the assumption that the generative stage is mood-selective. Thus, positive traits (e.g., a bank teller's being reliable) should be inferred more readily under positive mood than negative traits (e.g., cold). The reverse should hold for negative mood, which should, however, give rise to fewer inferences. This case of mood-selective stereotype judgment was simulated using a lower noise factor for encoding of mood-congruent ($i = 0.1$) than for

Table 10.1. *Simulated Influence of Encoding Inferences in Positive and Negative Mood States on Stereotypical Judgments*

	Positive Mood		Negative Mood	
Simulated Process	*Trait 1*	*Trait 2*	*Trait 1*	*Trait 2*
Unselective inferences during encoding	0.73	0.75	0.64	0.68
Mood-congruent inferences during encoding	0.89	0.42	0.34	0.85

incongruent inferences ($i = 0.4$). The theoretically predicted outcome is an asymmetric interaction, reflecting higher judgments on mood-congruent traits, with a generally stronger congruency effect under positive than under negative mood.

Consistent with this expectation, the simulated trait judgments (bottom panel of Table 10.1) reflect both a congruency effect, $F(1,99) = 393.72$, $p < 0.001$, and a generally stronger impact on stereotype judgments in positive than negative mood states, $F(1,99) = 6.46$, $p < 0.05$. When both tendencies work in the same direction (i.e., positive trait judged under positive mood), the judgment is especially strong ($r = 0.89$). When they work against each other (e.g., negative trait judged under positive mood), the reduced judgments ($r = 0.42$) reflect a conflict between the incongruent valence and the enhanced inferential activity under positive mood (as compared with $r = 0.34$ for positive trait judged under negative mood).

Mood and Persuasive Communication

The persuasive-communication paradigm may serve to illustrate the idealizing inference type whereby impoverished input vectors are completed and replaced by more informative or less ambigous patterns. A cue matrix was generated covering 10 columns (a 10-argument message), using a 6-cue prototype for the attitude label (i.e., the linguistic address used for prompting) and 10-cue ideal type segment denoting strong arguments for the attitude in question (e.g., legislation of abortion). In the strong-argument conditions, the second segment deviated only slightly from the ideal ($i = 0.2$). In contrast, in the weak-argument condition, the arguments differed markedly from the ideal ($i = 0.4$).

A 2 × 2 design was employed, involving the manipulation of positive versus negative mood and of strong versus weak arguments. Accordingly, each simulation case involves one quadruple of related cases. The impact of mood was again simulated by the number of encoding inferences that were based on a knowledge vector with the linguistic address (name) of an attitude in the first segment and an ideal pattern for a convincing argument (cogent evidence for the attitude) in the other segment. As a stimulus argument resembled this knowledge vector in the first segment (above threshold), the inference module was invoked and the stimulus pattern was replaced by the idealized pattern (with $i = 0.1$). This module turns weak points for an attitude (mere allusions, related jokes, ill-articulated arguments) into self-generated strong arguments. In positive mood, the inference threshold was lower ($+2$) than in negative mood ($+4$). Thus, the active cooperation of message receivers in good mood should compensate for weaknesses in the stimulus input.

Given these assumptions, the theoretcially and predicted pattern can be confirmed. Messages consisting of strong arguments are more effective than weak arguments, as measured by the correlation between the aggregate across all encoded arguments and inferences and the ideal type of an optimally persuasive argument in the second segment. However, the impact of message quality is stronger in negative than in positive mood in which more inferences are elicited that turn weak arguments into strong ones.

Mood Effects on Recall

Since recalling an item involves naming and communicating that item, one segment must be assumed for a name or label. Recall means to respond with that label when the item has been found in memory; this presupposes that a concept must be permanently stored in long-term memory. In free recall, when the task provides no explicit retrieval cue, the recall process can be conceived as being prompted by an internal activation pattern that can be termed a retrieval structure (Kintsch, 1988). Within the present framework, a retrieval structure is conceived as an aggregate of all cue values in all segments that have been been inferred during encoding.

To illustrate, the learning stage might provide 20 positive and 20 negative behavior descriptions. Each stimulus vector has to include at least one segment for the name or verbal label, one segment for valence, and additional segments to denote the semantic attributes that define the particular stimulus behavior. For instance, several negative items might be related to the category "dishonesty" so that the dishonesty pattern would be inferred several times. On aggregate, this should provide a strong retrieval cue on subsequent recall, making recall of dishonesty-related stimuli quite likely. Among all dishonesty-related stimuli, one item might refer to cheating on an exam and another one to stealing money. These specific attributes should be represented much weaker in the aggregate and they might be totally lost (owing to lack of attention or noise in the system). The effective retrieval structure on free recall is the aggregate of all encoding inferences in all semantic segments.

The free-recall simulation, then, starts with the presentation of all stimulus vectors and the encoding of stimulus vectors. In addition to the name and valence segment, further segments are appended for new semantic dimensions, resulting in a matrix that may have many row segments. Not every stimulus will have entries in all segments, but the entire matrix will afford segments for a variety of semantic aspects. The aggregate of this matrix can be considered the (internal) prompt or retrieval structure for free recall, something like the activation pattern across all stimulus aspects. Free recall involves a search for concepts in memory which resemble this prompt.

How can mood congruency be explained within this free-recall algorithm? On the one hand, the impact of *mood at the time of retrieval* is easily understood. Assuming, as before, that the affective valence segment of the current mood is included in the recall prompt, it is clear that mood-congruent stimuli are more likely to match the prompt than incongruent concepts. As a consequence, more congruent than incongruent items can be found.

On the other hand, BIAS also predicts a congruency effect for *encoding mood*. As explained in a previous section, this prediction derives from the assumption that encoding inferences are likely to be of similar valence as the encoder's affective state. Thus, the attribute "dishonesty" is more likely to be inferred in negative than in positive mood, whereas a segment for "charming" is more likely inferred in positive mood. As a consequence, the retrieval structure that is constructed during encoding should be biased toward mood-congruent semantic aspects. To the extent that the retrieval structure determines subsequent recall, the output will exhibit (encoding) mood congruency. Note, however, that this process is dependent on active mood-congruent inferences during encoding; if only the original stimulus details were encoded, rather than active inferences, there would be no congruency bias. Thus, the depicted algorithm is in close agreement with the finding that (encoding) mood congruency increases with the degree of inferential activity (Fiedler, 1990, 1991). Moreover, given that inferential activities are assumed to be stronger in positive than negative mood, the model correctly predicts an asymmetrically stronger congruency effect for positive than for negative mood.

Discussion

The purpose of the present chapter was to explicate a theory of the affect-cognition interface in terms of a transparent, fully specified computer algorithm. The proposed algorithm, BIAS, was not only able to simulate the two major classes of empirical findings – mood congruency and mood effects on cognitive style – but also accounted for a variety of interactions and more refined predictions derived from a dual-force approach to affect and cognition. Since the BIAS algorithm is precise and not contingent on verbal rhetoric, it clearly specifies the assumptions and processes of the underlying theory. In particular, the crucial assumption that positive mood supports assimilation (top-down inferences based on internalized knowledge) whereas negative mood supports accommodation (bottom-up stimulus fidelity) was explicated through clearly specified steps of the algorithm.

On the one hand, the assimilative style under positive mood may reflect any of the following knowledge-based operations: (a) extending a stimulus vector by inferred segments, (b) replacing a stimulus fragment by an inferred ideal type, and (c) encoding inferred stimuli in addition to experimenter-provided stimuli. On the other hand, the accommodation tendency under negative mood can be due to (a) abstinence from the above type of inferences and/or (b) a reduced parameter i for information loss. Although the reported simulations do not speak to all these possibilities entailing different operations, they clearly demonstrate that most empirical findings can in principle be explained through simple associative rules in a connectionist framework. To summarize, BIAS can account for mood-congruent judgment and recall, congruency effects of encoding mood and retrieval mood, increased stereotyping under positive mood, and the higher sensitivity to argument strength in negative than in positive mood. Furthermore, some refined predictions of the dual-force model are borne out, such as the stronger congruency effect for positive than negative mood or the enhanced congruency effect on highly inferential tasks.

Several simplifying assumptions were imposed on the BIAS algorithm. Thus, binary cue values (+ vs. −) were assumed rather than continuous values, arbitrary similarity functions (correlations, dot products) were used, and the segment length was chosen arbitrarily. It should be emphasized, however, that the qualitative pattern of predictions is robust over a reasonable range of parameters. Also, convergent results could be obtained with other connectionist models (Kruschke, 1992; McClelland & Rumelhart, 1985; Metcalfe-Eich, 1982), which suggests that the present results are not peculiar to BIAS alone.

Theoretical Assets of the BIAS Approach

Does BIAS only paraphrase a conventional associative approach to mood priming (Bower, 1981; Clark, Milberg, & Ross, 1983)? Or does it have unique implications that cannot be reduced to a standard associative network? Suffice it to mention two innovative ideas. First, a central feature of BIAS is its sensitivity to aggregation effects; that is, any latent information pattern will be more apparent with an increasing number of encoded matrix columns. Aggregation means to filter out noise and to make systematic variance visible. Without this feature, the impact of encoding inferences (i.e., assimilation vs. accommodation) on memory in general (i.e., the generation effect; Dosher & Russo, 1976; Fiedler et al., 1992), mood-congruent memory (Fiedler & Stroehm, 1986), and creativity (Isen et al., 1982) could not be explained by a unitary principle. It is aggregation that explains the creation of new ideas and the enriched encoding under positive moods.

The second important feature is the subsymbolic level of representation (Smith, 1996; Smolensky, 1988). While the nodes in a traditional network are themselves meaningful, the units of a connectionist model such as BIAS (i.e., the individual cues) do not themselves carry meaning, but meaning is distributed over patterns of cue units. (Only for convenience, the cues used in figures have been named, to avoid too high a level of abstractness.) It is this subsymbolic level that explains the interface of an individual's mood and the valence of a stimulus. Although these two constructs are categorically different at the symbolic level, they are mediated by similar, overlapping cues at the subsymbolic level.

In addition to the mood–valence interface, the subsymbolic representation can cope with empirical problems that are hard to overcome in a symbolic network. Thus, to explain mood congruency, a traditional model has to predict that the associative distance is shorter between nodes of same valence. However, free recall protocols are rarely clustered by pronounced valence patterns, but positive and negative stimuli alternate in close succession. This is not surprising given that opposites such as warm–cold or good–bad are close associates. Within a subsymbolic, distributed memory framework, this can be easily explained because opposites differ only in one or two features while sharing many other semantic features.

It remains to be shown in future research whether such assets of connectionist approaches lead to fundamentally new insights and empirical progress. The purpose here was merely to illustrate that an integrative algorithmic account of the affect-cognition interface is possible and that its potential should not be ignored. Since recent research advances in this area are characterized by many intriguing phenomena but little theoretical innovation, looking for new theoretical devices appears to be timely and promising.

References

Anderson, J. R. (1983). *The architecture of cognition.* Cambridge, MA: Harvard University Press.
Barsalou, L. W. (1985). Ideals, central tendency, and frequency of instantiation as determinants of graded structure in categories. *Journal of Experimental Psychology: Learning, Memory & Cognition, 11,* 629–649.
Blaney, P. H. (1986). Affect and memory: A review. *Psychological Bulletin, 99,* 229–246.
Bless, H., Bohner, G., Schwarz, N., & Strack, F. (1980). Mood and persuasion: A cognitive response analysis. *Personality and Social Psychology Bulletin, 16,* 331–345.
Bless, H., Clore, G. L., Schwarz, N., Golisano, V., Rabe, C., & Wölk, M. (1996). Mood and the use of scripts: Does a happy mood really lead to mindlessness? *Journal of Personality and Social Psychology, 71,* 665–679.
Bless, H., & Fiedler, K. (1995). Affective states and the influence of activated general knowledge structures. *Personality and Social Psychology Bulletin, 21,* 766–778.
Bless, H., Schwarz, N., & Kemmelmeier, M. (1997). Mood and stereotyping: Affective states and the use of general knowledge structures. *European Review of Social Psychology, 7,* 63–93.
Bodenhausen, G. V., Kramer, G. P., & Süsser, K. (1994). Happiness and stereotypic thinking in social judgment. *Journal of Personality and Social Psychology, 66,* 621–632.
Borkenau, P. (1990). Traits as ideal-based and goal-derived social categories. *Journal of Personality and Social Psychology, 58,* 381–396.
Bower, G. H. (1981). Mood and memory. *American Psychologist, 36,* 129–148.
Brunswik, E. (1956). *Perception and the representative design of experiments.* Berkeley: University of California Press.
Clark, H. H., & Haviland, S. E. (1977). Comprehension and the given-new contract. In R. O. Freedle (Ed.), *Discourse production and comprehension* (pp. 1–40). Norwood, NJ: Ablex.
Clark, M. S., Milberg, S., & Ross, J. (1983). Arousal cues arousal-related mate-

rial in memory: Implications for understanding effects of mood on memory. *Journal of Verbal Learning and Verbal Behavior, 22,* 633–649.

Clore, G. L., Schwarz, N., & Conway, M. (1994). Cognitive causes and consequences of emotion. In R. S. Wyer & T. K. Srull (Eds.), *Handbook of social cognition* (2nd ed., pp. 323–417). Hillsdale, NJ: Erlbaum.

Craik, F. I. M., & Tulving, E. (1975). Depth of processing and the retention of words in episodic memory. *Journal of Experimental Psychology: General, 104,* 268–294.

Dosher, B. A., & Russo, J. E. (1976). Memory for internally generated stimuli. *Journal of Experimental Psychology: Human Learning and Memory, 2,* 633–640.

Ellis, H. C., & Ashbrook, P. W. (1988). Resource allocation model of the effects of depressed mood states on memory. In K. Fiedler & J. P. Forgas (Eds.), *Affect, cognition, and social behavior* (pp. 25–43). Toronto: Hogrefe.

Fiedler, K. (1985). Zur Stimmungsabhaengigkeit kognitiver Funktionen. *Psychologische Rundschau, 36,* 125–134.

Fiedler, K. (1988). Emotional mood, cognitive style, and behavior regulation. In K. Fiedler, & J. P. Forgas (Eds.), *Affect, cognition, and social behavior* (pp. 100–119). Toronto: Hogrefe.

Fiedler, K. (1990). Mood-dependent selectivity in social cognition. In W. Stroebe & M. Hewstone (Eds.), *European Review of Social Psychology* (Vol. 1). New York: Wiley.

Fiedler, K. (1991). On the task, the measures, and the mood in research on affect and social cognition. In J. P. Forgas (Ed.), *Emotion and social judgments.* Cambridge: Cambridge University Press.

Fiedler, K. (1996). Explaining and simulating judgment biases as an aggregation phenomenon in probabilistic, multiple-cue environments. *Psychological Review, 103,* 193–214.

Fiedler, K. (in press). Affective states trigger processes of assimilation and accommodation. In L. L. Martin & G. L. Clore (Eds.), *Moods and information processing.* Hillsdale, NJ: Erlbaum.

Fiedler, K., Asbeck, J., & Nickel, S. (1991). Mood and constructive memory effects on social judgment. *Cognition and Emotion, 5,* 363–378.

Fiedler, K., & Bless, H. (1998). The formation of beliefs in the interface of affective and cognitive processes. In N. H. Frijda, S. R. Manstead, & S. Bem (Eds.), *Emotions and beliefs.* Unpublished manuscript.

Fiedler, K., & Forgas, J. P. (Eds.) (1988). *Affect, cognition, and social behavior.* Toronto: Hogrefe.

Fiedler, K., Lachnit, H., Fay, D., & Krug, C. (1992). Mobilization of cognitive resources and the generation effect. *Quarterly Journal of Experimental Psychology, 45A,* 149–171.

Fiedler, K., Nickel, S., & Mühlfriedel, T. (1997). *Is mood congruency a matter of discrimination or response bias?* Unpublished research, University of Heidelberg.

Fiedler, K., Pampe, H., & Scherf, U. (1986). Mood and memory for tightly organized social information. *European Journal of Social Psychology, 16,* 149–164.

Fiedler, K., & Stroehm, W. (1986). What kind of mood influences what kind of memory: The role of arousal and information structure. *Memory & Cognition, 14,* 181–188.

Fiedler, K., & Walka, I. (1993). Training lie detectors to use nonverbal cues instead of global heuristics. *Human Communication Research, 20,* 199–223.

Forgas, J. P. (1992). On mood and peculiar people: Affect and person typicality in impression formation. *Journal of Personality and Social Psychology, 62,* 863–875.

Forgas, J. P. (1995). Mood and judgment: The affect infusion model (AIM). *Psychological Bulletin, 116,* 39–66.

Forgas, J. P., & Fiedler, K. (1996). Mood effects on intergroup discrimination: The role of affect in reward allocation decisions. *Journal of Personality and Social Psychology, 70,* 28–40.

Forgas, J. P., & Moylan, S. J. (1991). Affective influences on stereotype judgments. *Cognition & Emotion, 5,* 379–395.

Isen, A. M. (1984). Toward understanding the role of affect in cognition. In R. S. Wyer & T. K. Srull (Eds.), *Handbook of social cognition* (Vol. 3, 2nd ed, pp. 179–236). Hillsdale, NJ: Erlbaum.

Isen, A. M., Means, B., Patrick, R., & Nowicki, G. P. (1982). Some factors influencing decision-making and risk taking. In M. S. Clark & S. T. Fiske (Eds.), *Affect and cognition* (pp. 243–261). Hillsdale, NJ: Erlbaum.

Kintsch, W. (1988). The role of knowledge in discourse comprehension: A construction-integration model. *Psychological Review, 95,* 163–182.

Kruschke, J. K. (1992). ALCOVE. *Psychological Review, 99,* 22–44.

McClelland, J. L., & Rumelhart, D. E. (1985). Distributed memory and the representation of general and specific information. *Journal of Experimental Psychology: General, 114,* 159–188.

Mackie, D. M., & Worth, L. T. (1989). Cognitive deficits and the mediation of positive affect in persuasion. *Journal of Personality and Social Psychology, 57,* 27–40.

Mayer, J. D., & Salovey, P. (1988). Personality moderates the interaction of mood and cognition. In K. Fiedler & J. P. Forgas (Eds.), *Affect, cognition, and social behavior* (pp. 87–99). Toronto: Hogrefe.

Metcalfe-Eich, J. (1982). A composite holographic associative recall model. *Psychological Review, 89,* 627–661.

Ostrom, T. M. (1988). Computer simulation: The third symbol system. *Journal of Experimental Social Psychology, 24,* 381–392.

Piaget, J. (1952). *The origins of intelligence in children.* New York: International University Press.

Schwarz, N., & Clore, G. L. (1983). Mood, misattribution, and judgments of well-being: Informative and directive functions of affective states. *Journal of Personality and Social Psychology, 45,* 513–523.

Schwarz, N., & Clore, G. L. (1988). How do I feel about it? The informative function of affective states. In K. Fiedler & J. P. Forgas (Eds.), *Affect, cognition, and social behavior* (pp. 44–62). Toronto: Hogrefe.

Simon, H. A. (1982). Affect and cognition: Comments. In M. S. Clark & S. T. Fiske (Eds.), *Affect and cognition* (pp. 333–342). Hillsdale, NJ: Erlbaum.

Slamecka, N. J., & Graf, P. (1978). The generation effect: Delineation of a phenomenon. *Journal of Experimental Psychology: Learning, Memory and Cognition, 4,* 592–604.

Smith, E. R. (1996). What do connectionism and social psychology offer each other? *Journal of Personality and Social Psychology, 70,* 893–912.

Smolensky, P. (1988). On the proper treatment of connectionism. *Behavioral and Brain Sciences, 11,* 1–74.

Strack, F., Schwarz, N., & Gschneidinger, E. (1985). Happiness and reminiscing: The role of time perspective, mood, and role of thinking. *Journal of Personality and Social Psychology, 49,* 1460–1469.

Wittgenstein, L. (1953). *Philosophical investigations.* New York: Macmillan.

Zuckerman, M., DePaulo, B. M., & Rosenthal, R. (1981). Verbal and nonverbal communication of deception. In L. Berkowitz (Ed.), *Advances in experimental social psychology* (Vol. 14, pp. 1–59). New York: Academic Press.

11. Affect and Information Processing Strategies

An Interactive Relationship

JOSEPH P. FORGAS

Introduction: Affect and Processing Strategies

Affect is an integral part of how we deal with the social world. The cumulative evidence from the chapters included in this volume, as well as other extensive research clearly shows that affect has a major impact on social cognition, judgments, and reasoning (Damasio, 1994; Oatley & Jenkins, 1992, 1996). Making sense of the social world typically requires us to go "beyond the information given." Affective influences occur because social thinking necessarily involves highly constructive, generative mental operations (Asch, 1946; Bruner, 1957; Heider, 1958). It is in the course of such constructive thinking that affect may either indirectly (through affect priming mechanisms) or directly (through affect-as-information mechanisms) influence the kind of information we process, and the way we process it. It is due to such affective influences that when in a bad mood we may see an entertainer such as Jerry Seinfeld as an irritating twerp, yet may laugh wholeheartedly at his jokes when in a more positive affective state. Positive mood may even help us see our intimate relationships in a more rosy light as deep, involving, and rewarding one day, whereas negative affect produces a much more critical assessment of the same partner on another (Forgas, 1994a; Forgas, Levinger, & Moylan, 1994).

This work was supported by a Special Investigator award from the Australian Research Council, and the Research Prize by the Alexander von Humboldt Foundation to Joseph P. Forgas. The contributions of Stephanie Moylan and Joan Webb to this project are gratefully acknowledged.

Please address all correspondence in connection with this paper to Joseph P. Forgas, at the School of Psychology, University of New South Wales, Sydney 2052, Australia; e-mail: jp.forgas@unsw.edu.au.

However, such examples of affect congruence present only half the story of how affect is linked to social judgments and reasoning. Although both affect-congruency and incongruency effects have been demonstrated, at times affect may have no effect at all on social thinking. How can we explain these apparently elusive effects?

This chapter will argue that different processing strategies adopted by people in response to different circumstances are the key to understanding why we sometimes observe congruency, incongruency, or no affective influences on social cognition and judgments. The relationship between processing style and affect is not unidirectional, however. Just as different processing styles can influence the presence and extent of affect congruence in thinking, affective states can in turn also influence how information is processed. The chapter will briefly outline a multi-process theory, the Affect Infusion Model (AIM; Forgas, 1995a), designed to explain some of these effects. Next, evidence for the process sensitivity of affective influences on cognition and judgments, and interpersonal behaviors is presented. Finally, some of our recent studies demonstrating the reverse mechanism, when affect influences processing styles and judgments will be considered.

The Affect Infusion Model is a comprehensive multiprocess framework designed to explain the different ways in which affect can have an impact on social cognition, judgments, and reasoning. The basic assumption behind AIM, consistent with much of the evidence presented in this book, is that affect can have both informational and processing effects on cognition. Informational effects occur because affect influences the content of cognition (*what* people think). Processing effects occur because affect influences the process of cognition (*how* people think). In contrast to alternative models of affect and cognition, the AIM assigns a central role to different processing strategies in the mediation of mood effects. The AIM assumes that people may deploy a number of alternative processing strategies when dealing with a cognitive task, depending on a range of situational and contextual influences. Thus, the *kind* of processing strategy used is the key to understanding how and why affect influences some cognitive tasks and not others. The empirical studies discussed in this chapter were selected to illustrate such an interactive relationship between processing style and affect.

A Multiprocess Framework: The Affect Infusion Model

The AIM predicts that affect infusion is most likely to occur whenever circumstances promote elaborative, open, constructive information processing style (Fiedler, 1991; Forgas, 1991a, 1991c, 1995a). Only a brief summary of the AIM will be given here, as a more detailed treatment of these ideas is available elsewhere (Forgas, 1992a, 1995a). *Affect infusion* refers to the process whereby affectively loaded information exerts an influence on, and becomes incorporated into cognitive and judgmental processes, entering into a person's deliberations and eventually coloring the outcome (see Forgas, 1995a). The incorporation of affectively loaded information into thinking is less likely to occur when a cognitive task can be performed using simple, directed, or highly motivated processing strategies that do not call for, or allow the use of, affectively primed material. Thus, the AIM assumes that (a) the extent and nature of affect infusion should be dependent on the kind of processing strategy that is used, and (b) that all things being equal people will use the least effortful and simplest processing strategy capable of producing a response.

Alternative Processing Strategies

Four distinct processing strategies were identified within the Affect Infusion Model: *direct access, motivated, heuristic,* and *substantive* processing. The theory predicts that two of these strategies, direct access and motivated processing, involve relatively directed and closed information search and selection strategies that limit the scope for incidental affect infusion to occur. The direct access strategy is the simplest way of producing a response and involves the direct retrieval of a preexisting reaction. People possess a rich store of such crystallized, preformed responses and are likely to use this strategy whenever possible, according to the principle of effort minimization. From the perspective of the AIM, such direct access responses are most likely to occur when the task is well known or familiar, and when no strong cognitive, affective, situational, or motivational cues call for more elaborate processing. Because direct access involves highly cued retrieval strategies and little cognitive elaboration, it allows little opportunity for affectively colored information to be incorporated.

The motivated processing strategy also involves highly selective and targeted information search strategies, directed by a specific motivational objective. Affect infusion is again unlikely. Affect itself may trigger motivated processing, to achieve objectives such as mood maintenance or mood improvement. Other goals that were found to produce motivated processing leading to an absence or even reversal of affect infusion include self-evaluation maintenance, ego enhancement, achievement motivation, affiliation, or ingroup favoritism (Forgas, 1990, 1991b; Forgas & Fiedler, 1996; Forgas, Bower, & Moylan, 1990). Although motivated thinking is extremely common in social situations, little has yet been done to document the exact cognitive information search strategies people use in such instances (but see, e.g., Forgas, 1989, 1991b).

The remaining two processing strategies, heuristic and substantive processing, require more constructive and open-ended processing and information search strategies and thus facilitate affect infusion. The heuristic processing strategy is used when neither stored responses nor a motivational goal can guide judgments, and people seek to compute a constructive response with minimal effort. In such instances, people may rely on limited information and employ cognitive shortcuts or heuristics when responding. Heuristic processing is most likely when the task is simple or highly typical, it is of low personal relevance, cognitive capacity is limited, and there are no motivational or situational pressures for more detailed processing. Responses in such cases may simply be based on superficial or irrelevant associations (Griffitt, 1970). Heuristic processing is most likely to produce affect infusion when judges misattribute their affective state as being informative about their evaluative reactions (Clore, Schwarz, & Conway, 1994; Schwarz & Clore, 1988).

The fourth, substantive processing strategy, occurs when people need to actually select, learn, and interpret novel information and relate this information to their preexisting knowledge structures in order to construct a response. Substantive processing is more likely when the task is complex, novel, or atypical; there is no motivational goal to dominate processing; there is adequate cognitive capacity; and/or the situation calls for constructive, elaborate processing. Affect-priming mechanisms are chiefly responsible for affect infusion in the course of substantive processing. Because substantive processing is an inherently constructive, generative strategy, affect may selectively prime access to, and the use of, related thoughts, ideas, memories, and interpretations. The AIM also makes the counterintuitive prediction that affect infusion should be greater whenever more extensive and constructive processing is required to deal with a more complex, demanding, or novel task. Specific evidence linking more substantive processing to greater affect infusion comes from processing latency and memory data (Forgas & Bower, 1987).

The variables determining processing choices are an integral part of the affect infusion model and comprise characteristics of the *target*, the *judge*, and the *situation*. For example, greater target familiarity, complexity, and typicality are likely to recruit more substantive processing. Important judge features include personal relevance, motivational goals, cognitive capacity, habitual processing styles (as indicated by certain personality traits), and temporary affective state. Situational features influencing processing strategy include a perceived need for accuracy, social desirability expectations, and the availability of objective criteria.

A key aspect of the Affect Infusion Model is the recognition that *affect* itself can play a dual role in social cognition, influencing both the processing choices people make (how they think) as well as the kind of information they are likely to consider (what they think). The AIM, consistent with other theories (see Bless, this volume; Fiedler, this volume), predicts that positive affect should generate more top-down, schematic, and heuristic processing, whereas negative affect triggers more piecemeal, bottom-up, and vigilant processing styles. As discussed in Chapter 1, this positive–negative processing asymmetry can be due to a variety of factors, such as cognitive capacity effects (Mackie & Worth, 1991), functional, evolutionary mechanisms, or motivational influences (Clark & Isen, 1982). Unlike other theories, the AIM also suggests that the processing consequences of positive and negative affect are generally weaker than, and secondary to, the processing requirements associated with target, judge, and situation features. Several experiments show that more demanding, complex, or ambiguous targets do recruit more extensive, substantive processing strategies and thus greater affect infusion in *both* positive and negative mood states (Forgas, 1992b, 1993, 1995b).

The main point emphasized by the AIM is that processing differences are the key to understanding affective influences on cognition. It is also important to recognize, however, that processing choices are multidetermined, and antecedent variables can interact with one another. The processing requirements of task features such as familiarity, complexity, or typicality are quite robust, as suggested by recent experiments (Forgas, 1993, 1995b). The careful analysis of processing variables such as memory, processing latency, and judgmental latency is an essential requirement for testing the predictions of the AIM, as it is only in this way that we can empirically distinguish between affect infusion due to heuristic processing, or substantive processing.

Some Supporting Evidence

The model predicts the *absence* of affect infusion when direct access or motivated processing is used, and the *presence* of affect infusion during heuristic and substantive processing. Consistent with the model, crystallized, direct access responses do not show affect infusion. Thus, judgments that can be performed by accessing crystallized evaluations, such as judgments about highly familiar products (Srull, 1984), familiar health events (Salovey & Birnbaum, 1989), familiar living quarters (Schwarz, Strack, Kommer, & Wagner, 1987), and well-known, focal aspects of the self (Sedikides, 1995) are resistant to affect infusion. Affect infusion is also absent when motivated processing is used. Drawing people's attention to their internal states may often be enough to produce motivated thinking (Berkowitz et al., this volume). Affect itself, and negative affect in particular, may trigger such motivated processing in the service of mood repair (Clark & Isen, 1982). There is clear evidence for motivated processing when sad, but not happy, persons engaged in a personally relevant decision task (selecting a partner for themselves) (Forgas, 1989; 1991b).

The tendency to engage in motivated processing is also related to individual difference variables. Recently, it was found that people who score highly on measures of social desirability and Machiavellianism are more likely to employ motivated processing in interpersonal tasks such as bargaining and negotiation and to show significantly less affect infusion in their judgments and behaviors than do low scorers on these measures (Forgas, 1998a). High trait anxiety may also produce motivated processing and reverse negative mood effects on judgments about threatening outgroups (Ciarrochi & Forgas, 1998a). Motivated processing can thus frequently produce an opposite, affect-incongruent outcome (Sedikides, 1994). It may be that the ability to spontaneously adopt motivated processing to control the aversive consequences of negative affect is a key feature of everyday affect management strategies (Forgas & Ciarrochi, 1998). Motivated processing may also be recruited by situational variables, such as the presence of a group. We found that the infusion of affect into stereotype judgments about groups such as Catholics, Jews, doctors, and farmers were markedly reversed when the judgmental task was carried out in a group rather than alone (Forgas, 1990).

However, affect infusion should be present whenever some degree of open, constructive thinking is required to complete a task. According to the AIM, affect infusion under heuristic processing occurs owing to the affect-as-information mechanism (Schwarz & Clore, 1988). Current affect may then become a convenient (but mistaken) source of inference about an evaluative reaction. Typically, affect infusion due to heuristic processing occurs when the task is of limited relevance, and judges have little time, capacity, and motivation to process more extensively. This can happen when judges are contacted over the telephone (Schwarz & Clore, 1988) or are asked on the street (Forgas & Moylan, 1987) to make quick, off-the-cuff judgments about issues they have not thought much about before. These effects are also easily eliminated simply by making judges aware of the source of their affect (Schwarz & Clore, 1988).

The AIM suggests, however, that most everyday instances of affect infusion of real interest occur in the course of substantive processing. Affect can then act as a prime, facilitating access to affect-congruent thoughts and associations ready to be used in constructive processing (see also Eich & Macaulay, this volume). Indeed, the more extensive the processing, the greater the potential for affect infusion (Bower, 1981; Forgas & Bower, 1987), a counterintuitive prediction now supported by numerous experiments. In the next section we will review some of the evidence indicating the process-dependence of affective influences on cognition and judgments, before turning to studies showing that affective influences on social behaviors are similarly process sensitive.

Processing Strategy Mediates Affect Infusion into Cognition

Task Complexity and Affect Infusion

To directly demonstrate that longer processing produces greater affect infusion, in several recent experiments we varied the extent to which social cognitive tasks required substantive processing. For example, in one series of studies, participants were asked to make judgments about more or less weird, unusual versus prototypical persons. Atypical individuals are harder to process and should thus recruit more extensive judgmental strategies (Forgas, 1992b, Experiment 1). Indeed, judgments of atypical targets showed significantly greater affect infusion and mood congruence than did impressions of easy-to-process, typical targets (Figure 11.1). As expected, memory data confirmed that recall was better for atypical than typical targets, consistent with the more extensive processing of these stimuli (Forgas, 1992b, Experiment 2). An analysis of actual judgmental latencies further confirmed the process mediation of these mood effects (Forgas, 1992b, Experiment 3). Consistent with the AIM, it took longer to judge atypical rather than typical persons, and there was correspondingly greater affect infusion into these more elaborately processed judgments. Because affect infusion increased as processing became more substantive, the greater incidental use of affectively primed material was the most likely mechanism responsible for these effects.

In a series of follow-up studies, nonverbal stimuli rather than verbal descriptions were used to control for possible semantic priming effects. Judgmental targets were pictures of well-matched or badly matched couples. In the first experiment (Forgas, 1995b), pictures of

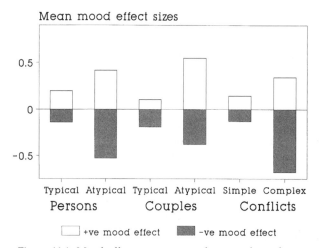

Figure 11.1. Mood effects are greater when people perform more atypical and complex cognitive tasks that require more elaborate, substantive processing. Both positive and negative mood effects were significantly greater (vs. the control condition) when judgments were made about (a) atypical rather than typical others; (b) atypical rather than typical couples; and (c) complex, serious rather than simple interpersonal conflicts (data based on results reported by Forgas, 1992a, 1994a, 1995b).

typical (well-matched for attractiveness) or atypical (mismatched for attractiveness) couples were judged by people feeling good or bad after watching happy or sad films. Affect infusion was again significantly greater for atypical couples (Figure 11.1). Consistent with the AIM, a second experiment found that recall was also better for such mismatched couples likely to recruit greater processing effort. In further studies, couples who were matched or mismatched in terms of two distinct features (physical attractiveness and race) were used to create well-matched, partly matched, and unmatched targets. Again, the greater the degree of mismatch, the more substantive the processing required, and the greater the extent of affect infusion and mood congruence in judgments. A mediational analysis confirmed a significant relationship between the extent of affect infusion and the kind of processing strategy used (the time taken to produce a judgment).

Interestingly, social judgments about highly complex and involving real-life issues, such as relationship conflicts, show similar process specificity. When happy or sad persons were asked to make causal attributions for recent actual conflicts in their relationships (Forgas, 1994a), negative affect produced more critical, self-blaming attributions. In contrast, positive affect resulted in more optimistic explanations, blaming external, and unstable causes for the conflicts. Once again, in a counterintuitive pattern, these mood effects were consistently greater when more extensive, constructive processing was required to deal with more complex, serious rather than simple, everyday events (Figure 11.1). The evidence that judgments about problematic and complex social episodes – even highly familiar ones – are especially prone to affect infusion is of particular interest to clinical and relationship research. The surprising principle predicted by the AIM, and supported in these studies, is that affect infusion in social cognition and judgments may be greatest when perceivers need to think most substantively and constructively about social judgments.

The same pattern was also confirmed recently by Sedikides (1995) in a study of self-judgments. In these experiments, familiar, central aspects of the self-concept required less extensive processing and were less influenced by affect, whereas judgments about less familiar, peripheral aspects of the self-concept required more extensive processing, and showed greater affect sensitivity. These experiments provide clear and convergent evidence for the process sensitivity of affect infusion effects. Contrary to intuition, it appears that cognitive tasks that require more extensive and constructive processing are also likely to produce greater affect infusion and affect congruence, as they provide greater scope for affectively primed information to be used.

Affect Infusion and Intergroup Judgments

The process-sensitivity of mood effects on social judgments and decisions can be further illustrated by a series of experiments conducted on intergroup judgments (Forgas & Fiedler, 1996). In these experiments, people feeling happy or sad were asked to make reward allocation decisions between members of an ingroup and an outgroup, using the traditional minimal group paradigm developed by Tajfel (see Tajfel & Forgas, 1981). To test the predictions of the AIM, the key variable manipulated to induce different processing strategies was the personal relevance of the decision. In the first study, when group membership was of little personal significance, happy people were actually more likely than sad people to unfairly allocate rewards to their ingroup. This effect occurred because positive mood in this instance promoted a more simple, heuristic processing style, leading to a greater reliance on simple group category information when allocating rewards. In the second and third studies, processing strategy was manipulated by emphasizing the personal significance of group membership to some participants, and not to others. Those for whom group membership was of low relevance continued to show greater ingroup favoritism in a happy than in a sad mood, consistent with a heuristic processing style, as also found in Experiment 1. When group relevance was high, however, sad subjects were more likely than happy subjects to discriminate against the outgroup, consistent with their greater constructive access and use of discriminatory information in the course of substantive processing. A series of regression analyses specifically supported predictions made by the AIM that the relationship between affect and these intergroup decisions was significantly mediated by different processing strategies, recruited by the personal relevance manipulations.

Individual Differences and Affect Infusion

Whether affect infusion occurs may also depend on individual differences between people in how they process social information.

Whereas some individuals are habitually open to affective influences, others may have a strong tendency to rely on motivated processing to control and limit their affective reactions. Two recent experiments compared affective influences on consumer judgments between people who scored high or low on the Openness to Feelings scale (Costa & Macrae, 1985). In modern industrial societies, the ownership of objects is heavily imbued with emotional meaning, and material possessions are a major source of work motivation and satisfaction for most people. When many social relationships are superficial and are based on surface characteristics, the things we own may take on a special emotional significance in defining and displaying our claimed status and social identity to others. Indeed, the mere act of owning an object may increase its subjective value. This so-called endowment effect has been defined as the premium people expect for giving up an object already owned. Subjective feelings about the prospect of losing a possession seem to play a dominant role in generating the endowment effect. Interestingly, affective influences on the endowment effect have not been investigated previously.

According to the AIM, positive affect should facilitate access to positive information about the pleasure of owning an object (Bower, 1981; Forgas & Bower, 1987) and should produce an overvaluation effect. When in a negative mood, people might selectively access negative information related to an object and thus should value it less. However, these affect infusion effects should be reduced or eliminated for people who habitually use motivated strategies to disregard their affective states, such as those scoring low on Openness to Feelings.

In two experiments (Ciarrochi & Forgas, 1998b), participants induced to feel good or bad estimated the subjective and objective value of a number of consumer items they owned or wanted to own. Participants also completed the Openness to Feelings (OF) scale. Both experiments predicted and found a significant interaction between personality (OF) and mood on consumer evaluations. Individuals scoring high on OF showed a clear mood-congruent pattern: Positive mood increased, and negative mood decreased their valuation of their material possessions. In contrast, people scoring low on OF showed the opposite, mood-incongruent bias. These effects were confirmed both in Experiment 1, using an autobiographical mood induction, and in Experiment 2, using exposure to happy or sad films to induce moods. These results clearly illustrate not only that affect has a mood-congruent influence on consumer judgments, but also that these effects are significantly moderated by different processing strategies linked to enduring personality characteristics.

To the extent that many everyday social behaviors (such as strategic communication and bargaining) also require open, constructive processing for their planning and execution, they might also be subject to process-dependent affect infusion effects. The process dependence of mood effect on strategic social behaviors has also been explored in some more recent experiments, described next.

Processing Strategy Mediates Affect Infusion into Strategic Behaviours

Strategic social judgments and reasoning are often performed as part of behavior planning, as an antecedent to intended purposive action (Heider, 1958). Given the strong evidence for affective influences on social judgment and decisions, affect may also influence actual strategic behaviors. The infusion of affect into strategic behaviors should produce the same kind of valenced effects demonstrated with the preceding section. Positive affect and more favorable judgments should produce more confident, friendly, and cooperative "approach" behaviors, whereas negative affect and unfavorable judgments would be expected to precede avoidance, defensive, or unfriendly behaviors. Although numerous studies have looked at affective influences on thinking and judgments, the behavioral consequences of affect have received surprisingly little attention. In the past several years, we have conducted a series of experiments examining the role of affect in a variety of strategic social behaviors (Forgas, 1998a-b, in press-a-b). The role of different processing strategies in mediating these effects was a particular focus of attention.

Affect Infusion into Strategic Responses

The first question investigated was how affect influences simple, automatic behavioral responses to unexpected strategic situations, such as an unexpected request. One study was carried out in a realistic field setting, in a library, using an unobtrusive procedure. Affect was manipulated simply by placing folders containing positively or negatively valenced images or text on empty library desks, with a written message encouraging arriving students to look at the contents. As students arrived and sat at the desks, they were surreptitiously observed. Those who looked through the images (and were thus exposed to the affect induction) were approached shortly afterward by another student (in fact, a confederate) who made an apparently casual, impromptu request for some writing paper. The request was phrased either in a conventional, polite manner (e.g., "Please, may I . . .") or in an unconventional, impolite manner (e.g., "Give me . . ."). Responses to the request were noted, and a few minutes later, participants were approached by a second experimenter and were asked to complete a brief questionnaire indicating their perceptions of the request, the requester, and their recall of the request itself.

We reasoned that the affective state induced by prior exposure to the emotional pictures should have a mood-congruent influence on how students interpret and respond to such requests. Further, we also expected that unconventional, impolite requests should elicit more extensive and substantive information processing as they deviate from expectations (Forgas, 1985; Gibbs, 1985). In contrast, polite, conventional requests can be processed almost mindlessly (Langer, Blank, & Chanowitz, 1978). Accordingly, affect should have a greater influence on responding to impolite requests than to polite requests. Consistent with the AIM, evaluations of, recall of, and compliance with the impolite request showed significantly greater affect congruence than did evaluations of, recall of, and compliance with polite requests. Similarly, judgments and impressions about the requester also showed greater mood congruency when the request was impolite rather than polite. These results confirm the significant process sensitivity of affect infusion into highly realistic interpersonal behaviors in a field setting. Further, affective influences were greater when more constructive processing was required to deal with an unusual, problematic social situation (such as an unconventional request). The kind of constructive thinking that produced affect infusion here was likely to be automatic and largely subsconscious – after all, there is little opportunity to consciously deliberate before responding to an unexpected request. Would affect have a similar process-mediated influence on more deliberate, and extensively planned social behaviors? This possibility was examined in another series of studies.

Affect Infusion into Planned Behaviors

The influence of affect on *negotiator cognition* and *bargaining behaviors* was the focus of a subsequent set of experiments (Forgas, 1998a). By definition, bargaining and negotiation are complex, indeterminate, and unpredictable events. Preparing for and planning a bargaining encounter is likely to require open, constructive thinking as people prepare their approach and plan their strategies. To the extent that substantive processing is required, we may expect affect to significantly influence the kind of bargaining strategies people plan, and actually use. In this series of experiments, mood was induced by informing participants that they did well or badly on a test. After the mood induction, as part of an allegedly unrelated study, subjects planned and participated in an interpersonal, informal, and a formal intergroup bargaining encounter. In three experiments, the results indicated that a positive affective state produced more cooperative, integrative thoughts and plans for the encounter, such a state generated more optimistic perceptions of the partner, and participants actually used more constructive, cooperative bargaining behaviors (Figure 11.2). Perhaps most interesting, positive affect not only influenced planned and actual bargaining strategies, but it also had a beneficial effect on outcomes. Individuals who were feeling good were not only more cooperative, but also seemed to obtain significantly better results owing to their more integrative approach.

There was also clear evidence that these mood effects on negotiation were a direct consequence of the prenegotiation plans and judgments formed, indicating a close link between affect infusion into cognition and subsequent behaviors. In addition, there was some evidence for the process mediation of these effects. For example, individuals who are inclined to approach a bargaining encounter from a predetermined, motivated perspective, and who thus employ less open, substantive processing strategies, may also be less influenced by their prevailing affective state. Just such a pattern was obtained when differences in mood sensitivity between different individuals were analyzed. People who scored high on measures likely to predict a habitually motivated approach to interpersonal tasks (such as high need for approval and high Machiavellianism) were significantly less influenced by affect when planning and executing the negotiation task than were low scorers on these measures. This result is consistent with the key argument proposed here, that the infusion of affect into social

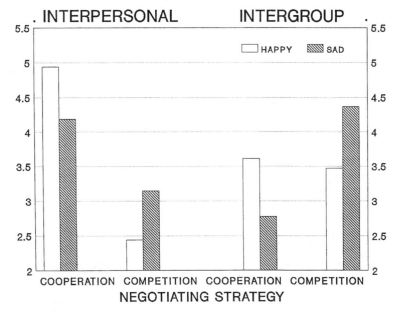

Figure 11.2. Mood effects on bargaining and negotiation strategies: Positive mood increases cooperation, and negative mood increases competitive strategies, both in interpersonal and in intergroup negotiation (data based on Forgas, 1998a).

thinking and behavior is highly process sensitive and tends to be reduced whenever more targeted, motivated, and "closed" information processing is adopted as a result of personal, or situational variables.

Affect Infusion into Communication Strategies

Further experiments sought to provide additional support for these theoretical arguments, by investigating how affect can influence people's planned and actual communication strategies, such as the production of requests (Forgas, in press-a). Requesting is an intrinsically complex and demanding behavioral task, characterized by uncertainty and ambiguity. Requesters typically need to formulate their messages so as to be sufficiently direct in order to maximize compliance, yet be polite enough to avoid giving offence. As long as an open, constructive processing strategy is used, affect should have an informational influence on request formulations. Positive affect should produce a more confident, direct strategy, consistent with the greater availability of positively valenced thoughts and associations. Negative affect in turn should result in more cautious, polite request strategies owing to the selective priming and greater availability of negative memories and information. In terms of the AIM, these mood effects should be greater when more substantive and elaborate processing is required to deal with a more complex and demanding requesting task.

In the first experiment, people feeling happy or sad after thinking about positive or negative personal episodes (Forgas, in press-a) selected more or less polite requests that they would use in easy and in difficult request situations. Induced mood had a significant influence on their request preferences: Happy participants preferred more direct, impolite request forms, and sad persons used more indirect, polite requests. Further, these affective influences on requesting were significantly greater in the more difficult, demanding request situations that presumably required more extensive, substantive processing strategies (Figure 11.3). In a follow-up experiment, participants were asked to formulate their own open-ended requests in easy or difficult situations. Once again, significant mood effects were found (Forgas, in press-a). A third experiment predicted and found that affect also had a relatively greater influence on decisions about using unconventional, impolite, and direct requests that deviate from the norm and thus require more substantive processing (Forgas, in press-a). These experiments provide convergent evidence for significant affective influences

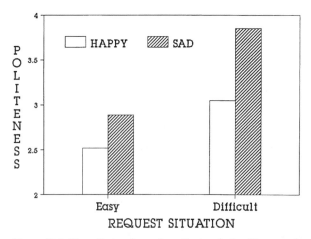

Figure 11.3. The effects of mood on the level of politeness of preferred requests in easy and difficult situations: Mood effects are greater on request politeness in more difficult situations likely to require more substantive processing (data based on Forgas, in press-a).

on strategic interpersonal behaviors such as requesting. These results also show that mood effects on social behaviors are indeed process dependent: Paradoxically, affect infusion seems to be enhanced rather than reduced when more constructive processing is required to deal with a more difficult and demanding interpersonal task (Fiedler, 1991; Fiedler & Forgas, 1988; Forgas, 1995a).

The experiments on requesting described so far relied on controlled laboratory methods and the use of hypothetical, simulated situations. Clearly it is important to show that similar mechanisms also operate when naturalistic requests are made. We used an unobtrusive procedure to elicit and observe spontaneous requests by happy and sad people in a real-life situation (Forgas, in press-b). Participants signed up for a study of social judgments and received an audiovisual mood induction using films to generate good or bad moods. Immediately afterward, in an apparently impromptu development, the experimenter asked participants to get a file from a neighboring office while the next part of the experiment was being set up. Participants' exact words when requesting the file from a confederate were recorded by a concealed tape recorder. Results showed a significant affective influence on these natural, unobtrusively elicited requests. Those induced into a negative mood by watching sad films used significantly more polite, elaborate, and hedging request forms than did happy people, who employed more direct and less polite forms (Figure 11.4). Interestingly, negative affect also produced an increased latency (delay)

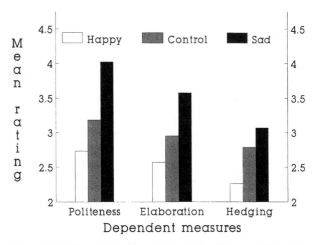

Figure 11.4. Mood effects on the level of politeness, elaboration, and hedging in naturally produced requests: Positive mood produces less polite, less elaborate, and less hedging request forms (data based on Forgas, in press-b).

before posing the request, a pattern that is again consistent with the more cautious, defensive interpersonal strategies induced by negative mood. Recall data confirmed that unconventional requests were in fact remembered significantly better, consistent with the more substantive and in-depth processing of these more problematic messages. These experiments further confirm that the infusion of affect into the planning and execution of real-life strategic behaviors, such as formulating and responding to requests and planning and executing negotiating encounters, is significantly mediated by the kind of processing strategy people employ. In particular, the production of more complex and demanding interpersonal behaviors seems to be especially affect sensitive, as suggested by the AIM.

The Processing Consequences of Affect

Although different processing strategies significantly influence affect infusion, the reverse relationship is equally important: Affective states also have processing consequences. The kind of vigilant, systematic attention to stimulus details recruited by negative moods (see also Fiedler, and Bless, this volume) tends to reduce or even eliminate such common judgmental biases as the fundamental attribution error (Forgas, 1998c). Furthermore, positive affect tends to increase, and negative affect reduce, the likelihood of other kinds of cognitive mistakes in social thinking, such as the corruption of eyewitness recollections (Forgas, 1998d).

Affective Influences on Attribution Errors

Explaining the behavior of others is one of the most critical and demanding social cognitive tasks people face in everyday social life (Heider, 1958). The fundamental attribution error (FAE) refers to a pervasive tendency by people to underestimate the impact of situational forces and overestimate the role of dispositional factors in attributions. A recent set of experiments explored the possibility that good moods can accentuate, and bad moods can inhibit the FAE, owing to the information-processing consequences of these affective states. Cognitive strategies play a major role in producing the FAE (Gilbert & Malone, 1995), as observers seem to pay selective attention to the most conspicuous information – the actor – and neglect important situational information when making inferences. This suggests a two-stage process in attributions: Judges first assume dispositions, a natural "unit relation" between the actor and his/her behavior, and may only correct for situational pressures subsequently, if at all (Gilbert, 1991; Jones, 1979; Quattrone, 1982). If the capacity or motivation to systematically process situational information is in some way impaired – owing to a positive affective state, for example – the adjustment for external constraints may be compromised, with a resulting increase in the FAE.

Previous studies of how mood affects attributions have focused mainly on informational effects. One of their findings is that happy persons tend to identify stable, internal causes when doing well and blame unstable, external causes for doing badly in achievement situations, such as a recent exam (Forgas et al., 1990). In contrast, temporarily depressed people make more internal and stable attributions for their failures than for their successes. As already mentioned, subsequent work has shown that the infusion of affect into attributions can even influence explanations for highly familiar and deeply involving events, such as inferring the causes of real interpersonal conflicts with one's intimate partner (Forgas, 1994a). Thus, affect-priming processes in the course of substantive processing can exert a powerful *informational* influence on the content of attributions.

The processing consequences of affect on attributions may be equally important but have received far less attention so far. In a series of recent experiments, we expected that the kind of processing style typically produced by good moods should make it more likely that salient and captivating information about the actor will dominate inferences, with less accessible information about situational constraints ignored (Forgas, 1998c). Further, these mood effects should be most pronounced when the behavior of the actor is particularly informative and salient as it deviates from popular expectations. In Experiment 1, mood was induced by providing participants with positive or negative feedback about their performance on a sentence-completion task. Next, participants were asked "to carefully read an essay written by a student participating in a debate," who either chose to represent this position (free choice) or was assigned the position (coerced choice) and argued "for" or "against" the French nuclear tests in the South Pacific. This was a highly topical issue in Australia at the time, and almost everybody strongly opposed the tests.

Judgments showed a marked FAE: Even when the essays were assigned, the attitudes expressed were thought to indicate the writer's genuine beliefs, and those arguing for the tests were judged more negatively. The key finding was that positive affect significantly increased, and negative mood decreased, the incidence of the FAE, and it did so most when the essays advocated a highly salient, pro-testing position (Figure 11.5). A similar pattern was obtained on evaluative judgments of the writer. These results support the theoretical prediction that more top-down and less situation-focused processing promoted by positive affect increases the FAE. In contrast, negative affect produced more careful and systematic attention to the stimulus information, and a reduction in the FAE.

The next experiment was designed as an unobtrusive field study. Participants feeling good or bad after seeing happy or sad films were asked to read and make judgments about the writers of popular and unpopular essays in an ostensible "street survey." The essays argued for or against the desirability of recycling. There was again clear evidence for the FAE. Positive affect increased and negative affect decreased the FAE both in attitude judgments and in evaluative judgments when highly salient information about the target (an antirecycling essay) was presented. Experiment 3 sought to provide specific evidence for the predicted processing consequences of good and bad mood, using recall memory data. Mood was induced by positive or

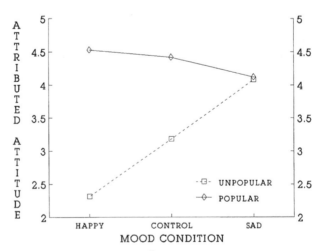

Figure 11.5. The effects of mood on the fundamental attribution error: Positive mood produces stronger correspondent inferences and the attribution of more negative attitudes based on coerced essays advocating unpopular opinions (data based on Forgas, 1998c).

negative feedback about performance on a visual estimation task. Immediately afterward, participants read a coerced or freely chosen essay arguing for or against exploiting native forests, then rated the attitudes and gave their evaluation of the writer.

Positive affect again increased, and negative affect decreased the FAE, and these effects were strongest when conspicuous and unpopular essays made it easier for judges to draw strong correspondent inferences (Jones & Harris, 1967). Surprisingly, those committing this error also reported greater confidence in their judgments, suggesting that judges were not aware that their information-processing strategies were in any way compromised by their affect. Memory results provided critical support for the role of positive affect in producing less attention to situational details, and greater subsequent judgmental errors. Mediational analyses confirmed that affect had a significant influence on the FAE, and that these effects were due to affect-induced differences in processing strategies.

Inferring the causes of behavior is one of the most complex and demanding cognitive tasks we face in everyday social life. These three experiments showed that affect has a marked influence on processing strategies, and on the commission of the fundamental attribution error. These results are consistent with multiprocess theories of affect and cognition such as the AIM and confirm the interdependence between affective states and cognitive processing strategies, as also argued by Fiedler (ch. 10) and Bless (ch. 9) in this volume.

Affective Influences on Eyewitness Memory

We often witness various incidents in everyday life and later rely on our recollections of what happened to describe the event to others. Such eyewitness descriptions play an important role in interpersonal behavior, as well as in the legal system. Questioning people about such experiences is a common occurrence in everyday life, as well as in investigative practice, in police work, and in the courts. Most of us implicitly assume that our recollections of personally witnessed events are fundamentally correct and reliable. Consistent with this belief, eyewitness testimony is accorded special evidential status by the legal system.

However, we also know from past research that social perceivers use highly constructive strategies to select, recall, and interpret information about people and events (Asch, 1946; Heider, 1958). This suggests, that eyewitness testimonies may also be easily contaminated by subsequent, unrelated information. Studies by Loftus (1979) showed that eyewitness accounts can be easily corrupted when people are exposed to misleading information about an incident in the course of subsequent questioning. Recently, we (Forgas, 1998d) investigated the possibility that positive affect might increase, and negative affect might reduce, such eyewitness errors, as a result of the different processing strategies recruited by these affective states.

In these studies the events to be remembered were presented to participants on brief videotapes showing either a happy, positive event (a wedding), or a negative event (a burglary). Positive and negative mood states were next induced using films, or an autobiographical recall method. Next, participants were exposed to questions that either included or did not include misleading details about the witnessed episodes (e.g., Did you see the burglars hit the shopkeeper /true/ after they handcuffed him/incorrect, planted information/?). After an interval of more than an hour comprising several interference tasks, participants' ability to correctly remember details of the incidents was tested. As predicted, there was a significant tendency for people who were exposed to false information in the course of prior questioning to report false eyewitness memories, as also found by Loftus (1979). However, we also found that positive mood significantly increased and negative mood decreased, the incidence of these eyewitness memory errors. It appears that the experience of positive affect produced a less stimulus-oriented, and more constructive and generative processing style, increasing the likelihood that false information suggested by the questioning would be incorporated in the top-down processing of eyewitness memories. In contrast, negative affect triggered a more attentive and externally focused processing strategy, reducing the incidence of eyewitness errors.

In another study, a "natural" incident was staged during a lecture, when some 200 students witnessed an unusual altercation between a lecturer and a young woman who entered the theater unexpectedly. About a week later, students received a positive or negative mood induction before exposure to misleading information about the incident in the guise of some questions. A test of their ability to correctly recognize details of the incident later on showed a significant mood effect. Once again, those feeling good were more likely to show eyewitness distortions due to the misleading questions, while negative affect improved eyewitness memory.

These results confirm the suggestion that even relatively mild, transient affective states may have a marked influence on the way people process social information. Attributions and eyewitness memory were more reliable and accurate in a negative mood and less accurate in a positive mood, consistent with the different processing consequences of these affective states. These results – consistent with other contributions to this volume (e.g., Bless, Fiedler) – support the contention that there is a complex, interactive relationship between affective states and strategies for processing social information.

Summary and Conclusions

The main point argued in this chapter is that a complete account of the role of affect in social cognition requires a clear understanding of how information-processing strategies and affective states interact. It was suggested that the complex pattern of mood congruence or incongruence found in the empirical literature can be best explained in terms of the different information-processing strategies that mediate these effects. The extensive research reviewed here specifically suggests that the infusion of affect into cognition is neither a necessary nor a universal process. Different processing strategies hold the key to explaining the absence or presence of the infusion of affect into cognition. A multiprocess theory, the Affect Infusion Model, offers a comprehensive explanation of exactly when and why affect will or will not infuse our thoughts and judgments.

The experiments described here suggest that affect infusion is absent whenever a social cognitive task could be performed using a simple, well-rehearsed direct access strategy or a highly motivated strategy. In these conditions, there is little need, and indeed little opportunity for incidentally primed mood-congruent information to infuse constructive information processing (Fiedler, 1991; Forgas, 1995a). By assuming that affect infusion is limited to circumstances involving constructive processing, the multiprocess model can account for most of the empirical evidence in the literature demonstrating mood congruence or its absence. Counterintuitive results showing that more extensive, substantive processing enhances mood congruity provides especially strong support for the AIM. As the research reviewed here shows, affect infusion is more likely when people must use more elaborate processing to compute judgments about atypical rather than typical people, badly matched rather than well-matched couples, and complex rather than simple personal conflicts (Forgas, 1992b, 1992c, 1994a, 1994b, 1995b). The same kinds of mechanisms determine whether affect is infused into constructive social behaviors. Responding to a casual request, planning and executing a negotiation, and producing strategic verbal messages were all found to be more affect-sensitive in circumstances that demand more substantive processing (Forgas, 1998a, 1998b, in press-a, in press-b).

Affect infusion occurs not only in the laboratory, but also in many real-life situations. Affective influences can be an important part of organizational decisions, appraisal judgments, consumer preferences, and health-related judgments (Forgas & Moylan, 1987; Mayer, Gaschke, Braverman, & Evans, 1992; Salovey, O'Leary, Stretton, Fishkin, & Drake, 1991; Sedikides, 1992). Indeed, the evidence reviewed here suggests that the more judges need to engage in open, constructive processing, the more likely that affect will infuse their responses. Even such highly involved and complex tasks as judging intimate relationship conflicts showed such mood-congruent biases (Forgas, 1994b). Conversely, other studies have shown the disappearance of mood congruity whenever people approach a cognitive task from a motivated perspective (Forgas, 1991a, 1991b; Forgas & Fiedler, 1996; Sedikides, 1995).

Indeed, we recently argued that the tendency to alternate between substantive and motivated processing strategies – and thereby to produce affect control, respectively – may also be thought of as part of an ongoing homeostatic strategy of controlled mood management (Forgas & Ciarrochi, 1998; Forgas, Johnson, & Ciarrochi, 1998). Thus, different cognitive information–processing strategies may not only mediate affect infusion, but could also function as an effective and self-correcting affect management system, producing affect congruence or incongruence in our thoughts and associations to regulate and "tune" our everyday mood states.

Much of the material discussed here indicates the effects of different information-processing strategies in mediating the infusion of affect into judgments and behavior. The final section of this chapter described some of our recent experiments that demonstrated the opposite effect: affective influences on processing strategies. These studies have shown that positive and negative affective states have an important and asymmetrical effect on cognition. We found that positive mood increases and negative mood decreases judgmental errors, such as the fundamental attribution error, as well as memory mistakes, such as the accuracy of eyewitness performance.

To conclude, by emphasizing the interactive links between distinct information processing strategies and affect, multiprocess theories such as the Affect Infusion Model offer a parsimonious account for a variety of mood effects observed in the literature. Generally, the evidence reviewed here confirms that the infusion of affect into judgments and decisions is most likely in conditions requiring constructive, substantive processing. Other processing strategies may result in the absence, or even reversal of affect infusion, as several contributions to this volume also suggest (Berkowitz et al., Martin). I hope that by highlighting the crucial role different processing strategies play in linking affect to social cognition and behavior, this chapter will be successful in encouraging further research into this important area of inquiry.

References

Asch, S. E. (1946). Forming impressions of personality. *Journal of Abnormal and Social Psychology, 41*, 258–290.

Bower, G. H. (1981). Mood and memory. *American Psychologist, 36*, 129–148.

Bruner, J. S. (1957). On perceptual readiness. *Psychological Review, 64*, 123–152.

Ciarrochi, J. V., & Forgas, J. P. (1998a). *The effects of mood and trait anxiety on intergroup judgments*. Unpublished manuscript.

Ciarrochi, J. V., & Forgas, J. P. (1998b). *The pleasure of possessions: Affect and consumer judgments*. Unpublished manuscript.

Clark, M. S., & Isen, A. M. (1982). Towards understanding the relationship between feeling states and social behavior. In A. H. Hastorf & A. M. Isen (Eds.), *Cognitive social psychology* (pp. 73–108). New York: Elsevier-North Holland.

Clore, G. L., Schwarz, N., & Conway, M. (1994). Affective causes and consequences of social information processing. In R. S. Wyer & T. K. Srull (Eds.), *Handbook of social cognition* (2nd ed.). Hillsdale, NJ: Erlbaum.

Costa, P. T., & Macrae, R. R. (1985). *The NEO Personality Inventory Manual*. Odessa, FL: Psychological Assessment Resources.

Damasio, A. R. (1994). *Descartes' error*. New York: Grosset/Putnam.

Fiedler, K. (1991). On the task, the measures and the mood in research on affect and social cognition. In J. P. Forgas (Ed.), *Emotion and social judgments* (pp. 83–104). Oxford: Pergamon Press.

Fiedler, K., & Forgas, J. P. (Eds.). (1988). *Affect, cognition and social behavior*. Toronto: Hogrefe International.

Forgas, J. P. (Ed.). (1985). *Language and Social situations*. New York: Springer.

Forgas, J. P. (1989). Mood effects on decision-making strategies. *Australian Journal of Psychology, 41*, 197–214.

Forgas, J. P. (1990). Affective influences on individual and group judgments. *European Journal of Social Psychology, 20*, 441–453.

Forgas, J. P. (Ed.). (1991a). *Emotion and social judgments*. Oxford: Pergamon Press.

Forgas, J. P. (1991b). Mood effects on partner choice: Role of affect in social decisions. *Journal of Personality and Social Psychology, 61,* 708–720.

Forgas, J. P. (1991c). Affect and cognition in close relationships. In G. Fletcher & F. Fincham (Eds.), *Cognition in close relationships* (pp. 151–174). Hillsdale, NJ: Erlbaum.

Forgas, J. P. (1992a). Affect in social judgments and decisions: A multi-process model. In M. Zanna (Ed.), *Advances in Experimental Social Psychology* (Vol. 25, pp. 227–275). New York: Academic Press.

Forgas, J. P. (1992b). On bad mood and peculiar people: Affect and person typicality in impression formation. *Journal of Personality and Social Psychology, 62,* 863–875.

Forgas, J. P. (1992c). Mood and the perception of unusual people: Affective asymmetry in memory and social judgments. *European Journal of Social Psychology, 22,* 531–547.

Forgas, J. P. (1993). On making sense of odd couples: Mood effects on the perception of mismatched relationships. *Personality and Social Psychology Bulletin, 19,* 59–71.

Forgas, J. P. (1994a). Sad and guilty? Affective influences on the explanation of conflict episodes. *Journal of Personality and Social Psychology, 66,* 56–68.

Forgas, J. P. (1994b). The role of emotion in social judgments: An introductory review and an affect infusion model (AIM). *European Journal of Social Psychology, 24,* 1–24.

Forgas, J. P. (1995a). Mood and judgment: The affect infusion model (AIM). *Psychological Bulletin, 117*(1), 39–66.

Forgas, J. P. (1995b). Strange couples: Mood effects on judgments and memory about prototypical and atypical targets. *Personality and Social Psychology Bulletin, 21,* 747–765.

Forgas, J. P. (1998a). On feeling good and getting your way: Mood effects on negotiation strategies and outcomes. *Journal of Personality and Social Psychology, 74,* 565–577.

Forgas, J. P. (1998b). Asking nicely? Mood effects on responding to more or less polite requests. *Personality and Social Psychology Bulletin, 24,* 173–185.

Forgas, J. P. (1998c). Happy and mistaken? Mood effects on the fundamental attribution error. *Journal of Personality and Social Psychology, 75,* 318–331.

Forgas, J. P. (1998d). *Mood effects on eyewitness accuracy.* Unpublished manuscript.

Forgas, J. P. (in press-a). Feeling good and being rude? The effects of mood on request formulations. *Journal of Personality and Social Psychology.*

Forgas, J. P. (in press-b). On being sad and polite: Mood effects on the use of more or less polite requests. *Personality and Social Psychology Bulletin.*

Forgas, J. P., & Bower, G. H. (1987). Mood effects on person perception judgements. *Journal of Personality and Social Psychology, 53,* 53–60.

Forgas, J. P., Bower, G. H., & Moylan, S. J. (1990). Praise or blame? Affective influences on attributions for achievement. *Journal of Personality and Social Psychology, 59,* 809–818.

Forgas, J. P., & Ciarrochi, J. (1998). Mood congruent and incongruent thoughts over time: The role of self-esteem in mood management efficacy. Manuscript submitted for publication.

Forgas, J. P., & Fiedler, K. (1996). Us and them: Mood effects on intergroup discrimination. *Journal of Personality and Social Psychology, 70,* 36–52.

Forgas, J. P., Johnson, R., & Ciarrochi, J. (1998). Affect control and affect infusion: A multi-process account of mood management and personal control. In M. Kofta, G. Weary, & G. Sedek (Eds.), *Personal control in action: Cognitive and motivational mechanisms* (pp. 155–189). New York: Plenum Press.

Forgas, J. P., Levinger, G., & Moylan, S. (1994). Feeling good and feeling close: Mood effects on the perception of intimate relationships. *Personal Relationships, 2,* 165–184.

Forgas, J. P., & Moylan, S. J. (1987). After the movies: The effects of transient mood states on social judgments. *Personality and Social Psychology Bulletin, 13,* 478–489.

Gibbs, R. (1985). Situational conventions and requests. In J. P. Forgas (Ed.), *Language and social situations* (pp. 97–113). New York: Springer.

Gilbert, D. T. (1991). How mental systems believe. *American Psychologist, 46,* 107–119.

Gilbert, D. T., & Malone, P. S. (1995). The correspondence bias. *Psychological Bulletin, 117,* 21–38.

Griffitt, W. (1970). Environmental effects on interpersonal behavior: Ambient effective temperature and attraction. *Journal of Personality and Social Psychology, 15,* 240–244.

Heider, F. (1958). *The psychology of interpersonal relations.* New York: Wiley.

Jones, E. E. (1979). The rocky road from acts to dispositions. *American Psychologist, 34,* 107–117.

Jones, E. E., & Harris, V. A. (1967). The attribution of attitudes. *Journal of Experimental Social Psychology, 3,* 1–24.

Langer, E. J., Blank, A., & Chanowitz, B. (1978). The mindlessness of ostensibly thoughtful action: The role of "placebic" information in interpersonal interaction. *Journal of Personality and Social Psychology, 36,* 635–642.

Loftus, E. (1979). *Eyewitness testimony.* Cambridge, MA: MIT Press.

Mackie, D., & Worth, L. (1991). Feeling good, but not thinking straight: The impact of positive mood on persuasion. In J. P. Forgas (Ed.), *Emotion and social judgments* (pp. 201–220). Oxford: Pergamon Press.

Mayer, J. D., Gaschke, Y. N., Braverman, D. L., & Evans, T. W. (1992). Mood congruent judgment is a general effect. *Journal of Personality and Social Psychology, 63,* 119–132.

Oatley, K., & Jenkins, J. M. (1992). Human emotions: Function and dysfunction. *Annual Review of Psychology, 43,* 55–85.

Oatley, K., & Jenkins, J. M. (1996). *Understanding emotions.* Oxford: Blackwell.

Quattrone, G. (1982). Overattribution and unit formation: When behavior engulfs the person. *Journal of Personality and Social Psychology, 42,* 593–607.

Salovey, P., & Birnbaum, D. (1989). Influence of mood on health-related cognition. *Journal of Personality and Social Psychology, 57,* 539–551.

Salovey, P., O'Leary, A., Stretton, M., Fishkin, S., & Drake, C. A. (1991). Influence of mood on judgments about health and illness. In J. P. Forgas (Ed.), *Emotion and social judgments* (pp. 241–262). Oxford: Pergamon Press.

Schwarz, N., & Clore, G. L. (1988). How do I feel about it? The informative function of affective states. In K. Fiedler & J. P. Forgas (Eds.), *Affect, cognition, and social behavior* (pp. 44–62). Toronto: Hogrefe.

Schwarz, N., Strack, F., Kommer, D., & Wagner, D. (1987). Soccer, rooms and the quality of your life: Mood effects on judgments of satisfaction with life in general and with specific life domains. *European Journal of Social Psychology, 17*, 69–79.

Sedikides, C. (1992). Changes in the valence of self as a function of mood. *Review of Personality and Social Psychology, 14*, 271–311.

Sedikides, C. (1994). Incongruent effects of sad mood on self-conception valence: It's a matter of time. *European Journal of Social Psychology, 24*, 161–172.

Sedikides, C. (1995). Central and peripheral self-conceptions are differentially influenced by mood: Tests of the differential sensitivity hypothesis. *Journal of Personality and Social Psychology, 69*(4), 759–777.

Srull, T. K. (1984). The effects of subjective affective states on memory and judgment. In T. Kinnear (Ed.), *Advances in Consumer Research* (Vol. 11, pp. 530–533). Provo, UT: Association for Consumer Research.

Tajfel, S., & Forgas, J. P. (1981). Social categorisation: Cognitions, values and groups. In J. P. Forgas (Ed.), *Social Cognition* (pp. 113–140). London: Academic Press.

PART IV

Affect and Social Knowledge Structures

12. Self-Organization in Emotional Contexts

CAROLIN J. SHOWERS

A man has as many social selves as there are individuals who recognize him and carry an image of him in their mind . . . it may be a perfectly harmonious division of labor, as where one tender to his children is stern to the soldiers or prisoners under his command.

—James, 1890, p. 294

Self-identifications . . . should be regarded as activities . . . that reflect the transaction of the person, the situation, and an audience.

—Schlenker and Weigold, 1989, p. 247

Introduction

For more than a century, self theorists have emphasized the complexity and multiplicity of self-representations. Early views recognized that the selves we present to others are context dependent (James, 1890). Modern views see our various self-presentations as an individual's solution to the problem of how to behave in response to the converging forces of person, situation, and audience (Mischel, 1973; Schlenker & Weigold, 1989; Snyder, 1979). In the modern view, these self-presentational solutions are treated as real and valid components of who we are, not just false or actor selves. More generally, it is not just public behaviors, but the way *we see ourselves* in specific situations, or in the past or in the future, that form our different self-representations, and that come together to constitute who we are (Markus & Wurf, 1987).

From a contemporary information-processing perspective, the self-

Correspondence about this chapter should be addressed to Carolin J. Showers at the Department of Psychology, University of Oklahoma, Norman, OK 73019-0535. E-mail: cshowers@ou.edu.

concept consists of an enormous repertoire of self-relevant information, including both episodic and semantic knowledge (Kihlstrom &
Cantor, 1984). To use such a large body of knowledge efficiently,
people need an effective organizational structure. One basic unit of
organization is the working self-concept, namely, a subset drawn from
the repertoire of knowledge that is relevant to the current situation
(Cantor, Markus, Niedenthal, & Nurius, 1986). In addition, both the
working self-concept and the entire repertoire are organized by a set
of categories, often called "self-aspects" (Linville, 1985). These self-
aspect categories are idiographic and may reflect an individual's roles
in life (professor, environmentalist), specific situations (with children,
with soldiers), emotional states, personality traits, interpersonal relationships, and so on. Each category contains specific items of self-
knowledge that are closely associated with one another and with the
category label.

From an information-processing perspective, feelings about the self
should correspond to the positive or negative content of the beliefs in
the self-repertoire, perhaps weighted by their frequency of activation
in the working self-concept (e.g., Greenwald, Bellezza, & Banaji, 1988;
Pelham & Swann, 1989). An information-processing view implies that
change in feelings about the self (if, say, a person is depressed) could
be accomplished by changing the content of specific self-beliefs. This
view of self-change seems optimistic compared with earlier perspectives in which feelings about the self were embedded in the psychody-
namics of early childhood relationships (Freud, 1917/1966). In practice,
however, changing the content of the self even from a social-cognitive
perspective may be fraught with obstacles. On one hand, the negative
self-beliefs of individuals who are depressed or low in self-esteem may
be relatively accurate (Alloy, Albright, Abramson, & Dykman, 1990).
On the other hand, change may be resisted by others in the environment who share an individual's negative perceptions (Safran & Segal,
1990), or because there are benefits to self-consistency that seemingly
outweigh the costs of continuing to feel bad (Swann, 1990).

If negative beliefs about the self are resistant to change, an alternate
route to improving mood or self-esteem might be to minimize their
impact. In the model described in the next section, it is not just the
content of positive or negative self-beliefs, but how that knowledge is
organized, that determines its impact. People who hold ingrained
negative beliefs about the self may be able to reorganize them in order

to improve mood or self-esteem without changing or denying their negative content.

A Model of Evaluative Organization

A growing body of literature examines organizational (structural) features of the self-concept. These features include self-complexity (Linville, 1987; Margolin & Niedenthal, 1997), differential importance and differential certainty (Pelham, 1991), self-clarity (Campbell, 1990), self-discrepancies (Higgins, 1987), and self-differentiation (Donahue, Robins, Roberts, & John, 1993), although this list is by no means exhaustive. There is also a substantial literature on self-schemas that illustrates the importance of understanding organizational structures because of their influence on the accessibility of specific beliefs. Of particular relevance to the present work are studies of negative self-schemas and depression (Bargh & Tota, 1988; Hammen, Marks, deMayo, & Mayol, 1985; Kuiper, Olinger, & MacDonald, 1988). As pointed out by Segal (1988), however, the evidence for self-schemes consists of data on accessibility (i.e., response latencies), rather than the underlying thought processes or organizational structures that create the interconnections between specific beliefs.

The present model focuses on evaluative organization and, specifically, the interconnections between positive and negative self-beliefs (Showers, 1992a, 1992b, 1995). For example, a depression-prone person who is feeling shy at a dinner party may think: "I'm shy, I'm acting awkwardly and saying the wrong thing, and I feel naive." This person may also know that he is a kind and loyal friend, but those thoughts are not accessible to him in this context. In contrast, imagine another individual who has all the same beliefs about the self, but has organized them differently, so that the knowledge about her shyness is closely linked to the knowledge that she is a loyal friend. At the dinner party this person also may feel shy, but the thought that comes to mind is "I'm shy, but I'm also a loyal friend." The associative link between the self-beliefs "shy" and "loyal" helps this individual avoid the stream of negative thought that is typical of depressed persons.

According to the present model, the individual who thinks "I'm shy, awkward, and naive" demonstrates evaluatively compartmentalized organization of self-knowledge. Each negative characteristic is linked with other characteristics of the same valence. However, the person who thinks "I'm shy, but I'm also a loyal friend" demonstrates evaluatively integrative organization. The negative attribute "shy" is closely linked to an attribute of a different valence, "loyal."

To illustrate further, consider the two college students whose beliefs about themselves in academic contexts are represented in Table 12.1. These two individuals, identified as "Harry" and "Sally," have all of the same specific self-beliefs but organize those beliefs in distinctive ways. Harry shows compartmentalized organization, because his positive self-beliefs and his negative self-beliefs are in separate categories (i.e., self-aspects): "me as a Renaissance scholar" and "me before exams." Sally's organization is evaluatively integrative, with both positive and negative beliefs appearing in each category.

What are the consequences of these types of organization? Presumably, most of the time that he is at school, Harry thinks of himself as a Renaissance scholar, and all of the positive attributes associated with that self-aspect are easily accessible to him. For Sally, positive and negative attributes come to mind all the time, although the specific content changes, depending on whether she is working on her science classes or her humanities classes. Thus, on an ordinary school day,

Table 12.1. *Examples of Compartmentalized Organization ("Harry") and Integrative Organization ("Sally") for Identical Items of Information About Self as Student*

"Harry" Compartmentalized Organization		"Sally" Integrative Organization	
Renaissance Scholar (+)	*Taking Tests, Grades (−)*	*Humanities Classes (+/−)*	*Science Classes (+/−)*
+curious	−worrying	+creative	+disciplined
+disciplined	−tense	−insecure	+analytical
+motivated	−distracted	+motivated	−competitive
+creative	−insecure	−distracted	−worrying
+analytical	−competitive	+expressive	+curious
+expressive	−moody	−moody	−tense

Note: A positive or negative valence is indicated for each category and each item. The symbol (+/−) denotes a mixed-valence category.
Source: Adapted from Showers (1992a).

Harry may feel better about himself than Sally, because only his positive attributes are activated. However, during exams, when Harry's negative compartment is activated, his thoughts will focus on his negative self-beliefs and he may feel much worse than Sally. Thus, the consequences of a compartmentalized type of organization depend on whether the positive or the negative compartments are activated. Over a long period of time, the cumulative impact of this type of organization may depend on the relative importance of positive and negative categories: When positive categories are most important or frequently activated, compartmentalization should be advantageous because this type of organization minimizes access to negative self-beliefs; when negative categories are most important, integrative organization should be advantageous because it minimizes the impact of negative beliefs that cannot be avoided.[1]

To summarize, the compartmentalization model predicts an interaction of type of organization with the relative importance of positive and negative self-aspect categories. The terms *positive compartmentalization* and *negative compartmentalization* are used to describe self-structures in which the positive compartments and the negative compartments, respectively, are most important. Integrative structures can also be identified as positive-integrative and negative-integrative, depending on the relative importance of the more positive and more negative self-aspects. The model predicts that for individuals whose self-concepts are basically positive and for whom positive self-aspects are important, positive compartmentalization will be associated with higher self-esteem and less negative mood than positive integration. For individuals whose self-concepts contain many important negative self-beliefs, negative compartmentalization will be associated with lower self-esteem and more negative mood than negative integration.[2]

Evidence for the Basic Model

In an initial series of studies, the relation between type of self-organization and current mood and self-esteem was examined by using a card-sorting task to assess the organization of participants' self-concepts (Showers, 1992a). In this task, participants are presented with a stack of 40 index cards, each containing an adjective that might describe them. There are 20 positive adjectives and 20 negative adjectives. Participants are asked to think of the different aspects of themselves and their lives, and to sort the cards into groups so that each group represents an aspect of themselves or their lives. They may generate as many or as few groups as they desire, depending on what is meaningful to them. They may use the adjectives in more than one group or, if an adjective does not describe them, they may simply set it aside. On average, participants generate between 6 and 8 groups, with about 7 or eight adjectives in each group. Participants may label their groups either as they sort the cards or when they are finished. They also provide Likert ratings of the importance of each group for their overall concept of themselves, and its positivity and negativity.[3]

The measure of compartmentalization is a phi coefficient (Cramer's V; Cramer, 1945/1974; Everitt, 1977). Phi is based on a chi-square statistic and compares the observed frequencies of positive and negative attributes in each group with those that would be expected owing to chance, given the overall proportion of positive and negative attributes in the card sort. Phi ranges from 0 to 1, where 1 represents perfectly compartmentalized organization, and 0 represents a sort that is no different from chance (i.e., contains the same proportion of positive and negative attributes in each group). Average values for phi are around .7.

In order to assess the relative importance of positive and negative self-aspect groups, a measure of differential importance (DI; Pelham & Swann, 1989) is computed using the importance, positivity, and negativity ratings provided by the participants for each of their groups. DI is the correlation (computed for each individual) of the importance ratings and positivity – negativity difference scores for their set of groups This measure ranges from +1.0 to −1.0, where positive values indicate that the individual perceives his or her positive groups to be more important than the negative ones, and negative values indicate that the individual perceives the negative groups to be more important than the positive ones. Average values of DI are around .5. Note that this measure is still valid if a person's most negative groups are actually more neutral than negative (as commonly occurs).

Table 12.2 presents an actual card sort generated by a participant in one of these studies. This is an example of perfectly compartmentalized organization, phi = 1.0. The DI score for this individual was .69, so this is positive compartmentalization.

An initial study of college students, selected for high and low proneness to depression, obtained the expected interaction of compartmentalization and differential importance for two measures of

Table 12.2. *Actual Card Sort Illustrating Positive Compartmentalization: Phi = 1.0, Differential Importance = .69*

Helpful	Not Always "Perfect"	Funny	Responsible	Lovable	Looking at the Good in Everyone
Giving Friendly Capable Hardworking	−Indecisive −Lazy −Isolated −Weary −Sad & blue −Insecure	Intelligent Happy Energetic Outgoing Fun & entertaining Communicative	Mature Independent Organized Interested Hardworking	Lovable Needed Friendly	Optimistic Giving Interested
Good Work Ethic	Making Decisions	Taking Disappointment Hard	Good Student	Talented	
Hardworking Capable Intelligent Interested Successful Confident Mature Independent Organized Energetic	−Indecisive −Uncomfortable −Tense −Insecure	−Sad & blue −Insecure −Like a failure −Hopeless −Inferior −Isolated −Incompetent	Intelligent Interested Organized Hardworking	Successful Capable Confident Fun & entertaining	

Note: − indicates negative attributes.

current feelings about the self, namely, self-esteem and mood (Showers, 1992a). When differential importance was high (positive groups were important), positive compartmentalization was associated with higher self-esteem and less negative mood than positive integration. However, when differential importance was low (negative groups were important), negative integration was associated with higher self-esteem and less negative mood than negative compartmentalization. Figure 12.1 illustrates this interaction, with the negative content of self-descriptions held constant.

Findings consistent with this basic model have been obtained in at least five other data sets, including noncollege student populations, and using alternative measures, such as nomothetic rating scales of specific self-domains and self-generated lists instead of the card-sorting task (Showers, 1992b; Showers, Abramson, & Hogan, Showers & Kevlyn, in press; Showers & Kling, 1996b; Showers & Ryff, 1996).

The Hidden Vulnerability of Compartmentalization

A follow-up study (Showers & Kling, 1996a) examined how these different self-structures function in specific contexts. Recall, that in contrast to the predictions of the basic model, Harry's positively compartmentalized structure was expected to lead to strong negative feelings about the self when his negative compartment was activated during exams. Thus, although people with positively compartmentalized structures may feel very good most of the time, they may also be vulnerable to intense negative moods when their negative aspects are salient. Showers and Kling tested this prediction in the laboratory by assessing type of self-structure, then activating participants' negative self-aspects by means of a sad mood induction. We predicted that, when negative self-aspects were primed, both positively and negatively compartmentalized individuals would get stuck in their negative compartments and would recover more slowly from the negative mood than individuals with integrative self-structures, whose negative self-aspects would bring at least some positive attributes to mind. This prediction was confirmed in a condition in which participants were self-focused rather than distracted during the mood recovery period (Figure 12.2). This finding demonstrates the "hidden vulnerability" of compartmentalized organization. When participants were distracted by performing easy numerical tasks, compartmentalized

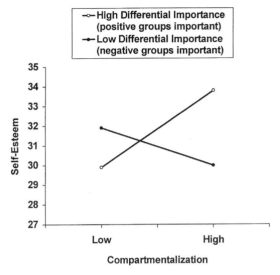

Figure 12.1. Adjusted predicted values for self-esteem (Rosenberg, 1965), supporting the basic model of evaluative organization. Negative content of self-descriptions is held constant. The predicted values are calculated at values that are 1 SD above and below the means. For compartmentalization, *M* = .71, *SD* = .21; for differential importance, *M* = .46, *SD* = .42. Source: Showers (1992a).

individuals recovered relatively quickly from their sad moods, presumably because these tasks activated their positive compartments.

Can the Organization of Self-Knowledge Change?

The basic model of evaluative organization predicts that compartmentalization is advantageous for individuals with a basically positive self-concept, whereas integrative organization is advantageous for those who have many important negative self-beliefs (i.e., those whose negative attributes cannot be avoided). However, individual circumstances may change. Stress or negative experience may change the content of a person's self-beliefs, or may make existing negative beliefs more salient and more important (Sedikides, 1992). If so, people who have basically positive self-concepts may either (a) become increasingly compartmentalized to avoid negative self-beliefs, or (b) if salient negative characteristics are unavoidable, may shift to integrative organization to minimize their impact. For individuals with important negative self-beliefs, self-organization that is ordinarily integrative may give way to negative compartmentalization if stress is over-

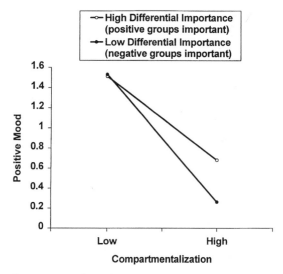

Figure 12.2. Adjusted predicted values for positive mood (Izard, 1971), illustrating the hidden vulnerability of compartmentalization. Negative content of self-descriptions is held constant. The predicted values are calculated at values that are 1 SD above the below the means. For compartmentalization, M = .73, SD = .23; for differential importance, M = .53, SD = .36. Source: Showers & Kling (1996a).

whelming and a depressive episode occurs. Individuals who are depression-prone may either (c) show this shift from integration to negative compartmentalization with change in mood, or (d) show rigid negative compartmentalization of the self, regardless of their level of stress or mood.

An inital study conducted to examine the possibility of change in self-organization used a sample of college students who were either high or low in cognitive vulnerability to depression (Showers, Abramson, & Hogan, 1998).[4] The self-descriptive card-sorting task used to assess self-organization was administered to each student twice over a 2-year period, once during the freshman year and once between 3 and 30 months (M = 19.6 months) later. Some of these students (Mood Change) were more stressed and in a more negative mood during the freshman year than they were at the second assessment. Others (Mood Stable) experienced low stress and relatively positive mood at both times. (The incidence of stress and negative mood in college students after their freshman year is relatively low.) Cognitive vulnerability to depression was defined as the tendency to interpret negative events in depressogenic ways, and participants were selected from the upper and lower quartiles on two cognitive measures of vulnerability (Alloy, Abramson, Murray, Whitehouse, & Hogan, 1997). Although High Vulnerables were especially likely to be depressed in their freshman year, and therefore to fall in the Mood Change group, there were sufficient numbers of participants to analyze the data as a 2 (Vulnerability to Depression: High/Low) × 2 (Mood Change Status: Stable/Change) design with repeated measures of self-organization at Time 1 and Time 2.

The results showed significant change in self-organization for only one of the groups, the Low Vulnerable, Mood Change group. (This group experienced high stress and a mild negative mood at Time 1.) These individuals were more compartmentalized when they were stressed than when they were not (Figure 12.3). It is important to note that the participants in this group had basically positive self-concepts, and although they endorsed more negative attributes under stress than not under stress, their organization was still positively compart-

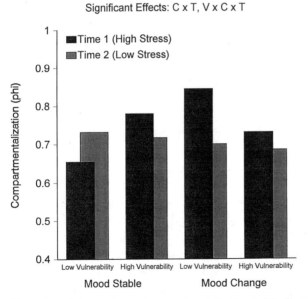

Figure 12.3. Mean values of compartmentalization (phi), illustrating change in compartmentalization for the Low Vulnerable, Mood Change group. These are cell means from 2 × 2 × 2 ANOVAs: V = Vulnerability Status (High/Low); C = Mood Change Status (Stable/Change); T = Time (Time 1/Time 2). Significant effects are $p < .05$. Source: Showers, Abramson, & Hogan (1998).

mentalized. Additional analyses confirmed that compartmentalization was correlated with less negative mood when stress was high, suggesting that compartmentalization either contributed to successful coping or was a consequence of it. These findings support option (a), namely, that individuals with a basically positive self-concept increase in compartmentalization under stress. High Vulnerables did not show a significant change in compartmentalization with stress and tended to be negatively compartmentalized at both times, consistent with option (d) (but note that this is a null effect).

These findings appear to expand the role of positively compartmentalized organization and show no particular advantage for integrative organization in any group. However, the participants in this study represent extremes of vulnerability: Low Vulnerables have a basically positive self-concept; High Vulnerables have a basically negative self-concept and, given their proneness to depression, are not likely to be especially good at coping with their negative self-beliefs. According to the basic model, integrative thinking should be most common in individuals who not only have important negative self-beliefs, but are handling them well. Additional support for the benefits of integrative thinking as well as an expanded role for compartmentalization were obtained in a study, not of the organization of self-knowledge, but rather of the organization of beliefs about someone else, namely, a partner in a close relationship.

Organization of Knowledge About a Relationship Partner

In this study (Showers & Kevlyn, in press), 99 participants completed a card-sorting task to generate a description of their relationship partner. Participants were college students who had been in an exclusive dating relationship for at least 3 months. The average age of the participants was 19.6 years, and the average length of the relationship was 20.7 months (it ranged from 3 to 60 months). Organization of knowledge about the relationship partner predicted feelings about the partner (i.e., loving) in a way that was consistent with the basic model of compartmentalization. Compartmentalization of partner knowledge interacted with the negativity of partner descriptions such that when partners were described with a high proportion of negative attributes, integrative organization was associated with greater loving than compartmentalized organization. When partner descriptions were basically positive, however, compartmentalization was associated with greater loving than was integrative organization.[5]

Interestingly, on additional measures the interaction just described was moderated by the length of the relationship. One such measure assessed individuals' attributions for negative behaviors that their partners might do (Fincham & Bradbury, 1987). Attributions may be closely tied to evaluative organization because the thought processes that influence attributions resemble those that may underlie evaluative structure. When beliefs about a partner are negatively compartmentalized, the activation of one negative belief is likely to bring to mind a whole set of other negative characteristics. This could lead to overgeneralization of a negative characteristic or behavior, a well-known feature of a pessimistic attributional style. In contrast, integrative organization should isolate a partner's negative characteristics and perhaps result in less stable, global, internal attributions for negative behaviors (a more positive attributional style). On the attributional measure, findings similar to those described for loving were obtained only for older relationships: When partner descriptions were relatively negative, integrative organization was associated with more positive attributions for negative behaviors; when partner descriptions were relatively positive, compartmentalized organization was associated with more positive attributions (see Figure 12.4). This interaction pattern for older relationships fits the basic model of compartmentalization.

For newer relationships, however, the relation between evaluative organization and attributions was different. Where partner descriptions were negative, compartmentalized (less integrative) organization was associated with more positive attributions. This suggests that compartmentalization may be an effective strategy for handling a partner's negative characteristics in new relationships. Compartmentalization may effectively keep these negative characteristics out of mind. Moreover, negative compartments may represent aspects of a partner's life that are rarely encountered. As the relationship continues, it may become difficult to avoid these negative aspects or domains, so the effectiveness of compartmentalization may break down. To summarize, the attributional measure suggests that when a partner is perceived as having many important negative characteristics, compartmentalization of those characteristics may be effective when the relationship is new, but integrative thinking is required to maintain a positive view of the partner in a long-term relationship.

Additional measures suggested that compartmentalized organization of partner knowledge in older relationships was associated with a lack of shared activities, which may account for how some partners

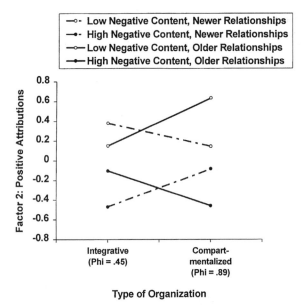

Figure 12.4. Adjusted predicted values for positive attributions, a measure of attributions for a partner's negative behaviors (Fincham & Bradbury, 1987), illustrating the interaction of compartmentalization, negative content of partner descriptions, and months in relationship at values that are 1 SD above and below the means. For compartmentalization, $M = .67$, $SD = .22$; for negative content, $M = .26$, $SD = .12$; for months in relationship, $M = 20.71$, $SD = 13.56$. Source: Showers & Kevlyn (in press).

develop a compartmentalized style of organization. The lack of shared activities may also explain how these relationships survive despite negative beliefs. These interpretations must be examined further, with longitudinal data. An analysis of a follow-up of the sample described here is under way.

Linking Cognitive Structure to Brain Physiology

An additional study supports an expanded role for compartmentalized organization. This study examined the relation between cognitive organization of self-beliefs and brain physiology (Showers, McMahon, Sutton, & Davidson, 1998). Research on the physiology of emotion finds that brain asymmetry – that is, a physiological asymmetry in left- and right-side anterior brain activation – is associated with positive and negative emotionality (e.g., Davidson, 1992). Such asymmetries may represent biological predispositions to positive or negative emotion. The present study replicated previous work associating relative left-side activation at midfrontal and anterior temporal sites with positive affect (e.g., Tomarken, Davidson, Wheeler, & Doss, 1992). In addition, we considered whether the association between brain asymmetry and affect would be moderated by cognitive organization. In other words, might different types of self-organization facilitate positive affect or ameliorate negative affect in individuals who are predisposed to positive and negative emotions, respectively?

The sample for this study was 75 individuals who had previously participated in the Longitudinal Individual Differences (LID) project conducted at the University of Wisconsin Laboratory for Affective Neuroscience.[6] For the LID project, 220 participants were recruited from introductory psychology classes over a 3-year period, to participate in one or more laboratory sessions. In two of the laboratory sessions, baseline (resting) electroencephalographic (EEG) measures of anterior brain symmetry were collected. The present study involved the administration of the self-descriptive card-sorting task in a laboratory session that took place between 6 months and 4 years after the EEG assessments ($M = 19.6$ months, $SD = 13.2$). Affect and personality measures, including the PANAS scales (Watson, Clark, & Tellegen, 1988), Self-Esteem (Rosenberg, 1965), Depression (Beck, Ward, Mendelson, Mock, & Erbaugh, 1961), and Extraversion and Neuroticism (Eysenck & Eysenck, 1964) were also administered at this time.

Two measures of brain asymmetry were constructed from the EEG data. One, AVF3F7, represents the average of standardized asymmetry scores for two pairs of sites in the midfrontal (F3, F4) and the lateral frontal (F7, F8) regions. The second measure, AVT3, represents the asymmetry score for one pair of anterior temporal sites (T3, T4). Positive asymmetry scores represent greater left-side activation and negative scores reflect greater right-side activation. In addition, the affect and personality measures were factor-analyzed to produce composite measures of positive affect and negative affect.

Regression analyses examined the relation among brain asymmetry, evaluative organization, and affect. For individuals with relative right-side midfrontal activation and many negative self-beliefs, a compartmentalized self-structure was associated with more positive affect than would be expected, given their brain asymmetry (Figure 12.5). Similarly, in individuals with relative right-side anterior temporal activation and high differential importance, a compartmentalized self-

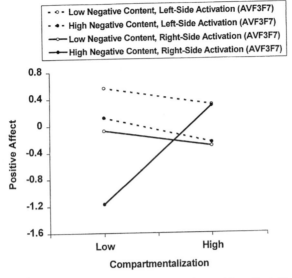

Figure 12.5. Adjusted predicted values for positive affect, illustrating the interaction of compartmentalization, negative content of self-descriptions, and midfrontal activation asymmetry (AVF3F7) at values that are 1 SD above and below the means. For compartmentalization, $M = .76$, $SD = .22$; for negative content, $M = .31$, $SD = .14$; for AVF3F7, $M = .03$, $SD = .90$. Source: Showers, McMahon, Sutton, & Davidson (1998).

structure was associated with less negative affect than would be expected, given their brain asymmetry. In other words, these compartmentalized individuals do not report levels of affect that would be consistent with their physiological predisposition to negative emotionality.

This result is somewhat surprising because one might think that individuals who are biologically predisposed to negative emotion would have chronically activated negative beliefs and feelings – a circumstance in which integration should be advantageous. How is it that compartmentalization is associated with more positive and less negative affect? One possibiliy is that the person's affective experience lends itself to compartmentalization. If negative emotions stem from biological factors, for example, those emotions may be strikingly inconsistent with the person's current life experience. A person with a biological predisposition to negative emotion may well have a successful career and solid relationships that seem unrelated to their mood episodes. Current life experience, including positive achievements and interpersonal relationships may form the basis of positive compartments, whereas negative moods (stemming from biological factors and seemingly inconsistent with current life events) may form separate negative compartments. The negative emotion episodes are isolated from other self-beliefs, thereby minimizing their impact on general affectivity. Thus, some people who have a biological predisposition to negative emotionality may be especially good candidates for compartmentalized organization, because of clear discrepancies between their emotionality and other facets of their experience. Rightside activated individuals who cannot achieve this separation may find that their negative emotions intrude on a wide range of self-aspects, lowering their general affect and increasing the incidence of neurotic feelings and behaviors.

An Expanded Model of Evaluative Organization

Taken together, the studies described here suggest that the model of evaluative organization should be expanded to give compartmentalization a broader role. There is still substantial support for the basic model. However, these recent studies indicate that compartmentalization may be useful and effective in a wider range of contexts than the basic model might suggest. Evaluative integration may be a strategy that requires more effort and attentional resources than compartmentalization, in part because the spreading activation of similarly valenced items of knowledge needs to be overridden if integration is to take place (Showers & Kling, 1996a). The findings of all of the studies in our laboratory to date make sense if compartmentalization is viewed as an organizational strategy of first resort. It is an easy strategy (because it is easy to group specific items of knowledge according to their affective valence) and can be very effective, because it isolates negative knowledge and keeps it completely out of mind. However, compartmentalization can break down, consistent with its "hidden vulnerability," at any time when negative beliefs cannot be avoided. Perhaps only when compartmentalization breaks down is it worth the extra effort and cognitive resources required to engage in evaluatively integrative thinking and construct an integrative structure of self-beliefs.

The present studies suggest the following circumstances may facilitate compartmentalization: (1) when the self-concept is basically positive (Showers, 1992a); (2) when stresses are limited in time frame and linked to a specific (novel) context, such as the freshman year at college (Showers et al., 1998); (3) when negative beliefs can be easily avoided, such as negative characteristics of a new relationship partner (Showers & Kevlyn, in press); and (4) when the positive and negative features of experience are easily kept separate (Showers et al., 1998). These studies also help to define the conditions in which evaluative integration is most likely to be worthwhile: (1) when the self-concept includes many important, negative beliefs (Showers, 1992a, 1992b); (2) when there is time and cognitive resources are available to engage in successful integration (Showers & Kling, 1996a); (3) when negative beliefs must be confronted, as in long-term relationships (Showers & Kevlyn, in press).

Does Evaluative Organization Contribute to the Effects of Mood on Cognition?

The kinds of organizational structures described here could contribute to the effects of mood and emotion on information processing. Several affect-based phenomena are consistent with the view that the organization of knowledge changes with a person's affective state. For example, Niedenthal and Halberstadt (this volume) find that affective states influence the dimensions that perceivers use to categorize stimuli. People in emotional states are more likely than people in neutral states to rely on affective characteristics of stimuli (such as a person's happy or sad facial expression or the affective valence of an object like "trophy") in making similarity judgments. In other words, the category structures of people in emotional states are likely to be affectively or evaluatively based, that is, compartmentalized.

As another example, consider the effects of mood on memory. The phenomenon of mood-dependent memory also suggests that emotional state is a fundamental dimension used to organize information about affect-laden events. If events are most easily recalled when a person is in the emotional state in which they were experienced (Eich & Macaulay, this volume), then emotional states must influence the way in which memory is organized, making mood-congruent information more accessible. This is what compartmentalization does. A similar process may explain mood-congruency effects in general. If the organizing dimension is evaluative valence rather than emotional state per se, any information that is congruent with a perceiver's emotional state should be more accessible than information that is affectively incongruent, all other factors being equal.

More specifically, the phenomena of emotional response categorization, mood-dependent memory, and mood-congruent memory all suggest that positive and negative mood states should increase the evaluative compartmentalization of knowledge. However, my own studies examining the relation of mood and organization of the self-concept as a whole have not confirmed this hypothesis. A mood-induction procedure in the laboratory failed to influence the evaluative organization of self-knowledge, as assessed by the self-descriptive card-sorting task (Showers & Kling, 1996a, Study 1). Most likely, studies of mood and self-concept organization are confounded by people's motivation to get themselves out of negative moods. In fact, mood states can lead to incongruent cognitive outcomes, as people attempt to correct for their moods in regulating their behaviors and in presenting themselves to others (Berkowitz et al., this volume). Thus, the hypothesis that positive and negative moods increase compartmentalization may best be examined either in non-self-relevant contexts, or in circumstances in which motivation for mood repair is low.

Compartmentalized and integrative structures may also contribute to specific information-processing strategies. For example, given that mood functions as one input to subsequent evaluations (Martin, this volume), congruency or incongruency of mood with a target's fulfillment of an expected role may encourage integrative thinking (to resolve incongruencies) or compartmentalization (when current and expected feelings are congruent). In general, compartmentalization may be a simple type of organization that is associated with heuristic or simplified processing, whereas integration is more substantive or elaborative. This suggests some interesting empirical questions as to whether compartmentalized individuals are more likely to experience affect infusion in the form of mood-as-information, whereas integrative individuals may be more likely to be influenced by affective priming of mood-consistent beliefs (Forgas, this volume). Moreover, if a compartmentalized type of organization is associated with positive mood, then the structure itself may facilitate the use of heuristics and top-down processing in positive moods (Bless, this volume). The notion that bottom-up thinking occurs in problematic contexts seems to fit the present model, in which integrative thinking (presumably bottom-up) is most fruitful when a person must confront important negative self-beliefs. Integrative thinking should also preserve the detail of positive and negative information, whereas compartmentalization may involve assimilation of inconsistently valenced information into the dominant valenced structure (cf. Fiedler, this volume).

Conclusions

This chapter proposed an expanded model of evaluative organization that recognizes that the compartmentalization of positive and negative beliefs is an easy and efficient strategy for minimizing access to negative knowledge. Compartmentalization is likely to be beneficial when the content of relevant knowledge is basically positive, when stress occurs in novel, short-lived situations, or when it is easy to separate the positive and negative aspects of experience. Evaluative integration is described as a strategy that requires considerable effort and cognitive resources, and is most likely to be worthwhile when negative knowledge cannot be avoided and compartmentalization breaks down.

More broadly, this work suggests that the organization of knowledge structures bears an important correspondence to affective states. Moods and emotional states may encourage the reorganization of information. At the same time, preferences for one type of structure or another may influence a person's emotional reactions to events and overall feelings about the self. Further research is needed to explore the conditions under which people develop one type of structure or another, and whether those who suffer from negative moods or low self-esteem can learn alternative styles for organizing knowledge that will help them handle negative beliefs.

This volume documents the pervasive influence of affect on cognition. Such effects are most likely mediated by changes in the organizational structure of relevant knowledge. Identification of alternative styles of organization informs our understanding of affective processes and, ultimately, provides a mechanism for the interface of affect and cognition.

Notes

1. The example suggests that compartmentalized individuals may be vulnerable to swings in mood or self-esteem. This notion is consistent with the model. For a related finding, see Showers and Kling (1996a; described in the next section). Also, Rhodewalt, Madrian, & Cheney (1998) find that com-

partmentalized narcissists show high fluctuations on daily measures of self-esteem.

2. A related model of self-complexity also considers how the organization of self-knowledge into multiple self-aspects may influence people's reactions to positive and negative events (Linville, 1985, 1987). In contrast to the present model, which argues that affective reactions depend on the positive or negative content of the self-knowledge activated, Linville's model suggests that affective reactions are influenced by the amount of the self (i.e., number of self-aspects) that is implicated. In the model of compartmentalization, the self-structure determines the content of the self-knowledge that comes to mind; in the self-complexity model, self-structure determines the amount of the self that is implicated, without regard for its content.

   Although the model of compartmentalization treats the valence of self-beliefs as given, it accommodates shifts of meaning for specific attributes in the following way. A characteristic like "outspoken" may sometimes be perceived as positive and sometimes negative. Presumably, such a shift in meaning involves the reorganization of knowledge, so that the characteristic in question is linked to other positive or negative attributes. Thus, "outspoken" refers to a set of behaviors that do not change, whereas the implications of those behaviors depend on other features of self-knowledge to which this attribute is linked at the time. The shifts in meaning associated with the phenomenon of affective priming presumably result from this kind of reorganization of an attribute in relation to other beliefs.

3. To what extent does the card-sorting task reflect the way self-information is ordinarily processed? Presumably, although the groups that an individual generates may vary across time and context, they are filled in a systematic way that reflects the underlying thought processes of the individual. In other words, the specific groups that come to mind may change, but the tendency to generate compartmentalized groups may not. Over a 2-year period, the stability of the measure of compartmentalization (phi) is .58 (Showers et al., 1998). Moreover, the model of compartmentalization assumes that the content of self-aspect categories reflects the associative links between items of information – links that are generated by thought processes. For example, an individual who thinks "I'm shy, but I'm a loyal friend" may generate a card-sort category, "Myself in social situations" that includes the attributes "shy" and "loyal." The underlying thought processes (as opposed to the abstract categories) are surely the proximal cause of any impact that these cognitive structures have on mood or self-esteem.

4. The Cognitive Vulnerability to Depression Study was funded by National Institute of Mental Health Grant 1RO1MH43866, awarded to Lyn Y. Abramson, and National Institute of Mental Health Grant 1R01MH48216, awarded to Lauren B. Alloy. Collection of the self-organization data described here was supported by National Institute of Mental Health Fellowship F32MH10058 and funds from the University of Wisconsin Graduate School, awarded to Carolin J. Showers.

5. A recent study of attachment style and relationship complexity obtained a

similar result (Fishtein, Pietromonaco, & Feldman-Barrett, in press). Securely attached individuals (who may have relatively positive perceptions of their relationships) were more compartmentalized in their descriptions of their relationships than were insecurely attached individuals (whose perceptions may be more negative).

6. The LID project and the University of Wisconsin Laboratory for Affective Neuroscience are supported by National Institute of Mental Health Grant R01MH43454, awarded to Richard J. Davidson. The self-concept study described here was supported by funds from the University of Wisconsin Graduate School, awarded to Carolin Showers; National Institute of Mental Health (NIMH) Grant R01-MH43454, the Wisconsin Center for Affective Science (NIMH Behavioral Science Research Center P50-MH52354), and NIMH Research Scientist Award K05-MH00875 to Richard Davidson; and a Young Investigator Award from the National Alliance for Research on Schizophrenia and Affective Disorders to Steven Sutton.

References

Alloy, L. B., Abramson, L. Y., Murray, L. A., Whitehouse, W. G., & Hogan, M. E. (1997). Self-referent information processing in individuals at high and low cognitive risk for depression. *Cognition and Emotion, 11,* 539–568.

Alloy, L. B., Albright, J. S., Abramson, L. Y., & Dykman, B. M. (1990). Depressive realism and nondepressive optimistic illusions: The role of the self. In R. E. Ingram (Ed.), *Contemporary psychological approaches to depression: Treatment, research and theory* (pp. 71–86). New York: Plenum Press.

Bargh, J. A., & Tota, M. E. (1988). Context-dependent automatic processing in depression: Accessibility of negative constructs with regard to self but not others. *Journal of Personality and Social Psychology, 54,* 925–939.

Beck, A. T., Ward, C. H., Mendelson, M., Mock, J., & Erbaugh, J. (1961). An inventory for measuring depression. *Archives of General Psychiatry, 4,* 561–571.

Campbell, J. D. (1990). Self-esteem and clarity of the self-concept. *Journal of Personality and Social Psychology, 59,* 538–549.

Cantor, N., Markus, H., Niedenthal, P., & Nurius, P. (1986). On motivation and the self-concept. In E. T. Higgins & R. M. Sorrentino (Eds.), *Handbook of motivation and cognition: Foundations of social behavior* (pp. 96–121). New York: Guilford Press.

Cramer H. (1974). *Mathematical methods of statistics.* Princeton, NJ: Princeton University Press. (Original work published 1945)

Davidson, R. J. (1992). Emotion and affective style: Hemispheric substrates. *Psychological Science, 3,* 39–43.

Donahue, E. M., Robins, R. W., Roberts, B. W., & John, O. P. (1993). The divided self: Concurrent and longitudinal effects of psychological adjustment and social roles on self-concept differentiation. *Journal of Personality and Social Psychology, 64,* 834–846.

Everitt, B. S. (1977). *The analysis of contingency tables.* London: Chapman and Hall.

Eysenck, H. P., & Eysenck, S. G. B. (1964). *Eysenck personality inventory*. San Diego: Educational and Industrial Testing Service.

Fincham, F. D., & Bradbury, T. N. (1987). Assessing attributions in marriage: The relationship attribution measure. *Journal of Personality and Social Psychology, 62*, 457–468.

Fishtein, J., Pietromonaco, P. R., & Feldman-Barrett, L. (in press). The contribution of attachment style and relationship conflict to the complexity of relationship knowledge. *Social Cognition*.

Freud, S. (1966). *Introductory lectures on psychoanalysis*. (J. Strachey, Trans.). New York: Norton. (Original work published 1917)

Greenwald, A. G., Bellezza, F. S., & Banaji, M. R. (1988). Is self-esteem a central ingredient of the self-concept? *Personality and Social Psychology Bulletin, 14*, 34–45.

Hammen, C., Marks, T., deMayo, R., & Mayol, A. (1985). Self-schemas and risk for depression: A prospective study. *Journal of Personality and Social Psychology, 49*, 1147–1159.

Higgins, E. T. (1987). Self-discrepancy: A theory relating self and affect. *Psychological Review, 94*, 319–340.

Izard, C. E. (1971). *The face of emotion*. New York: Appleton-Century-Crofts.

James, W. (1890). *The principles of psychology* (Vol. 1). New York: Henry Holt.

Kihlstrom, J. F., & Cantor, N. (1984). Mental representations of the self. In L. Berkowitz (Ed.), *Advances in experimental social psychology* (Vol. 17, pp. 1–47). New York: Academic Press.

Kuiper, N. A., Olinger, L. J., & MacDonald, M. R. (1988). Vulnerability and episodic cognitions in a self-worth contingency model of depression. In L. B. Alloy (Ed.), *Cognitive processes in depression* (pp. 289–309). New York: Guilford Press.

Linville, P. W. (1985). Self-complexity and affective extremity: Don't put all of your eggs in one cognitive basket. *Social Cognition, 3*, 94–120.

Linville, P. W. (1987). Self-complexity as a cognitive buffer against stress-related illness and depression. *Journal of Personality and Social Psychology, 52*, 663–676.

Margolin, J., & Niedenthal, P. M. (1997). *Manipulating self-complexity through communication role assignment*. Manuscript submitted for publication.

Markus, H., & Wurf, E. (1987). The dynamic self-concept: A social psychological perspective. *Annual Review of Psychology, 38*, 299–337.

Mischel, W. (1973). Toward a cognitive social learning reconceptualization of personality. *Psychological Review, 80*, 252–283.

Pelham, B. W. (1991). On confidence and consequence: The certainty and importance of self-knowledge. *Journal of Personality and Social Psychology, 60*, 518–530.

Pelham, B. W., & Swann, Jr., W. B. (1989). From self-conceptions to self-worth: On the sources and structure of global self-esteem. *Journal of Personality and Social Psychology, 57*, 672–680.

Rhodewalt, F., Madrian, J. C., & Cheney, S. (1989). Narcissism, self-knowledge organization, and emotional reactivity: The effect of daily experiences on self-esteem and affect. *Personality and Social Psychology Bulletin, 24*, 75–87.

Rosenberg, M. (1965). Society and the adolescent self-image. Princeton, NJ: Princeton University Press.

Safran, J. D., & Segal, Z. V. (1990). Interpersonal process in cognitive therapy. New York: Basic Books.

Schlenker, B. R., & Weigold, M. F. (1989). Goals and the self-identification process: Constructing desired identities. In L. A. Pervin (Ed.), Goal concepts in personality and social psychology (pp. 243–290). Hillsdale, NJ: Erlbaum.

Sedikides, C. (1992). Changes in the valence of the self as a function of mood. In M. S. Clark (Ed.), Review of Personality and Social Psychology (pp. 271–311). Newbury Park, CA: Sage.

Segal, Z. V. (1988). Appraisal of the self-schema construct in cognitive models of depression. Psychological Bulletin, 103, 147–162.

Showers, C. (1992a). Compartmentalization of positive and negative self-knowledge: Keeping bad apples out of the bunch. Journal of Personality and Social Psychology, 62, 1036–1049.

Showers, C. (1992b). Evaluatively integrative thinking about characteristics of the self. Personality and Social Psychology Bulletin, 18, 719–729.

Showers, C. J. (1995). The evaluative organization of self-knowledge: Origins, processes, and implications for self-esteem. In M. H. Kernis (Ed.), Efficacy, agency, and self-esteem (pp. 101–120). New York: Plenum Press.

Showers, C. J., Abramson, L. Y., & Hogan, M. E. (1998). The dynamic self: How the content and structure of the self-concept change with mood. Journal of Personality and Social Psychology, 75, 478–493.

Showers, C. J., & Kevlyn, S. B. (in press). Organization of knowledge about a relationship partner: Implications for liking and loving. Journal of Personality and Social Psychology.

Showers, C. J., & Kling, K. C. (1996a). Organization of self-knowledge: Implications for recovery from sad mood. Journal of Personality and Social Psychology, 70, 578–590.

Showers, C. J., & Kling, K. C. (1996b). The organization of self-knowledge: Implications for mood regulation. In L. L. Martin & A. Tesser (Eds.), Striving and feeling: Interactions among goals, affect, and self-regulation (pp. 151–174). Mahwah, NJ: Erlbaum.

Showers, C. J., McMahon, P. D., Sutton, S. K., & Davidson, R. J. (1998). Cognitive compensations for negative mood: The interplay of self-structure and brain activation. Manuscript submitted for publication.

Showers, C., & Ryff, C. D. (1996). Self-differentiation and well-being in a life transition. Personality and Social Psychology Bulletin, 22, 448–460.

Snyder, M. (1979). Self-monitoring processes. In L. Berkowitz (Ed.), Advances in experimental social psychology (Vol. 12, pp. 85–118). New York: Academic Press.

Swann, W. B., Jr. (1990). To be adored or to be known? The interplay of self-enhancement and self-verification. In E. T. Higgins & R. M. Sorrentino (Eds.), Handbook of motivation and cognition: Foundations of social behavior (Vol. 2, pp. 408–448). New York: Guilford Press.

Tomarken, A. J., Davidson, R. J., Wheeler, R. E., & Doss, R. C. (1992). Individual differences in anterior brain asymmetry and fundamental dimensions of emotion. *Journal of Personality and Social Psychology, 62*, 676–687.

Watson, D., Clark, L. A., & Tellegen, A. (1988). Development and validation of brief measures of positive and negative affect: The PANAS scales. *Journal of Personality and Social Psychology, 54*, 1063–1070.

13. Prologue to a Unified Theory of Attitudes, Stereotypes, and Self-Concept

ANTHONY G. GREENWALD, MAHZARIN R. BANAJI,
LAURIE A. RUDMAN, SHELLY D. FARNHAM,
BRIAN A. NOSEK, AND MARSHALL ROSIER

Introduction

The theoretical analysis in this chapter connects social psychology's central cognitive constructs, *stereotype* and *self-concept*, to its central affective constructs, *attitude* and *self-esteem*. In addition to proposing this unified account of social psychology's major theoretical constructs, the chapter seeks to unify the competing affective-cognitive consistency principles of social psychology's classic consistency theories: Heider's (1958) balance theory, Osgood and Tannenbaum's (1955) congruity theory, and Festinger's (1957) cognitive dissonance theory.

Initial support for the unified theory comes from experiments that use a new latency-based procedure, the Implicit Association Test (IAT), to obtain indirect measures of *implicit* attitudes, stereotypes, self-concept, and self-esteem (Banaji & Greenwald, 1995). The IAT's findings reveal patterns of affective-cognitive consistency that are not readily observed with explicit (self-report) measures.

Decline of the Consistency Principle and Reliance on Self-Report Measures

The principle of affect-guided cognition was central to the major cognitive consistency theories of the 1950s: balance theory (Heider, 1958), congruity theory (Osgood & Tannenbaum, 1953), and cognitive dissonance theory (Festinger, 1957). Through the combined force of these

This research was supported by grants from the National Science Foundation (SBR-9422242, SBR-9710172, SBR-9422241, and SBR-9709924) and from the National Institute of Mental Health (MH-41328 and MH-001533). Please address correspondence to Anthony G. Greenwald, Department of Psychology, University of Washington, Seattle, WA.

theories, affective-cognitive consistency became a dominant theme in social psychology of the 1960s (see Abelson et al., 1968). Despite being widely regarded as valid, cognitive consistency theories diminished in importance in the late 20th century, never having established a position of broad scope and applicability. This chapter suggests that the success of consistency theories was limited in part by the necessity of using self-report measures to test them. At about the same time that consistency theories achieved prominence in the 1960s, self-report measures were under attack because of their susceptibility to artifacts in the form of *demand characteristics* (Orne, 1962), *evaluation apprehension* (Rosenberg, 1969), and *impression management* (Tedeschi, Schlenker, & Bonoma, 1971; see also Weber & Cook, 1972).

Complementing the empirical attack on self-report measures, Nisbett and Wilson (1977) constructed a strong theoretical critique of modern introspective (i.e., self-report) methods. During the period of concerted attack on self-report measures, social psychologists were attracted to indirect or nonreactive measures (Webb, Campbell, Schwartz, Sechrest, & Grove, 1981). However, this courtship with alternative measures was short-lived, being effectively sabotaged both by the labor-intensive character of these measures and by their remoteness from the cognitive constructs on which social psychological theory was increasingly focused in the late 20th century.

How might social psychology's reliance on self-report measures have adversely affected cognitive consistency theories? A critical characteristic of self-report measures is that they oblige conscious oversight. The respondent is asked both to retrieve and to report relevant knowledge. It is possible not only that respondents may report inaccurately what they can retrieve (i.e., may engage in impression management), but also that they may simply be unable to retrieve some of the knowledge requested for self-report (i.e., may lack introspective access). For either of these reasons, the conscious oversight that is intrinsic to self-report may obscure or obliterate the operation of consistency processes and thereby misleadingly make the theories appear limited in scope.

Not until the late 1980s and early 1990s did useful alternatives to self-report become available for social cognition research. A wide variety of new measures was inspired by the use of indirect measures in implicit cognition research (e.g., Jacoby, Lindsay, & Toth, 1992; Schacter, 1987). Following upon that development, Banaji and Greenwald (1995) described how concepts of implicit cognition could illuminate social cognition's major constructs of attitude, stereotype, and self-esteem. Subsequently, Greenwald, McGhee, and Schwartz (1998) developed a general method for research on implicit social cognition, the Implicit Association Test (IAT), which made possible the research to be reported in this chapter.

Assumptions Underlying a Unified Theory of Social Cognition

Associative Structure of Social/Semantic Knowledge

Social knowledge is knowledge of persons (including self) and groups. Social knowledge is here assumed to have an associative structure. This description of social knowledge as associative fits with various models for social cognition, including hierarchically connected prototype nodes, exemplar representations of categories, and parallel distributed process or connectionist networks. Associative models have the virtue of easily permitting representations of (a) connections among the structure's elements (persons, groups, concepts, traits, valence, etc.) and (b) multiple paths (and therefore variable strengths of connection) between representations. An associative social knowledge structure is a *semantic* structure of the sort that was contrasted with *episodic* knowledge by Tulving (1972). Whereas episodic knowledge is knowledge about experiences or events, semantic knowledge is the repository of repeated or enduring associations.

Centrality of Self

Much previous work has identified the *self* as a central entity in both the semantic and episodic structure of social knowledge (Greenwald, 1981; Greenwald & Pratkanis, 1984; Kihlstrom & Cantor, 1984; Koffka, 1935). In an associative knowledge structure, the self's property of centrality can be conceived by locating its representation (or node) associatively near other important nodes in the structure.

Cognitive Representation of Valence

In the social knowledge structure, negative and positive valence are themselves identified as nodes. This device is in the spirit of Bower's (1981) representation of moods as nodes in an associative structure.[1]

Self-Positivity

With valence represented in the associative structure of social knowledge, low and high self-esteem can be represented as connections of the self node with the negative or positive valence node. The observation that self-esteem is typically positive in normal populations translates to an assumption that the self node is, for most people, strongly connected to the positive valence node.

The Unified Theory

The principles of the associative structure of knowledge, centrality of self, and positive valence of self are so widely accepted as to form pieces of the paradigmatic common ground of modern social psychology. In using these principles, the unified theory therefore stays within familiar theoretical territory. The main novelty of the unified theory is its attempt to establish that these familiar theoretical principles suffice both (a) to locate all of social cognition's major theoretical constructs in a common structure and (b) to generate interesting predictions of interrelation among these constructs.

A Social Knowledge Structure

Figure 13.1 displays a schematic social knowledge structure (SKS) that is based on the background ("paradigmatic common ground") assumptions just stated. Although Figure 13.1 includes only a small fraction of the objects and attributes of any actual social knowledge structure, it does show structures corresponding to all of social psychology's main theoretical constructs: *self-concept, self-esteem, stereotype,* and *attitude.*

Three Consistency Principles

In order to describe expected relations among self-esteem, self-concept, stereotypes, and attitudes, the unified theory needs assumptions about constraints on relations within associative structures such as Figure 13.1's SKS. The following three principles have been named in ways that identify their debt to the 40-year tradition of consistency theories. Each principle is associated with the definition of a property of the associative knowledge structure.

SOCIAL KNOWLEDGE STRUCTURE

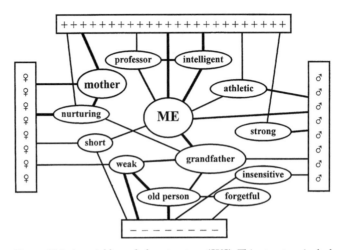

Figure 13.1. A social knowledge structure (SKS). This structure includes representations that correspond to social psychology's major constructs of self-concept,
self-esteem, stereotype, and attitude. Nodes (ovals) represent concepts and attributes, and links (lines) represent associative relations. The *self-concept* includes
links of the *Me* node to such things as roles (professor, grandfather) and traits
(intelligent, athletic). *Self-esteem* is the collection of links – either direct or mediated via components of the self-concept – of the *Me* node to valence (+ + + or
– – –). Parallel to the self-concept, *stereotypes* are group concepts, consisting of
collections of traits linked to nodes representing social categories such as mother,
grandfather, professor, male, female, and grandfather. Parallel to self-esteem,
attitude is the collection of links, either direct or mediated via components of a
stereotype, that connect a social category node to valence (+ + + or – – –).

Definition 1: Shared first-order link. Two nodes that are both linked to the
same third node are said to have a shared first-order link.

Principle 1: Balance-congruity. A new link tends to be formed between
two nodes that have a shared first-order link.

In Figure 13.1's structure, the balance-congruity principle tends to
produce (among others) several new links involving the *Me* node,
including *Me-mother, Me-strong, Me-nurturing, Me-old person,* and *Me-
weak.* Importantly, all but one (*Me-strong*) of these possible new direct
links is opposed by the next principle. Principle 1 is named to acknowledge its debt both to Heider's (1946, 1958) balance theory and
to Osgood and Tannenbaum's (1955) congruity theory.

Definition 2: Bipolar opposition of nodes. Two nodes that have fewer shared first-order links than expected by chance are described as bipolar-opposed.

As shown in Figure 13.1, SKS has two prominent pairs of bipolar-opposed nodes, those for valence (positive, negative) and gender (male, female). (SKS contains one other bipolar pair – weak and strong – and could easily be extended to include others, such as intelligent–stupid, short–tall.)[2]

Principle 2: Imbalance-dissonance. The network resists forming new links that would result in a node having first-order links to both of a pair of bipolar-opposed nodes.

The resistance to new links embodied in this imbalance-dissonance principle is theoretically necessary to oppose the otherwise inevitable effect of the balance-congruity principle, in conjunction with environmental influences, to produce links between all pairs of nodes. In Figure 13.1, for example, *Me* is linked to *short*, which is linked to *female*. The imbalance-dissonance principle resists the linkage of *Me* to *female*, which would otherwise be called for by the balance-congruity principle. Similarly, in Figure 13.1's SKS, the imbalance-dissonance principle should resist *Me-negative* and *Me-female*.

The unified theory's third consistency principle shares the imbalance-dissonance principle's function of avoiding configurations that link a single node to both of two bipolar-opposed nodes. However, the third principle encompasses an especially problematic class of situations in which circumstances provoke sustained pressures toward generating these imbalanced configurations. Consider the situation in which one's loved sibling (*A*) gets married to *B*, who happens to be a criminal (*C*). The existing association of *A* to positive valence should produce (by virtue of the balance-congruity principle together with an assumed new link of *A* to *B*) a link of *B* to positive valence. At the same time, the unalterable association of the concept criminal (*C*) with negative valence should (again, by virtue of balance congruity) tend to produce an association of *B* to negative valence. The resulting tendency for *B* to develop links to bipolar-opposed nodes (positive and negative valence) is clearly opposed by the imbalance-dissonance principle. This situation requires a more extreme solution than simple nonformation of the new link, because of expected sustained confrontation of the imbalancing influences.

Definition 3: Pressured concept. A concept is pressured when sustained or repeated influences, operating in accord with the balance-congruity principle, should cause it to develop links to both of two bipolar-opposed nodes.

Principle 3: Differentiation. Pressured concepts tend to split into subconcepts, each linked to one of the pressuring bipolar-opposed nodes.

In the example of the sibling's criminal spouse, the spouse (*B*) becomes a pressured concept. This pressure would be removable if *B* could split into two concepts, one linked to negative valence (e.g., *B*'s past life as criminal) and the other to positive (*B*'s current life as loving spouse). Differentiation of the concept may provide enough buffering to relieve the opposing pressures of the balance-congruity and imbalance-dissonance principles. The differentiation principle embodies the cognitive operation that has been identified as *subtyping* in research on stereotypes (e.g., Deaux, Winton, Crowley, & Lewis, 1985; Hewstone, Macrae, Griffiths, & Milne, 1994; Weber & Crocker, 1983).

Relations to Heider's Formulation of Balance Theory

The similarities between Heider's (1958) balance theory and the unified theory are far more compelling than are the differences. Insights corresponding to the unified theory's three principles can be seen in Heider's (1958) diagrams of balanced and imbalanced configurations for sentiment and unit relations. In his diagrams (see Figure 13.2) the balance-congruity principle appears in the balanced structures *b–d*, the imbalance-dissonance principle in diagram *a*, and the differentiation principle in diagram *e*. The chief differences between Heider's representations and those of the unified theory are that Heider (a) restricted attention to links that involved a person object (either self [*p*] or other [*o*]; (b) distinguished *unit* (association) from *sentiment* (liking) links, in contrast to the present use of only one type of link; (c) focused more on the role of consistency in modifying existing links than on its role in creating (or avoiding) new links; and (c) did not distinguish between unrelated and bipolar-opposed pairs of nodes.[3]

The differences of the present analysis from Heider's allow us to identify closer relatedness among social psychology's cognitive and affective constructs than was previously apparent. Heider took it as a goal to represent the complexity of consciously construed relations among psychological objects. To do that, he focused on person–object

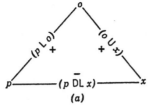

(a)

The given situation is unbalanced: two positive relations and one negative relation.

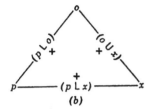

(b)

Change in sentiment relation resulting in a balance of three positive relations.

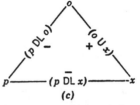

(c)

Change in sentiment relation resulting in a balance of two negative relations and one positive relation.

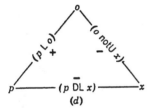

(d)

Change in unit relation resulting in a balance of two negative relations and one positive relation.

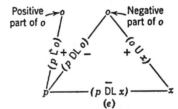

(e)

Change in unit relation through differentiation resulting in a balance of two negative relations and one positive relation.

Figure 13.2. Heider's representation of consistency principles. From Heider (1958, p. 208).

relations and distinguished unit from sentiment relations. His discovery that most person–object relations could be reduced to just the unit and sentiment relations was a remarkable and theoretically effective simplification. The present analysis seeks even broader scope by using an even more radical simplification: collapsing both (a) the distinction between person concepts and other concepts and (b) the distinction between unit and sentiment relations. This increased simplification has certainly been influenced by modern connectionist and neural network modeling, itself a form of theory that reduces mental representations to node and link structures (Rumelhart & McClelland, 1986; Smith, 1996).

Predicting Relations Among Self-Concept, Stereotypes, and Attitudes

The preceding section stated three principles, all based on consistency theories from the 1950s (especially on Heider's balance theory). These three principles are presumed to operate on a conceptual structure that can encompass social psychology's major affective (attitude, self-esteem) and cognitive (stereotype, self-concept) constructs. The rest of this chapter develops this theory's predictions for relationships among self-concept, self-esteem, stereotypes, and attitudes; describes a research method (the Implicit Association Test) that permits empirical tests of these predictions; and provides the results of new studies that test the unified theory's predictions.

Relations Among Self-Concept, Self-Esteem, and Ingroup Attitude

The balance-congruity principle tends to produce same-valenced attitudes toward self and concepts that are closely associated with self (i.e., components of self-concept or identity). Figure 13.3. illustrates this form of theoretical derivation for the gender self-concept. For women, self (*Me* in Figure 13.3) is typically associated with both positive valence and female identity. The balance-congruity principle calls for the further association of positive with the concept of female. More particularly, the strength of positive attitude toward female (i.e., of the *female-positive* link) should be a joint function of the strengths of the two links (*Me-positive* and *Me-female*) on which it depends.

Relations Among Self-Concept, Gender Stereotype, and Attitude Toward Math

The unified theory assumes that the knowledge base of major social stereotypes – for example, those involving sex and race categories – is approximately the same for all members of society. Therefore, men and women should have similar knowledge of the prevailing gender stereotypes that associate (for example) male identity with greater strength and female identity with greater nurturance. This similarity between gender-stereotype knowledge possessed by males and fe-males notwithstanding, the unified theory predicts various affective-cognitive sex differences because of sex-typing of the self-concept (i.e., male traits associated to self for males, female traits to self for fe-males). Figure 13.4 shows female and male structures involving the

Self-Esteem, Self-Concept, and Ingroup Attitude

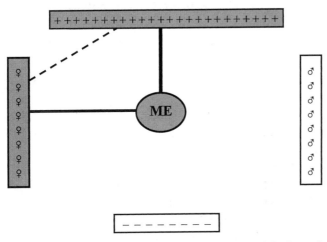

Figure 13.3. Operation of the balance-congruity principle. In conjunction with strong *Me-positive* and *Me-female* links, the balance-congruity principle should produce the *female-positive* link, which is indicated by the dashed line.

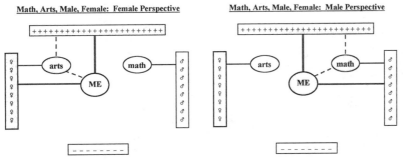

Figure 13.4. Effect of stereotypes and self-esteem on self-concept and attitudes. The dashed links are self-concept and attitude links generated by the balance-congruity principle, operating in conjunction with the *Me-positive* and either the *Me-male* link (for men) or the *Me-female* link (for women). The imbalance-dissonance principle, operating together with gender stereotypes that associate *male* with *math* and *female* with *arts*, opposes links of *math* to *Me* or to *positive* for women, and of *arts* to *Me* or *positive* for men.

concepts of *math, arts, male,* and *female.* Both the female and male structures incorporate gender stereotypes that associate *female* more with *arts* and *male* more with *math.* Also, both structures incorporate normal self-positivity. The critical difference between Figure 13.4's two structures is that the female version includes a strong *Me-female* link, whereas the male version includes a strong *Me-male* link. The different strengths of these sex self-concept links in the two figures, in conjunction with both the balance-congruity and imbalance-dissonance principles, lead to predictions of both (a) a self-concept difference – greater strength of *Me-arts* than *Me-math* for women than for men, and (b) an attitude difference – greater positive valence of *arts* than *math* for women than for men.

Relations Between Gender Identity and Valence of Gender Stereotypes

Figure 13.5 analyzes a structure similar to that of Figure 13.4. In parallel with the balance-congruity effect in the left panel of Figure 13.4, the configuration of Figure 13.5 should lead women (a) to develop a *Me-weak* association and (b) to associate *weak* with *positive.* At the same time, both of these links should be resisted by balance-congruity pressures derived from the cultural association of *weak* with *negative.* In this situation, the *weak* node is under pressure to become associated with the bipolar opposites, *positive* and *negative.* This situation calls for operation of the unified theory's third consistency prin-

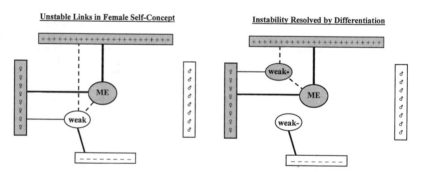

Figure 13.5. Expected effect of the differentiation principle on women's conception of *weak.* The left panel indicates, as dashed lines, two links involving *weak* that should be (a) strengthened by the balance-congruity principle, but (b) resisted by the imbalance-dissonance principle. The second diagram indicates a resolution achieved by splitting *weak* into a positively valenced subconcept that is associated with female, and a negatively valenced subconcept that is not.

ciple, differentiation, which can remove pressure on the *weak* concept by splitting it into separate positive- and negative-valenced representations.

The Implicit Association Test (IAT): A Technique for Measuring Associative Distance in the Social Knowledge Structure

The unified theory predictions of Figures 13.3 to 13.5 might be tested using self-report measures of the type that have been standard in social cognition research of the past several decades. For two reasons, however, self-report procedures are inappropriate for these tests. First, some of the associative links of SKS may not be available to introspection and may therefore not permit assessment by self-report. Second, self-report measures allow response artifacts (e.g., impression management) that could distort reporting of links that are introspectively available. Rather than using the direct measurement strategy of self-report, then, the unified theory's predictions are more suitably tested with indirect measures that avoid reliance on introspection and that are less susceptible to response artifacts.

Much recent research has focused on developing or applying indirect measures. In social cognition research, measures based on various cognitive priming techniques have been especially widely used. However, a limitation of these indirect measures is that their effect sizes have not been large enough to reflect individual differences. By contrast, the recently developed Implicit Association Test (IAT) method (Greenwald, McGhee, & Schwartz, 1998) does have the needed sensitivity.

The IAT Method

As it has been developed to this point, the Implicit Association Test measures *relative* strengths of associative links in a structure such as SKS. For example, rather than providing an absolute measure of strength of the *female-positive* link, it provides a measure that compares the strength of *female-positive* to that of *male-positive*.[4]

The IAT method works by obliging subjects to map four categories of stimuli onto just two responses. When the instructions are such that the two categories that share each response are conceptually close, the task is considerably easier than when the two categories that share each response are more distant. The IAT is illustrated in Figure 13.6 for the four categories of male, female, self, and other – a combination that provides an IAT measure of biological gender identity (or self-concept).

Using the IAT to Test Unified Theory Predictions

This section describes initial tests of the three predictions developed in the preceding section. In these tests, the IAT was used to obtain the needed measures of associative structure.

> *Prediction 1* (based on the balance-congruity principle). For women, the strength of positive attitude toward female should be a joint (interactive) function of the strength of the two links (*Me-positive* and *Me-female*) on which it depends.

This prediction was tested in a study of Farnham and Greenwald (1998). Participants were 63 undergraduate women at the University

Sample Implicit Association Test:
Gender Self-Concept (Identity)

	SELF	OTHER	MALE	FEMALE
IAT	• I	• They	• Male	• Female
Items in	• Me	• Them	• Man	• Woman
Four	• My	• Their	• Boy	• Girl
Cate-	• Mine	• Theirs	• He	• She
gories	• Self	• Other	• Sir	• Lady

	respond left	respond right
Task 1	SELF + OTHER	MALE + FEMALE
Task 2	SELF + MALE	OTHER + FEMALE
Task 3	SELF + FEMALE	OTHER + MALE

Figure 13.6. Illustration of the Implicit Association Test. The IAT starts by introducing subjects to the four categories used in the task. In this illustration, the categories are introduced by asking subjects to respond "left" to words representing either *male* or *female*, and to respond "right" to words representing either *self* or *other*. The IAT measure is obtained from the next two tasks, one in which *male* and *self* are assigned to "left" and *female* and *other* to "right," and another in which *female* and *self* are assigned to "left" and *male* and *other* to "right." The speed difference between the latter two tasks provides the desired measure. For example, if the subject responds more rapidly when *male* and *self* share a response, this indicates that *male* is associatively closer to *self* than is *female*.

of Washington. As summarized in Figure 13.7, each subject completed three IAT measures, one measuring gender self-concept (or identity), one measuring self-esteem, and one measuring attitude toward the (female) ingroup. The mean IAT results graphed in Figure 13.7 show implicit female identity and female positivity, both of which agree with unified-theory expectations due to operation of the balance-congruity principle together with self-positivity (which can also be seen in the figure). However, the test provided by these sample means is not nearly so stringent a test of the unified theory as is a test based on correlations among the three implicit measures. The expectation is that implicit attitude toward female will be a multiplicative function of the other two implicit measures. The prediction was confirmed in a multiple regression analysis in which the IAT measure of implicit female positivity was predicted from (a) the other two IAT measures and (b) the interaction of the two. In this analysis, both IAT predictors significantly and uniquely predicted attitude toward females (gender identity: beta $= .32$, $p = .01$; self-esteem: beta $= .36$, $p = .006$). The critical finding was a statistically significant effect of the interaction (product) term in the second step of this hierarchical regression analysis (beta $= .22$, $p = .05$).[5]

The interaction effect of the Farnham and Greenwald (1998) study supports the balance-congruity principle by showing that the positive relation between implicit gender identity and implicit attitude toward female is moderated by implicit self-esteem. The multivariate model (including the interaction effect) explained 33% of the variance ($R = .57$) in the female-positive link. By contrast, for the parallel analysis with explicit measures, neither of the univariate effects (beta $= -.15$, $-.21$) nor their interaction (beta $= .01$) was even in the expected positive direction. In summary, evidence for the balance-congruity principle was obtained with moderate clarity using implicit measures, but not at all with explicit measures. Similar findings in the domain of implicit racial attitudes, self-concept, and racial identity were obtained by Rosier, Banaji, and Greenwald (1998) in an investigation of Black undergraduate students at Yale University.

The balance-congruity principle was additionally tested in samples that included both men and women in a study by Lemm and Banaji (1998). Participants were 49 undergraduates (28 men and 21 women) at Yale University. Each subject completed two IAT measures (see Figure 13.8), one measuring gender self-concept (or identity), and one measuring attitude toward gender groups (male and female). Self and

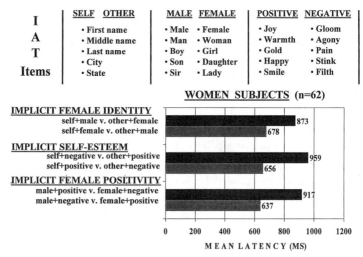

Figure 13.7. Design and results of the study by Farnham and Greenwald (1998). The self–other categories were composed of subject-generated items that, for *self*, included the subject's first, middle, and last names, hometown, and home state. The concept *other* was represented by similar items selected by the subject to be familiar but not self-related. The *IAT effect*, which indicates relative associative strengths, is measured by a latency difference between two tasks, latencies for which are shown in adjacent bars in the figure. Combinations of concepts that produced relatively low latency when sharing a response (see Figure 13.6) are thereby identified as being more closely associated than are combinations that yield higher latency. In the first pair of bars in the figure, the data indicated (unsurprisingly for the women subjects of this study) that self is more closely associated with female than male.

other items for the self-concept measure were generated using 10 standard categories (e.g., name, hometown, phone number, social se-curity number). The items for the "masculine" and "feminine" cate-gories were verbs (e.g., masculine: *controls, dares, employs, fixes, governs, profits*; feminine: *cleans, feels, irons, needs, prepares, senses, tolerates*). In support of the balance-congruity principle, the IAT results in Figure 13.8 show strong evidence of implicit gender identity for both males and females. (That is, males combine self with male more easily than female with self, and females do the reverse.) Similarly, the gender attitude IAT data also agreed with the balance-congruity expectation that women will implicitly prefer feminine to masculine, and males will do the reverse (see Figure 13.8). In addition, supporting the balance-congruity principle, a correlation of $r = .64$ was obtained between the gender-identity and gender-attitude measures; and posi-

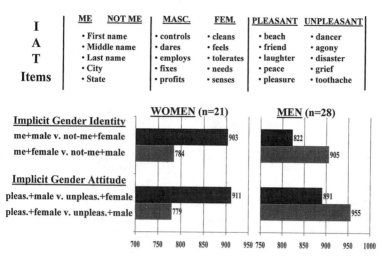

Figure 13.8. Design and results of the study by Lemm and Banaji (1998). Gender identity and gender attitude were measured in Yale men and women using the two tasks shown in the figure. Concepts that were more strongly associated (e.g., female + self for female subjects) were grouped more easily (rapidly) than concepts less associated (e.g., male + self for female subjects). The two IAT tasks revealed that males and females each identified more strongly with, and showed greater liking for, their ingroup.

tivity toward own gender was correlated with strength of own-gender identity.

Prediction 2 (based on the imbalance-dissonance principle). Compared with men, women should show a stronger link of *Me-arts* relative to *Me-math*, and greater positive valence for *arts* than *math*.

This prediction was tested in a series of studies by Nosek, Banaji, and Greenwald (1998). Participants were male and female undergraduate students at Yale University who provided data for four IAT measures, three of which included a contrast of concepts of mathematics and arts/literature (see Figure 13.9). As expected, both men and women yielded IAT data patterns that indicated the stereotypical association of mathematics more with male than female. Confirming Prediction 2, the male–female difference in relative strengths of *Me-math* and *Me-arts* (greater *Me-math* for men) was observed, as was the predicted difference in math attitude (math-positive stronger for men than women).

Some additional findings of the Nosek et al. study were consistent with expectations of the balance-congruity principle. Combining (a)

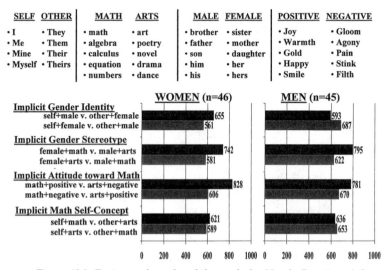

SELF	OTHER	MATH	ARTS	MALE	FEMALE	POSITIVE	NEGATIVE
• I	• They	• math	• art	• brother	• sister	• Joy	• Gloom
• Me	• Them	• algebra	• poetry	• father	• mother	• Warmth	• Agony
• Mine	• Their	• calculus	• novel	• son	• daughter	• Gold	• Pain
• Myself	• Theirs	• equation	• drama	• him	• her	• Happy	• Stink
		• numbers	• dance	• his	• hers	• Smile	• Filth

Figure 13.9. Design and results of the study by Nosek, Banaji, and Greenwald (1998). This study used a generic *Me–them* contrast in place of the idiographic self-other contrast of the studies shown in Figures 13.7 and 13.8. In addition, Nosek et al. added several IAT measures, including a *math–arts* contrast and collected data for both male and female subjects. Results confirmed predictions based on the imbalance-dissonance principle.

the balance-congruity principle with (b) assumed positive valence of self and (c) assumed implicit own-sex gender identity yields an expected correlation between content of implicit gender stereotype and implicit attitude toward the gender-stereotyped trait. For males, implicit favorability to math was correlated as expected with implicit association of math with male gender ($r = .36$, $p = .02$). For female participants, the expected opposite correlation was observed: that is, the stronger the math-masculine association, the more negative the attitude toward math ($r = -.35$, $p = .02$).

Prediction 3 (based on the differentiation principle). For women, the concept of weak should divide into a positively valenced subconcept that is associated with female, and a negatively valenced subconcept that is not associated with female.

This prediction was tested in a set of experiments by Rudman, Greenwald, and McGhee (1998). Their Experiment 2 showed that men and women alike possess a stereotype that associates strength more with male than female. In that experiment, *male* and *female* were represented by familiar first names (e.g., Beth, Marcia, Sara vs. Brian, Scott,

Kevin) and *strong* and *weak* were represented by words that were matched in evaluation. Evidence for the expected (male = strong) stereotype was found for both male and female subjects, regardless of whether strong and weak were represented by evaluatively negative words (e.g., destroy, violent vs. feeble, lame), neutral words (e.g., iron, durable vs. feather, quiet), or positive words (e.g., bold, mighty vs. gentle, flower).

In Rudman et al.'s (1998) third experiment, 42 undergraduate women and 27 undergraduate men at the University of Washington each responded to two IAT tasks in which the concepts *male* and *female* were again represented by familiar male and female first names. These two IATs differed in the manner in which the concepts *weak* and *strong* were represented. In one task, *strong* was represented by five evaluatively positive words (bold, mighty, power, robust, stamina) and *weak* by five evaluatively negative words (feeble, frail, lame, scrawny, sickly). In the second IAT, these evaluative assignments were reversed, with *strong* represented by five evaluatively negative words (destroy, fight, fury, rage, violent) and *weak* by five evaluatively positive words (delicate, fine, flower, gentle, lamb).

The predicted finding was that women should respond differently to these two tasks. Specifically, they should associate *female* with the positive aspects of *weak*, but not with the negative aspects of *weak*. The results clearly confirmed this expectation, as is shown in Figure 13.10. When *weak* was paired with positive words and *strong* with negative, women associated *Me* with *weak*. However, they did not at all associate *Me* with *weak* when the evaluative assignments were reversed. It was expected that men would not associate *Me* with *weak* even when *weak* was represented by evaluatively positive words. Surprisingly, however, men identified somewhat more with the negative *strong* category (contrasted with positive *weak*) than with the positive *strong* (contrasted with negative *weak*). The overall pattern indicates that the negative *strong* items are especially masculine and the positive *weak* items especially feminine. There was no indication that men differentiate the *strong* category in the way that women appear to differentiate the *weak* category. Rather, there was a slight indication that men differentiate *strong* in an unexpected way, associating male more with the negative than the positive aspects of *strong*. This unexpected outcome can be taken as an indication that the male stereotype strongly associates the aggressive aspects of strength with male.[6]

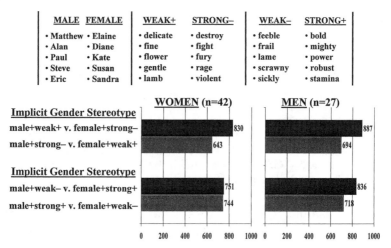

Figure 13.10. Design and results of the study by Rudman, Greenwald, and Mc-Ghee (1998). This study operationalized the male–female contrast using sex-typed names in place of the nouns and pronouns used by Nosek et al. (1998; see Figure 13.9). Women's different gender associations for the two evaluatively varied versions of the strength attribute were consistent with expectations based on the differentiation principle (see Figure 13.5).

Relations to Other Chapters in this Volume

Several of this volume's chapters deal with influences of current emotional state on cognitive processing (see chapters by Berkowitz et. al, Bless, Eich & Macaulay, Fiedler, Forgas, Martin, and Niedenthal & Holberstadt). Others examine the reverse connection, the effect of cognitive factors on affective experience (see chapters by Blascovich & Mendes, Leary, and Smith & Kirby). The present theory has not yet attempted to represent or analyze phenomena involving current emotional state either as a causal influence on cognition or as a consequence of cognitive processes. (It is similarly true that current emotional state was not a central focus of the classic cognitive consistency theories.) Bower's (1981) method of representing mood as a node in associative structure might serve as a starting point for incorporating mood into the unified theory. However, that approach would likely fall short of the goals of most of the present volume's authors, because Bower was concerned more with modeling the effects of knowledge about mood than with modeling effects of current mood on cognition or of cognition on mood (see chapters by Eich & Macaulay and Niedenthal & Halberstadt).

Conclusion

This chapter set out to develop a theoretical unification of social psychology's major cognitive constructs, stereotype and self-concept, with its major affective constructs, attitude and self-esteem. This obviously ambitious goal was prompted by the recent adaptation of cognitive psychology's implicit cognition concepts to describe implicit forms of the social-cognitive constructs of attitude, stereotype, and self-esteem (Greenwald & Banaji, 1995). The goal of unification was encouraged by an expectation that new measures of implicit attitudes, stereotypes, and self-concept would make it possible to identify closer relationships among these major constructs than had been apparent from decades of research conducted with self-report measures.

The chapter provides the first overview of findings obtained with a newly developed general method for measuring conceptual relations at the associative level, the Implicit Association Test (Greenwald et al., 1998). As data collection proceeded, it became apparent that it will not be necessary to create fundamentally new principles in order to make progress in the theoretical unification effort. Three principles originating in social psychology's cognitive consistency theories of the 1950s – especially that of Heider (1958) – appeared to be sufficient. This was a satisfying outcome of the research, because the resulting consistency-based unified theory is at once simpler and possibly broader in explanatory scope than the set of three cognitive consistency theories on which it was based.

Notes

1. This view intentionally sidesteps the question of relative processing priority of affect and cognition, which is a focus of chapters by Zajonc and by Smith and Kirby in this volume.
2. For this initial statement of the unified theory, the concept of bipolar opposition may not need any more precise statement than given in Definition 2. Nevertheless, to indicate how greater precision can be achieved, consider that the opposition of two nodes can be quantified in terms of their number of shared first-order links compared with the total number of links. For example, consider the *weak* and *nurturing* nodes in SKS (see Figure 13.1).

These two nodes have four shared first-order links in relation to eight total links (four for *weak* and four for *nurturing*). Sharing four of eight first-order links is substantial, given that the expected number of shared first-order links for *weak* and *nurturing* is just over one. (To calculate: there are 15 nodes with which these two might have shared first-order links. With each of *weak* and *nurturing* having four direct links, the expected number of shared first-order links is therefore $4/5 \cdot 4/15 \cdot 15 = 1.07$.) By contrast, *strong* and *weak* have zero shared first-order links in relation to six total links (four for *weak* and two for *strong*). Although a measure of bipolar opposition should be based on a more complete specification of associative structure than in Figure 13.1, the patterns just described indicate that *weak* and *nurturing* are positively associated (even though there is no direct link between them), whereas *weak* and *strong* are possibly in bipolar opposition.
3. Heider's struggle with the awkwardness of not having a distinction like that between unrelated and bipolar-opposed nodes can be seen in his discussion of "some difficulties with the notU (i.e., not-unit) relation" (Heider, 1958, p. 201).
4. Associative priming techniques also compare strengths of two categories of association. Priming techniques do this by comparing the effects of two contrasted categories of primes (e.g., evaluatively positive vs. negative; semantically related vs. unrelated; male vs. female) on responses to various target stimuli. Fortunately, such relative indicators of association strength are quite useful in testing the unified theory, especially for predictions that involve associations to bipolar-opposed concepts.
5. The interaction effect finding, although theoretically important, must be regarded as tentative both because of the low power of the study for an effect of the magnitude observed, and because even this effect would have been smaller without exclusion of two subjects who appeared to be outliers from the multivariate data pattern.
6. The analysis of *compartmentalization* in Showers's Chapter 12 in this volume is compatible with this chapter's use of differentiation as a consistency principle.

References

Abelson, R. P., Aronson, E., McGuire, W. J., Newcomb, T. M., Rosenberg, M. J., & Tannenbaum, P. (Eds). (1968). *Theories of cognitive consistency: A sourcebook*. Chicago: Rand-McNally.

Banaji, M. R., & Greenwald, A. G. (1995). Implicit gender stereotyping in judgments of fame. *Journal of Personality and Social Psychology, 68,* 181–198.

Bower, G. H. (1981). Mood and memory. *American Psychologist, 36,* 129–148.

Deaux, K., Winton, W., Crowley, M., & Lewis, L. L. (1985). Levels of categorization and content of gender stereotypes. *SocialCognition, 3,* 145–167.

Farnham, S. D., & Greenwald, A. G. (1988, May). *Implicit Balance of Personal and Social Identity: I am good + I am Female = Female is Good*. Paper presented at the meetings of the Midwestern Psychological Association, Chicago.

Festinger, L. (1957). *A theory of cognitive dissonance.* Palo Alto, CA: Stanford University Press.

Greenwald, A. G. (1981). Self and memory. In G. H. Bower (Ed.), *The psychology of learning and motivation* (Vol. 15, pp. 201–236). New York: Academic Press.

Greenwald, A. G., & Banaji, M. R. (1995). Implicit social cognition: Attitudes, self-esteem, and stereotypes. *Psychological Review, 102,* 4–27.

Greenwald, A. G., McGhee, D. E., & Schwartz, J. L. K. (1998). Measuring individual differences in implicit cognition: The implicit association test. *Journal of Personality and Social Psychology, 74,* 1464–1480.

Greenwald, A. G., & Pratkanis, A. R. (1984). The self. In R. S. Wyer & T. K. Srull (Eds.), *Handbook of social cognition* (pp. 129–178). Hillsdale, NJ: Erlbaum.

Heider, F. (1946). Attitudes and cognitive organization. *Journal of Psychology, 21,* 107–112.

Heider, F. (1958). *The psychology of interpersonal relations.* New York: John Wiley.

Hewstone, M., Macrae, C. N., Griffiths, R., & Milne, A. B. (1994). Cognitive models of stereotype change: 5. Measurement, development, and consequences of stereotyping. *Journal of Experimental Social Psychology, 30,* 505–526.

Jacoby, L. L., Lindsay, D. S., & Toth, J. P. (1992). Unconscious influences revealed: Attention, awareness, and control. *American Psychologist, 47,* 802–809.

Kihlstrom, J. F., & Cantor, N. (1984). Mental representations of the self. In L. Berkowitz (Ed.), *Advances in experimental social psychology* (Vol. 17, pp. 2–48). New York: Academic Press.

Koffka, K. (1935). *Principles of gestalt psychology.* New York: Harcourt, Brace, & World.

Lemm, K., & Banaji, M. R. (1998, May). *Implicit and explicit gender identity and attitudes toward gender.* Paper presented at the meeting of the Midwestern Psychological Association, Chicago.

Nisbett, R. E., & Wilson, T. D. (1977). Telling more than we can know: Verbal reports on mental processes. *Psychological Review, 84,* 231–259.

Nosek, B., Banaji, M. R., & Greenwald, A. G. (1998, May). *Math = Bad + Male, Me = Good + Female, Therefore Math = Me.* Paper presented at meeting of the American Psychological Society, Washington, DC.

Orne, M. T. (1962). On the social psychology of the psychological experiment: With particular reference to demand characteristics and their implications. *American Psychologist, 17,* 776–783.

Osgood, C. E., & Tannenbaum, P. H. (1955). The principle of congruity in the prediction of attitude change. *Psychological Review, 62,* 42–55.

Rosenberg, M. J. (1969). The conditions and consequences of evaluation apprehension. In R. Rosenthal & R. L. Rosnow (Eds.), *Artifact in behavioral research* (pp. 279–349). New York: Academic Press.

Rosier, M., Banaji, M. R., & Greenwald, A. G. (1998, May). *Implicit and explicit self-esteem and group membership*. Paper presented at the meetings of the Midwestern Psychological Association, Chicago.

Rudman, L. A., Greenwald, A. G., & McGhee, D. E. (1998). *Sex differences in gender stereotypes revealed by the Implicit Association Test*. Unpublished manuscript.

Rumelhart, D. E., & McClelland, J. L. (1986). *Parallel distributed processing* (2 vols). Cambridge, MA: MIT Press.

Schacter, D. L. (1987). Implicit memory: History and current status. *Journal of Experimental Psychology: Learning, Memory, and Cognition, 13*, 501–518.

Smith, E. R. (1996). What do connectionism and social psychology offer each other? *Journal of Personality and Social Psychology, 70*, 893–912.

Tedeschi, J. T., Schlenker, B. R., & Bonoma, T. V. (1971). Cognitive dissonance: Private ratiocination or public spectacle? *American Psychologist, 26*, 685–695.

Tulving, E. (1972). Episodic and semantic memory. In E. Tulving & W. Donaldson (Eds.), *Organization of memory* (pp. 149–165). New York: Academic Press.

Webb, E. J., Campbell, D. T., Schwartz, R. D., Sechrest, L., & Grove, J. B. (1981). *Nonreactive measures in the social sciences* (2nd ed.). Boston: Houghton Mifflin.

Weber, R., & Crocker, J. (1983). Cognitive processes in the revision of stereotypic beliefs. *Journal of Personality and Social Psychology, 45*, 961–977.

Weber, S. J., & Cook, T. D. (1972). Subject effects in laboratory research: An examination of subject roles, demand characteristics, and valid inference. *Psychological Bulletin, 77*, 273–295.

14. Affect, Cognition, and the Social Emotions

MARK R. LEARY

Introduction

For many years, researchers who were interested in emotional processes focused almost exclusively on the effects of cognition on emotion. Not only were the effects of thought on emotion demonstrated
earlier than the effects of emotion on thought (see e.g., Schachter &
Singer, 1962), but the popularity of attribution and other cognitive
approaches in social psychology sensitized researchers to the powerful
and pervasive effects of cognitive processes on emotion and behavior.
More recently, researchers have begun to explore the reciprocal effects
of feeling states on how people think about themselves and their social
worlds. To date, however, the vast majority of this work has focused
on the effects of positive versus negative affect (or good vs. bad
moods) on people's thought and behavior, with little attention to the
effects of specific emotions on cognition (for exceptions, see Bodenhausen, Sheppard, & Kramer, 1994; Keltner, Ellsworth, & Edwards,
1993).

The specific focus of this chapter is on *social emotions* – emotions
that are aroused by real, imagined, anticipated, or remembered encounters with other people. Although social emotions obviously share
many features with nonsocial ones, they possess a common set of
causes, concomitants, and consequences that distinguish them from
other emotions. The conceptualization introduced here traces one category of social emotions to the human need to maintain interpersonal

Address correspondence concerning this chapter to Mark R. Leary, Department of
Psychology, Wake Forest University, Box 7778, Reynolda Station, Winston-Salem, NC
27109. I thank Batja Mesquita and Kathleen Martin for their comments on an earlier
draft of this chapter.

connections with other people. After describing the theory and how it applies to common social emotions, we examine the mutual influences of cognitive and affective processes on the experience of social emotion. Along the way, we consider the implications of this view for how behavioral researchers study and understand affective influences on cognition.

Affect, Emotion, and Mood

Many terms have been used to describe subjectively experienced feeling states, but three such terms are relevant to this chapter. As usually defined, *affect* refers to the simple pleasant or unpleasant tone of a feeling. Affect is related to mere preference or value for a particular stimulus or even – what Frijda (1993a) called the "felt appraisal" of an event – and, thus, to an inclination to approach or avoid certain stimuli (Batson, Shaw, & Oleson, 1992). However, affect typically does not involve complex cognitive activity.

Emotions involve affect – a diffuse good or bad feeling – as well as other, more complex feelings that distinguish one emotion from another. A particular emotion is best regarded not as a unitary affective state but rather as a "family" of related feeling states (Ekman, 1994). A person who feels "embarrassed," for example, feels "bad" in a very specific way that is different from how a "lonely" person feels. Emotions also typically involve attentional processes that interrupt ongoing behavior and focus attention on the emotion-producing event, the activation of elaborate knowledge structures regarding the antecedents and consequences of particular emotions, and a readiness to respond in a particular fashion (Frijda, 1993b).

Unlike emotions, *moods* are diffuse and unfocused. A mood is a "general and pervasive feeling state that is not directed toward a specific target" (Wood, Saltzberg, & Goldsamt, 1990, p. 900). Like emotions, moods typically consist not only of affective valence (i.e., a "good" vs. "bad" mood) but also of feelings that give the experience a more specific quality (i.e., a sad, angry, or happy mood). Because they are generally mild, however, moods rarely interrupt ongoing thought or behavior, although they may "gently color and redirect ongoing thoughts and actions, influencing what will happen next but almost without notice" (Isen, 1984, pp. 186–187).[1]

Social Emotions

Some emotions occur only as a result of real, anticipated, remembered, or imagined encounters with other people.[2] For example, people experience the reaction that we call "hurt feelings" only because of how they believe other people have treated them; one's feelings cannot be hurt by inanimate objects or impersonal events. Likewise, embarrassment and shame both require a real or imagined audience of other people, and jealousy is inherently tied to interpersonal relationships. Similarly, the complex combination of emotions that we call loneliness arises from the perception of deficiencies in one's interpersonal relations. Certain positive emotions also arise solely from interpersonal factors. Feelings, such as pride, that people experience when they perceive that they are loved, admired, or respected by others, are inherently social emotions; one does not experience such feelings except in the context of interpersonal relationships.

Other emotions can occur in response to either social or nonsocial events. People may become angry, for example, either because of the actions of other people (such as being belittled by one's spouse in public) or because of frustration over a nonsocial event (the vending machine refuses to dispense the drink or refund one's money). Similarly, sadness may occur for interpersonal reasons (a loved one moves far away) or nonsocial ones (a treasured belonging is lost). Fear may arise from interpersonal threats (being summoned to the boss's office) as well as from noninterpersonal ones (stumbling upon a coiled and hissing snake in the woods). Yet, even among those emotions that can be caused by either social or nonsocial events, we may distinguish the socially induced variety from the nonsocial kind. For example, although people can feel anxious as the result of either interpersonal or impersonal events, researchers have found it useful to study *social anxiety* separately from other kinds. And, although the distinctions have rarely been made (Leary, 1990), we can similarly distinguish social from nonsocial anger, and social from nonsocial sadness.

Importantly, not all emotions that are caused by other people should be regarded as *social* emotions. If I am afraid because I have learned that the pilot of my flight has had a heart attack or because a sniper is firing randomly at pedestrians, my fear is caused by other people (the incapacitated pilot or the sniper), yet my reaction is not inherently interpersonal. Social emotions may be distinguished from nonsocial ones by the fact that they arise in response to events that have implications for a person's well-being in the context of socially constructed reality. As the symbolic interactionists have pointed out, the human being as a social interactant is largely a socially constructed creation, a conglomerate of abstract roles and identities. These constructions have no objective existence but emerge from the process of interaction itself. Social emotions are reactions to events that have implications for these social constructions, particularly one's viability as a social participant in relation to other people. Put differently, social emotions are reactions to events that the person views as relevant to his or her social concerns (Frijda & Mesquita, 1994).

Social emotions may be classified into two general categories. One category, which can be called social-evaluative emotions, has to do with how people feel about others (such as contempt, hatred, envy, and love). The second category, which we will call social-relational emotions, encompasses feeling states that arise as a result of how people perceive that others feel about them and their relationships with them. This chapter deals exclusively with this second category of social-relational emotions, which includes experiences such as shame, embarrassment, pride, hurt feelings, social anxiety, and jealousy.

Beginning with Darwin and James, virtually all emotion theorists have assumed that emotions evolved because they conferred adaptive advantages (Tooby & Cosmides, 1990). Thus, emotions that occur only in interpersonal encounters presumably evolved in response to a different set of adaptive challenges than did emotional responses to nonsocial events. Most nonsocial emotions appear to be connected with events that are relevant to either the individual's physical well-being or to the accomplishment of valued goals. For example, fear prepares individuals to respond to threats to their physical safety (primarily by motivating escape from the dangerous situation), and hope and frustration mediate reactions to goal attainment (see Frijda, 1986; Izard, 1993). Purely social emotions, in contrast, do not directly serve our physical well-being (although they may indirectly do so through their effects on our interpersonal relationships). Rather, social emotions arise as responses to our social well-being – specifically, as responses to how other people treat us as social interactants. Social-relational emotions (e.g., embarrassment, jealousy, hurt feelings) reflect our feelings about other people's reactions to us, and social-evaluative emotions (e.g., love, hate) reflect our feelings about other people. Presumably, social emotions that arise solely from encounters with other people play some role in helping us to manage our inter-personal lives (Miller & Leary, 1992).

A Theory of Social Emotion

In an earlier paper, Roy Baumeister and I proposed that the "need to belong" should be regarded as the fundamental interpersonal motive (Baumeister & Leary, 1995). Because solitary human beings are un-likely to survive and reproduce, natural selection has favored individ-uals who are inclined toward sociality and group living. As a result, human beings have evolved with a strong motivation to establish and maintain at least a minimum number of interpersonal relationships. Given the importance of this need to belong, a great deal of human thought, emotion, and behavior is dedicated to fostering and main-taining social bonds.

One psychological implication of this fundamental need to belong is that it makes people acutely sensitive to the degree to which they are being accepted by other people. In a primitive state, social exclu-sion has dire consequences, and people would be expected to be attuned to cues that indicate their viability as a group member is in jeopardy. In extreme cases, violations of group norms might result in total ostracism or exile that, in a primitive state, would typically result in death from predators, starvation, or accidents. In less extreme cases, disinterest by other people may limit one's access to important re-sources and sources of support. A peripheral group member may not have the benefit of others who will share their food, provide protec-tion or care, or form coalitions for mutual benefit. Furthermore, a person who is ignored, avoided, or excluded by others is not likely to attract or retain mates.

The Sociometer

To the extent that one's acceptance by other people can be jeopardized by all manner of indiscretions and violations of appropriate behavior, people are highly concerned about how they are perceived by other people. They monitor how others regard them and take care that they do not convey impressions of themselves – as incompetent, unattrac-tive, immoral, or otherwise undesirable individuals – that would jeop-ardize their social inclusion (Leary, 1995). People appear to be partic-ularly attuned to instances of real or potential *relational devaluation,* indications that others do not regard their relationship with the individual to be as important, close, or valuable as the individual desires.

It may well be that people possess a psychological monitor or gauge – a *sociometer* – that scans the social environment for cues indicating social exclusion (Leary & Downs, 1995; Leary, Tambor, Terdal, & Downs, 1995). This mechanism appears to operate largely on a preattentive level, allowing people to devote their conscious attention to other things, yet quickly and automatically alerting them to interpersonal cues that connote disinterest, disapproval, or rejection.

In our initial work, we were interested in the role of the sociometer in self-esteem (Leary & Downs, 1995). When cues connoting relational devaluation are detected, people experience an aversive drop in state self-esteem, accompanied by an increased motivation to be accepted. Viewed in this way, feelings of self-esteem are a subjective readout of relational valuation and devaluation (or what can also be called perceived inclusionary status) (Leary, Haupt, Strausser, & Chokel, 1998). From the standpoint of sociometer theory, events threaten self-esteem when people perceive that they jeopardize their social inclusion (Leary, 1999; Leary & Downs, 1995; Leary, Schreindorfer, & Haupt, 1995).

Social Emotions and Relational Devaluation

However, a close look at people's psychological reactions to perceived relational devaluation suggests that the sociometer monitors more than feelings of self-esteem. Specifically, perceived relational devaluation invariably produces not only changes in state self-esteem but also one or more *negative social emotions*. Viewed in this way, certain social emotions – namely, social-relational emotions – are responses to real, potential, remembered, or imagined relational devaluation. A closer examination of a few examples will clarify this point.

Shame and Embarrassment. Although theorists still disagree as to whether shame and embarrassment should be regarded as different emotions or as two labels for the same emotion, recent research suggests that they differ in important ways (Miller, 1996; Miller & Tangney, 1994; Tangney, Miller, Flicker, & Barlow, 1996). At the same time, they are both inherently social emotions in that their central concern is how one's behavior and/or character are regarded by other people

(Keltner & Buswell, 1997; Miller & Leary, 1992). The link to relational devaluation is obvious: People become ashamed or embarrassed when they are concerned that their behavior or personal characteristics have weakened their relational ties to other people.

Social Anxiety. Social anxiety – feelings of nervousness in interpersonal encounters – may arise in anticipation of an upcoming encounter or while engaged in interaction. People experience social anxiety when they believe they cannot make the impressions they desire to make on other people (Leary & Kowalski, 1995; Schlenker & Leary, 1982). People realize that the impressions they make have important implications for the degree to which they are accepted and valued by others. Whether one is making small talk with the boss, meeting strangers in a bar, being interviewed for a job, or performing on stage, making the right impression (whatever "right" happens to be in a particular context) can affect the degree to which one is valued and accepted by other people. As a result, people monitor and control how they are perceived by others and become anxious when they feel they cannot make the desired impressions.

Hurt Feelings. When people's feelings are "hurt," the precipitating factor appears to be their perception that another person does not regard his or her relationship with them to be as important, close, or valuable as they desire (Leary, Springer, Negel, Ansell, & Evans, 1998). In cases in which the other person has expressly ignored, avoided, or rejected the individual, relational devaluation is obvious. However, even when people are hurt by inconsiderate behavior – missed birthdays, unreturned phone calls, or hurtful teasing, for example – the victim is likely to conclude that the perpetrator's actions reflect insufficient concern for the relationship.

Jealousy. People feel jealous when they perceive that a third party poses a threat to their relationship with another individual. Although we tend to think of jealousy as arising from concerns that one's romantic partner is or may become involved in another relationship (Buunk, 1982; Pines & Aronson, 1983), people often feel jealous in nonromantic contexts as well. For example, a child may feel jealous because she believes that a parent favors her sibling, or a graduate student may feel jealous because his adviser focuses extra attention on another student. What all instances of jealousy have in common is the belief that the presence or intrusion of a third party has led another individual to devalue their relationship with the individual.

Sadness. People are saddened by the loss of important social relationships (Brown & Harris, 1978). According to Averill (1968), the social sadness that is characteristic of grief helps to ensure group solidarity by making separation distressing. Most, if not all, social sadness appears, like the other negative social emotions, to arise from perceived relational devaluation. In the case of rejection, the role of relational devaluation is easy to see. But even when one is saddened by the death of a loved one, part of one's grief arises from the loss of the relationship, one's role in it, and the accompanying sense of love and acceptance that the loved one formerly provided (Lofland, 1982). The survivor feels less valued and accepted than before the loved one died.

Loneliness. Loneliness is a particularly complex set of affective reactions that arises from the perception of deficiencies in one's social relationships (Peplau & Perlman, 1979). Importantly, loneliness depends on the person's perceptions of his or her relationships rather than on objective indices of a social network, such as the number or quality of the person's friendships (Williams & Solano, 1983). People who are lonely typically feel sad, anxious, and angry, as well as often hurt by the fact they are not being included in other people's plans. In many ways, loneliness is the ultimate reaction to a sense of social exclusion and relational devaluation.

Positive Social Emotions. People sometimes feel good because they believe others value them and their relationships but, in contrast to the negative emotions just described, we have a dearth of English words to refer to such feelings. People talk about "feeling loved" or "feeling accepted," but curiously, these phrases refer as much to the actions of the other person as to the emotions themselves. "Pride" is sometimes a positive emotional response to being valued, but in many instances pride involves private self-satisfaction rather than a reaction to how one is being regarded by other people.

Furthermore, the determinants and effects of positive emotions do not parallel those of negative emotions. Negative social emotions appear to be aroused quite easily; seemingly minor criticisms, slights, and embarrassments can induce very strong reactions. In contrast, positive social emotions require very strong indications of love, respect, or acceptance. Experimental studies consistently find that people who are accepted or included by others show little change in their emotional states, whereas those who are rejected or excluded (even in seemingly trivial ways) demonstrate markedly negative emotions and lowered self-esteem, (Leary Tambor et al., 1995). Research also shows that people are differentially sensitive to information relevant to acceptance as opposed to rejection (Leary, Haupt et al., 1998). Neurophysiological evidence suggests that positive and negative emotions are mediated by different systems of the brain and have markedly different effects on attention, judgment, motivation, and action readiness (e.g., Derryberry & Tucker, 1994; Frijda, 1986).

Positive social-relational emotions undoubtedly arise when people perceive that others value their relationships with the individual and, thus, are relevant to our discussion. However, because of the marked differences in people's emotional reactions to acceptance versus rejection, this chapter deals primarily with negative emotions that arise from real or imagined relational devaluation. Research on positive social-relational emotions is badly needed.

The Conceptual Status of Social Emotions

Emotion theorists have proposed a number of taxonomies of emotions, but most of them concur that the number of basic emotions is relatively small, typically between 6 and 16. One popular model identifies six fundamental emotions: happiness, disgust, surprise, sadness, anger, and fear (Ekman, 1992). Another has identified 12: interest, enjoyment, surprise, sadness, anger, disgust, contempt, fear, guilt, shame, shyness, and inward-directed hostility (Izard, 1993). Other theorists are critical of efforts to identify "basic" emotions such as these. Averill (1994, p. 14), for example, suggested that "basic emotions have no more place in psychology than basic animals in zoology or basic diseases in medicine." More recent dimensional models have tried to avoid taxonomies and typologies in favor of characterizing emotional experience along two or more bipolar dimensions, such as negative–positive and aroused–unaroused (for reviews, see Larsen & Diener, 1992; Ortony & Turner, 1990).

Some of the negative social emotions that interest us in this chapter appear in taxonomies and dimensional representations of emotions, but others do not. Shame, for one, appears on most lists of basic emotions, and these frameworks encompass the social varieties of emotions such as sadness and fear (or anxiety). However, the conceptual status of several other social emotions is unclear. Where, for example, do hurt feelings, embarrassment, jealousy, and loneliness figure in? Are they distinct emotions, blends of emotions, the same general emotional reaction accompanied by different patterns of cognition, or what? To fully explore this question would take us far from the main topic of this chapter, so I am going to skirt it here. For purposes of our discussion, it suffices to acknowledge two points.

First, people easily distinguish among these negative social emotions. Even when they experience more than one reaction simultaneously, they report them as distinct experiences. In our studies of hurt feelings, for example, respondents have reported that they felt "hurt, jealous, sad, and angry." Of course, the fact that people use different labels for these emotions does not indicate that they are necessarily distinct experiences (Frijda, Kuipers, & ter Schure, 1989) nor that the distinctions are theoretically valid or conceptually useful. Even so, it suffices here to accept that the distinctions among these emotions are phenomenologically meaningful to the people who experience them.

Second, however these social emotions may differ, all of them are precipitated by events that are relevant to relational devaluation, rejection, and exclusion (Leary, 1990). In a study by Spivey (1990), university students wrote about instances in which they had felt nervous, lonely, jealous, or sad "in response to a social situation or relationship." Participants rated their emotional reactions in the situation they described, as well as how accepted versus rejected they had felt. Ratings of perceived exclusion correlated very highly with the ratings of each emotion; correlations ranged from .54 for social anxiety to .97 for loneliness. In a second study, participants completed trait measures that assessed their tendency to experience social anxiety, loneliness, jealousy, and socially based sadness and a measure of how valued and accepted they typically felt. Again, individual differences in perceived relational devaluation correlated highly (from .53 to .71) with the tendency to experience these emotions. The single exception was jealousy, which was tied more closely to relational devaluation by a particular person in the context of a particular relationship rather than to a general perception of the degree to which one is valued and accepted. Other research has also demonstrated clear links between these emotions and people's concerns with being valued and accepted by other people (e.g., Leary, 1990; Leary, Springer et al., 1998; Miller, 1996).

The Influence of Social Emotions on Cognition

As mentioned at the outset, the relationship between cognition and emotion was for many years viewed as a one-way street on which traffic moved from cognition to emotion. As the chapters in this volume attest, the reciprocal effects of affective states on cognition are now widely acknowledged and better understood. Nevertheless researchers interested in the effects of affect on cognition have generally ignored the differences among various types of emotional states (see, however, Bodenhausen et al., 1994; Keltner et al., 1993). As we will see, states that are aroused by different kinds of social concerns have predictably different cognitive and emotional patterns.

Figure 14.1 shows the complex relationships among affective and cognitive processes involved in the experience of negative social-relational emotions. According to the model, the sociometer (depicted in Figure 14.1 as a gauge) monitors the interpersonal environment for cues relevant to the degree to which the individual is being valued, accepted, and included by other people. As noted earlier, theory and research suggest that people can monitor and detect cues that connote relational devaluation in an automatic and preconscious fashion. Perhaps the best empirical evidence of this comes from research showing that subliminal stimuli that connote disapproval or rejection can evoke negative affect and lower self-esteem (Baldwin, 1994; Baldwin, Carrell, & Lopez, 1990; Sommer, 1997).[3]

The sociometer operates automatically and preattentively until relational devaluation is detected. The stimuli that cause the sociometer to respond may be objective events in the person's social environment, cognitive events in which the person remembers past experiences or anticipates future encounters, or completely imaginary episodes that involve themes relevant to relational devaluation (Craighead, Kimball, & Rehak, 1979).

Focus of Attention

When the sociometer detects (real or imagined) relational devaluation, it produces negative affect that alerts the individual to the existence of a potential relational problem and diverts attention to the relevant interpersonal event. In drawing the person's attention to the interpersonal threat, negative affect appears to have two distinct effects.

First, it interrupts ongoing behavior to permit an assessment of the

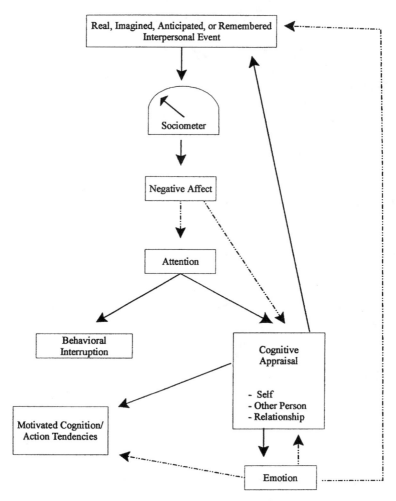

Figure 14.1. Cognitive and affective influences on social emotion. Cognitive influences are indicated by solid lines; affective influences are indicated by dashed lines.

situation (and, perhaps, to ensure that ongoing behavior does not compound the problem). Many theorists have pointed out that negative affect interrupts behavior to allow the individual to assess the nature of the threat (e.g., Frijda, 1986; Oatley, 1992). If the ongoing behavior is an important one that cannot be stopped, the person may persist, but with decreased attention devoted to it. The usefulness of such an attention-diverting mechanism is clear, but it can lead to failures in self-regulation such as when people choke under pressure because they cannot devote sufficient attention to the task at hand (Baumeister & Showers, 1986).

At the same time, attention is directed to the interpersonal event itself, eliciting a cognitive analysis of the situation (Derryberry & Tucker, 1994). The relational devaluation model suggests that people who are experiencing a negative social emotion will think specifically about the degree to which they are valued (accepted, liked, loved, or respected) by other people. As shown in Figure 14.1, some of these thoughts deal with oneself, some with the other individual, and some with self-in-relation-to-other. Such cognitive effects have been demonstrated in the case of social anxiety. People who feel socially anxious think about the impressions that others are forming of them, consider their interpersonal deficiencies, and worry about the implications of their self-presentational difficulties for their relationship with the other person (Leary, 1986).

As appraisal theories of emotion suggest, the specific ways in which people appraise self and relationship determine the precise emotion that is experienced (Ellsworth & Smith, 1988; Smith, 1989; Blascovich & Mendes, Smith & Kirby, this volume). Different patterns of appraisal of oneself and relevant relational factors elicit different emotions, with different salient features and different action tendencies. I will return to these emotion-specific differences in appraisal and action tendencies later in the chapter.

The model in Figure 14.1 is consistent with the suggestion that appraisal can occur at different cognitive levels (Frijda, 1993b; Smith & Kirby, this volume). As we have seen, the sociometer can monitor the social environment and produce negative affect automatically and nonconsciously. Thus, the cognitive processes that occur at this stage of the sequence are simple and not always conscious (see, for example, Zajonc, 1980; this volume). In contrast, the cognitive appraisals that occur after attention has been directed toward the interpersonal difficulty are more complex, explicit, and conscious (cf. Lazarus, 1982).

Affective-Emotional Influences on Cognition

As noted, most theories of emotion have viewed cognition as an antecedent of emotion. However, affect and emotion influence cognitive processes in the experience of social emotions in at least three ways. These are shown by the dotted lines in Figure 14.1.

Effects of Negative Affect on Cognitive Analysis. The initial affective response of the sociometer to perceived relational devaluation can influence the tenor of the subsequent cognitive analysis (as indicated by the dotted line from *Negative Affect* to *Cognitive Appraisal*). Considerable research (much of it reviewed in this volume) shows that cognition is influenced by affective valence – whether the person feels good or bad. Most studies have obtained valence-congruency (often called mood-congruency) effects in which people attend to and remember information that is consistent with their positive or negative feelings more readily than information that is inconsistent with their feelings. People who are experiencing negative affect, whatever its source, tend to think about things in more negative ways than those who are experiencing positive affect. They are more attuned to negative information about themselves and others, expose themselves to stimuli and situations that are consistent with their bad mood, pay greater attention to mood-congruent stimuli, and remember information that is consistent with their negative moods better than mood-incongruent information (Bower, 1991). Importantly, people judge themselves and their relationships more negatively when they are in a bad mood (see Forgas, Levinger, & Moylan, 1994; Salovey & Rodin, 1985; Sedikides, 1992). (For discussions of mood-congruency effects and the conditions under which they occur, see chapters by Bless, Fielder, Forgas, and Martin in this volume.)

Along these lines, people who are experiencing negative social-relational emotions tend to regard episodes of relational devaluation as more disastrous and traumatic than the events themselves seem to dictate. Writing about people's reactions to embarrassment, Goffman (1955) observed that people tend to give a "worst-case reading" to embarrassing predicaments, believing that their social images are more severely damaged and others' reactions are more negative than is the case. As a result, they not only fret more about the event than appears warranted to observers, but they tend to overcompensate for it by apologizing more than necessary. A similar worst-case reading appears to occur for other emotional reactions to relational devaluation as well. For example, people who feel socially anxious overestimate the negativity of the impressions others have of them: People whose feelings are hurt believe that the perpetrator feels less positively toward them than is the case, and people who are saddened by the loss of a relationship overestimate the long-term impact of the loss (see Gilbert & Wilson, this volume; Leary & Kowalski, 1995; Leary, Springer et al., 1998).

Several processes may underlie this effect. Tomkins (1963) and others have suggested that strong emotions amplify the perceived importance or seriousness of events. Beyond that, affective-priming explanations suggest that affect primes or activates concepts in memory that are associated with the affective state, thereby rendering certain thoughts more accessible than others (e.g., Forgas, Bower, & Moylan, 1990), and affect-as-information explanations suggest that people use their feelings as a source of information from which they make inferences about themselves, other people, and the world (Martin, this volume; Schwarz, 1990). Forgas (1995; this volume) has explained such effects in terms of the "infusion" of negative affect into the person's cognitive appraisals of the event. We do not need to choose among these explanations; evidence suggests that all of them may occur. For our purposes, the important point is that the negative affect generated by the sociometer may bias subsequent judgments of oneself and of the relationship in a negative direction.

These negatively biased appraisals of oneself and one's relationships that occur in conjunction with negative social emotions run contrary to the widespread assumption that people are inherently motivated to preserve their self-esteem and maintain positive moods, and engage in a wide array of self-serving behaviors in order to do so (e.g., Taylor & Brown, 1988). People are often more ashamed, embarrassed, hurt, anxious, jealous, lonely, and sad than they seemingly "ought" to be, and they often insist on appraising events in ways that maintain these negative emotions and lower their self-esteem (Leary, 1999). Their steadfast adherence to a worst-case reading despite its hedonic consequences raises the possibility that these negative appraisals are more than an accidental byproduct of negative affect and may serve some adaptive function.

One possibility is that this negative bias may be functional, in that it prevents people from underestimating the seriousness of situations that threaten their well-being and prods them to deal fully with whatever has transpired. In the case of interpersonal difficulties, for example, people are typically better served by overestimating than underestimating the seriousness of situations that threaten their connections with other people. Taking the prospect of relational devaluation seriously leads people to take steps to repair, maintain, and bolster their relationships.

Effects of Specific Emotions on Appraisal. Consistent with the notion that each emotion has particular cognitive antecedents and action tendencies (Frijda et al., 1989; Smith & Kirby, this volume), the specific emotion experienced in response to relational devaluation – shame, jealousy, hurt, social anxiety, or whatever – is determined by the pattern of cognitions regarding self, other, and self-in-relation-to-other. A full discussion of the differences among these social emotions goes beyond the scope of this chapter, but Table 14.1 presents a summary of these differences.

The important point here is that emotion-specific patterns of cognition, feeling, and motivational tendencies prime particular thoughts. Thus, people's assessments of themselves and the situation may be influenced by features of the specific emotion that they are experiencing. The experience of a particular social emotion will channel

Table 14.1. *Salient Features and Action Tendencies of Negative Social Emotions*

Social Emotion	Salient Feature of Relational Devaluation	Emotional Action Tendency
Shame/ embarrassment	Socially undesirable behavior or personal characteristic has led (or may lead) others to value their relationship with the individual less.	Engage in remedial behaviors (e.g., apologize, make excuses, seek forgiveness, show oneself to be acceptable).
Hurt feelings	Another person does not view his or her relationship with the individual to be as important, close, or valuable as the individual desires.	Promote value of relationship if possible; if not, withdraw and seek alternative relationships.
Jealousy	The presence or intrusion of a third party has led another person to value his or her relationship with the individual less than before.	Eliminate the presence or influence of the third party.
Social anxiety	The individual fears that others may value their relationship less because of the impressions they may form of him or her.	Employ self-presentational tactics to forestall relational devaluation.
Social sadness	The individual has lost a relationship with a peson who valued the relationship (e.g., through death, distance, or relationship termination).	Withdraw temporarily; give attention to alternative relationships.
Loneliness	An insufficient number of people value their relationships with the individual.	Seek additional relationships, if possible; if not, withdraw.

thoughts toward themes of devaluation and rejection that are consistent with that emotion. It also seems likely that particular emotions will directly prime the detection of interpersonal devaluation and facilitate thoughts that involve imagined, anticipated, and remembered devaluation.

For example, the socially anxious individual tends to assume that the impressions others are forming of him or her are not optimal (Leary, 1986; Leary, Kowalski, & Campbell, 1988). The jealous lover seems predisposed to interpret seemingly innocuous cues as evidence of betrayal (White & Mullen, 1989). The embarrassed person seriously overestimates how negatively other people view the embarrassing event (Miller, 1996). The person whose feelings were hurt by an inconsiderate friend reads far more foreboding implications into the slight than the perpetrator insists are warranted (Leary, Springer et al., 1998).

The fact that social emotions may have these specific effects on cognition raises an important methodological issue for the study of affective influences on thought. Many experiments that have examined the effects of affect on judgments of oneself and others have induced mood in ways that would be expected to evoke emotions associated with relational devaluation. For example, some researchers have created good and bad moods by leading participants to believe they succeeded or failed on a laboratory task (e.g., Mischel, Ebbesen, & Zeiss, 1976), events that have implications for the degree to which people feel valued. Other researchers have used imagery relating to acceptance and rejection to induce good and bad moods. Kavanagh and Bower (1985), for instance, led hypnotized participants to recall romantic successes or romantic failures. Other researchers have induced mood by asking participants to recall or imagine situations that would make them feel happy, sad, or neutral. Data from Wright and Mischel (1982) suggest that these recalled or imagined situations often involve interpersonal events and, presumably, social emotions. When asked to imagine a happy situation, 69% of their participants imagined an event that connoted acceptance (e.g., friendship, sexual experiences, academic achievement); and when asked to imagine a sad event, 36% imagined relational devaluation, such as loss of friendship, romantic breakup, failure, or social rejection.

Even manipulations that do not, on the surface, appear to involve acceptance and rejection may potentially evoke relational thoughts. For example, Sedikides (1994) had participants imagine their friends experiencing particularly good or bad events (such as winning a lottery or dying in a fire). Not only do such inductions tap into relational themes and thus potentially prime the sociometer, but themes of disease and death (a popular theme of imagery and videotaped inductions in mood research) can arouse thoughts regarding one's social relationships as well as one's personal acceptability (Solomon, Greenberg, & Pyszczynski, 1991). The same may be said of movie clips that, in the process of inducing positive and negative affect, may prime thoughts related to acceptance and rejection.[4]

These ways of inducing mood potentially confound mood with relational devaluation. Success and failure have obvious implications for acceptance, rejection imagery obviously primes relational thoughts, and personalized recall of past events appears to elicit a high proportion of memories that are relevant to relational evaluation. Even music, which on the surface may appear to induce moods with little cognitive mediation, nonetheless may elicit mood-congruent thoughts that often involve relational themes. Thus, these ways of inducing mood might be expected to evoke negative social emotions and their attendant concerns with relational devaluation. As a result, when studies find that participants who imagined a "sad" situation subsequently evaluated themselves or others differently than did participants who imagined a "happy" event, we are unable to tell the degree to which the effect is due to the general effects of mood as opposed to the priming of thoughts related to relational devaluation specifically.

The problems of using mood induction procedures that access specific kinds of content has been acknowledged by several researchers (Salovey & Rodin, 1985). It is notably difficult, however, to induce moods without priming emotion-specific cognitions. In fact, according to Frijda (1986), positive and negative appraisals are an inherent part of mood states. The best solution appears to be for researchers to use multiple mood-induction paradigms, some of which do not involve interpersonal events (see, e.g., Forgas, 1991). When multiple mood inductions are used, researchers typically find that affective influences do generalize across the different methods, but we should not assume that different ways of inducing positive and negative feelings will always produce the same effects. This may be particularly true when the behavior under investigation involves judgments of oneself or familiar others (e.g., Forgas et al., 1994; Sedikides, 1992). As we have seen, social emotions are accompanied by predictable patterns of appraisals regarding oneself and one's relationships.

Cognitive Appraisal and Perception of Relational Devaluation. We have seen that affective-emotional processes can influence individuals' perceptions of the interpersonal landscape. In turn, these cognitive appraisals and the accompanying emotions can provide new input to the sociometer. This effect may contribute to the preoccupation and cognitive rumination that accompany negative social emotions. People persevere in their cognitive analysis, often long after the interpersonal event itself is over. People who feel embarrassed, for example, often continue to think about the situation in which they conveyed undesired impressions of themselves. People who feel ashamed may agonize over their indiscretion for a long time afterward. Jealousy is particularly notable in its ability to hold the jealous individual's attention, often taking on an obsessional character, with the result that the person cannot stop thinking about the jealousy-provoking event.

Although preoccupation with real or imagined relational devaluation may be painful to the individual, it may be functional as well. A person who has experienced relational devaluation might be advised to examine his or her inclusionary status carefully. Relational devaluation in one context may signal the presence of personal qualities that might jeopardize one's acceptance in other situations. Thus, the person is wise to consider his or her interpersonal value and general includability, and intrapsychic cognitive and emotional feedback to the sociometer may help to maintain this assessment process.

Motivated Cognition. Finally, social emotions are also accompanied by thoughts about how one should respond to the threat to relational valuation and by heightened motivation to enhance one's social bonds. When people feel ashamed, embarrassed, socially anxious, jealous, hurt, sad, or lonely, they invariably consider behavioral options.

People who have experienced events that connote relational devaluation often show evidence of being particularly motivated to obtain social approval and acceptance. Sometimes they are motivated to regain the attention, affection, or acceptance of the person who does not appear to sufficiently value his or her relationship with them (Walster, 1965). At other times, they give up trying to obtain the other's acceptance, even using "sour grapes" rationalization to convince themselves that they did not really want the other person to accept them anyway (Leary et al., 1995). Such a tactic may be functional in hastening the person's disengagement from relationships in which they are not sufficiently valued, thereby allowing them to pursue alternatives.

Furthermore, people who have been rejected by one person are increasingly motivated to be accepted by others. For example, people who are embarrassed in front of one person try to convey more acceptable images of themselves to others who were not involved in the embarrassing event (Apsler, 1975), and, of course, rejected lovers often rebound quickly into new relationships. Relational devaluation also affects people's perceptions of relational alternatives. When people "need" acceptance, they may regard those who can provide that acceptance more favorably than they otherwise would. This effect may underlie Pennebaker et al.'s (1979) finding that men and women in a single's bar rated members of the other sex as increasingly more attractive as the bar's closing time approached. Such changes in social perception may motivate the individual to initiate social contact or respond positively to the overtures of those who might enhance their sense of social valuation.

Conclusions

This chapter argued that specific emotional states are accompanied by predictable cognitive patterns. Although this is likely true of all emotions (Smith, 1989), we have specifically focused here on emotions that arise in response to perceived relational devaluation. Once alerted to the possibility that others do not regard their relationship to be as important, close, or valuable as they desire, people appraise themselves and their relationship and think about ways to handle the interpersonal threat. Equally important, the content of these thoughts may differ depending on the specific emotion that is experienced.

The idea that relational devaluation is the common denominator underlying several different social emotions provides an overarching framework for understanding this particular category of emotional experience. Theory and research on emotion have tended to adopt either a macrolevel approach that focuses on general principles common to all emotion or else a microlevel approach that focuses on specific emotions. The relational devaluation perspective reflects a midlevel approach that bridges the gap between the macro and micro approaches by identifying the commonalities within particular *categories* of emotion. At least four distinct categories of emotions can be identified, involving affective responses to (a) immediate threats to the organism's physical well-being (such as fear), (b) progress toward valued goals (such as hope, disappointment, and anger), (c) the hedonic relevance of particular people and events (such as love, hatred, and contempt), and (d) the degree to which other people value one's relationship (such as hurt feelings, shame, pride, and jealousy).[5]

Theory and research regarding the influences of affect on cognition have focused primarily on the effects of affective valence (good vs. bad mood, positive vs. negative affect) and have tended to disregard the specific nature of the feeling states involved. Yet, as we have seen, many experimental manipulations that are used to induce positive and negative emotions clearly elicit social emotions (and their attendant themes of relational devaluation). As a result, it is difficult to determine with certainty whether obtained effects are due to affect per se or to the cognitive patterns that are elicited naturally by these manipulations.

Nothing in this chapter should be taken to suggest that feeling states do not have effects separate from their accompanying cognitions. Indeed, studies using multiple mood inductions show that many affective influences generalize across different emotional states. However, researchers should take greater care to ensure that their findings are not specific to particular emotions. This is particularly important when studying affective influences on self-evaluations and social judgments because, as we have seen, an inherent aspect of social emotions is thinking about oneself and one's relationships, often in negatively biased ways.

Notes

1. Beck (1997) has suggested that the distinction between moods and emotions is best conceptualized as the difference between implicit and explicit affect. Implicit affect (i.e., mood) is a feeling state for which the individual cannot easily identify the source. The result is a vague, pervasive feeling that has no focal object, nor any particular behavioral intention. An explicit emotion is a feeling state for which the individual can identify the source. The (attributed) cause is in focal attention, resulting in a clearly defined emotion and an action readiness that is consistent with it.
2. What I am calling social emotions includes states that others have labeled "self-conscious" emotions (e.g., shame, embarrassment, pride). For example, Lewis (1993) distinguished self-conscious emotions from other kinds by virtue of the fact that they involve self-reflexive cognitions (specifically attributions and evaluations about oneself). Fischer and Tangney (1995) distinguished self-conscious emotions by the fact that they are responses to events that have implications for evaluations of oneself as worthy or unworthy. As we will see, all negative social emotions involve a cognitive appraisal of oneself (particularly in relation to other people), yet acute self-

consciousness is characteristic of only some of them. My tentative suggestion is that so-called self-conscious emotions are a subset of social emotions.

3. Cooley (1902), best known for his concept of the "looking glass self," acknowledged the preattentive nature of this system when he suggested that people live "in the minds of others without knowing it."

4. For example, one movie clip that has been used to induce sadness is the "choice scene" from *Sophie's Choice*, in which Sophie (played by Meryl Streep) must decide whether to turn her son or her daughter over to the Nazis. Much of the emotional impact of this scene seems to arise from the relational theme of rejection.

5. Some emotions, such as hurt feelings and shame, may fit neatly into a particular category, but others may not. A person may be disgusted, for example, by contact with rotten food (an emotional reaction to a potential threat to physical well-being) or by the crass behavior of a drunk and unruly relative (a social-evaluative response).

References

Apsler, R. (1975). Effects of embarrassment on behavior toward others. *Journal of Personality and Social Psychology, 32*, 145–153.

Averill, J. R. (1968). Grief: Its nature and significance. *Psychological Bulletin, 70*, 721–748.

Averill, J. R. (1994). In the eyes of the beholder. In P. Ekman & R. J. Davidson (Eds.), *The nature of emotion: Fundamental questions* (pp. 7–14). New York: Oxford University Press.

Baldwin, M. W. (1994). Primed relational schemas as a source of self-evaluative reactions. *Journal of Social and Clinical Psychology, 13*, 380–403.

Baldwin, M. W., Carrell, S. E., & Lopez, D. F. (1990). Priming relational schemas: My advisor and the Pope are watching me from the back of my mind. *Journal of Experimental Social Psychology, 26*, 435–454.

Batson, C. D., Shaw, L. L., & Oleson, K. C. (1992). Differentiating affect, mood, and emotion: Toward functionally based conceptual distinctions. In M. S. Clark (Ed.), *Emotion* (pp. 294–326). Newbury Park, CA: Sage.

Baumeister, R. F., & Leary, M. R. (1995). The need to belong: Desire for interpersonal attachment as a fundamental human motivation. *Psychological Bulletin, 117*, 497–529.

Baumeister, R. F., & Showers, C. J. (1986). A review of paradoxical performance effects: Choking under pressure in sports and mental tests. *European Journal of Social Psychology, 16*, 361–383.

Beck, R. C. (1997). *Hedonic theory of mood*. Unpublished manuscript, Wake Forest University, Winston-Salem, NC.

Bodenhausen, G., Sheppard, L. A., & Kramer, G. P. (1994). Negative affect and social judgment: The differential impact of anger and sadness. *European Journal of Social Psychology, 24*, 45–62.

Bower, G. H. (1991). Mood congruity of social judgments. In J. P. Forgas (Ed.), *Emotion and social judgments* (pp. 31–53). Oxford: Pergamon Press.

Brown, G. W., & Harris, T. (1978). *Social origins of depression: A study of psychiatric disorder in women.* New York: Free Press.

Buunk, B. (1982). Anticipated sexual jealousy: Its relationship to self-esteem, dependency, and reciprocity. *Personality and Social Psychology Bulletin, 8,* 310–316.

Cooley, C. H. (1902). *Human nature and the social order.* New York: Scribner.

Craighead, W. E., Kimball, W. H., & Rehak, R. S. (1979). Mood changes, physiological responses, and self-statements during social rejection imagery. *Journal of Consulting and Clinical Psychology, 47,* 385–396.

Derryberry, D., & Tucker, D. M. (1994). Motivating the focus of attention. In P. Niedenthal & S. Kitayama (Eds.), *The heart's eye: Emotional influences in perception and attention* (pp. 167–196). New York: Academic Press.

Ekman, P. (1992). An argument for basic emotions. *Cognition and Emotion, 6,* 169–200.

Ekman, P. (1994). All emotions are basic. In P. Ekman & R. J. Davidson (Eds.), *The nature of emotion* (pp. 15–19). Oxford: Oxford University Press.

Ellsworth, P. C., & Smith, C. A. (1988). From appraisal to emotion: Differences among unpleasant feelings. *Motivation and Emotion, 12,* 271–302.

Fischer, K. W., & Tangney, J. P. (1995). Self-conscious emotions and the affect revolution: Framework and overview. In J. P. Tangney & K. W. Fischer (Eds.), *Self-conscious emotions: The psychology of shame, guilt, embarrassment, and pride* (pp. 3–24). New York: Guilford Press.

Forgas, J. P. (1991). Mood effects of partner choice: Role of affect in social decisions. *Journal of Personality and Social Psychology, 61,* 708–720.

Forgas, J. P. (1995). Mood and judgment: The affect infusion model (AIM). *Psychological Bulletin, 117,* 39–66.

Forgas, J. P., & Bower, G. H. (1987). Mood effects of person perception judgments. *Journal of Personality and Social Psychology, 53,* 53–60

Forgas, J. P., Levinger, G., & Moylan, S. J. (1994). Feeling good and feeling close: Affective influences on the perception of intimate relationships. *Personal Relationships, 2,* 165–184.

Frijda, N. H. (1986). *The emotions.* Cambridge: Cambridge University Press.

Frijda, N. H. (1993a). Moods, emotion episodes, and emotions. In M. Lewis & J. M. Haviland (Eds.), *Handbook of emotions* (pp. 381–404). New York: Guilford Press.

Frijda, N. H. (1993b). The place of appraisal in emotion. *Cognition and Emotion, 7,* 357–388.

Frijda, N. H., Kuipers, P., & ter Schure, E. (1989). Relations among emotion, appraisal, and emotional action readiness. *Journal of Personality and Social Psychology, 57,* 212–228.

Frijda, N. H., & Mesquita, B. (1994). The social roles and functions of emotions. In S. Kitayama & H. R. Markus (Eds.), *Emotion and culture: Empirical studies of mutual influence* (pp. 51–87). Washington, D.C.: American Psychological Association.

Goffman, I. (1955). On facework. *Psychiatry, 18,* 213–231.

Isen, A. M. (1984). Toward understanding the role of affect in cognition. In

R. S. Wyer, Jr., & T. K. Srull (Eds.), *Handbook of social cognition* (Vol. 3, pp. 179–236). Hillsdale, NJ: Erlbaum.

Izard, C. (1993). Organizational and motivational functions of discrete emotions. In M. Lewis & J. M. Haviland (Eds.), *Handbook of emotion* (pp. 631–641). New York: Guilford Press.

James, W. (1890). *Principles of psychology.* New York: Dover.

Kavanagh, G. F., & Bower, G. H. (1985). Mood and self-efficacy: Impact of joy and sadness on perceived capabilities. *Cognitive Therapy and Research, 9,* 507–525.

Keltner, D., & Buswell, B. N. (1997). Embarrassment: Its distinct form and appeasement functions. *Psychological Bulletin, 122,* 250–270.

Keltner, D., Ellsworth, P. C., & Edwards, K. (1993). Beyond simple pessimism: Effects of sadness and anger on social perception. *Journal of Personality and Social Psychology, 64,* 740–752.

Larsen, R. J., & Diener, E. (1992). Promises and problems with the circumplex model of emotion. In M. S. Clark (Ed.), *Emotion* (pp. 25–59). Newbury Park, CA: Sage.

Lazarus, R. S. (1982). Thoughts on the relation between emotion and cognition. *American Psychologist, 37,* 1019–1024.

Leary, M. R. (1986). The impact of interactional impediments on social anxiety and self-presentation. *Journal of Experimental Social Psychology, 22,* 122–135.

Leary, M. R. (1990). Responses to social exclusion: Social anxiety, jealousy, loneliness, depression, and low self-esteem. *Journal of Social and Clinical Psychology, 9,* 221–229.

Leary, M. R. (1995). *Self-presentation: Impression management and interpersonal behavior.* Boulder, CO: Westview Press.

Leary, M. R. (1999). The social and psychological importance of self-esteem. In R. M. Kowalski & M. R. Leary (Eds.), *The social psychology of emotional and behavioral problems: Interfaces of social and clinical psychology.* (pp. 120–143) Washington, DC: APA Books.

Leary, M. R., & Downs, D. L. (1995). Interpersonal functions of the self-esteem motive: The self-esteem system as a sociometer. In M. Kernis (Ed.), *Efficacy, agency, and self-esteem* (pp. 123–144). New York: Plenum.

Leary, M. R., Haupt, A. L., Strausser, K. S., & Chokel, J. L. (1998). Calibrating the sociometer: The relationship between interpersonal appraisal and state self-esteem. *Journal of Personality and Social Psychology, 74,* 1290–1299.

Leary, M. R., & Kowalski, R. M. (1995). *Social anxiety.* New York: Guilford Press.

Leary, M. R., Kowalski, R. M., & Campbell, C. (1988). Self-presentational concerns and social anxiety: The role of generalized impression expectancies. *Journal of Research in Personality, 22,* 308–321.

Leary, M. R., Schreindorfer, L. S., & Haupt, A. L. (1995). The role of self-esteem in emotional and behavioral problems: Why is low self-esteem dysfunctional? *Journal of Social and Clinical Psychology, 14,* 297–314.

Leary, M. R., Springer, C. S., Negal, L., Ansell, E., & Evans, K. (1998). The causes, phenomenology, and consequences of hurt feelings. *Journal of Personality and Social Psychology, 74,* 1225–1237.

Leary, M. R., Tambor, E. S., Terdal, S. J., & Downs, D. L. (1995). Self-esteem as an interpersonal monitor: The sociometer hypothesis. *Journal of Personality and Social Psychology, 68,* 518–530.

Lewis, M. (1993). Self-conscious emotions: Embarrassment, pride, shame, and guilt. In M. Lewis & J. M. Haviland (Eds.), *Handbook of emotions* (pp. 563–574). New York: Guilford Press.

Lofland, L. H. (1982). Loss and human connection: An exploration into the nature of the social bond. In W. Ickes & E. S. Knowles (Eds.), *Personality, roles, and social behavior* (pp. 219–242). New York: Springer-Verlag.

Miller, R. S. (1996). *Embarrassment: Poise and peril in everyday life.* New York: Guilford Press.

Miller, R. S., & Leary, M. R. (1992). Social sources and interactive functions of emotion: The case of embarrassment. In M. S. Clark (Ed.), *Emotion and social behavior* (pp. 202–221). Newbury Park, CA: Sage.

Miller, R. S., & Tangney, J. P. (1994). Differentiating embarrassment and shame. *Journal of Social and Clinical Psychology, 13,* 273–287.

Mischel, W., Ebbesen, E. E., & Zeiss, A. (1976). Determinants of selective memory about the self. *Journal of Consulting and Clinical Psychology, 44,* 92–103.

Oatley, K. (1992). *Best laid schemes: The psychology of emotions.* Cambridge: Cambridge University Press.

Ortony, A., & Turner, T. J. (1990). What's basic about basic emotions? *Psychological Review, 97,* 315–331.

Pennebaker, J. W., Dyer, M. A., Caulkins, R. S., Litowitz, D. L., Ackreman, P. L., Anderson, D. B., & McGraw, K. M. (1979). Don't the girls get prettier at closing time: A country and western application to psychology. *Personality and Social Psychology Bulletin, 5,* 122–125.

Peplau, L. A., & Perlman, D. (1979). Blueprint for a social psychological theory of loneliness. In M. Cook & G. Wilson (Eds.), *Love and attraction.* Oxford: Pergamon Press.

Pines, A., & Aronson, E. (1983). Antecedents, correlates, and consequences of sexual jealousy. *Journal of Personality, 51,* 108–135.

Salovey, P., & Rodin, J. (1985). Cognitions about the self: Connecting feeling states and social behavior. In P. Shaver (Ed.), *Self, situations, and social behavior* (pp. 143–166). Beverly Hills, CA: Sage.

Schachter, S., & Singer, J. (1962). Cognitive, social, and physiological determinants of emotional state. *Psychological Review, 65,* 379–399.

Schlenker, B. R., & Leary, M. R. (1982). Social anxiety and self-presentation: A conceptualization and model. *Psychological Bulletin, 92,* 641–669.

Schwarz, N. (1990). Feelings as information: Informational and motivational functions of affective states. In E. T. Higgins & R. Sorrentino (Eds.), *Handbook of motivation and cognition: Foundations of social behavior* (Vol. 2, pp. 527–561). New York: Guilford Press.

Sedikides, C. (1992). Changes in the valence of self as a function of mood. In

M. S. Clark (Ed.), *Emotion and social behavior* (pp. 271–311). Newbury Park, CA: Sage.

Sedikides, C. (1994). Incongruent effects of sad mood on self-conception valence: It's a matter of time. *European Journal of Social Psychology, 24*, 161–172.

Smith, C. A. (1989). Dimensions of appraisal and physiological response in emotion. *Journal of Personality and Social Psychology, 56*, 339–353.

Solomon, S., Greenberg, J., & Pyszczynski, T. (1991). A terror management theory of social behavior: The psychological functions of self-esteem and cultural worldviews. *Advances in Experimental Social Psychology, 24*, 93–159.

Sommer, K. (1997, October). *Rejection priming and self-esteem.* Paper presented at the meeting of the Society for Experimental Social Psychology, Toronto.

Spivey, E. (1990). *Social exclusion as a common factor in social anxiety, loneliness, jealousy, and social depression: Testing an integrative model.* Unpublished master's thesis, Wake Forest University, Winston-Salem, NC.

Tangney, J. P., Miller, R. S., Flicker, L., & Barlow, D. H. (1996). Are shame, guilt, and embarrassment distinct emotions? *Journal of Personality and Social Psychology, 70*, 1256–1264.

Taylor, S. E., & Brown, J. D. (1988). Illusion and well-being. *Psychological Bulletin, 103*, 193–210.

Tomkins, S. S. (1963). *Affect, imagery, and consciousness: Vol. 2. The negative affects.* New York: Springer-Verlag.

Tooby, J., & Cosmides, L. (1990). The past explains the present: Emotional adaptations and the structure of the ancestral environment. *Ethology and Sociobiology, 11*, 375–424.

Walster, E. (1965). The effect of self-esteem on romantic liking. *Journal of Experimental Social Psychology, 1*, 184–197.

White, G. L., & Mullen, P. E. (1989). *Jealousy: Theory, research, and clinical strategies.* New York: Guilford Press.

Williams, J. G., & Solano, C. H. (1983). The social reality of feeling lonely: Friendship and reciprocation. *Personality and Social Psychology Bulletin, 9*, 237–242.

Wood, J. V., Saltzberg, J. A., & Goldsamt, L. A. (1990). Does affect induce self-focused attention? *Journal of Personality and Social Psychology, 58*, 899–908.

Wright, J., & Mischel, W. (1982). Influence of affect on cognitive learning person variables. *Journal of Personality and Social Psychology, 43*, 901–914.

Zajonc, R. B. (1980). Feeling and thinking: Preferences need no inferences. *American Psychologist, 35*, 151–175.

15. Grounding Categories in Emotional Response

PAULA M. NIEDENTHAL AND JAMIN H. HALBERSTADT

Introduction

Beginning in part with the work of Cantor and Mischel (1977, 1979), cognitive social psychologists have recognized the value of conceptualizing social perception and social judgment (including attribution, impression formation, and stereotyping) as processes that rely on – indeed, are grounded in – social categorization (Fiske & Taylor, 1991). Volumes of work by cognitive psychologists concerned with the acquisition and use of artifactual and taxonomic categories have provided social psychologists with theory and method with which to explore social categorization. As a consequence of this intellectual history, social categories have been conceptualized largely as object categories that contain people and social situations. Of course, one important difference between social and object categories, it has been argued, is that persons, even more so than objects, can be placed in multiple categories. Thus, social psychologists have had to address the question: Why and under what conditions do we classify this person as a "woman" instead of as a "Northerner" or a "jazz musician" (Macrae, Bodenhausen, & Milne, 1995; Smith, Fazio, & Cejka, 1996). In addition, social categorization is more often, and perhaps more consequentially, motivated than object categorization. Thus, social categories are almost never devoid of emotion, and motivation determines the use and the evaluation of categories of persons and situations. Nevertheless, in general, it is fair to say that the study of social cate-

Address correspondence concerning this chapter to Paula M. Niedenthal, Department of Psychology, Indiana University, Bloomington, Indiana 47405. E-mail: pniedent@indiana.edu.

gorization has received more than it has given back to the study of basic categories.

We believe that social psychology can now return the intellectual favor. The study of the interactions between affect and cognition has revealed much that cognitive psychology has (perhaps studiously) neglected in the quest to adequately model mental processes involved in the acquisition and use of categories. As the researchers in this volume and others studying affect and cognition (e.g., Fiedler & Forgas, 1988; Forgas 1991; Mackie & Hamilton, 1993; Niedenthal & Kitayama, 1994) attest, the study of mental processes must proceed with the explicit acknowledgment that affect shapes, constrains, and organizes even those categorization processes considered to be at a "low level" (e.g., Niedenthal & Kitayama, 1994). As a contribution along these lines, the research presented in this chapter demonstrates that traditional theories and models of categorization have failed to take into account one basis of, or grounds for, forming categories per se, namely, emotional response. We propose that individuals group together not only those things that are perceptually similar (Rosch, 1975; Rosch, Mervis, Gray, Johnson, & Boyes-Braem, 1976; see also Goldstone, 1994; and Medin, Goldstone, & Gentner, 1993), that share a similar theory of cause and effect (Murphy & Medin, 1985; Wattenmaker, Nakamura, & Medin, 1987), and that serve a common goal (e.g., Barsalou, 1983), but also those things that elicit in them a common emotional response. Objects and events that have evoked happiness, for example, may be treated as equivalent and categorized as the same sort of thing, even if they are otherwise perceptually, functionally, and theoretically diverse. This idea was first explicitly proposed in the psychological literature by Bruner, Goodnow, and Austin (1956) in their classic book on categorization, *A Study of Thinking*. As Bruner et al. put it, "A group of people, books, whether of a certain kind, and certain states of mind are all grouped together as 'alike,' the 'same kind of thing.' . . . What holds them together and what leads one to say that some new experience 'reminds one of such and such weather, people, and states' is the evocation of a defining affective response" (p. 4). Unfortunately, the idea was never elaborated, pursued empirically, or integrated into models of category learning and use.

This chapter develops a theoretical and empirical argument for considering emotional response a basis for categorization (for a more detailed treatment, see Niedenthal, Halberstadt, & Innes-Ker, in press). To make the case, we must start by addressing another question: Which emotions could serve this purpose? In theory, any emotional response could be the ground for a category, but an unlimited set of emotional response categories would not be useful. We argue, using prior theory and data, that certain emotions are most likely to lead people to organize objects and events into emotional response categories. The second step, then, will be to determine the conditions under which individuals favor emotional equivalence over other bases of categorization; the experiments we describe demonstrate that during emotional states individuals increase their use of emotional response categorization. Finally, we explore the mechanisms of emotional response categorization. We suggest that during emotional states people selectively attend to their emotional response to novel stimuli and to representations of their responses to previously encoded objects and events. Attention to this aspect of the stimuli produces a clustering of the stimuli into groups based on the emotional response that they evoke.

Defining Emotional Response Categories

In the present account, emotional response categorization means the mental grouping together of objects and events (stimuli) that elicit the same emotion in a given perceiver, and lead to the representation of those stimuli in terms of the emotional response to them. Although it has not been interpreted as evidence of emotional response categorization, a body of data indeed suggests that emotions serve as primes to information related to those emotions by virtue of having produced the same emotional response, and to linguistic tags linked to that information (see, e.g., Clark & Teasdale, 1982; Laird, Cuniff, Sheehan, Shulman & Strumm, 1989; Laird, Wagener, Halal, & Szegda, 1982; Lloyd & Lishman, 1975; Madigan & Bollenbach, 1982; Natale & Hantas, 1982; Salovey & Singer, 1988, Experiment 2; Snyder & White, 1982; Teasdale & Fogarty, 1979; for reviews, see Blaney, 1986; and Singer & Salovey, 1988). Emotions do not simply prime information, however; they actually lead individuals to reorganize conceptual space according to emotional equivalences. This reorganization then determines how people perceive similarities and differences among objects and events, and how they respond to them. Thus, emotions affect not only memory but also category construction and use.

The primary purpose of emotional response categorization is to motivate adaptive behavior. Of course, emotions may motivate adaptive behavior in both humans and animals without the mediation of mental representations of things that have elicited that emotion (e.g., Averill, 1968; Buck, 1985; Ekman, 1984; Frijda, 1986; Izard, 1977; Johnson-Laird & Oatley, 1992; MacLean, 1993; Oatley, 1992; Plutchik, 1980; Tomkins, 1962, 1963). However, we are talking about much more than reflex-like responses. A category of things that have elicited a particular emotion facilitates the perceiver's understanding of the meaning of a particular category exemplar in terms of their own personal learning histories and objectives (see also Greenwald et al., this volume), and it facilitates the perceiver's ability to imagine the consequences of his or her reactions to new objects (see also Blascovich and Mendes, this volume). Before we address the viability of this account, however, we first must answer the question: which emotions can be grounds for categories?

Which Emotional Responses Ground Categories?

In a nationally syndicated cartoon, Matt Groening once depicted "The 77 Moods of Akbar and Jeff." He included among them *demure, sassy, giddy, testy, peevish,* and *cranky.* Does each of these affective states or feelings provide the basis for a category? Put differently, if there is a word for a feeling, is there a category of things that have elicited that subjective state? Although a reasonable argument could no doubt be made in support of the idea, theory and data on the structure of emotional experience suggest another possibility. We briefly review the different accounts of the structure of emotional experience and then argue in favor of one view with respect to emotional response categorization.

Some psychologists believe that emotional experiences are reducible to a small number of bipolar dimensions. In their view, the greatest variance in the apprehension of meaning (e.g., Osgood & Suci, 1955), in the perception of emotional objects (e.g., Abelson & Sermat, 1962; Schlosberg, 1952) and in the self-report of mood (e.g., Mayer & Gaschke, 1988; Russell, 1980) is due to a bipolar pleasant–unpleasant dimension. This valence dimension usually accounts for 50% to 60% of the variance in ratings of mood (e.g., Feldman, 1995a). Although a unidimensional model cannot fully account for emotional experience, a valence model is often adopted in the study of the semantic processing of emotion. The model suggests that there are two emotional response categories that correspond to positive feelings and negative feelings, and that these general categories may consist of subcategories of positive and negative people, positive and negative foods, and positive and negative features of the self (see also Showers, this volume).

Other researchers have proposed a more complete, two-dimensional model of affective experience. In the modal two-dimensional model, the valence dimension is supplemented by a dimension of perceived arousal or intensity (i.e., high to low arousal) (Feldman, 1995b; Lang, Bradley, & Cuthbert, 1990; Reisenzein, 1994; Russell, 1980, 1989; Schlosberg, 1952; although see also Larsen & Diener, 1992; Thayer, 1989; Watson & Tellegen, 1985 for an alternative account of the two dimensions). The arousal dimension typically accounts for about half as much of the variance in emotional state as that accounted for by the valence dimension (e.g., Feldman, 1995a; Mayer & Gaschke, 1988; Meyer & Shack, 1989). Such a model might suggest that there are four emotional response categories, which correspond to things that elicit high and low positive arousal, as well as high and low negative arousal.

A second major account of emotional experience is that there are a number of discrete emotional states that are not further reducible to a small number of common dimensions. Although emotion theorists disagree as to which experiences count as discrete emotional states, they consistently point to at least five: happiness, sadness, anger, disgust, and fear (e.g., Ekman, 1984; Izard, 1977; Johnson-Laird & Oatley, 1992; Plutchik, 1980; Tomkins, 1962, 1963). Among other things, these emotions emerge early in human development (Sroufe, 1979), seem to be communicated through universally recognized facial gestures (Ekman & Friesen, 1971; for reviews, see Ekman, 1994, and Izard, 1994; but see also Russell, 1994), and are reflected in the organization of generic knowledge about the emotions (e.g., Shaver, Schwartz, Kirson, & O'Connor, 1987). These facts have led some to propose that these are biologically basic emotions, although there is still much debate on this matter. Note, however, that emotions may best be modeled as discrete nondecomposable states, even if they are not basic in a biological sense.

When one considers the function of categorization, there is good reason to believe that emotional response categories are organized by the discrete emotional states rather than more general affective dimensions. To be useful, categories must be general enough to permit abstraction to new exemplars, but specific enough to offer accurate information about how to respond to those exemplars (Rosch, 1975). Furthermore, they must reflect the fact that the behavioral implications of the stimuli that cause fear, for example, are quite different from those that cause anger, sadness, or disgust (e.g., Frijda, 1986; Izard, 1977; Plutchik, 1984; Tomkins, 1962, 1963). Thus, in terms of the function of categorization, an organization of concepts by discrete emotions is likely to be the most useful, and discrete emotional states probably provide the best map of emotional response categories (for other evidence supportive of this cognitive organization, see, e.g., Gernsbacher, Goldsmith, & Robertson, 1992; Halberstadt, Niedenthal, & Kushner, 1995; Laird et al., 1989; Laird et al., 1982; Niedenthal, Halberstadt, & Setterlund, 1997; Niedenthal & Setterlund, 1994). Working from this assumption, our research on emotional categorization involves the manipulation of discrete emotions as well as the use of stimuli previously found to be associated with those emotions (see also Niedenthal, Setterlund, & Jones, 1994).

Conditions of Use of Emotional Response Categories

Most perceived and already-represented stimuli can be categorized in multiple ways (e.g., Barsalou, 1983, 1991). Thus, while taxonomists may group together trees into categories based on the presence of certain morphological features, landscape workers may group trees into very different categories, according to the functions that the trees serve, such as providing shade or privacy (Medin, Lynch, Coley, & Atran, 1997). Like the temporary conceptual reorganization induced by goal states, discrete emotional states reorganize the conceptual space according to emotional response equivalences, and thus emotional response categories can be observed when individuals are experiencing those states.

We expect the reorganization of the conceptual space into emotional response categories to be functional for the individual, but in a way that differs from goal-based categorization. Because individuals are often unaware of the source of their emotions, the onset of an emotion can prompt a search for its cause (see also chapters by Fiedler, this volume; Bless, this volume). When information and stimuli are (re)organized in terms of the emotional responses they elicit, the source of an emotional state can be more readily determined. By sorting stimuli into emotion categories, fearful people (for example) can more readily identify potential causes of their emotion and in turn better determine the stimuli that will be useful for coping with the emotion (Frijda, 1986, 1993). Consistent with this account, Derryberry (1993) found evidence of emotion-congruence in an attention task such that success and failure motivated attention to spatial locations associated with positive and negative values, respectively. However, Derryberry also found evidence of *incongruence* such that the failure of feedback increased attention to positive cues, and success feedback increased attention to negative cues (Derryberry, 1989). In other words, participants attended to emotional information that was both similar and dissimilar in emotional tone to their current emotional state. As Derryberry and Tucker (1994, p. 175) note: "By promoting both kinds of complementary influences, the motivational state can promote more balanced and flexible processing. The individual is prepared for improving as well as deteriorating conditions." Such findings, as well as the functional reasoning discussed earlier, suggest that emotions reorganize conceptual space into groups of concepts associated with each discrete emotion, not only the emotion currently experienced by the individual. In other words, although automatic processes such as perceptual encoding often reveal facilitated processing of emotion-congruent stimuli (e.g., Niedenthal et al., 1997), unspeeded categorization behavior is likely to reveal emotional response categorization in general, or the enhanced use of the range of emotional response categories during states of emotion.

Experimental Evidence

In their experiments, Savitsky and Izard (1970) showed children aged 4, 5, 6, 7, and 8 triads of pictures of human faces. Two of the faces in each triad expressed the same emotion. Another pair of the faces were both wearing hats. When asked which two faces were alike or the same, 4-year-olds showed a slight preference for the hat grouping over the emotion grouping. By age 6 and increasing with development, children preferred to call faces alike that expressed the same emotion. Interestingly, this preference was strongest for faces that expressed anger, fear, and joy, which are typically considered discrete emotions, and was less pronounced for faces that expressed "distress," which is not. The authors' interpretation was that this result demonstrates an increase in the interest in and recognition of emotional expression over development. We also believe that the increased use of emotional groupings may reflect implicit learning about the usefulness of emotional equivalences.

Our research program on the existence and conditions of using emotional response categorization also relied on a triad task similar to the one employed by Savitsky & Izard (1970). In the studies, college undergraduates were presented over numerous trials with a target concept, X, followed by two comparison concepts, A and B. Their task was to indicate which concept, A or B, was most similar to X. In the triads, X was related to A in a nonemotional, taxonomic or associative way, whereas X and B shared an emotional association; that is, both X and B were associated with the same discrete emotional response. Examples of triads in which the emotional association was based on happiness, sadness, and fear are presented in Table 15.1. The general procedure for the experiments we describe here involved inducing a discrete emotion (e.g., happiness, sadness, fear) or a "neutral" (control) state, and then to ask participants to respond to a large set of triads. Triads of interest, those just described, were always presented within a larger set of neutral triads in which A and B were associated with X in different abstract (but emotionally neutral) ways.

In the first experiment (Niedenthal et al., in press) 107 participants were randomly assigned to happiness, sadness, or control conditions. Emotions were manipulated with the use of films seen prior to the triad task and music heard during the triad task (for details of the emotion induction procedure, see, e.g., Halberstadt & Niedenthal, 1997; Niedenthal et al., 1997). Happy, sad, and control condition participants then responded to 45 triads, 9 of which were "happy" triads, and 9 of which were "sad" triads (see Table 15.1). A manipulation check showed that the emotion induction procedures had been effective (indeed, for all experiments reported here, emotion induction procedures were highly effective). The data of interest, graphed in Figure 15.1, are the mean percentage of happy and sad triads in which the emotional comparison concept (B) was selected as being most similar to the target, X. As seen in Figure 15.1, emotion condition had a significant effect: Participants in both the happy and sad conditions chose B as more similar to X significantly more often than did participants in the control condition. In other words, participants experiencing happiness and sadness were more likely to base their groupings of the triad concepts on the discrete emotional responses with which

Table 15.1. *Example Triads Presented in the Order* {X: A, B} *Where* X *Is the Target Concept,* A *Is the Emotion Alternative, and* B *Is the Taxonomic Alternative*

Triad Type	Examples
Happy triads . . .	joke: sunbeam, speech
	puppy: parade, beetle
	waterski: celebration, elevator
	kiss: fortune, handshake
Sad triads . . .	cancer: divorce, pulse
	ambulance: poverty, wheelbarrow
	bankruptcy: tomb, teller
	tears: disease, breath
Fear triads . . .	nightmare: punishment, thought
	vulture: insanity, parakeet
	electric chair: tumor, sofa
	snake: guillotine, armadillo

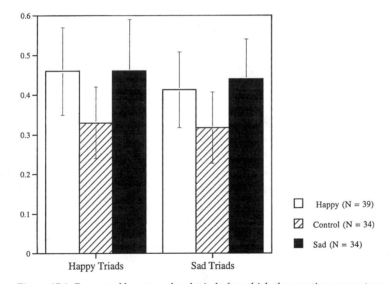

Figure 15.1. Percent of happy and sad triads for which the emotion concept was judged as most similar to the target concept (Experiment 1). (Adapted from P. M. Niedenthal, J. B. Halberstadt, and A. H. Innes-Ker, Emotional Response Categories, in press, *Psychological Review*.)

the concepts were associated. This strongly suggests that emotional states are indeed associated with the reorganization of concepts into emotional response categories that correspond to discrete emotions.

However, the data could also be interpreted to mean that people form categories of emotional or emotionally arousing stimuli when in an emotional state, without regard to whether the target and comparison concepts are associated with the *same* emotion. The use of an all-inclusive category such as "arousing things" is inconsistent with the reasoning about the structure of emotional response categories presented earlier. To test this alternative interpretation, a follow-up study was conducted in which participants (N = 181) judged whether a target word (e.g., *bankruptcy*) was more similar to a taxonomically or associatively related concept (e.g., *teller*) or to a concept that was emotional but was related to a *different* discrete emotion (e.g., *parade*). Thus, in happy "mixed triads," the target was associated with happiness, whereas the emotional alternative, B, was associated with sadness; the reverse was true for sad "mixed triads." The nonemotional associates in mixed triads were the same as in the original stimulus set.

Results of the follow-up study revealed that for the mixed triads the different-emotion associate was considered most similar to the target far less often than was the nonemotional alternative. More important for the present concerns, judgments were not mediated by emotional state (see Figure 15.2). The follow-up experiment therefore indicates that people do not use emotionality or arousal per se as a basis of categorization when they are experiencing an emotion; they do not group happy stimuli with sad stimuli just because both are emotionally arousing.

It should be emphasized that these first studies manipulated only the emotions of happiness and sadness, and the concepts in the critical triads were related only to happiness or sadness as well. Happiness and sadness could be special in that they are considered "opposite" emotions, if not in a statistical or dimensional way, at least in a cultural way. It is therefore possible that the tendency for happy and sad people to form both groups of happy things and groups of sad things is due to a special relationship between happiness and sadness and is not characteristic of individuals in other emotional states or for other emotional response categories. Moreover, the relationship between happiness and sadness may have been particularly salient when both happy and sad concepts were present in the task. If this were the

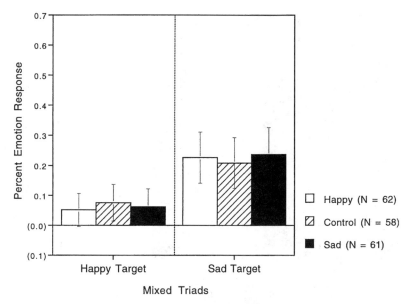

Figure 15.2. Percent of happy and sad mixed triads for which the emotion concept was judged as most similar to the target concept (first follow-up study to Experiment 1). (Adapted from P. M. Niedenthal, J. B. Halberstadt, and A. H. Innes-Ker, Emotional Response Categories, in press, *Psychological Review*.)

case, then the "reorganization" of concepts into emotional response categories could not be said to be a general effect.

One way to address the salience objection is to make triad type (happy vs. sad triads) a between-subjects variable. Such a strategy makes the relationship between the two kinds of stimuli less obvious. (Admittedly, this solution does not address the possibility that happiness and sadness independently motivate heightened attention to information associated with both feeling states.) In a second follow-up study, therefore, half of the participants (total N = 169) in each of three emotion conditions (happy, sad, or neutral control) saw happy triads intermixed with neutral triads, and the remaining participants saw sad triads intermixed with neutral triads (refer to Table 15.1 for examples).

Results of the second follow-up revealed that both happy and sad participants used happiness as a basis for categorization significantly more than control participants. That is, consistent with the results of the first experiment, emotional participants based their judgments on the emotional associations among the concepts (see Figure 15.3), even

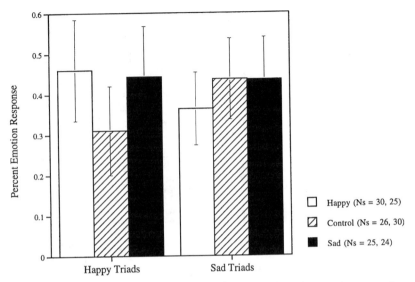

Figure 15.3. Percent of happy and sad triads for which the emotion concept was judged as most similar to the target concept (second follow-up study to Experiment 1). Triad type was varied between participants. (Adapted from P. M. Niedenthal, J. B. Halberstadt, and A. H. Innes-Ker, Emotional Response Categories, in press, *Psychological Review*.)

when the happy triads were presented in the absence of sad triads. However, this finding did not extend to the conditions in which participants saw only sad triads. Happy, sad, and control condition participants all responded to the sad triads in the same way, apparently because control participants increased their use of sadness as a basis of categorization. In fact, individuals in the control condition who saw only sad triads grouped concepts together on the basis of emotional equivalence significantly more than did control participants who saw only happy triads. This was a surprising finding, and it suggests the possibilities that either the sad triads strongly afforded sadness as grounds for categorization, regardless of the emotional state of the perceiver, or that the sad triads altered the emotional state of the control participants (although this was not detected by a manipulation check). The former interpretation is reminiscent of the finding that negative information automatically captures the attention of perceivers in attention and perception tasks of other kinds (e.g., Hansen & Hansen, 1994; Pratto & John, 1991).

The results of this study argue against the possibility that the specific stimuli used in the first experiment made both happy and sad participants more inclined to use both happiness and sadness as a basis of categorization. However, the results do not address the possibility that both happy and sad information is particularly salient to both happy and sad people, regardless of the context in which the information is presented, and whether the emotional categorization effects observed in the first experiment are thus limited to those emotions. A second experiment was therefore conducted to investigate the generalizability of the emotional similarity effect. In this experiment, participants (N = 166) were exposed to either a sad or a fear (or a control) emotion induction and then solved a set of sad and fear triads (refer to Table 15.1 for examples), embedded (as in the previous studies) in a set of nonemotional triads. As can be seen in Figure 15.4, the same general emotional categorization effect was obtained once again. Participants in the sad and fear conditions indicated that B (the emotionally related concept) was more similar to the target concept X than A (the taxonomically related concept) significantly more often than did participants in the neutral condition. They did this regardless of whether X and B were both related to sadness or to fearfulness.

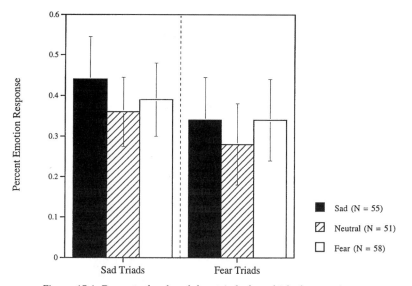

Figure 15.4. Percent of sad and fear triads for which the emotion concept was judged as most similar to the target concept (Experiment 2). (Adapted from P. M. Niedenthal, J. B. Halberstadt, and A. H. Innes-Ker, Emotional Response Categories, in press, *Psychological Review*.)

To summarize, the research discussed thus far found that individuals experiencing discrete states of happiness, sadness, and fearfulness grouped together concepts according to emotional equivalence significantly more than individuals who were experiencing relatively neutral feelings. The latter individuals were more likely to base their judgments on distant taxonomic or associate relationships. Emotional response categorization was also in evidence when individuals in emotional states were exposed only to happy triads (intermixed with neutral triads) and were not exposed to sad triads as a comparison. An alternative account of the data, which holds that people in emotional states group all emotional objects into a single "emotion" or "arousal" category, was not supported by the results of a follow-up study in which participants failed to group together emotional items that were related to different emotions. In a divergence from the basic finding, when happy, sad, and control participants solved sad triads intermingled with neutral triads (i.e., in the absence of happy triads), all groups used emotional categorization to the same, rather elevated, degree. It appears that, when presented in the absence of happy triads, either the sad associations of the sad triads became particularly salient, or the stimuli themselves induced sadness in the participants.

However, there is a troubling alternative account of these findings. Perhaps the observed effects are not due to emotion at all, but rather to the priming of generic knowledge about emotions. That is, stimuli (such as films and music) that are used to induce emotions may prime concepts about emotion, perhaps generic categories of emotion knowledge, and this priming may be responsible for the observed effects. Emotional feelings, in this view, are superfluous. To address this possibility, we conducted a third major experiment designed to test the specific hypothesis that the content of the films used in our emotion induction procedures enhanced the detection of emotional equivalences, even in the absence of the induction of emotional feelings. An ideal way to test this hypothesis is to expose individuals to the emotion-inducing and control films, but to prevent some participants from having emotional reactions to them. In this way, the pure "cognitive" effects of the concepts and ideas contained in the films on categorization behavior can be observed. We therefore gave some participants a processing goal that would interfere with their emotions but ensure that they were paying attention to the films (e.g., Blascovich et al., 1993). The processing goal was to count (in their heads) the number of times the camera changed point of view within each film segment.

Substantial testing and debriefing of the participants indicated that the point-of-view instructions did not interfere with their ability to comprehend and remember the content of the films. In a pilot study, for instance, participants with and without the processing goal remembered equal numbers of details about events that took place in the films and also did not differ in their ratings of the emotions expressed in the scenes and the emotions likely to be typically evoked by the scenes. In the main experiment, participants watched the happy, sad, and control films with either no instructions or with instructions to watch for changes in the point of view of the camera. Then all participants performed a triad task that contained happy and neutral triads.

There were two reasonable predictions about the solution of the happy triads by participants in the point-of-view conditions. One prediction was that because emotions were not manipulated, no effect of film condition would be observed. This is because all participants in all film conditions under point-of-view instructions would be equally (non)emotional and would therefore not attend to emotional equivalences. A second prediction was that participants in the point-of-view condition who were exposed to the happy films would demonstrate elevated emotional response categorization in responding to the happy triads, compared with participants who were exposed to the sad and neutral films. This "emotion-congruence" prediction was somewhat weaker than the first because conceptual knowledge might not enhance the tendency to detect emotional response equivalences between concepts in terms of the emotions typically evoked by their exemplars.

Results of the study showed, first, that the point-of-view instructions were successful in short-circuiting emotional responses to the films. That is, participants who watched the happy movie under point-of-view instructions were no more happy than were those who watched the sad films under the same instructions. It appeared that the instructions caused participants to process the films in a more analytical, less emotional, way. The results of the triad task, presented in Figure 15.5, indicate that the no-instruction conditions replicated the previously observed finding that emotions enhance the use of emotional similarity. Compared with participants in a more neutral mood, happy and sad participants were more likely to report that concepts associated with the same emotion (happiness) were more similar than concepts that had a taxonomic or associative relation. For

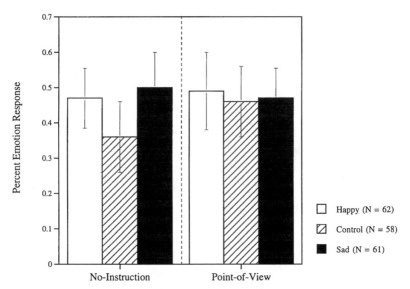

Figure 15.5. Percent of triads for which the happy concept was judged as most similar to the target concept (Experiment 3). (Adapted from P. M. Niedenthal, J. B. Halberstadt, and A. H. Innes-Ker, Emotional Response Categories, in press, *Psychological Review*.)

the participants in the point-of-view condition, however, the content of the movie had no effect on the use of emotional similarity. Point-of-view participants who saw happy, sad, and neutral films performed the triad task in a similar way.

The results thus do not support an alternative account of the previous findings that invokes a mechanism of nonemotional priming of concepts related to "good" and "bad" or "happy" and "sad." If the films primed emotion concepts, and such priming was responsible for the results of the first two experiments, then we should have found the same pattern of similarity judgments in both the no-instruction and the point-of-view conditions.

Our second, weaker, hypothesis regarding the point-of-view conditions was that individuals who were exposed to the happy films would tend to equate happy concepts because generic knowledge about happiness was primed by the films. This emotion-congruence effect was not in fact observed. Thus, perhaps the films did not actually prime generic knowledge about emotions, even though they induced emotional states among those who were not counting changes in the point-of-view of the camera. Or perhaps such priming does not motivate emotional response categorization at all.

There is, however, a condition under which a type of emotion-congruent categorization might be anticipated. Individuals who are chronically depressed might be expected to use sadness as a basis of equating stimuli, but perhaps not happiness. In addition to the presence of a negativity bias, depression is characterized by the absence of a positivity bias, an apparent disruption in the processing of positive information (e.g., Alloy & Abramson, 1988; Sanz, 1996; see also Bless, this volume, and Fiedler, this volume, for a related processing account).

In an effort to identify a condition in which emotion-congruent categorization might be observed, individuals who scored high or low on the Beck Depression Inventory (BDI) in a mass-testing session at the beginning of an academic term were invited into the laboratory. Although the name of the BDI refers to depression, in order to avoid confusion with the assessment of clinical levels of depression, we hereafter refer to high and low *dysphoria* (Coyne, 1994). There were approximately 30 participants in each group. The average BDI score for the low-dysphoria group was 1.27 (mode = 0, median = 1) and the range was 0 to 4. The average BDI score for the high-dysphoria group was 14.06 (both the mode and the median were 14) and the range was 7 to 26. The BDI was also administered at the experimental session as a check on the initial selection. The correlation between BDI scores at Times 1 and 2 was .84, indicating good reliability of the measure. When they arrived at the laboratory session, all participants performed the triad task containing happy, sad, and nonemotional filler triads. Emotional state was not manipulated.

Analysis of the triad data revealed a significant interaction between dysphoria status and the percentage of triads in which emotional response determined the concept groupings (see Figure 15.6). Compared with nondysphoric individuals, high dysphorics were more likely to group together concepts on the basis of sadness and less likely to group together concepts on the basis of happiness. That is, dysphoric participants, unlike participants in whom sadness was manipulated, did not attend to the happy associations of the items in the happy triads. This finding is consistent with a diverse literature showing that depression is defined by a deficiency in the processing of positive information in addition to a negativity bias (Alloy & Abram-

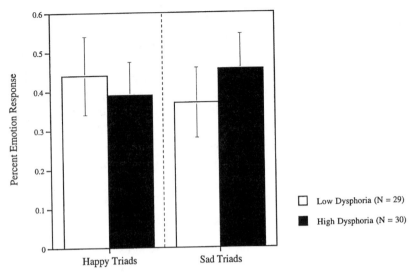

Figure 15.6. Percent of happy and sad triads for which the emotion concept was judged as most similar to the target concept (Experiment 4). Participants were dysphoric and non-dysphoric individuals. (Adapted from P. M. Niedenthal, J. B. Halberstadt, and A. H. Innes-Ker, Emotional Response Categories, in press, *Psychological Review*.)

son, 1988; Alloy, Abramson, Murray, Whitehouse, & Hogan, in press; Sanz, 1996).

The research project just reviewed strongly suggests that during emotional states individuals are more likely to group together those things that have elicited in them the same emotional response in the past. Individuals in more neutral states rely relatively more on distant taxonomic or associative relations when they perform the same task. Obviously, the triad task used in these initial experiments is not the only, or even necessarily the best, measure of categorization. Thus, it is incumbent upon future work to provide additional evidence that emotional states cause enhanced emotional response categorization. At this point, however, we are convinced enough that emotional states alter conceptual connections to explore the mechanism of this effect. Just why do people find more similarities between emotionally equivalent objects and events during discrete emotional states?

A Mechanism for Emotional Response Categorization

To answer this question, one must look to the cognitive and social cognitive literature on category formation. In many influential theories (e.g., Kruschke, 1992; Medin & Schaffer, 1978; Nosofsky, 1986, 1992; Smith & Zárate, 1992; Smith, 1989), category learning and use depend on selective attention to category-relevant stimulus features, or to representations of those features. Specifically, these theories assume that attention to different classes of stimulus features, such as shape or size, changes their discriminability. Stimuli have become relatively more distinct on aspects that receive greater attention, and at the same time relatively indistinguishable on aspects that are ignored. These changes in discriminability are reflected in perceptions of similarity, and in turn, category formation and structure. For example, a perceiver attending to shape (and ignoring color) would tend to judge a blue square as more similar to a red square than to either a blue or red triangle (Nosofsky, 1992). More generally, this perceiver would also tend to categorize new stimuli in terms of their shape.

We argue that emotional response is a stimulus aspect that can receive more or less attentional weight in judgments of similarity and categorization. That is, stimulus representations include not only perceptual features such as size and shape, but also the emotional response the stimulus has elicited (Zajonc, 1998). For example, a perceiver's representations of *puppy*, *parade*, and *beetle* include the happiness associated with these concepts. To the extent that the perceiver attends to this aspect (and ignores other aspects), *puppy* and *parade*, which are emotionally equivalent, will seem more similar overall, and less similar to *beetle*. Thus, it is proposed that emotional states influence solutions to the triad problem by directing attention to the emotional aspects of the triad concepts.

In fact, there is already a good deal of evidence that emotional, particularly negative, stimuli attract attention. For instance, Pratto and John (1991) found that negative words categorically interfered with processing in a Stroop task, a traditional measure of the automatic allocation of attention. Furthermore, there is evidence that this effect is greater for people in emotional states or with emotional traits. MacLeod, Mathews, and Tata (1986), for example, had participants monitor their computer screen for a small dot, which sometimes followed the appearance of either threat or neutral words. Anxious, but not nonanxious or depressed individuals, were faster to detect the probe when it replaced a threat word (see also Broadbent & Broadbent, 1988), indicating that attention is particularly likely to be drawn to emotional stimuli that match the perceiver's state in emotional tone.

Unfortunately, emotion-biased attentional orientation, as reported in the studies cited earlier, cannot confirm the current hypothesis that emotional people give emotion-associated stimulus aspects greater weight in judgment, because orientation to a stimulus aspect and use of that aspect in judgment do not always co-occur. Dalgleish and Watts (1990) have noted that, even if participants' attention is drawn to a particular stimulus or stimulus aspect, as indicated (for example) by distraction from a primary task, this fact alone does not provide information about how – or even if – the stimulus was processed. A stimulus can even draw attention for the purpose *avoiding* further processing, as in the phenomenon of perceptual defense.

Therefore, to examine the proposed mechanism of emotional response categorization, one needs a method of quantifying not only the orientation of attention to emotion-related stimulus aspects, but also the weight given to those aspects in similarity and categorization judgments. Individual difference multidimensional scaling (INDSCAL; Carroll & Chang, 1970) is ideal for this purpose. In an INDSCAL model, similarities among stimuli are represented as distances in a multidimensional space: The model calculates both a "group space," based on similarity judgments across all experimental participants, as well as a set of dimension weights for each participant, which provide an estimate of that participant's unique *use* of the stimulus aspects (see Arabie, Carroll, & DeSarbo, 1987, for more details). Thus, one advantage of the INDSCAL approach is simply that the group space can verify the psychological validity of emotional response as a stimulus aspect; one cannot merely assume that the emotion-related stimulus aspects established by the experimenter are actually perceived as stimulus aspects by the experimental participants. More important, the perceiver-specific weights produced by the model provide a measure of how each participant uses those aspects in judgment. If selective use of emotional aspects accounts for the effects observed in the triad studies, then we would expect an interaction on the INDSCAL weights between the stimulus aspects and the emotional state of the perceiver. Compared with control participants, participants in emotional states should attend to and use (i.e., weight more heavily) emotion-related stimulus aspects and should tend to ignore aspects unrelated to emotion.

Halberstadt and Niedenthal (1997) tested this hypothesis using as stimuli high-resolution photographs of the faces of male and female actors expressing happiness and sadness. These stimuli were chosen because of the strong associations between emotional expressions and emotional feeling states. Indeed, emotional expressions have been shown to produce corresponding emotions in the perceiver through processes of mimicry and contagion (e.g., Hatfield, Cacioppo, & Rapson, 1993; Laird et al., 1994). The procedure was straightforward: Participants were induced to feel happiness, sadness, or neutral emotion, after which they made similarity judgments between every pair of stimulus faces. The participants' similarity data were then submitted to an INDSCAL analysis to determine which aspects were most important in their judgments.

The number of dimensions used to model the data in multidimensional scaling depends both on the interpretability of each dimension and on the extent to which the dimension improves the fit of the overall model (see Kruskal, 1964; Kruskal & Wish, 1978). In this case, it was determined that a three-dimensional model provided the best balance between interpretability and fit. The two dimensions that accounted for the most variance were emotional expression and gender, and a third was tentatively interpreted as "head orientation." The weights participants gave to these three aspects of the faces are illustrated in Figure 15.7. As can be seen, regardless of emotional state, the stimuli were judged largely on the basis of their emotional expressions. Although consistent with other research on the importance of evaluative or valenced information in judgment, this result is important, because it provides direct evidence that emotional response is a psychologically valid stimulus category. More important, and consistent with a selective attention account of the triad effects, the aspects interacted with emotional state. Happy and sad participants weighted emotional expressions more heavily, and the other two dimensions less heavily, than neutral participants, and, as in the triad studies, the happy and sad groups did not differ from each other. These effects replicated across three different studies, using faces expressing both dichotomous and continuous emotions, and using both music and film emotion inductions (Halberstadt & Niedenthal, 1997). Furthermore, an examination of the similarity ratings themselves revealed that these different weighting schemes were reflected in the perceived similarity of same-emotion faces. That is, participants in both the happy and sad conditions judged pairs of faces expressing the same emotion (regard-

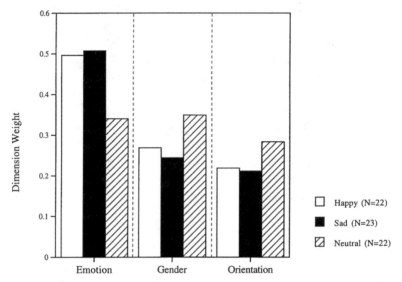

Figure 15.7. Attention weights revealed by an INDSCAL analysis of similarity judgments between pairs of faces, as a function of emotional state (happy, sad, neutral). (Adapted from Halberstadt and Niedenthal, 1997.)

less of whether that emotion matched the participant's own state) as more similar than did control participants.

Thus, the INDSCAL analyses replicate our earlier findings and provide evidence consistent with our proposed mechanism of emotional response categorization. In the triad studies, emotional participants were more likely to base forced choice similarity judgments on the emotional response relationships among the target and comparison concepts. Similarly, in the face studies, they appeared to base their paired similarity judgments on the faces' emotional equivalence. Consistent with our selective attention account, INDSCAL modeling of the face judgments indicated that participants in emotional states were overweighting (in relation to neutral emotion controls) the faces' emotional expressions and underweighting other aspects of the faces. This, in turn, led to greater perceived similarity between faces expressing similar emotions, and overall to a clustering in psychological space of emotionally equivalent faces: that is, to emotional response categories.

Why Use Emotional Response Categories?

Perhaps a better question to ask is why *not* use emotional response categories? The fact that other types of concepts and problem-solving strategies cannot take the place of emotional response in guiding socially appropriate action has been amply noted of late (e.g., Damasio, 1994; Goleman, 1995; Salovey & Sluyter, 1997; Zajonc, 1998; see also Zajonc, this volume). A man who evokes in a woman the same happy feelings that she experienced long ago while watching a beautiful sunset or drinking pastis in a Provençal café will receive different treatment and take on a different meaning to the woman than will a man who reinvokes the feelings of being attacked by a swarm of hornets or cornered by a snarling dog (see also Greenwald et al., this volume). The difference is not a matter of instinct. The reactions and the ideas brought to mind in the first case suggest to the woman that the man is rewarding and potentially special in the context of her life. Categorization with the hornets suggests something very different, for example, that there is something quite wrong with a person who instills these emotions in others. If the woman is smart, she will use the emotional response categorization to help her escape the latter situation (Zajonc, 1998).

Emotional Response Categories and Generic Emotion Knowledge

In this chapter we distinguished between generic emotion concepts and emotional response categories. Generic emotion knowledge refers to the explicit beliefs individuals hold about what emotions are, what produces them, and what they lead to. On the other hand, emotional response categories are the mental groupings of objects and events that have evoked the same emotional response in the past.

The differences between these two types of processes are accounted for in LeDoux's (1987, 1993) theory that emotional learning is mediated by a different memory system from that which represents and processes explicit knowledge about emotions. Hierarchical theories of emotion, such as those associated with Buck (1985) and Leventhal (1984), also differentiate between these types of knowledge. In Leventhal's approach, for example, emotions are represented at three processing levels (see also Smith & Kirby, this volume). At the *expressive-motor* level, sensory inputs are processed by innate neuromotor templates. These produce the output we recognize as emotional responses. The output is integrated with stored memories of emotional experiences at the *schematic* level. Such schemes represent the memories and physiological responses associated with emotional experiences. The third, *conceptual* level, contains rules, beliefs, and expectations about emotional experience, such as the belief that pain can be reduced through distraction (Leventhal & Everhart, 1979). Within Leventhal's framework, members of emotional response categories might be represented as schematic memories for specific emotion-eliciting episodes and stimuli, whereas generic emotion knowledge constitutes what is represented at the conceptual level.

As Leventhal and others note, a model of emotion processing must allow for interaction among these levels (see also Niedenthal et al., 1994). In Leventhal's theory, emotional responses organize input into the schematic and conceptual levels to determine the full subjective emotional experience, while the schematic and conceptual levels organize the input and guide attention and behavior toward other people and objects during emotional episodes (e.g., Ahles, Blanchard, & Leventhal, 1983). Empirical evidence is consistent with these notions. For example, some priming of the conceptual level by the activation of schematic memories for emotion is necessary to account for the phemonenon of emotion-congruent recall (i.e., the tendency for people in specific emotional states to retrieve more easily words and ideas associated with the same emotion). Activation of the schematic level by the conceptual level is necessary to account for the success of the Velten mood manipulation (Velten, 1968) in which people read emotional statements and consequently experience the emotional state suggested by the statements. Finally, the structure of emotion language corresponds well to the structure of emotion itself (e.g., Fehr & Russell, 1984; Shaver et al., 1987). For example, in the Shaver et al. (1987) study of emotion terms, results of hierarchical cluster analysis revealed that people think about emotions and organize the emotion lexicon in terms of the basic categories of joy, love, anger, sadness, fear, and possibly surprise. Given these connections, it is possible that individuals differ not only in the content of emotional response categories but also in the consciousness of their use of emotional response as a basis of categorization.

Conclusion

We have argued that emotional response is a type of conceptual glue, theoretically and functionally distinct from the similarity- and theory-based views dominant in the categorization literature. Although it is true that even social stimuli are often equated because of their physical or functional similarity, or because of their fit to a personal theoretical model, we have observed that stimuli can cohere as a category even when they have nothing in common other than the emotional response they elicit. The experiments reviewed in this chapter provide strong evidence that when people are experiencing specific emotions, they are more likely to attend to the emotional response equivalence of otherwise dissimilar abstract concepts (i.e., those presented in the triad experiments), as well as perceptually similar stimuli such as the faces of different individuals. We believe that cognitive models of basic categorization will benefit by attention to this basic categorization process and that as a consequence future models of categorization will be more ecologically valid, more predictive of behavior, and therefore more complete.

References

Abelson, R. P., & Sermat, V. (1962). Multidimensional scaling of facial expressions. *Journal of Experimental Psychology, 63,* 546–554.

Ahles, T. A., Blanchard, E. B., & Leventhal, H. (1983). Cognitive control of pain: Attention to the sensory aspects of the cold pressor stimulus. *Cognitive Therapy and Research, 7,* 159–178.

Alloy, L. B., & Abramson, L. Y. (1988). Depressive realism: Four theoretical perspectives. In L. B. Alloy (Ed.), *Cognitive processes in depression* (pp. 111–140). New York: Guilford Press.

Alloy, L. B., Abramson, L. Y., Murray, L. A., Whitehouse, W. G., & Hogan, M. E. (in press). Self-referent information processing in individuals at high and low cognitive risk for depression. *Cognition and Emotion.*

Arabie, P., Carroll, J. D., & DeSarbo, W. S. (1987). *Three-way scaling and clustering.* Sage University Paper Series on Quantitative Applications in the Social Sciences 07–065. Beverly Hills, CA: Sage.

Averill, J. R. (1968). Grief: Its nature and significance. *Psychological Bulletin, 70,* 721–748.

Barsalou, L. W. (1983). Ad hoc categories. *Memory and Cognition, 11,* 211–227.

Barsalou, L. W. (1991). Deriving categories to achieve goals. In G. H. Bower (Ed.), *The psychology of learning and motivation.* New York: Academic Press.

Blaney, P. H. (1986). Affect and memory: A review. *Psychological Bulletin, 99,* 229–246.

Blascovich, J., Ernst, J. M., Tomaka, J., Kelsey, R. M., Salomon, K. L., & Fazio, R. H. (1993). Attitude accessibility as a moderator of autonomic reactivity during decision making. *Journal of Personality and Social Psychology, 64,* 165–176.

Broadbent, D. E., & Broadbent, M. (1988). Anxiety and attentional bias: State and trait. *Cognition and Emotion, 2,* 165–183.

Bruner, J. S., Goodnow, J. J., & Austin, G. A. (1956). *A study of thinking.* New York: Wiley.

Buck, R. (1985). Prime theory: An integrated view of motivation and emotion. *Psychological Review, 92*, 389–413.

Cantor, N., & Mischel, W. (1977). Traits as prototypes: Effects on recognition memory. *Journal of Personality and Social Psychology, 35*, 38–48.

Cantor, N., & Mischel, W. (1979). Prototypes in person perception. In L. Berkowitz (Ed.), *Advances in experimental social psychology* (Vol. 12, pp. 3–52). New York: Academic Press.

Carroll, J. D., & Chang, J. J. (1970). *A "quasi-non-metric" version of INDSCAL, a procedure for individual differences in multidimensional scaling.* Paper presented at meetings of the Psychonomic Society, Stanford, CA.

Clark, D. M., & Teasdale, J. D. (1982). Diurnal variation in clinical depression and accessibility of positive and negative experiences. *Journal of Abnormal Psychology, 91*, 87–95.

Coyne, J. C. (1994). Self-reported distress: Analog or ersatz depression? *Psychological Bulletin, 116*, 29–45.

Dalgleish, T., & Watts, F. N. (1990). Biases of attention and memory disorders of anxiety and depression. *Clinical Psychology Review, 10*, 589–604.

Damasio, A. R. (1994). *Descartes error: Emotion, reason, and the human brain.* New York: Grosset/Putnam.

Derryberry, D. (1989). Effects of goal-related motivational states on the spatial orienting of attention. *Acta Psychologica, 72*, 199–220.

Derryberry, D. (1993). Attentional consequences of outcome-related motivational states: Congruent, incongruent and focusing effects. *Motivation and Emotion, 17*, 65–89.

Derryberry, D., & Tucker, D. M. (1994). Motivating the focus of attention. In P. M. Niedenthal & S. Kitayama (Eds.), *The heart's eye: Emotional influences in perception and attention* (pp. 167–196). San Diego, CA: Academic Press.

Ekman, P. (1984). Expression and the nature of emotion. In K. Scherer & P. Ekman (Eds.), *Approaches to emotion* (pp. 319–343). Hillsdale, NJ: Erlbaum.

Ekman, P. (1994). Strong evidence for universals in facial expressions: A reply to Russell's mistaken critique. *Psychological Bulletin, 115*, 268–287.

Ekman, P., & Friesen, W. V. (1971). Constants across culture in the face and emotion. *Journal of Personality and Social Psychology, 17*, 124–129.

Fehr, B., & Russell, J. A. (1984). The concept of emotion viewed from a prototype perspective. *Journal of Experimental Psychology: General, 113*, 464–486.

Feldman, L. A. (1995a). Variations in the circumplex structure of mood. *Personality and Social Psychology Bulletin, 21*, 806–817.

Feldman, L. A. (1995b). Valence focus and arousal focus: Individual differences in the structure of affective experience. *Journal of Personality and Social Psychology, 68*, 153–166.

Fiedler, K., & Forgas, J. P. (Eds.). (1988). *Affect, cognition and social behavior.* Toronto: Hogrefe.

Fiske, S. T., & Taylor, S. E. (1991). *Social Cognition.* New York: McGraw-Hill.

Forgas, J. P. (1991). Affective influences on partner choice – role of mood in social decision. *Journal of Personality and Social Psychology, 61*, 708–720.

Frijda, N. H. (1986). *The emotions.* London: Cambridge University Press.

Frijda, N. H. (1993). The place of appraisal in emotion. Special issue: Appraisal and beyond: The issue of cognitive determinants of emotion. *Cognition and Emotion, 7,* 357–384.

Gernsbacher, M. A., Goldsmith, H. H., & Robertson, R. R. (1992). Do readers mentally represent characters' emotional states? *Cognition and Emotion, 6,* 89–111.

Goldstone, R. L. (1994). The role of similarity in categorization: Providing a groundwork. *Cognition, 52,* 125–157.

Goleman, D. (1995). *Emotional intelligence.* New York: Bantam Books.

Halberstadt, J. B., & Niedenthal, P. M. (1997). Emotional state and the use of stimulus dimensions in judgment. *Journal of Personality and Social Psychology, 72,* 1017–1033.

Halberstadt, J. B., Niedenthal, P. M., & Kushner, J. (1995). Resolution of lexical ambiguity by emotional state. *Psychological Science, 6,* 278–282.

Hansen, C. H., & Hansen, R. D. (1994). Automatic emotion: Attention and facial efference. In P. M. Niedenthal & S. Kitayama (Eds.), *The heart's eye: Emotional influences in perception and attention* (pp. 217–243). San Diego, CA: Academic Press.

Hatfield, E., Cacioppo, J. T., & Rapson, R. L. (1993). Emotional contagion. *Current Directions in Psychological Science, 2,* 96–99.

Izard, C. E. (1994). *Human emotions.* New York: Plenum.

Izard, C. E. (1994). Innate and universal facial expressions: Evidence from developmental and cross-cultural research. *Psychological Bulletin, 115,* 288–299.

Johnson-Laird, P. N., & Oatley, K. (1992). Basic emotions, rationality, and folk theory. *Cognition and Emotion, 6,* 201–223.

Kruschke, J. K. (1992). ALCOVE: An exemplar-based connectionist model of category learning. *Psychological Review, 99,* 22–44.

Kruskal, J. B. (1964). Multidimensional scaling by optimizing goodness of fit to a nonmetric hypothesis. *Psychometrika, 29,* 1–27.

Kruskal, J. B., & Wish, M. (1978). *Multidimensional scaling.* Sage University Paper Series on Quantitative Applications in the Social Sciences, 11. Newbury Park, CA: Sage.

Laird, D. L., Alibozak, T., Davainis, D., Deignan, K., Fontanella, K., Hong, J., Levy, B., & Pacheco, C. (1994). Individual differences in the effects of spontaneous mimicry on emotional contagion. *Motivation and Emotion, 18,* 231–247.

Laird, J. D., Cuniff, M., Sheehan, K., Shulman, D., & Strumm, G. (1989). Emotion specific effects of facial expression on memory for life events. *Journal of Social Behavior and Personality, 4,* 87–98.

Laird, J. D., Wagener, J. J., Halal, M., & Szegda, M. (1982). Remembering what you feel: Effects of emotion on memory. *Journal of Personality and Social Psychology, 42,* 646–657.

Lang, P. J., Bradley, M. M., & Cuthbert, B. N. (1990). Emotion, attention and the startle reflex. *Psychological Review, 97,* 377–395.

Larsen, R. J., & Diener, E. (1992). Promises and problems with the circumplex model of emotion. In M. S. Clark (Ed.), *Emotion. Review of personality and social psychology* (No. 13, pp. 25–59). Newbury Park, CA: Sage.

LeDoux, J. E. (1987). Emotion. In F. Plum (Ed.), *Handbook of physiology. Section I: The nervous system: Vol. 5. Higher functions of the brain, part I.* (pp. 419–459). Bethesda, MD: American Physiological Society.

LeDoux, J. E. (1993). Emotional memory systems in the brain. *Behavioral Brain Research, 58,* 69–79.

Leventhal, H. (1984). A perceptual-motor theory of emotion. In L. Berkowitz (Ed.), *Advances in Experimental Social Psychology* (Vol. 17, pp. 118–182). Orlando, FL: Academic Press.

Leventhal, H., & Everhart, D. (1979). Emotion, pain, and physical illness. In C. E. Izard (Ed.), *Emotion and psychopathology.* New York: Plenum Press.

Lloyd, G. G., & Lishman, W. A. (1975). Effect of depression on the speed of recall of pleasant and unpleasant experiences. *Psychological Medicine, 5,* 173–180.

Mackie, D. M., & Hamilton, D. L. (1993). *Affect, cognition and stereotyping: Interactive processes in group perception.* San Diego: Academic Press.

MacLean, P. D. (1993). Cerebral evolution of emotion. In M. Lewis & J. M. Haviland (Eds.) *Handbook of emotions* (pp. 67–83). New York: Guilford Press.

MacLeod, C., Mathews, A. M., & Tata, P. (1986). Attentional bias in emotional disorders. *Journal of Abnormal Psychology, 95,* 15–20.

Macrae, C. N., Bodenhausen, G. V., & Milne, A. B. (1995). The dissection of selection in person perception: Inhibiting processes in social stereotypes. *Journal of Personality and Social Psychology, 69,* 397–407.

Madigan, R. J., & Bollenbach, A. K. (1982). Effects of induced mood on retrieval of personal episodes and semantic memories. *Psychological Reports, 50,* 147–157.

Mayer, J. D., & Gaschke, Y. N. (1988). The experience and meta-experience of mood. *Journal of Personality and Social Psychology, 55,* 102–111.

Medin, D. L., Goldstone, R. L., & Gentner, D. (1993). Respect for similarity. *Psychological Review, 100,* 254–278.

Medin, D. L., Lynch, E. B., Coley, J. D., & Atran, S. (1997). Categorization and reasoning among tree experts – Do all roads lead to Rome? *Cognitive Psychology, 32,* 49–96.

Medin, D. L., & Schaffer, M. M. (1978). Context theory of classification learning. *Psychological Review, 85,* 207–238.

Meyer, G. J., & Shack, J. R. (1989). Structural convergence of mood and personality: Evidence for old and new directions. *Journal of Personality and Social Psychology, 57,* 690–706.

Murphy, G. L., & Medin, D. L. (1985). The role of theories in conceptual coherence. *Psychological Review, 92,* 289–316.

Natale, M., & Hantas, M. (1982). Effect of temporary mood states on selective memory about the self. *Journal of Personality and Social Psychology, 42,* 927–934.

Niedenthal, P. M., Halberstadt, J. B., & Innes-Ker, Å. H. (in press). Emotional response categorization *Psychological Review.*

Niedenthal, P. M., Halberstadt, J. B., & Setterlund, M. B. (1997). Being happy and seeing "happy": Emotional state facilitates visual encoding. *Cognition and Emotion, 11,* 403–432.

Niedenthal, P. M., & Kitayama, S. (1994). *The heart's eye: Emotional influences in perception and attention.* San Diego: Academic Press.

Niedenthal, P. M., & Setterlund, M. B. (1994). Emotion congruence in perception. *Personality and Social Psychology Bulletin, 20,* 401–410.

Niedenthal, P. M., Setterlund, M. B., & Jones, D. E. (1994). Emotional organization of perceptual memory. In P. M. Niedenthal & S. Kitayama (Eds.), *The heart's eye: Emotional influences in perception and attention* (pp. 87–113). San Diego, CA: Academic Press.

Nosofsky, R. M. (1986). Attention, similarity, and the identification-categorization relationship. *Journal of Experimental Psychology: General, 115,* 39–57.

Nosofsky, R. M. (1992). Exemplar-based approach to relating categorization, identification and recognition. In F. G. Ashby (Ed.), *Multidimensional models of perception and cognition* (pp. 363–393). Hillsdale, NJ: Erlbaum.

Oatley, K. (1992). *Best laid schemes: The psychology of emotions.* New York: Cambridge University Press.

Osgood, C. E., & Suci, G. J. (1955). Factor analysis of meaning. *Journal of Experimental Psychology, 50,* 325–338.

Plutchik, R. (1980). *Emotion: A psychoevolutionary synthesis.* New York: Harper & Row.

Plutchik, R. (1984). A psychoevolutionary theory of emotions. *Social Science Information, 21,* 529–553.

Pratto, F., & John, O. P. (1991). Automatic vigilance: The attention-grabbing power of negative information. *Journal of Personality and Social Psychology, 61,* 381–391.

Reisenzein, R. (1994). Pleasure-arousal theory and the intensity of emotions. *Journal of Personality and Social Psychology, 67,* 525–539.

Rosch, E. (1975). Cognitive representations of semantic categories. *Journal of Experimental Psychology: Human Perception and Performance, 1,* 303–322.

Rosch, E., Mervis, C., Gray, W., Johnson, D., & Boyes-Braem, P. (1976). Basic objects in natural categories. *Cognitive Psychology, 8,* 382–439.

Russell, J. A. (1980). A circumplex model of affect. *Journal of Personality and Social Psychology, 39,* 385–408.

Russell, J. A. (1989). Measures of emotion. In R. Plutchik & H. Kellerman (Eds.), *The measurement of emotions: Vol. 4. Emotion: Theory, research, and experience* (pp. 83–111). Toronto: Academic Press.

Russell, J. A. (1994). Is there universal recognition of emotion from facial expression? A review of the cross-cultural studies. *Psychological Bulletin, 115,* 102–141.

Salovey, P., & Singer, J. A. (1988). Mood congruency effects in recall of childhood versus recent memories. *Journal of Social Behavior and Personality, 89,* 99–120.

Salovey, P., & Sluyter, D. J. (1997). *Emotional development and emotional intelligence.* New York: Basic Books.

Sanz, J. (1996). Memory biases in social anxiety and depression. *Cognition and Emotion, 10,* 87–105.

Savitsky, J. C., & Izard, C. E. (1970). Developmental changes in the use of emotion cues in a concept-formation task. *Developmental Psychology, 3,* 350–357.

Schlosberg, H. (1952). The description of facial expressions in terms of two dimensions. *Journal of Experimental Psychology, 44,* 229–237.

Shaver, P., Schwartz, J., Kirson, D., & O'Connor, G. (1987). Emotion knowledge: Further exploration of a prototype approach. *Journal of Personality and Social Psychology, 52,* 1061–1086.

Singer, J. A., & Salovey, P. (1988). Mood and memory: Evaluating the network theory of affect. *Clinical Psychology Review, 8,* 211–251.

Smith, E. R., Fazio, R. H., & Cejka, M. A. (1996). Accessible attitudes influence categorization of multiply categorizable objects. *Journal of Personality and Social Psychology, 71,* 888–898.

Smith, E. R., & Zárate, M. A. (1992). Exemplar-based model of social judgment. *Psychological Review, 99,* 3–21.

Smith, L. B. (1989). From global similarities to kinds of similarities: The construction of dimension in development. In S. Vosniadou & A. Ortony (Eds.), *Similarity and analogical reasoning* (pp. 146–178). New York: Cambridge University Press.

Snyder, M., & White, P. (1982). Moods and memories: Elation, depression, and the remembering of events in one's life. *Journal of Personality, 50,* 149–167.

Sroufe, L. A. (1979). The coherence of individual development: Early care, attachment, and subsequent developmental issues. *American Psychologist, 34,* 834–841.

Teasdale, J. D., & Fogarty, S. J. (1979). Differential effects of induced mood on retrieval of pleasant and unpleasant events from episodic memory. *Journal of Abnormal Psychology, 88,* 248–257.

Thayer, R. E. (1989). *The biopsychology of mood and arousal.* New York: Oxford University Press.

Tomkins, S. S. (1962). *Affect, imagery, consciousness: Vol. 1. The positive affects.* New York: Springer Verlag.

Tomkins, S. S. (1963). *Affect, imagery, consciousness: Vol. 2. The negative affects.* New York: Springer Verlag.

Velten, E. (1968). A laboratory task for induction of mood states. *Behavior Research and Therapy, 6,* 473–482.

Watson, D., & Tellegen, A. (1985). Toward a consensual structure of mood. *Psychological Bulletin, 98,* 219–235.

Wattenmaker, N. D., Nakamura, G. V., & Medin, D. L. (1987). Relationships between similarity-based and explanation-based categorization. In D. Hilton (Ed.), *Contemporary science and natural explanation: Commonsense conceptualizations of causality* (pp. 204–240). Brighton, England: Harvester Press.

Zajonc, R. B. (1998). Emotions. In D. T. Gilbert & S. T. Fiske (Eds.), *Handbook of social psychology* (Vol. 2, pp. 591–632). Boston: McGraw Hill.

16. Feeling and Thinking

Summary and Integration

JOSEPH P. FORGAS

Introduction

By any standard, we have much cause to be fundamentally satisfied with the achievements of affect/cognition research during the past two decades. There has been a steady progression of interesting empirical findings, an exemplary development of ever-more sensitive and inclusive theories, and the discovery of important and reliable effects that have widespread theoretical and practical implications, as illustrated by many of the chapters here. It is indeed gratifying to note that perhaps for the first time ever, we are making real progress toward understanding the influence of affective states on our thoughts, judgments, and decisions, a question that has long been a source of interest and fascination to laypersons and philosophers alike.

As noted in the introduction to this volume, psychologists were relatively late to turn their attention to investigating the multifaceted links between affect, cognition, and behavior. This probably has a great deal to do with the traditional practice of separating affect, cognition, and conation, the three "faculties of mind," throughout most of the history of our discipline (Hilgard, 1980). As we have seen in the introduction to this volume, explanations of affect/cognition phenomena have evolved from earlier speculative, philosophical approaches through psychoanalytic and conditioning theorising (Clore & Byrne, 1974; Feshbach & Singer, 1957), to the more recent cognitive,

Correspondence concerning this article should be addressed to Joseph P. Forgas, School of Psychology, University of New South Wales, Sydney 2052, Australia. Electronic mail may be sent to jp.forgas@unsw.edu.au.

information-processing accounts. The past 20 years saw a rapid development in our understanding of how affective states and cognition interact. These two decades were marked by several major "landmark" research achievements. In a sense, the contributions included in this volume present an up-to-date discussion and integration of the major achievements of recent affect-cognition research.

The first major impetus towards renewed empirical research linking feeling and thinking, affect and cognition came from striking research evidence that demonstrated affect-congruent influences on learning, memory, associations, and judgments in the early 1980s (Bower, 1981; Fiedler & Forgas, 1988; see also Eich & Macaulay, Fiedler, Zajonc, this volume). The affect priming hypothesis (Bower, 1981, 1991) offered a particularly appealing and parsimonious account of many mood-congruent phenomena, including judgmental effects (Forgas & Bower, 1987; Sedikides, 1995). From the initial fascination with affect congruence, research rapidly developed to explore a variety of other issues linking affect and cognition. This included some of the main themes surveyed in this volume, such as research on the information-processing consequences of affect (see chapters by Bless, Fiedler, Forgas), and work on the role of cognitive appraisal processes in affective experience (see chapters by Blascovich & Mendes, Smith & Kirby, Leary). Rapid progress was also made in exploring the cognitive and motivational mechanisms producing affect-incongruent outcomes (see chapters by Berkowitz et al., Eich & Macaulay, Gilbert, Martin) and the study of affect in the representation and use of social knowledge structures (Showers, Niedenthal & Halberstadt, Greenwald et al.). Having surveyed this broad and expanding field in this volume, it is now time to draw some conclusions, identify some integrative themes, and consider the future prospects of this exciting research domain. This is the task of this final chapter.

Affect and Cognition: Toward a New Synthesis

One of the key integrative themes of this book is the way several of the chapters here converge in arguing for a new, dynamic, and interactive conceptualization of affective and cognitive phenomena. Affect was placed on the agenda for most social psychologists as a result of the debate in the 1980s about its status in relation to cognition. The chapter by Zajonc included here provides a mature overview and recapitulation of the main issues considered then, and the current status of the empirical evidence. It turns out that physiological, neuropsychological, and neuroanatomical evidence about the role of affect in social thinking and behavior has provided substantial input into contemporary conceptualizations of the affect/cognition interface (Damasio, 1994; DeSousa, 1987; LeDoux, 1995). The role of affective states as fundamentally adaptive, evolutionary response systems is now increasingly accepted, consistent with the growing influence of functional ideas on psychological theorizing in general (Oatley & Jenkins, 1992, 1996). Thus, our view of affect has undergone a fundamental shift in the past 20 years. Rather than viewing affect as a source of disruptive influence on proper – that is, affect-less – thinking, there is now a growing consensus that affective responses are a useful and even essential means of dealing with the social environment (Damasio, 1994). There is now strong evidence that evaluative, affective responses can often be produced in a fast, automatic, and highly adaptive manner even in the absence of inferential cognitive deliberations, as argued by Zajonc here.

Research during the past 20 years thus helped to fundamentally change how we think about the nature and functions of affect. In contrast with the relative neglect of affective phenomena during most of psychology's brief history (Hilgard, 1980), affect has now been reintegrated into mainstream psychological research. In other words, one way of viewing the developments during the past 20 years is as the gradual move of affective phenomena from the periphery to the center of psychological theorizing, accompanied by the emancipation of affect research from the earlier dominance of cognitive, information-processing metaphors. It would be a mistake, however, to insist on viewing the relationship between affect and cognition as fundamentally about the question of primacy and independence, as some of the early debates in the 1980s suggested (Lazarus, 1984; Zajonc, 1980, this volume). The work reported in most of the chapters here strongly suggests that the affect/cognition relationship is fundamentally an interactive one (see, e.g., chapters by Bless, Blascovich & Mendes, Fiedler, Forgas, Gilbert, Leary, Greenwald et al., Niedenthal & Halberstadt, Showers). Cognitive appraisal processes do, for instance, seem to make a critical difference to mediating even visceral reactions to subtly different challenge and threat situations, as the work reported by Blascovich and Mendes suggests.

The rapid development of affect/cognition research surveyed here had a major impact not only on our understanding of affective phenomena, but also on contemporary views of the nature of basic social cognitive processes. For the first time, affective states could be seen as an important and independent source of functional information and input into realistic judgmental and information-processing tasks, rather than merely as a source of noise and disturbance in idealized affect-less cognition (Bruner, 1957; Neisser, 1982). By radically expanding the scope of cognitive information-processing theories, the careful and precise analysis of the role of affective reactions in thinking and behavior became possible for the first time. Once again, this expanded view of cognition as necessarily incorporating affective inputs has been hastened by the growing popularity of functionalist, evolutionary ideas, and accumulating neuroanatomical evidence indicating the close involvement of affective inputs as a source of adaptive information in complex cognitive processing tasks (Damasio, 1994; DeSousa, 1987; LeDoux, 1995). In a sense, then, this book is about the emerging patterns of exactly how affective and cognitive phenomena interact in everyday social life. Several integrative themes and ideas can be discerned in the work presented here.

Affect as a Source of Adaptive Information

A key integrative theme touched upon in a number of chapters relates to the adaptive, informational role of affect in cognition. Many of the most fruitful ideas in affect/cognition research were adopted from information processing cognitive psychology, and have been concerned with fundamental memory effects (see chapter here by Eich and Macaulay). Perhaps the most important early development in affect/cognition research was the discovery, documentation, and initial theoretical explanation of basic affect congruence phenomena in memory in the early 1980s. By expanding the principle of state dependence in memory to include affective states, the associative network model of Bower (1981) provided perhaps the first truly integrative theoretical treatment of these findings. The notion that affective experiences and states are closely and intricately involved in how we know and represent the social world continues to be among the most powerful ideas linking affect and cognition. For example, in Chapter 13 Greenwald and his colleagues describe an integrative theory based on associative network principles linking affective responses to attitudes, stereotypes, and the self. In Chapter 15, Niedenthal and Halberstadt propose that the affective characteristics of social categories play a key role in organizing our mental representations about them. These sophisticated theories have close links with pioneering research on mood congruence and mood-state dependence in memory carried out during the past two decades.

However, after the intense and enthusiastic initial interest in affect congruence, with the accumulation of empirical findings there came a growing recognition that affect congruence is not as robust or reliable a phenomenon as first assumed. It turned out that mood-state dependence in memory is itself subject to boundary conditions and can be highly context dependent (Blaney, 1986). The next period of research and theorizing could be described as one of growing complexity and even confusion about the role of affect in cognition. Inevitably, the kind of robust and universal predictions about mood congruence in thinking initially made by cognitive psychologists needed to be qualified and modified as the theories were tested in ever more complex and realistic social circumstances. Not surprisingly, there was some initial disappointment among cognitive psychologists – who were accustomed to probing and discovering fairly universal cognitive mechanisms of information processing – that predictions of affect congruence proved to be relatively context dependent (Bower & Mayer, 1985).

In contrast, social psychologists, accustomed as they are to dealing with complex and realistic cognitive tasks, and habitually fascinated by the "power of the situation" to influence social behavior, were much less surprised. Context sensitivity is the rule rather than the exception in social cognition research (Forgas, 1981). Discovering the solution to the puzzle of exactly when and why affect congruence in thinking occurs was always going to be a highly exciting enterprise. Several of the chapters here clearly indicate that persevering with attempts to understand precisely how, why, and when affect may be a source of adaptive social information can be a highly profitable and intellectually exciting research enterprise (see, for example, chapters by Eich and Macaulay, Berkowitz et al., Gilbert, Forgas, and Martin).

The initial interest in the adaptive informational role of affect in memory representations soon developed in a number of stimulating directions. The discovery and empirical demonstration of the boundary conditions for mood-state dependency and mood congruence in memory represents one highly successful research enterprise, as the chapter by Eich and Macaulay here illustrates. Other researchers became more interested in extending the principle of affect congruence to the related areas of social perception, social judgment, and decision making. It was argued that to the extent that social thinking is highly constructive and necessarily involves the active use of memory-based representations (Asch, 1946; Kelly, 1955; Heider, 1958), the same kind of mechanisms first identified by Bower (1981) should also play a role here. Numerous studies conducted in our laboratory documented mood congruence in social judgmental tasks (Forgas, 1990, 1992a, 1992b, 1994, 1995b, 1998c; Forgas & Bower, 1987; Forgas et al., 1984; Forgas, Bower, & Moylan, 1990). More recently, the principle of mood congruence first proposed for memory representations has been further expanded to account for affective influences on the performance of constructive social behaviors, such as negotiation, bargaining and the production of and responses to verbal messages such as requests as discussed in the chapter by Forgas here (see also Forgas, 1998a, 1998b, in press-a, in press-b.)

Of course, affect congruence in memory, judgments, and social thinking turned out to be neither a simple nor a uniform phenomenon. Several of the chapters included here document the complex and context-sensitive nature of this relationship. Berkowitz and his colleagues (Chapter 6) describe an ingenious research program directed at understanding just how and why affect sometimes has a profound influence on people's thoughts and judgments, and sometimes does not. They show that even minor shifts in attentional focus can bring about quite dramatic changes in the extent to which people are willing and able to rely on their affective states as a source of useful information. Simply focusing on the self seems often sufficient to eliminate and even reverse this process, according to Berkowitz et al. It appears, then, that the informational role of affect is not absolute but is subject to configural interpretation, as also suggested by Martin in Chapter 7.

The cumulative evidence reviewed here in the chapters by Eich and Macaulay, Berkowitz et al., Fiedler and Forgas suggests that affect is most likely to serve as a useful source of adaptive information when people need to engage in open, constructive processing to solve an inherently uncertain, complex, and demanding social cognitive task. One of the most common instances when we need to draw on affectively colored information is when we anticipate our reactions to future events, according to the stimulating chapter by Gilbert and Wilson (Chapter 8). Such affective forecasting mechanisms, they argue, can be open to a number of predictable distortions. These have mainly to do with the fact that people seem to have an inadequate appreciation of exactly how strong and how enduring their anticipated affective reactions are likely to be. This should come as no surprise in the light of recent discoveries concerning the mechanisms responsible for the informational influence of affect. The more open, uncertain, and unpredictable the judgmental target – as is the case in forecasting future reactions – the greater the likelihood that affectively colored information will have a disproportionate impact on its outcome. Just as judgments and explanations of the self, others, and social situations show affect sensitivity (Forgas, 1992b, 1995b; Sedikides, 1995), so too should the forecasting of future events, as Gilbert and Wilson show.

Extrapolating for these chapters demonstrating the informational role of affect we may conclude by observing that affect is now widely accepted as a key component of social knowledge. However, its informational value is neither simple nor absolute. Rather, people seem to rely on affectively colored information in circumstances when they need to engage in open, constructive and generative thinking about a social task, when they have the necessary cognitive and motivational resources to do so, and when there are no external or internal reasons compelling them to engage in more restricted and targeted information-processing strategies. We shall have more to say about this issue later. First however, we will briefly focus on a complementary theme covered in this book: the role of cognitive appraisal strategies in the generation of affective experiences.

Appraisal and Affect

Just as research on mood congruence has told us about how affect may inform cognition, appraisal research has shown the reverse process: how cognition may inform affective experiences. A further integrative theme considered in several of the chapters here is the shared emphasis on cognitive appraisal processes as the antecedents of affective experiences. By the second half of the 1980s, research on the informational consequences of affect was well established. At around the same time, an important, and largely complementary research tradition emerged, focusing on the cognitive mechanisms involved in the generation of emotional experiences and reactions and relying on appraisal theoretical principles. In Chapter 4, Smith and Kirby provide a major new contribution to this literature by suggesting that in addition to static appraisal rules, dynamic, information-processing variables should also be considered in appraisal research. Appraisal research initially evolved to specify the situation-specific production rules that apparently regulate affective reactions (Roseman, 1984; Smith & Ellsworth, 1985). As such, the *content* of appraisal rules was the primary focus of interest, and the *processing mechanisms* necessary to implement them received less attention. Smith and Kirby now argue that a complete understanding of cognitive appraisal mechanisms must necessarily include close attention to the dynamic aspects of how appraisal processes operate. Such a shared focus on information-processing strategies should present a unique opportunity to finally link the two largely isolated areas of affect/cognition research: work on the cognitive antecedents of emotions, and work on the affective consequences of cognition.

Until recently, appraisal research was interested mainly in the role of emotion production mechanisms in eliciting various affective reactions, and in the knowledge structures associated with different affective states (Roseman, 1984; Smith & Ellsworth, 1985). In extending this notion, Blascovich and Mendes in Chapter 3 argue that even visceral, autonomic response patterns associated with different emotional states are strongly dependent on the cognitive appraisal mechanisms employed. They note, for example, that the difference between situations experienced as challenging and those experienced as threatening is a subtle one, and that it depends largely on an individual's cognitive evaluation of his or her ability to cope with and overcome a challenge. This is by definition a highly elaborate, inferential appraisal process. Yet the evidence collected by Blascovich and Mendes clearly shows that these subtle cognitive differences produce remarkably distinct visceral consequences. This work provides a challenging counterpoint to the arguments presented by Zajonc. Even though affective reactions may often be distinct from, and primary to, cognitive responses, as Zajonc proposed, subtle changes in cognitive processing and inferences can in turn produce significant differences, not only in the experience but also in the physiological reactions associated with an affective state.

Of course, most affective reactions arise in a social context, and actual or anticipated reactions by others are a major source of appraisals and affective responses, as argued by Leary (Chapter 14). Human beings are intensely social creatures. Indeed, one may speculate that the spectacular evolutionary success of our species has much to do with our intense sociability and our gregariousness. It makes good sense therefore to assume that human beings should be closely attuned to how others react to them and be especially sensitive to indications of relational devaluation. Leary proposes an ingenious device he calls the "sociometer" (in a sense, an on-line appraisal mechanism) to describe our continuous monitoring of signs of disapproval, disinterest, and devaluation by others. Negative social emotions such as social anxiety, shame, or loneliness represent typical affective reactions to appraisals of relational devaluation. Leary's work nicely illustrates the dynamic, interactive character of affect and cognition: Social emotions may be elicited by subtle swings of the "sociometer" and associated appraisal processes, but they in turn influence cognitive processes such as attention, thinking, and inferences about the social world.

Affect and Information-Processing Strategies

The fourth major integrative theme highlighted in several contributions to this book concerns the information-processing consequences of affective states. After early speculations about the role of affect in triggering more or less automatic or controlled processing strategies by Clark and Isen (1982), by the late 1980s this question has also become the focus of concentrated research attention. Although there has been clear evidence that positive and negative affective states do tend to have very different information-processing consequences, the nature of this difference is still incompletely understood. The chapters by Bless (Chapter 9), Fiedler (Chapter 10), and to some extent Martin (Chapter 7) offer a major reconceptualization of the links between affective states and cognitive information-processing strategies.

The processing consequences of affect were traditionally conceptualized in terms of a simple processing dichotomy. It was argued that positive affect typically produces more heuristic, simple, superficial, and less systematic and effortful processing strategies, whereas negative affective states often result in more effortful, analytic, and systematic thinking styles. This distinction was closely related to other popular processing dichotomies traditionally proposed in the social cognition literature (Brewer, 1988; Petty & Cacioppo, 1986). Several theoretical explanations were offered to explain why positive and negative affect should produce such very different information-processing styles. One suggestion was couched in terms of functional, evolutionary theorizing and argued that positive affect signals a safe, nonthreatening environment calling for reduced vigilance, whereas negative affect calls for greater preparedness and increased vigilance (Schwarz, 1990). Alternatively, affect itself may have motivational consequences. Thus, positive affect may produce reduced processing effort in order to safeguard a pleasant emotional state (mood maintenance), whereas negative affect leads to increased vigilance and processing effort in order to control and improve an aversive state (mood repair) (Clark & Isen, 1982). Finally, the processing effects of affect were also attributed to cognitive capacity factors, as both positive affect (Mackie & Worth, 1991) and negative affect (Ellis & Ashbrook, 1988) may impinge on processing resources. However, this explanation seems increasingly implausible in the light of recent evidence suggesting that positive affect at least does not seem to impair performance on secondary cognitive tasks (Bless, this volume).

Several chapters included here challenge this simple processing dichotomy. In particular, both Bless and Fiedler argue that positive affect need not necessarily lead to an impairment in processing efficacy. Indeed, tasks requiring creativity, generative thinking, and more inclusive categorization may well be facilitated by a positive affect (Isen, 1987). Bless proposes that positive mood does not simply produce a more superficial processing style; rather, it promotes a general, schematic way of thinking that relies more on the deductive use of existing general knowledge structures but is less focused on the inductive use of external, piecemeal information. Thus, individuals in a positive mood may be more creative and may also be more inclined to rely on general knowledge structures such as scripts, heuristics, and stereotypes in dealing with social information. Negative affect in turn may signal problematic situations and may motivate more detailed and attentive processing.

In a somewhat similar vein, Fiedler introduces a fundamental distinction between accommodation and assimilation as basic and complementary cognitive processes. Whereas accommodation requires close attention to, and conservation of, the stimulus details so as to avoid mistakes in stimulus-driven tasks, assimilation involves the imposition of existing and internalized knowledge structures on the stimulus world. Fiedler suggests that positive affect promotes assimilation, and that negative affect promotes accommodation as the dominant processing strategy (see also Fiedler, in press). The key argument here is that neither positive nor negative mood should be regarded as having an inherently beneficial or deleterious effect on thinking. Rather, the processing consequences of affect depend on the nature of the task to be performed. Inherently creative, constructive tasks may be facilitated by a positive affect, but tasks requiring close attention to stimulus details are better performed in a negative affective state. For example, it has been found that positive mood increases the incidence of judgmental biases such as the fundamental attribution error, as people in a good mood are less likely to pay due attention to, and process fully information about external constraints impinging upon an actor (Forgas, 1998c). Likewise, positive affect increases and negative affect decreases the likelihood that eyewitness memory will become contaminated by incorrect information provided subsequently (Forgas, 1998d). The chapters in this volume thus testify to the rapid evolution of theorizing about the information-processing consequences of affect. We have moved from a simple, dichotomous conceptualization to an integrative account that more accurately reflects the processing costs and benefits of both positive and negative affect.

Affect and the Structure of Mental Representations

In addition to the informational and processing role of affect in social cognition, there is a further integrative theme emphasized by the contributions here: affect also plays a key role in the structural representation of social knowledge. Psychologists such as George Kelly (1955) have always maintained that the study of how individuals develop and maintain their unique ways of seeing the world, their representative knowledge structures, or "personal constructs," is the key to understanding social thinking and social behavior. In their various ways, Showers (Chapter 12), Greenwald and his colleagues (Chapter 13), and Niedenthal and Halberstadt (Chapter 15) all emphasize the key role of affect in the way everyday social knowledge is represented and organized. Niedenthal and Halberstadt make the fundamental point that the affective characteristics of social stimuli can serve as an important source of cognitive categorization. As these authors suggest, emotional response is "a type of conceptual glue" that is both theoretically and functionally different from cognitive bases of categorization. Social stimuli that have conceptually nothing to do with each other can nevertheless form coherent categories simply on the basis of the similar emotional reactions they elicit. Interestingly, researchers have arrived at a very similar conclusion when studying people's cognitive representations of common social episodes. The representational categories people formed of their social encounters had little to do with the actual features of these situations and were almost entirely based on the similarities of affective reactions they produced (Forgas, 1979, 1982).

To the extent that affect is a significant source of cognitive categorization, we may predict close associative links between all kinds of affectively loaded representations. This is one of the main themes of Chapter 13, by Greenwald and his colleagues, who propose an integrative theory linking affect, attitudes, stereotypes, and the self. Well-established and affectively based associative links between various mental representations lie at the heart of Greenwald et al.'s model, and principles derived from cognitive balance theory are used to predict how dynamic judgments and evaluations are produced. There is more than a passing similarity between Greenwald's model, and the fundamental representational mechanisms assumed by associative network theories of memory reviewed by Eich and Macaulay (Chapter 5). Ingenious empirical techniques, such as the Implicit Associations Test, were developed by Greenwald and his colleagues to measure precisely the strength and direction of implicit associative links between valenced mental representations about attitude objects, stereotyped groups, and the self.

Naturally, once mental representations are established, they need to be continuously monitored, maintained, and updated in the light of new experiences, a point that was forcefully argued by George Kelly (1955) some decades ago in his theory of personal constructs. Showers in her intriguing chapter suggests a distinction between the compartmentalized and integrated organization of self-related knowledge structures. Compartmentalized structures work well when access to negative knowledge needs to be minimized. However, a more effortful and resource-intensive cognitive strategy – evaluative integration – is required when compartmentalized representations come under strain because of exposure to inconsistent information. Showers's work also points to the importance of individual differences between people in how they represent affective loaded information. Such individual variations between people who predominantly rely on compartmentalized or integrated representations may have significant consequences for their affective reactions to social stimuli, their ability to incorporate new information into existing categories, and their personal experience of themselves. A shared emphasis on the affective structure of mental representations about the social world is thus a key integrative theme running through several chapters in this book (e.g., Eich & Macaulay, Leary, Showers, Niedenthal and Halberstadt and Greenwald et al.).

Toward Integrative Theories

Early research on affect and cognition was driven by a few appealingly simple and robust theoretical ideas and predictions, derived largely from information-processing cognitive psychology. In keeping with the traditions of cognitive theorizing, most of these early theories assumed relatively invariant and universal effects. The network theory of affect (Bower, 1981), the affect as information model (Schwarz & Clore, 1988), early appraisal theories (Roseman, 1984; Smith & Ellsworth, 1985), and initial interest in the processing consequences of affect (Clark & Isen, 1982) were all characterized by an implicit assumption that relatively reliable and context-independent effects would be obtained. In reality, with the rapid accumulation of empirical findings, it soon became apparent that the relationship between affect and cognition is neither simple nor straightforward. The history of affect/cognition theorizing during the past 20 years has been a history of ever-more inclusive, complex, and integrative theoretical formulation capable of accounting for the emerging evidence. Again, this process is particularly well illustrated by the contributions to this volume.

Thus, the network theory of affect soon came to be qualified by the addition of affect production rules and the requirement of causal belonging between affect and cognition (Bower, 1991; Eich & Macaulay, this volume). Eventually, researchers identified a variety of mechanisms that can qualify, inhibit, or even reverse the kind of simple affect-priming predictions initially proposed (Fiedler, 1991), as the chapters by Berkowitz et al., Forgas, and Gilbert also suggest. Appraisal theories became more and more attuned to the importance of subtle variations in cognitive, situational and interpersonal variables and are about to incorporate dynamic information-processing variables in their formulations (Blascovich & Mendes, Leary, and Smith & Kirby, this volume). We can also discern a straight line of development from the appealingly simple ideas incorporated in Schwarz and Clore's (1988) affect-as-information model to the kind of context-dependent, configural informational effects predicted by Martin in Chapter 7. And Clark and Isen's (1982) early speculations about a possible distinction between automatic and controlled processing eventually led to the kind of sophisticated process theories proposed by Bless, Fiedler, and Martin in this volume.

One of the common themes throughout this book is that the relationship between affect and cognition is complex, context sensitive, and clearly bidirectional. The work described by Berkowitz and his colleagues indicates how even slight changes in phenomenological focus may produce dramatic shifts in affective influences on cognition and judgments. Simply directing people's attention to their internal states seems sufficient to reduce or even reverse affect infusion. The strong evidence reviewed by Forgas in Chapter 11 indicates that information-processing strategies play a key role in mediating affective influences on thinking. However, affect itself also has a strong influence on both the process and the content of social cognition, influencing the outcome of inferential attributions as well as social memory. Perhaps one of the key messages of this book is that the stage is now set for genuinely interactive and dynamic conceptualizations of the links between affect and social cognition.

In one recent attempt at producing such a comprehensive multiprocess theory, the Affect Infusion Model was put forward by Forgas (1995a) to account for both the informational and processing role of affect in social thinking. This model, briefly considered in Forgas's chapter here, emphasizes the role of different processing strategies in producing affect congruence or incongruence. Theories such as the Affect Infusion Model also seek to reconcile theories of affect congruence, such as the associative network theory (Bower, 1981), with the growing evidence in the literature that there are important boundary conditions that regulate affect-congruence in cognition. Whereas some theorists moved toward emphasizing things like "causal belonging" between affect and cognitive representations for the effect to occur (Bower, 1991), the AIM suggests that the critical requirement for affect-priming is that people must engage in genuinely constructive, generative processing strategies.

It is only in the course of constructive thinking that affectively primed information has a good chance of being incidentally used. It is interesting that given the highly constructive nature of most social cognitive tasks, mood congruence was always more reliably obtained with social judgments than in memory tasks (Forgas & Bower, 1987). Others, like Fiedler (1991), explicitly drew attention to a processing dichotomy contrasting constructive versus nonconstructive processing, paving the way for theories such as the AIM. In a sense what the AIM does is to emphasize and systematize the contextual circumstances within which substantive, constructive processing is most likely to occur, and indicates when affect-priming effects should most reliably be obtained. Berkowitz's finding that self-directed attention eliminates affect congruence is entirely consistent with the AIM's prediction that motivated processing elicited by self-directed attention should inhibit constructive processing and thus should reduce affect infusion.

Consistent with Fiedler's (1991) suggestions, the AIM predicts that affect is most likely to be infused into social cognition when people adopt a processing strategy that facilitates the use of internally generated and affectively colored information. Two of the processing strategies identified by the AIM – *direct access* and retrieval of a previously stored response, and *motivated processing* dominated by a preexisting objective – do not involve open and constructive thinking and have often been shown to be resistant to affect infusion (Forgas, 1989, 1990, 1991a, 1991b). In contrast, *heuristic processing* and *substantive processing* are strategies that require constructive thinking and that allow affect infusion to occur. A number of studies have now found that differences in processing do have a major impact on affect infusion, as predicted by the AIM (Forgas, 1992b, 1993, 1995b, 1998a; Sedikides, 1995).

Another integrative theory is proposed by Greenwald and his colleagues (Chapter 13), who seek to explain the links between affective, evaluative reactions and such key concepts in social psychology as attitudes, stereotypes, and self-concept. Their model is also an associative network theory in which existing excitatory and inhibitory links between stored mental representations about the social world provide the structural foundations. However, Greenwald et al. reach back to Heider's dynamic balance principles to account for the pattern of implicit and incidental positive and negative associative links often demonstrated in research with attitudes and stereotypes. New methods, such as the Implicit Associations Test (IAT), developed by Greenwald and his colleagues offer clever way of empirically measuring the strength of such implicit evaluative associations. With the emergence of more comprehensive integrative theories of affect and cognition, there is now a rapid extension of affect-cognition research into a variety of applied areas in clinical, social, developmental, and organizational psychology.

Conclusions

We started this book with a brief overview of the historical roots and antecedents to interest in affect and cognition in Chapter 1. The way our feelings influence our thoughts and actions has always been a source of intense fascination to philosophers and laypersons alike. For the first time, the last 20 years saw the rapid emergence of dedicated psychological research into this domain. The aim of this book has been to provide an integrative overview of where this research came from, how far we have progressed, and also provide some pointers as to future directions.

Affect/cognition research is likely to be influenced by several major developments during the next 10 years. One of these is the very rapid advances now being made in neuropsychology and neurophysiology, which should help us to understand the interaction between affective and cognitive functions in ever more accurate detail (Damasio, 1994; LeDoux, 1995; Oatley & Jenkins, 1992, 1996). The second likely development will be the more precise exploration of how affective states and different information-processing strategies interact. It is probably fair to say that most research up to now has been concerned with unidirectional relationships, the exploration of how affect influences cognition, and how cognition influences affective experience. There is now also strong evidence that positive and negative affective states produce very different information-processing strategies, although there is not yet clear agreement as to the mechanisms responsible for this.

The stage is just about set for theories that will start looking at affect and cognition in a genuinely interactive, dynamic way. For example, it may be possible that continuous and gradual shifts in information-processing style (producing affect congruence or affect incongruence) are a key element in how people control and manage their everyday mood fluctuations. We already know that different affective states facilitate different processing strategies (e.g., Bless, Fiedler, Forgas, this volume). We also know that different processing strategies produce different levels of affect infusion and affect congruence (e.g., Berkowitz et al., Eich & Macaulay, this volume). If we put these two ideas together, we may be on the way toward developing genuinely interactive, dynamic cognition/emotion theories. Indeed, we have found some interesting evidence for the operation of such a homeostatic, automatic affect management system in some recent studies (Forgas, Johnson & Ciarrochi, 1998). Such an interactive cognition/emotion system has obvious evolutionary, adaptive character- istics that we are only just beginning to appreciate.

In conclusion, we can indeed be well pleased with what has been achieved, and we have reason to be optimistic about the future. We now have a better understanding of the delicate interplay between affect and social cognition than at any time before. A substantive body of empirical evidence has been accumulated about such fascinating phenomena as the infusion of affect into cognition, the appraisal mechanisms that trigger various emotional reactions, the processing consequences of affective states, and the role of affect in mental rep- resentations. Our theories have become more subtle, comprehensive, and integrative and are better able to account for the empirical evi- dence. The work accomplished has significant implications for many spheres of human life where dealing with affect is of great practical concern: Clinical psychology, health psychology, and organizational psychology are just three areas in which affect/cognition research has been rapidly expanding. There seems thus ample reason to close this book on an optimistic note. We know more about affect and cognition than at any time before, and we have every reason to believe that progress in the future will be similarly rapid. If this book has contrib- uted to stimulating further interest in this exciting area of research, and has helped the reader to share the sense of excitement about work in this field, it will have achieved its objective.

References

Asch, S. E. (1946). Forming impressions of personality. *Journal of Abnormal and Social Psychology, 41,* 258–290.

Blaney, P. H. (1986). Affect and memory: A review. *Psychological Bulletin, 99,* 229–246.

Bower, G. H. (1981). Mood and memory. *American Psychologist, 36,* 129–148.

Bower, G. H. (1991). Mood congruity of social judgments. In J. P. Forgas (Ed.), *Emotion and social judgments* (pp. 31–53). Oxford: Pergamon Press.

Bower, G. H., & Mayer, J. D. (1985). Failure to replicate mood-dependent retrieval. *Bulletin of the Psychonomic Society, 23,* 39–42.

Brewer, M. (1988). A dual-process model of impression formation. In T. K. Srull & R. S. Wyer (Eds.), *Advances in Social Cognition* (Vol. 1, pp. 1–36). Hillsdale, NJ: Erlbaum.

Bruner, J. S. (1957). On perceptual readiness. *Psychological Review, 64,* 123–152.

Clark, M. S., & Isen, A. M. (1982). Towards understanding the relationship between feeling states and social behavior. In A. H. Hastorf & A. M. Isen (Eds.), *Cognitive social psychology* (pp. 73–108). New York: Elsevier-North Holland.

Clore, G. L., & Byrne, D. (1974). The reinforcement affect model of attraction. In T. L. Huston (Ed.), *Foundations of interpersonal attraction* (pp. 143–170). New York: Academic Press.

Damasio, A. R. (1994). *Descartes' error*. New York: Grosset/Putnam.

De Sousa, R. J. (1987). *The rationality of emotion*. Cambridge, MA: MIT Press.

Ellis, H. C., & Ashbrook, T. W. (1988). Resource allocation model of the effects of depressed mood state on memory. In K. Fiedler & J. P. Forgas (Eds.), *Affect, cognition and social behaviour* (pp. 25–43). Toronto: Hogrefe.

Feshbach, S., & Singer, R. D. (1957). The effects of fear arousal and suppression of fear upon social perception. *Journal of Abnormal and Social Psychology, 55,* 283–288.

Fiedler, K. (1991). On the task, the measures and the mood in research on affect and social cognition. In J. P. Forgas (Ed.), *Emotion and social judgments* (pp. 83–104). Oxford: Pergamon Press.

Fiedler, K. (in press). Affect and processing strategies. In L. L. Martin & G. Clore (Eds.), *Affect theories*. Mahwah, NJ: Erlbaum.

Fiedler, K., & Forgas, J. P. (Eds.). (1988). *Affect, cognition and social behavior*. Toronto: Hogrefe.

Forgas, J. P. (1979). *Social episodes: The study of interaction routines.* San Diego, CA: Academic Press.

Forgas, J. P. (Ed.). (1981). *Social cognition: Perspectives on everyday understanding.* San Diego, CA: Academic Press.

Forgas, J. P. (1982). Episode cognition: Internal representations of interaction routines. In L. Berkowitz (Ed.), *Advances in experimental social psychology* (Vol. 15, pp. 59–100). San Diego, CA: Academic Press.

Forgas, J. P. (1989). Mood effects on decision-making strategies. *Australian Journal of Psychology, 41,* 197–214.

Forgas, J. P. (1990). Affective influences on individual and group judgments. *European Journal of Social Psychology, 20,* 441–453.

Forgas, J. P. (Ed.). (1991a). *Emotion and social judgments*. Oxford: Pergamon Press.

Forgas, J. P. (1991b). Mood effects on partner choice: Role of affect in social decisions. *Journal of Personality and Social Psychology, 61,* 708–720.

Forgas, J. P. (1992a). Affect in social judgments and decisions: A multi-process model. In M. Zanna (Ed.), *Advances in experimental social psychology* (Vol. 25, pp. 227–275). New York: Academic Press.

Forgas, J. P. (1992b). On bad mood and peculiar people: Affect and person typicality in impression formation. *Journal of Personality and Social Psychology, 62,* 863–875.

Forgas, J. P. (1993). On making sense of odd couples: Mood effects on the perception of mismatched relationships. *Personality and Social Psychology Bulletin, 19,* 59–71.

Forgas, J. P. (1994). Sad and guilty? Affective influences on the explanation of conflict episodes. *Journal of Personality and Social Psychology, 66,* 56–68.

Forgas, J. P. (1995a). Mood and judgment: The affect infusion model (AIM). *Psychological Bulletin, 117* (1), 39–66.

Forgas, J. P. (1995b). Strange couples: Mood effects on judgments and memory about prototypical and atypical targets. *Personality and Social Psychology Bulletin, 21,* 747–765.

Forgas, J. P. (1998a). On feeling good and getting your way: Mood effects on negotiation strategies and outcomes. *Journal of Personality and Social Psychology, 74,* 565–577.

Forgas, J. P. (1998b). Asking nicely? The effects of mood on responding to more or less polite requests. *Personality and Social Psychology Bulletin, 24,* 173–185.

Forgas, J. P. (1998c). On being happy and mistaken: Mood effects on the fundamental attribution error. *Journal of Personality and Social Psychology, 75,* 318–331.

Forgas, J. P. (1998d). *Mood effects on eyewitness accuracy.* Unpublished manuscript, University of New South Wales, Sydney, Australia.

Forgas, J. P. (in press-a). On being sad and polite? Affective influences on language use and requesting strategies. *Personality and Social Psychology Bulletin.*

Forgas, J. P. (in press-b). On feeling good and being rude: Affective influences on language use and request formulations. *Journal of Personality and Social Psychology.*

Forgas, J. P., & Bower, G. H. (1987). Mood effects on person perception judgments. *Journal of Personality and Social Psychology, 53,* 53–60.

Forgas, J. P., Bower, G. H., & Krantz, S. (1984). The influences of mood on perceptions of social interactions. *Journal of Experimental Social Psychology, 20,* 497–513.

Forgas, J. P., Bower, G. H., & Moylan, S. J. (1990). Praise or blame? Affective influences on attributions for achievement. *Journal of Personality and Social Psychology, 59,* 809–818.

Forgas, J. P., Johnson, R., & Ciarrochi, J. (1998). Affect control and affect infusion: A multi-process account of mood management and personal control. In M. Kofta, G. Weary, & G. Sedek (Eds.), *Personal control in action: Cognitive and motivational mechanisms* (pp. 155–189). New York: Plenum Press.

Heider, F. (1958). *The psychology of interpersonal relations.* New York: Wiley.

Hilgard, E. R. (1980). The trilogy of mind: Cognition, affection, and conation. *Journal of the History of the Behavioral Sciences, 16,* 107–117.

Isen, A. (1987). Positive affect, cognitive processes and social behavior. In L. Berkowitz (Ed.), *Advances in experimental social psychology* (Vol. 20, pp. 203–253). New York: Academic Press.

Kelly, G. A. (1955). *The psychology of personal constructs.* New York: Norton.

Lazarus, R. S. (1984). On the primacy of cognition. *American Psychologist, 39,* 124–129.

LeDoux, J. E. (1995). Emotions: Clues from the brain. *Annual Review of Psychology, 46,* 209–235.

Mackie, D., & Worth, L. (1991). Feeling good, but not thinking straight: The impact of positive mood on persuasion. In J. P. Forgas (Ed.), *Emotion and social judgments* (pp. 201–220). Oxford: Pergamon Press.

Neisser, U. (1982). Memory: What are the important questions? In U. Neisser (Ed.), *Memory observed.* San Francisco: Freeman.

Oatley, K., & Jenkins, J. M. (1992). Human emotions: Function and dysfunction. *Annual Review of Psychology, 43*, 55–85.

Oatley, K., & Jenkins, J. M. (1996). *Understanding emotions*. Oxford: Blackwell.

Petty, R. E., & Cacioppo, J. T. (1986). *Communication and persuasion: Central and peripheral routes to attitude change.* New York: Springer.

Roseman, I. (1984). Cognitive determinants of emotion: A structural theory. *Review of Personality and Social Psychology, 5*, 11–36.

Schwarz, N. (1990). Feelings as information: Informational and motivational functions of affective states. In E. T. Higgins & R. Sorrentino (Eds.), *Handbook of motivation and cognition: Foundations of social behaviour* (Vol. 2, pp. 527–561). New York: Guilford Press.

Schwarz, N., & Clore, G. L. (1988). How do I feel about it? The informative function of affective states. In K. Fiedler & J. P. Forgas (Eds.), *Affect, cognition, and social behavior* (pp. 44–62). Toronto: Hogrefe.

Sedikides, C. (1995). Central and peripheral self-conceptions are differentially influenced by mood: Tests of the differential sensitivity hypothesis. *Journal of Personality and Social Psychology, 69* (4), 759–777.

Smith, C., & Ellsworth, P. (1985). Patterns of cognitive appraisal in emotion. *Journal of Personality and Social Psychology, 48*, 813–838.

Zajonc, R. B. (1980). Feeling and thinking: Preferences need no inferences. *American Psychologist, 35*, 151–175.

Author Index

407

Subject Index